TRANSFORMING CHINA

Anthem Studies in Political Economy and Globalization

Other titles in the series

TRANSFORMING CHINA

GLOBALIZATION, TRANSITION AND DEVELOPMENT

Peter Nolan

Anthem Press

This edition first published by Anthem press 2004
Reprinted 2005

Anthem Press is an imprint of
Wimbledon Publishing Company
75–76 Blackfriars Road
London SE1 8HA

or

PO Box 9779, London SW 19 7ZG

British Library Cataloguing in Publication Data
Data available

Library of Congress in Publication Data
A catalogue record has been applied for

ISBN 1 84331 122 4 (HB)
ISBN 1 84331 123 2 (PB)

3 5 7 9 10 8 6 4 2

Typeset by Regent Typesetting, London

For Xiaoming

Also by Peter Nolan:

with T J Byres, *Inequality: India and China compared, 1950–1970*

Growth Processes and Distributional Change in a South Chinese Province: the case of Guangdong

The Political Economy of Collective Farms: an analysis of China's post-Mao rural economic reforms

State and Market in the Chinese Economy: essays on controversial issues

China's Rise, Russia's Fall: politics and economics in the transition from Stalinism

Indigenous Large Firms in China's Economic Reform: the case of Shougang Iron and Steel Corporation

Coca-Cola and the Global Business Revolution

with Wang Xiaoqiang, *Strategic Reorganisation* (in Chinese)

China and the Global Business Revolution

China and the Global Economy

Looking at China's enterprises (in Chinese)

China at the Crossroads

with Dong Fureng, eds, *Market Forces in China: competition and small business, the Wenzhou debate*

with S Paine, eds, *Re-thinking Socialist Economics*

with Dong Fureng, eds, *The Chinese Economy and its Future*

with Fan Qimiao, eds, *China's Economic Reforms in the 1980s: the costs and benefits of incrementalism*

with H J Chang, eds, *The Transformation of the Communist Economies: against the mainstream*

CONTENTS

ACKNOWLEDGEMENTS

The following chapters have previously appeared in the corresponding publications indicated below. The author and Anthem Press are grateful to the respective publishers for their permission to reproduce the essays in question.

Chapter 1: from *Industrial Transformation in Eastern Europe* in the Light of the East Asian Experience, ed. Jeffrey Henderson et al., Palgrave, 1998.

Chapter 2: *The Chinese Economy and its Future*, eds Peter Nolan and Dong Fureng, Polity Press, 1990.

Chapter 3: *The Role of the State in Economic Change*, eds Ha-Joon Chang and Robert Rowthorn, Oxford, 1995, pp. 237–61.

Chapter 4: *Democratization*, vol. 1, no. 1 (1994), Frank Cass, pp. 73–99.

Chapter 5: *World Development*, vol. 27, no. 1 (1998), Elsevier Science Ltd, pp. 169–200.

Chapter 7: *The Challenge of Globalization for Large Chinese Firms*, Discussion Paper, UNCTAD, no. 162, July 2002.

Chapter 8: *The Journal of Peasant Studies*, vol. 21, no.1 (1993), pp. 1–28.

Epilogue: *Challenge*, May–June 2003.

INTRODUCTION:
CHINA AT THE CROSSROADS

For the past two decades, the Chinese leadership has been groping its way forward, away from the 'planned' economy of the Maoist period. In the sharpest contrast to the reform path of the former USSR, China has been 'groping for stones to cross the river'. China's approach was deeply influenced by the disasters that the country has experienced since the middle of the nineteenth century, not least the massive famine after the 'Great Leap Forward', and the great suffering during the Cultural Revolution. China's policymakers were determined to avoid such policy-induced disasters. The process of reform has throughout been treated as a complex process of comprehensive 'system transformation', in which economic, social, political and psychological factors are considered as a seamless whole. Unlike the former USSR, China decided to address economic reform before considering political reform, though this was not inconsistent with making great efforts to improve the capability of the bureaucratic apparatus.

In economic reform, the watchword has been consistent experimentation before widespread adoption of a particular policy. Reform began in the countryside in the late 1970s and early 1980s with the system of contracting land to the individual household. It spread to the urban areas in the 1980s with the widespread introduction of the 'contract system' for individual enterprises. By the 1990s this had been replaced by a system of even wider enterprise autonomy, with taxation substituted for profit handovers to the state, corporatization and flotation of part of companies' equity on domestic and international stock markets. Controls over foreign investment were lifted slowly, and were followed by a surging tide of FDI in the 1990s. By 2002, China was the world's largest recipient of FDI, and had around US$400 billion in accumulated FDI. Rural 'township and village enterprises' were allowed increased freedom in resource allocation, becoming a highly dynamic part of the economy in the late 1980s and early 1990s.

Market forces, including market-determined prices, and entrepreneurship gradually permeated the economy. Private business activity was gradually accepted and spread into all corners of the economy, though still not given formal protection. However, in July 2002 private businessmen became eligible formally to join the communist party. At the Sixteenth Party Congress in 2002, Party General Secretary Jiang Zemin announced that citizens should be judged on their contribution to society and not penalized for their property holdings: 'Mr. Jiang's statement provides support for the speedier development of legal institutions for protecting private property and the wealth generated by the emerging middle class of entrepreneurs'.[1] Controls over foreign trade were relaxed slowly over the course of two decades, and given a final impetus by China finally joining the WTO at the end of 2001. Foreign exchange controls also were only slowly relaxed, and by 2003, the renminbi was still not convertible on the capital account.

The outcome of China's reform strategy, inititated by Deng Xiaoping in the late 1970s, has been the most explosive and long-sustained period of economic advance that the world has ever seen. Even the Asian Financial Crisis made no dent in China's forward momentum. Moreover, this growth has taken place in a vast country, whose population comprises more than one-fifth of the world's total. Therefore, the significance of China's unprecedentedly successful development eclipses that of all other latecomer countries.

From 1978 to 2001, China's average annual growth rate of GDP per capita was 8.1 per cent, and its rate of industrial growth was 11.5 per cent , placing China at the top of the world's growth performance in this period.[2] When one considers the huge diversity of conditions of China's different regions, this was a remarkable performance. It went far beyond merely 'taking up the slack' from the inefficiencies of the Maoist period. No other former planned economy remotely achieved this performance.

Such growth went far beyond simply benefiting from the 'advantages of backwardness'. By 2001, China had climbed to first place in the world in the production of a wide array of products, including cereals, meat, cotton lint, fruit, crude steel, coal, cement, chemical fertilizer and TV sets.[3] It was the world's largest production base for a wide range of household appliances. In 2001, China produced 96 million electric fans, 60 million cameras, 41 million colour TV sets, 25 million mobile phones, 14 million household refrigerators, 14 million household washing machines, 11 million vacuum cleaners, 11 million household freezers and 11 million video recorders.[4]

China's exports grew from US$18.1 billion in 1978 to over US$266 billion in 2001, an average annual growth rate of over 12 per cent. Its manufactured exports in same period rose from US$9 billion to US$240 billion, an average annual growth rate of over 15 per cent. Manufactured exports' share in

China total exports rose from 50 per cent in 1978 to over 90 per cent in 2001.[5]

China had become the largest single focus for global firms' foreign direct investment. The total stock of FDI in the Mainland had reached US$395 billion in 2001, and US$452 billion in Hong Kong Special Administrative Region, totalling more than US$847 billion.[6] This combined total was significantly greater than that in the whole of Latin America and the Caribbean, which stood at US$693 billion in 2001. It greatly exceeded the stock of FDI in the rest of Asia: the total stock of FDI for the whole region, including East Asia (including Japan), South East Asia and South Asia, amounted to US$434 billion in 2001. It eclipsed that in the former USSR and Eastern Europe, which totalled just US$163 billion in 2001.

Even more importantly, this period of exceptional growth saw a comprehensive transformation of Chinese people's livelihood. Real average per capita consumption by Chinese people rose by over 7 per cent per annum from 1978 to 2001. This achievement was all the more remarkable in view of the fact that the Chinese population grew by over 313 million people during the same period. Not only was the standard of living transformed during this period, but the early years of reform and opening up saw the most remarkable reduction in absolute poverty that the world has ever seen. The World Bank estimates that the number of absolutely poor people in China fell from 270 million in 1978 (28 per cent of the total) to just 97 million (9.2 per cent of the total) in 1985.[7]

There are radically different interpretations of the causes and significance of this performance. At an international meeting held in Beijing in 2001, one Chinese economist delivered an impassioned speech. He said that although China had achieved a great deal in the previous two decades, the growth rate could be double or more that of the previous period if only the government would stop interfering in the economy. The statement was met with loud applause from the international businessmen attending the meeting. My own view is that the reason China has been so successful is that despite great strains and numerous policy shortcomings, the state has continued to play a critical role in maintaining social stability, resolving problems of market failure, regulating the distribution of income, wealth and life opportunities, and regulating the way in which China interacts with the global economy.

Despite the fact that China's incremental system reform produced outstanding results, the country faces deep economic, political and social challenges as it moves into the next period in its development. By the time of the Sixteenth Party Congress in November 2002, China had decisively left one 'bank' of the river, that of the old Maoist system, but the 'other bank' was only dimly visible. At the end of 2002, at the Congress, a new generation of leaders was appointed, including a new Party General Secretary, Hu Jintao. In his first speech after being elected, he likened China's current situation to that facing the leadership under Chairman Mao at the end of the Civil War.

In March 1949 at the Second Plenum of the Seventh Central Committee of the Chinese Communist Party Mao Zedong made a highly significant speech outlining the tasks ahead. The victory over the Guomindang (KMT) was basically complete. The Party was entering a new phase in its development. Chairman Mao warned that it should guard against complacency and realize that a long, arduous struggle lay ahead: 'To win countrywide victory is only the first step in a long march of ten thousand *li*. Even if this step is worthy of pride, it is comparatively tiny; what will be more worthy of pride is yet to come'. The central theme of the speech was the need for the Party to find a path through the enormous tasks that confronted them in the face of great challenges both at home and abroad. In the same way, China now stands at a crossroads. It must grope its way forward in the face of these immense challenges, fully aware that there is a serious danger of system disintegration. This would be disaster for the Chinese people. It would render previous achievements meaningless.

There are challenges of numerous types that confront the new Chinese leadership. These include: the vast extent of poverty and rapidly growing inequality; the challenge to Chinese businesses from the global business revolution; a deeply degraded natural environment; declining capabilities of the state; a comprehensive challenge in international relations; widespread corruption within the Chinese Communist Party; and extreme dangers – vividly exposed during the Asian Financial Crisis – in engaging closely with the global financial system. The leadership is trying to deal simultaneously with the challenges of globalization, transition and development. No other country has ever faced such a set of challenges, and there are no textbooks to guide China along this path. The responsibilities for the leadership are massive, because the price of failure is so huge. The possibility of social and political disintegration is real. Every effort of policy has to be directed towards avoiding this potentially catastrophic outcome.

There is intense debate in China, among Chinese policymakers, scholars and society at large, about each of these issues. There is a widespread feeling that the country has arrived at a crossroads in its long journey away from the administratively planned economy. At a crossroads in the middle of nowhere the traveller cannot stay put. He can turn to the left, to the right, or even turn around and go home. The other option is to keep on in the same direction as the road he has come down.

Some people argue that China has no alternative but to accept that this phase of development will be characterized by a harsh political-economic order. They compare this with the phase of 'primitive capitalist accumulation' in volume one of Marx's *Capital*. Few people dispute that the main task for China's policymakers is to ensure social stability. Many argue that the only way to achieve this in such a turbulent, challenging environment is through the exercise of harsh social control: the process of accumulation must come first or there will be no 'development'. Such arguments are typically supported with historical examples from early industrialization elsewhere.

Many people, both inside and outside the country, argue for a 'regime change'. They believe that the hard tasks that lie ahead can only be resolved with Western democratic institutions. A significant proportion of this camp believes that the model for China to aim at is the USA, not the 'bankrupt' models of the European welfare states or 'quasi-socialist' Japan. Almost invariably, those advancing such arguments claim the authority of Adam Smith who, they argue, demonstrated that the only rational way to organize the economy is through the free market. Frequently, it is asserted that China's long economic history provides a powerful object lesson for today's policymakers: China's achievement in technical progress in medieval times was blocked from making further progress by a despotic state that prevented China taking the capitalist path that was followed in Europe. They believe that the smaller the role for the state, the faster China will progress in the period ahead.

A third group, the 'new left wing', argues that the country has taken a fundamentally wrong turning by moving towards a market economy, increasingly integrated with and 'dependent' on the global economy. The 'new left wing' believes that the country can only solve the growing tensions by reducing the country's reliance on international trade and capital inflow, and returning to the policies of the Maoist years of the mid-1950s to the mid-1970s.

Another perspective is that China must continue along the path it has trodden for the past two decades, 'groping for a way forward', but adapting this approach to the fresh challenges that the country faces.

As China stands at a crossroads in its development, there are profound issues for the country's leaders to consider. Is it possible for China to build a civilized, socially cohesive society over the next few decades, during what is still the early phase of China's industrialization, and during which time there will still be a huge rural reserve army of labour? Will China be condemned to pass through a long phase of harsh political rule in order to meet the imperative of the accumulation process? If China fails to achieve a socially cohesive path of development, will the society and political structure remain stable? Does the fact that China is trying to industrialize at the beginning of the 21st century make this task more or less difficult? Is this task made more difficult by the fact that China faces numerous other deep development challenges, including a wide-ranging threat to the natural environment? Is it made more difficult by the fact that China faces a massive international relations challenge, notably in its relationship with the USA? What is the impact of the fact that China's large firms face a deep threat to their survival from the global giant firms headquartered in the high-income countries? Is this task more or less difficult in a huge country such as China, with its long history of economic development and its highly sophisticated culture?

In their search for a way forward, China's leaders are looking to the lessons from the country's own past, as well as to those from other countries, in order to find a way to build a stable, cohesive and prosperous society. This effort is of vital importance, not only for China, but also for the whole world.

Notes

1   *Financial Times*, 10 November 2002.
2   State Statistical Bureau 2002, p. 54.
3   State Statistical Bureau 2002, p. 932.
4   State Statistical Bureau 2002, pp. 478–9.
5   State Statistical Bureau 2002, p. 613.
6   OECD 2002.
7   Nolan 1995, p. 14.

References

Nolan, P, 1995, *China's Rise, Russia's Fall*, Basingstoke, Macmillan.
OECD, 2002, *World Investment Report*, Geneva, OECD.
State Statistical Bureau (SSB), 2002, *Chinese Statistical Yearbook (Zhongguo tongji nianjian)*, Beijing, Tongji chubanshe.

1

THE STARTING POINT OF LIBERALIZATION: CHINA AND THE FORMER USSR ON THE EVE OF REFORM[1]

The contrast in performance of China and the former USSR under reform policies has been dramatic. In China there was explosive growth, a large reduction in poverty and a major improvement in most 'physical quality of life indicators' (Banister 1992, World Bank 1992a). The economy of the former USSR collapsed, alongside massive psychological disorientation and a large deterioration in physical quality of life indicators, including a huge rise in death rates (Ellman 1994). The contrast in reform paths is well known. China's approach to economic reform was experimental and evolutionary, under an authoritarian political system. The USSR followed the 'transition orthodoxy' of revolutionary political change under Gorbachev, followed by shock therapy and rapid privatization in the Russian Federation under Yeltsin.

Systematic comparison of the two countries' experience under reform is still limited (but see, for instance, Aslund 1989, Sachs and Woo 1994, Goldman 1994: chapter 9, Nolan 1994, 1995). Much the most influential proposition in this literature is the argument that the difference in results is explained not by the difference in reform policies but, rather, by the different starting-points:

> It was neither gradualism nor experimentation, but rather China's economic structure, that proved so felicitous to reform. China began reform as a peasant agricultural society, EEFSU [Eastern Europe and the former Soviet Union] as urban and overindustrialised ... In Gerschenkron's famous phrase [China] had the 'advantage of backwardness' (Sachs and Woo 1994: 102–4).

This proposition has been absorbed rapidly into the mainstream of popular perception of the reasons for the difference in outcome from post-Stalinist reform in China and the former USSR.

This chapter examines the two systems of political economy on the eve of their respective system reforms in order to evaluate their respective possibilities for accelerated growth. It concludes that there were indeed large system differences. However, many of these were to China's disadvantage. It argues that despite the differences, the systems each possessed large possibilities for accelerated growth with the introduction of market forces in an incremental fashion, in a stable political environment with an effective state apparatus. These possibilities stemmed to a considerable degree from common features of the communist system. The chapter concludes that on the eve of reform China did not on balance possess greater possibilities for improved system performance than did the USSR. It argues that the main explanation for the differences in outcome must, therefore, be sought in the policies chosen, not in system differences. We begin by comparing both societies on the basis of economic factors crucial to the possibility of accelerated growth.

ECONOMIC FACTORS

Advantages of the Latecomer

There are three main 'advantages of the latecomer'. Firstly, it may be advantageous to have a large share of the population in agriculture, since a rural labour surplus provides the potentiality for rapid 'Lewis-type' growth in labour-intensive industries. Secondly, latecomers can draw upon a much greater pool of international savings than was available to the early starters. Thirdly, a latecomer can employ more advanced technology than was available to the early industrializers. However, there are many problems with these arguments as applied to the Sino-Soviet comparison.

Economic Structure

Industry   In the early 1980s a reported 62 per cent of Soviet GDP came from the industrial sector, which is a higher share than even for the advanced industrial economies (Table 1.1). However, China also was hugely 'over-industrialized'. In China in the early 1980s, industry reportedly produced 47 per cent of GDP, ahead of even the advanced capitalist countries (Table 1.1). There were serious inefficiencies in both Chinese and Soviet industry, but 'over-industrialization' may have been an even greater burden for China than for the USSR, since in China's case the 'over-industrialization' was in a vastly poorer country, with a much lower income level from which to generate savings to finance investment.

In the USSR in the early 1980s the proportion reportedly employed in

Table 1.1 **Economic Structure of Pre-reform China, the USSR, Compared to the Non-communist Countries, 1980 (%)**

	GDP					Employment				
	USSR	China	LIEs	MIEs	IMEs	USSR	China	LIEs	MIEs	IMEs
Agriculture	16	31	45	15	4	14	71	73	44	6
Industry	62	47	17	40	37	45	17	11	22	38
Services	22	22	38	45	62	41	12	19	34	56

Notes

LIEs = Low Income Economies (excluding China and India)

MIEs = Middle Income Economies

IMEs = Industrial Market Economies

Source: World Bank, World Development Report 1982

industry (around 45 per cent: Table 1.1) was higher than in the advanced economies. However, the difference was not large, and it stood at a similar figure in several of the advanced capitalist economies. Moreover, to some degree the relatively high proportion employed in industry reflected the high levels of over-manning in industry in all the communist countries.[2] This was a form of 'disguised unemployment' (Arnot 1988). Suitable institutional reform could have raised labour productivity and encouraged state enterprise managers to release labour to be employed in other sectors.

Agriculture China's employment structure was close to that of a typical low-income country, with around three-quarters of the population still employed in agriculture. Although the USSR had a much lower proportion of the workforce employed in the farm sector, the share was still large compared to the advanced capitalist countries (Table 1.1) and was probably much higher than the usually reported figure (see Table 1.13 for a much higher estimate). There were large possibilities in Soviet agriculture, as in Soviet state industry, for releasing surplus labour to undertake useful work in other sectors.

Having a large proportion of national output and employment generated in agriculture is not necessarily an advantage for a reforming communist country. An important reason for the success of the East Asian Four Little Dragons was that each had a relatively small farm sector at the start of their phase of accelerated growth (Little 1979: 450). In a densely populated economy such as China's the capital needs for expanding agriculture are large. If a sufficient condition of rapid growth was having a large share of output and employment in the farm sector, impoverished countries would long ago have 'caught up'.

Services   Both China and the USSR had a low proportion of employment in the service sector (Table 1.1). They each had large possibilities for improvements in welfare and for attracting surplus labour from industry, agriculture and from the state bureaucracy, simply by allowing people to set up service sector businesses. Under China's reforms the service sector's share of employment rose from 14 per cent in 1978 to 23 per cent in 1991 (derived from SSB, ZGTJNJ 1992: Section 4). In the USSR in the late 1980s, the Law on Individual Labour Activity (1986) and the Law on Cooperatives (1988) were followed by a rapid growth of small-scale service-sector activity.

State Sector   Most Soviet workers were employed in the state sector, which included industry, state services, notably government administration, as well as state farms. These workers had secure jobs, incomes and housing, and welfare provision. In China, only a small proportion of the workforce was in these sectors. Most of the growth in employment in the non-state sector during reform came from rural dwellers, and only a small part from the state sector. Obviously in this respect successful reform in the USSR would have taken a different path from that in China.

The Soviet state sector was far from homogeneous. Although the 'Pareto tails' of extreme inequality in income distribution were missing, there were wide differences in income and standard of living between different occupations and sectors (Yanowitch 1977: chapter 2). Moreover, there were quite wide differences in average income and large differences in labour force growth rates between regions (Feshbach 1983). Generally speaking, income levels were lower and population growth rates much higher in central Asia than in the European republics. As new employment opportunities emerged outside the state sector during a successful economic reform programme, then, it is not difficult to imagine how workers might have begun to migrate between sectors, occupations and regions. This could have happened in many ways, including the following:

- Direct bidding of full-time permanent labour out of the state sector through higher wages.
- 'Part-time' work in the non-state sector by state-sector workers.
- State-sector workers might retain their right to work in the state-sector enterprise but cease to be paid wages from that enterprise, and being allowed to more or less permanently work full-time in the non-state sector.
- Workers in the state sector could be allowed to retain their rights to work in the state enterprise and their social security benefits from it in return for some form of fee paid to their original enterprise.

- State enterprises could themselves invest in new enterprises (either directly or as joint ventures with capital from other sectors) in the production of goods and services, the areas for which demand was growing rapidly, allowing the redeployment of surplus labour from the original enterprise.

Some form of all these arrangements occurred in China during its reforms, but the rapid growth in the new entrants to the workforce and the huge rural labour surplus in farm employment tended to reduce the extent of migration from the state to the non-state sector.

Capital Markets

The accelerated globalization of capital after the 1970s provided a large potential 'catch-up' opportunity for reforming communist countries. Post-1978 China attracted substantial direct foreign investment because it provided political stability, cheap labour costs with a low probability of strike action, reliable investment guarantees and rapid growth behind high protectionist barriers which made it attractive as a potentially huge market. China did enjoy an advantage of having a large amount of capital in the hands of the Chinese diaspora. Some other reforming countries also have large diaspora. For example, the Indian diaspora's financial resources probably exceed those of overseas Chinese. However, only a small proportion of this has been invested in India despite India's economic liberalization. Clearly, a large diaspora is insufficient. The reforming country needs to implement policies which encourage its overseas citizens to invest in their native land.

At the start of its reform, the USSR had high potential to attract direct foreign investment. The core of the Russian economy to the West of the Urals was essentially a part of Europe, which was to become the largest single market in the world in 1992. It had vast natural resources and a much more educated and skilled labour force than China's (see below). They were prepared to work hard for much lower incomes than comparably skilled people in the advanced capitalist countries. Moreover, its infrastructure was vastly more developed than that of China. A successful reform strategy would have generated huge needs for foreign capital. The fact that it failed miserably to attract foreign direct investment (rated as the second riskiest country for investments in 1993: *The Economist*, 21 August 1993) is attributable to massive instability caused by policy choices in politics and economics.

Technological Catch-up

Both China and the USSR achieved low returns in terms of civilian technical progress from their investment in science. Scientific research workers were isolated in institutions and universities. Enterprise managers had a strong interest in resisting technical progress, let alone themselves attempting to pursue it (Nove 1983: 76). By introducing the profit motive to industry (alongside other necessary reforms), large increases in output could in principle have been achieved from existing scientific personnel. The potential for the USSR to gain from this was considerably greater than was the case for China.

In both cases a large share of scientific expertise was allocated to the military sector. This reflected the USSR's frontline position in the Cold War and China's post-1960 'war on two fronts' against both the US and the Soviet Union. In the early 1980s Soviet defence expenditure amounted to around 15 per cent of GNP (USCJEC 1983: 306), and the defence sector claimed a large share of the best resources (USCJEC 1982: 340). China's defence sector was much less technically advanced than that of the USSR in the 1970s. However, the share of industrial resources pre-empted by the military sector was at least as great as in the USSR, accounting for around 21 per cent of industrial output value in 1980 (USCJEC 1975: 477). In both cases there existed a large 'peace dividend' from the end of the Cold War which could have released scientific and material resources for civilian use. This dividend could have been especially large if the end of the Cold War had coincided with well-devised policies to introduce competition to industry leading to the intensive use (in order to make profits) of scientific skills and capital stock formerly tied up in the military sector. The USSR's scientific expertise would have been hugely attractive to foreign investors if the correct institutional environment, such as peace and a suitable, enforceable legal framework, could have been constructed and steady growth of demand ensured. Tragically, under the conditions of collapsed domestic demand and shattered political institutions, foreign countries often preferred to import scientists rather than organize production within Russia.

Despite the 'turn to the West' in the 1970s resulting in increases in the USSR's technology imports, equipment imports still accounted for only around 2 per cent of total domestic equipment investment (Hanson 1978: 31). In the 1950s most of China's technology imports had come from the USSR. In the 1960s 'self reliance' had become the watchword and imports of equipment and technology were reduced to the selective acquisition of the most advanced technology: '[China's] stock of Soviet equipment was rapidly becoming obsolete and domestically produced equipment was primitive' (USCJEC 1978: 311). Both China and the USSR possessed a large opportunity for technical catch-up, provided the foreign exchange could be generated to pay for technology-enhancing imports. China was in a much less favourable position than the Soviet Union to select and absorb foreign technology, since its scientific capabilities had been badly damaged during the Cultural Revolution.

Size

The vast size of China and the USSR provided a considerable potential advantage compared to other reforming Stalinist economies. This provided them with the opportunity to restructure with a relatively small loss of efficiency behind protectionist barriers. Domestic industries could potentially move towards profitability at world market prices within a relatively closed economy with growing internal competition while simultaneously achieving economies of scale.

Social Capability

Poor economies mostly have failed to catch up with advanced ones. Catch-up tends to occur only above a certain income level (Gomulka 1991). In order to 'catch up', countries need a certain level of 'social capability' to be able to exploit advanced technology: '[A] country's potential for rapid growth is strong not when it is backward without qualification but rather when it is technologically backward but socially advanced' (Abramowitz 1986, 388).

The Labour Force

General Educational Level   Socialist ideals of the communist countries were reflected in the relative equality of access to education. China's level of general education in the 1970s was advanced for a low-income country, at least in the urban areas (Table 1.2). However, a mere 17 per cent of the labour force worked in industry (Table 1.1). In the mid-1970s the vast bulk of the Chinese population was a semi-literate peasantry, over one-third of whom lived in dire poverty (Nolan 1983, World Bank 1992a). Around 35 per cent of the adult population was estimated to have been illiterate, around the same figure as for Indonesia (Eberstadt 1986: 315). Moreover, the country's primary and secondary education was hugely disrupted by the Cultural Revolution, which led to schools being closed across much of the country for two to three years and, even when they reopened, ideological education took a high priority in the curriculum.

The USSR by the 1980s was a highly urbanized country. Its achievements

Educational Achievements in China and the Former USSR, 1978

	No. enrolled in primary school as % of age group	No. enrolled in secondary school as % of age group	No. enrolled in higher education as % of population aged 20–4	Adult literacy rate %
Low-income countries*	74	20	2	43
Middle-income countries	95	41	11	72
Industrial market economies	100	89	37	99
China	93	51	1	66
India	79	28	8	36
USA	98	97	56	99
Austria	100	72	21	99
USSR	97	72	22	100

Note: * excluding India and China

Source: World Bank, World Development Report 1981

in basic education compare favourably even with those of the advanced capitalist countries (Table 1.2). In the mid-1970s the USSR's per capita consumption of educational services was ahead of all Western countries except the USA (Schroeder 1983: 319).

Higher Education   Maoist China concentrated its limited educational resources upon primary and (to a lesser extent) secondary schools. In 1978 only 1 per cent of the relevant age group were studying in higher educational institutions, compared to 2 per cent in lower-income countries as a whole, and 8 per cent in India (Table 1.2). Moreover, during the Cultural Revolution higher educational institutions had been closed for several years, resulting in an estimated loss of two million middle-level technicians and a million university graduates (World Bank 1981a: 106). In the late 1970s the ratio of scientific and technical personnel to total manpower was low. Moreover, even this fact conceals the:

poor quality and out-of-date character of much technical knowledge – the result of ten years of educational disruptions and isolation from the rest of the world ... In relation to China's desire and need to modernize, its supply of skilled manpower is inadequate (World Bank 1981a: 107).

The USSR had a vastly greater pool of scientific and technical personnel than did China. A consequence of its poor record in utilizing scientific skills to produce technical progress was that it allocated a large amount of resources in order to enable the supply of scientific and technical workers to grow rapidly. In the early 1950s the USSR possessed just 15 scientists and engineers per 1000 people compared to 26 per 1,000 people in the USA. By the mid-1970s the USSR had overtaken the USA, with the respective figures standing at 66 and 62 per 1,000 people (Bergson 1983: 56).[3]

In neither case was the stock of scientists and engineers used well. The absence of competition and profit-seeking greatly reduced the incentive of enterprises to undertake technical progress and even led enterprises to resist new technology. Pervasive shortages led to a widespread sellers' market so that in both capital goods and final consumption goods there was little incentive for enterprises to use available scientific skills to improve product quality. In the belief that technical progress was a public good, a large part of scientific capacities were located away from the enterprises.

A common consequence of the difficulties of the command economy was that both countries possessed a large stock of capital goods per unit of final product. In both cases, capital goods were unreliable, with a high propensity to break down. Compared to market economies, there was much less reliability in obtaining spare parts from specialist producers. These factors led to widespread engineering failures.

Motivation   A large array of factors combined to produce a workforce in both China and the USSR that was operating well inside its capacity.

The penalty of dismissal was virtually absent. Managers had a strong incentive to hoard labour as well as capital, since this made it easier to achieve the key planning targets, namely gross value or physical quantity of output. The absence of timely delivery of needed inputs prevented production running smoothly at full capacity. Consequently, the workpace was very uneven throughout each production period.

The slow workpace and low work effort which resulted from these factors were not fixed parameters. Rather, they represented a potential windfall gain if workers' motivation could have been harnessed through suitable policies. An important factor which was available to enable this force to be released was the widespread disappointment with the standard of living attained after long years with high rates of saving and investment. The introduction of suitable incentive systems could have released a greatly increased intensity of labour, and hugely raised output from existing resources.

Entrepreneurship

China possessed a powerful capitalist tradition. It had a highly developed entrepreneurial system for many centuries before the European industrial revolution. In the first three decades of the twentieth century in those areas in which there was some semblance of political order, rapid industrial growth did occur (Bergere 1981, Rawski 1989). Because the Chinese revolution had occurred relatively recently, in the 1970s the memory of capitalism was still alive. Over much of the Russian empire there had been severe natural barriers to commerce. By 1914, capitalist development had still 'as yet touched little more than the hem of Russia's economic system' (Dobb 1966: 35–6). Subsequently, the Soviet Union experienced almost 60 years under anti-capitalist policies.

However, the view that China possessed a much stronger base of entrepreneurship from which to launch its post-Stalinist reforms is erroneous. In Maoist China the private sector came under repeated attack as a 'snare both to poor peasants and to party cadres who still had bourgeois aspirations' (Walker 1965: 75). 'Capitalism' was likened to a 'dog in the water to be beaten and drowned'. During Soviet collectivization the Soviet rural private sector was crudely suppressed. However, the policies were quickly reversed. By the late 1930s the private sector was producing a large part of rural personal income. The USSR had no subsequent attack on the rural private sector to match the severity of that in China.

In European Russia before 1860 capitalism was much more advanced than was once supposed (Gatrell 1986: 144–50; Blackwell 1983). From the 1880s to 1914, Russian industry grew at around 4 to 5 per cent per annum (Gatrell 1986: 143). A powerful group of big businesses emerged, benefiting from foreign technology, often involving foreign capital, and centred particularly around St Petersburg (Blackwell 1983: 17). Alongside them went a continued growth of more primitive small-scale *kustar* industry involving as many as 15 million urban and rural craftsmen in the 1880s (Gatrell 1986: 154).

In both China and the USSR the Stalinist command economy produced simultaneous shortages and surpluses without the possibility legally to reconcile them through the market. As a result there was a powerful tendency towards illegal (black) market and quasi-legal (grey) market activity (Grossman 1979). In Berliner's view, much of the activity of the 'second economy' consisted of 'entrepreneurship of the classically Marshallian kind – redirecting resources towards an equilibrium state' (Berliner 1983: 196). Within the state sector of all of the Stalinist economies an army of people ('pushers') scoured the country to obtain desired inputs in exchange for unwanted surpluses. The second economy often provided personal services or produced consumer

Table 1.3   **Intermediate Inputs per Dollar of GNP (1979/1980)**

	Steel (g)	Sulphuric acid (g)	Cement (g)	Energy consumption (kg of coal equivalent)
USSR	136	21	116	1.49
China	146	31	319	3.21
USA	42	17	27	1.16
West Germany	61	7	47	0.56
Japan	109	7	87	0.48

Source: World Bank 1981a, SSB, ZGTJNJ 1981

goods. In addition there was a large illegal output both from enterprises themselves as well as from private illegal factories using stolen materials and often employing many workers. In the USSR in the 1970s between 30 and 40 per cent of personal income came from the private sector (Aslund 1991: 155). Indeed, due to the pervasiveness of shortages, ordinary individuals in command economies needed to be far more entrepreneurial in the conduct of their daily lives than the bulk of wage earners in the West.

Industry

Heavy Industry Bias

The extreme inefficiency of the Stalinist economies meant that both China and Russia required a large amount of heavy industrial output to produce a unit of final product (Table 1.3). China was even more profligate in its use of inputs than was the USSR. The quality of much heavy industrial output, especially machinery, was below that required to compete on world markets. Both economies had large potential, through the introduction of competition, to greatly reduce the amount of inputs needed to produce a unit of output and to raise the quality of capital goods, with multiple efficiency gains for the users of these goods.

However, the share of heavy industry in industrial output in neither country was particularly large compared to the advanced capitalist economies (Table 1.4). Output per capita of key heavy industrial products was much higher in the USSR than in China, but was not especially large relative to the advanced capitalist countries (Table 1.4). A large part of heavy industrial output in most economies consists of intermediate inputs, such as basic chemicals, steel, cement and glass, in which the product is relatively homogeneous and quality often is a less important element in competitiveness than in other

Table 1.4   Output Per Capita of Selected Industrial Products in the Late 1980s and Early 1990s

	electric power '000s kwh	coal '000s kg	steel '000s kg (a)	paper '000s kg (a)	cement '000s kg (a)	sulphuric acid '000s kg (b)	chemical fibre '000s kg (b)	TV sets no 1000 people (b)	motor vehicles no 1000 people (b)(c)	share of heavy industry in GVIO* (%)
USSR	5.6	2.3	557	22	471	94	5.1	36	7	74
China	0.4	0.8	45	8	137	10	1.6	23	0.4	64
USA	11.1	3.4	339	136	321	147	15.8	60	35	70
Japan	5.5	0.1	872	99	621	56	14.5	122	107	70

Notes
(a) 1985
(b) 1991
(c) including both commercial and passenger vehicles
* various years
n.a. not available

Sources: (i) Liu 1988: 56–7 and 116; (ii) SSB, ZGTJNJ 1993, appendix; (iii) World Bank 1981: 16

Table 1.5 **Role of Very Large Establishments (Over 5000 Employees) in Chinese and Soviet Industry**

	No. of establishments	Employment No. (m)	(%)	Fixed assets (%)	GVIO (%)	Employees/ establishment ('000)
USSR (1983)	1316	14.4	38.1	46.7	35.9	10.9
China (1987)	885	11.9	16.8	33.9	18.9	13.4

Sources: Li 1988: 120, 145, 436 and SSB, ZGGYJJTJNJ 1989: 293

industrial product markets. In both countries there was a huge pent-up demand for the products of sectors that directly used large quantities of inter-mediate inputs. These included housing, motor vehicles and the associated investment in road networks. In both countries levels of production and con-sumption of these items were relatively very low indeed. Moreover, a rapid growth in demand for other lower-value industrial consumer goods, such as textiles, toys, sports goods and household electrical goods, all created demand for upstream inputs from heavy industries such as power, steel, chemical fibres, and plastics. Although the USSR's level of consumer durable and clothing consumption was much greater than that of China,[4] it is likely that there was a high income elasticity of demand for the replacement of old, unre-liable and unstylish items purchased in the Soviet command economy period.

In sum, while it might be expected that successful growth would have caused a faster growth rate of output in heavy industry in China than in the USSR, it is not self-evident that even in the USSR successful reform would have been accompanied by the absolute decline of the heavy industrial sector (Table 1.4). What both countries needed were policies that caused the quality of heavy industrial output to rise and increased the efficiency with which heavy industrial products were used.

Industrial Organization: Similarities

Very Large Plants   In the early 1980s in both China and the USSR around one thousand very large plants (over 5,000 employees) employed 12–14 million workers, accounted for around one-third to one-half of the total value of industrial fixed assets, and produced around one-fifth to one-third of the total gross value of industrial output (Table 1.5).

Table 1.6 **Industrial Concentration by Size of Establishment in China (1987) and the USSR (1983) (%)**

Size of establishment (employees)	Establishments		Employees		Fixed assets		Gross value of industrial output	
	China	USSR	China	USSR	China	USSR	China	USSR
under 100	68.5	27.2	14.0	1.6	5.8	1.1	9.6	1.9
100–500	25.6	42.4	32.6	12.6	18.1	8.8	26.6	12.8
500–1000	3.6	13.1	14.7	11.2	12.2	9.0	15.5	10.8
1000–10000	2.2	16.3	27.5	52.4	38.2	51.8	36.5	54.1
over 10000	0.1	1.0	11.2	22.2	25.7	29.3	11.7	20.4
Aggregate	100	100	100	100	100	100	100	100

Source: Liu 1988: 120, 145, 145 and SSB, ZGGYJJNTJNJ 1988: 7, 293

Large Plants   In both cases, large plants (over 1000 employees) massively dominated the total value of fixed assets, occupying 64 per cent in China's case and 81 per cent in that of the USSR (Table 1.6). In China, large plants produced 48 per cent of the total value of industrial output compared to 75 per cent in the Soviet case (Table 1.6).

Small and Medium-sized Enterprises (SMEs)   In both China and the USSR, SMEs were under-represented in the size structure of industrial establishments (Table 1.7). In both cases, there were large possibilities for improved industrial efficiency, for meeting consumers' needs and for absorbing surplus labour from other sectors, simply by permitting entrepreneurial endeavour in the SME sector. There were many activities in the SME sector in both economies in which high profits could have been made as market forces began to take effect, especially in quick-gestating investments requiring small amounts of capital (for example, personal services, restaurants, leisure services, small-scale manufacturing as with toys, furniture, clothing, etc.). The potential for growth of SMEs was shown by the explosive growth of China's township and village enterprises (TVEs) in the reform period (see Chapter 7 in this volume). Such a possibility was not confined to China. If anything, these potential opportunities were greater in the USSR than in China due to the even greater degree of under-representation of SMEs in the industrial size structure in the USSR compared to China. In the USSR, less than two years after the passage of the Law on Cooperatives (1988), the number of small

Table 1.7 **Distribution of Employment in Manufacturing Industry by Size of Establishment %**

Size of establishment	Capitalist countries				USA	India	China*	USSR
	Small type		Large type					
	1950	1970	1950	1970	1986	1987/88	1987	1983
10–100	40	35	23	20	31.0	27.6	14.0	1.6
101–500	30	33	30	30	32.0	23.8	32.6	12.6
501–1000	11	13	13	14	11.6	12.0	12.0	11.2
over 1000	19	19	34	36	25.4	36.7	38.7	74.6

Note: * 'Independent accounting enterprises' only. In 1978 independent accounting enterprises accounted for 96% of NVIO (SSB, ZGGYJJTJZL, 1949–84, 1985, 41–2.

Source: Erlich 1985, SSB, ZGGYJJTJNJ 1991, Acs and Audretsch 1993: 62, Liu 1988: 120, 145

business cooperatives had reached 150,000, employing five million people (3.7 per cent of the total workforce), producing an estimated 7 per cent of national income, and already attracting substantial numbers of skilled staff from state factories and government ministries (Miller 1993: 103).

The Nature of the Large Enterprise   In both cases, there was a high degree of vertical integration at the plant level. The difficulties of constructing the 'plan' were reduced by maximizing plants' self-sufficiency. Plants could not rely on the supply of inputs through the command system. Almost all enterprises in the massive machine-building sector produced their own iron and steel rather than purchasing it from specialized suppliers (Granick 1967: 157). A large proportion of spare parts and machinery needs were produced within the large plants. There was a large stock of general-purpose machine tools with low utilization rates used to produce a wide variety of inputs in small batches.

Far from benefiting from large-scale specialized production, large Chinese and Soviet plants produced a large amount of small-batch output with below-optimal scale. Within each large 'plant' were many relatively small-scale 'shops' undertaking activities which in a capitalist economy would be undertaken mainly by specialist producers, often on a much larger scale.

Both countries had large possibilities for improving industrial efficiency. These were illustrated vividly by China's reforms after the 1970s. Increasingly managers were selected on the basis of ability. Profit retention contracts led to the rise of profits as the main goal of enterprise managers. By the mid-1990s domestic price control and the material balance system had been virtually eliminated. State industry had moved 'upstream' into mainly large-scale, capital-intensive heavy industries, in which scientific and technical expertise is much more important to success than in the small-scale light industrial sector where entrepreneurship is much closer to that envisaged by the perfect competition model of economic behaviour. The small-scale state sector was allowed to shrink rapidly in relative terms, its place being taken over by a variety of non-state forms of enterprise. A group of large multi-plant state-owned firms began to emerge in each sector under a carefully orchestrated planning strategy intended to create a series of South Korean-style large corporations. Output in the large-scale state sector increased rapidly, growing at around 11 per cent per annum in real terms and even increasing its share of total industrial output (from 25 per cent by value in 1980 to 28 per cent in 1991 (Nolan 1995: ch. 6). Most studies show a rise in total factor productivity in state enterprises in the reform period (for example, Chen *et al.* 1992, Macmillan and Naughton 1992, Nolan 1995).

Table 1.8 **Distribution of Industrial Capital, Employment, and Output Between Coastal and Inland Provinces of China, 1952 and 1978 (%)**

	1952	1978
Workers:		
coastal	60.5	46.3 (1984)
inland	39.5	53.7 (1984)
Value of fixed assets:		
coastal	72.0	43.9
inland	28.0	56.1
Value of industrial output:		
coastal	69.4	60.9
inland	30.6	39.1
Capital-output ratio:		
coastal	0.45	0.54
inland	0.40	1.08

Source: SSB, ZGGYJJTJZL 1985: 137

Industrial Organization: Differences

Spatial Distribution of Industry   China's split with the USSR in 1960 and its isolation from the capitalist world left it deeply vulnerable in international affairs. A major economic consequence of this intense insecurity was the 'Third Front' policy, under which the share of total investment allocated to the inland provinces increased rapidly. Their share of total industrial capital stock rose from 28 per cent in 1952 to 56 per cent in the late 1970s (Table 1.8). The economic return to this investment was low (Table 1.8).

Self-reliance   Maoist China encountered special problems that led to a distinctively 'self-reliant' pattern of industrial development. China is huge and the transport system was backward. Widespread political turmoil during the Great Leap Forward (1958–9) and the Cultural Revolution (1966–76), increased the desire of administrative units for self-sufficiency since they could not rely on normal trade networks. Local self-sufficiency made it easier for the central authorities to retain some semblance of political order. In a feudal fashion, lower-level leaders were made responsible for all activities social, political and economic within their boundaries, minimizing contacts of ordinary citizens with the outside and making a direct and easy chain of command in all respects from higher- to lower-level authorities. These factors produced a high degree of 'self-reliance' at every level of the economic system, far beyond that normally characteristic even of a command economy.

Small Plants   The policy of self-reliance tended to cause the number of small plants to rise rapidly. This tendency was given further impetus by rapid growth in the production of modern farm inputs in the countryside after the disaster of the Great Leap Forward (Table 1.9). Much of this growth came from small rural plants. A large fraction of China's farm machinery was supplied by these plants by the mid-1970s (Yu 1984, Perkins 1977).

Table 1.9 **China's 'Green Revolution'**

	1957	1978	1992
arable area:			
total (m. ha.)	112	99.5 (1979)	95.4
per capita (ha.) (index)	0.173(100)	0.103(58)	0.081(47)
irrigated area (m. ha)	27.4	45.0	48.6
% of arable area	(24.5)	(45.2)	(50.9)
of which.			
mechanically irrigated (m. ha)	1.2	24.9	26.3
% of arable area	(1.1)	(25.0)	(27.6)
mechanically ploughed area (m. ha)	2.6	40.7	51.5
% of arable area	(2.3)	(40.9)	(54.0)
farm machinery (m. kwh)	1.21	117.5	303.1
large/medium tractors ('000s)	14.7	557.4	758.9
walking tractors (m)	–	1.37	7.51
combine harvesters ('000s)	1.8	19.0	51.1
farm-use trucks ('000s)	4	74	642
chemical fertiliser use (m. tons)	0.4	8.8	29.3

Source: SSB, ZGTJNJ 1993: 341, 349 and World Bank 1981c: 61

In the mid-1980s within the factory sector ('independent accounting enterprises'), there were 286,000 small enterprises with less than one hundred workers per enterprise (the average was 35 per enterprise), which produced just 9.6 per cent of the gross value of industrial output from factories (SSB, ZGGYJJTJNJ 1988:293). Data for 1979 show there were in addition 580,000 minuscule enterprises at the brigade or team level, employing an average of only 17 workers per plant, which produced under 4 per cent of total industrial output value (World Bank 1981b: 20–21).

Results   These policies produced a relatively widespread technical capacity in China's rural areas. They reinforced the role of local governments as a key economic agent over a wide array of activities rather than simply an administrator of agriculture. However, China's industry failed to benefit from economies of scale and the advantages of specialization and exchange, even more than was normal in a command economy. A large proportion of the output produced under this strategy was of low quality, using large amounts of power and raw materials. Costs of production were widely acknowledged to be very high in a large portion of the small factories. They produced a large volume of capital goods which are normally characterized by strong economies of scale at the plant level. Like the USSR, China faced large tasks in restructuring the large-scale industrial sector. However, it faced a special problem in that it needed also to undertake a large-scale restructuring of its small-scale sector.

Agriculture: Differences

Population Pressure on Farm Resources   China occupies less than 7 per cent of the world's cultivated area but its population is around 22 per cent of the world's total. The USSR occupied around 17 per cent of the world's cultivated area but accounted for only 6 per cent of the world's population (SSB, ZGNCTJNJ 1989: 417–18). By the late 1970s, the amount of farmland per person in China was among the lowest in the world, much below that even of India, let alone the USSR (Table 1.10).

Capital   The stock of large farm machinery in Maoist China was vastly below that in the USSR (Table 1.11). In the USSR, only a small fraction of farmland was irrigated (Li 1981, SLNYTJZLHB 1981: 6, 446). A major reason for China's ability to sustain its huge population on such a limited arable area was its highly developed irrigation works. China's high labour input per unit of farmland, high irrigation ratio, and rapid advance in farm modernization after the 1950s (Table 1.9), enabled China to attain high yields

Table 1.10 **Arable Area Per Capita in China and Other Selected Countries, 1979 (hectares)**

China	0.10	
within which:		
East	0.08	Shanghai, Jiangsu, Zhejiang, Anhui, Fujian, Jiangxi and Shandong
within which:		
'densely populated eastern provinces'*	0.05 (1992)	Jiangsu, Shanghai, Zhejiang, Fujian
Northeast	0.19	Liaoning, Jilin, Heilongjiang (4.1)
Northwest	0.18	Shaanxi, Gansu, Ningxia, Xinjiang
Southwest	0.07	Sichuan, Guizhou, Yunan, Tibet
Central-South	0.08	Henan, Hubei, Hunan, Guangxi, Guangdong
North	0.15	Beijing, Tianjin, Hebei, Shanxi, Inner Mongolia
Other countries:		
Japan	0.04	
USA	0.86	
India	0.26	
USSR	0.89	

Note: * Total population in 1993 was 156 million

Source: Ministry of Agriculture 1982: 12–13; SSB, ZGTJNJ 1993: 83,332

per unit of farmland. By 1987, China's annual grain yields per hectare of harvested land stood at 4.0 tons, compared to 2.4 tons in Bangladesh, 1.9 tons in the USSR, 1.8 tons in Mexico, and 1.5 tons in India (SSB, ZGNCTJNJ 1989: 419).

Demand for Food At the start of its reform process, China's level of food intake per capita was vastly below that of the USSR (Table 1.12). China's reforms resulted in large increases in per capita income which were reflected in increased demands for superior foodstuffs, taking China's food consumption towards that of Japan, the most relevant comparator country (Table 1.12).

China's limited (and falling) arable area, and the fact that yields were very high, placed severe technical constraints on raising farm output. Huge popu-

Table 1.11 **Size of Collective and State Farms in China and the USSR (average per farm)**

| | USSR (1985)* | | China (1980) | |
	Collective farms	State farms	Production teams	Production brigades
number of workers	488	529	56	449
sown area (hectares)	3485	4766	26	206
large animals	1930 (cows)*	1850 (cows)**	17	134
pigs	1109**	1163**	55	430
sheep/goats	1666**	2921**	33	263
large/medium tractors	20	57	0.1	1.1
walking tractors	–	–	0.3	2.6
combine harvesters	14	19	negl	negl
farm-use trucks	44	26	negl	0.2
agricultural water pumps	–	–	0.8	6.4
mechanical threshers	–	–	0.5	3.5
grain husking machines	–	–	0.5	4.3
fodder crushing machines	–	–	0.3	2.0
rubber-tired carts:				
animal-drawn	–	–	0.4	3.4
hand-drawn	–	–	6.4	49.6

Notes

* In 1985, state farms occupied 179 million hectares of sown area, and collective farms occupied 143 million hectares of sown area.

** publicly owned

Sources: Liu 1989: 287, 289, 303; SSB, ZGNCTJNJ 1985: 232–3, 244; SSB, SYC, section 3.

lation growth and improvements in diet meant that China in the 1980s needed large agricultural investments in order to sustain the required large growth of farm output. The 'Green Revolution' continued throughout the reform period (Table 1.9), pre-empting investment funds from other uses. China's farm output growth from the late 1970s to the early 1990s was not achieved simply through making better use of existing resources, or 'taking up the slack'. Although the efficiency with which resources were used was much greater than in the Maoist period, a big effort of saving and investment by individual farmers, local communities and the state, was needed to sustain the growth of farm output.

Table 1.12 **Nutrient Intake in China (1978), USSR, USA and Japan (1988/90) (per capita per day)**

	China	(China as % of Japan)	Japan	USSR	(USSR as %of USA)	USA
calories of which:	2311	(79)	2921	3379	(93)	3642
animal	142	(23)	616	949	(86)	1107
vegetable	2169	(94)	2305	2430	(96)	2535
protein of which:	71	(75)	95	107	(97)	110
animal	4	(8)	53	57	(81)	71
vegetable	67	(160)	42	50	(128)	39
fats of which:	30	(37)	81	106	(68)	155
animal	14	(37)	38	71	(89)	80
vegetable	16	(37)	43	35	(47)	75

Source: SSB, SYC 1983: 509; SSB, ZGTJNJ 1993: 896

At the start of its reform, the USSR's level of per capita consumption of farm products was vastly above China's and close to that of the USA (Table 1.12). The USSR's population was growing slowly. Even a large growth of per capita income in the USSR would not have led to a large growth in demand for farm produce. China's task in reforming the farm sector was both to improve efficiency and substantially increase farm output. The USSR's task was simply to increase efficiency.

Size of Collective Farms   The basic level of ownership of the means of production, of work organization and income distribution in China was the production team. This averaged only around 50–60 workers and 26 hectares of sown area (Table 1.11). The Soviet collective farm averaged almost 500 workers and around 3500 hectares of sown area (Table 1.11).

Labour Force: Growth   By the 1980s, the USSR's farm population was stagnant. China's rural workforce grew by more than 130 million (over 43 per cent)[5] over the same period. Despite a successful programme of rural industrialization and non-farm labour absorption, the agricultural labour force increased by 65 million (25 per cent) over the same period. The amount of farmland per person fell by around one quarter in these years (from 0.35 ha per worker to 0.27 ha per person). Both economies began their reform process with a large amount of surplus labour consequent upon the shortcomings of the Stalinist command economy. However, China faced vastly greater problems than the USSR in absorbing surplus labour due to the huge pressure of population growth which constantly added to the total numbers for whom employment needed to be found.

Labour Force: Skill Level A sharply rising share of the Soviet rural workforce was technically qualified. Alongside a fall in the total rural workforce from the 1950s through to the 1980s went a steady rise in the number of technically skilled personnel (Li R. 1981: 498–9). The proportion of illiterate workers was negligible. In China in the mid-1980s, a mere 0.05 per cent of the rural workforce had a high-level specialist education. Only 8.8 per cent had even been to upper middle school, while 21 per cent were reported to be illiterate (SSB, ZGNCTJNJ 1985: 232). The Cultural Revolution badly damaged China's rural research and extension service: 'The numbers of qualified staff, especially at the senior levels, are severely limited…' (World Bank 1981c: 46). The agricultural education system had still in the late 1970s not recovered from 'the long period of closure and anti-professional bias' and there were 'critical shortages of staff at all levels' (World Bank 1981c: 46).

Agriculture: Similarities

Institutional Setting The communist economies all based their agricultural policies on the erroneous assumption that agriculture contained wide possibilities for economies of scale in all aspects of the farm process. Although the Soviet collective and state farm was much larger than the Chinese production team, the latter was still a large institution compared to farms under capitalist systems. There are deep problems with the collective and state-farm method of farm organization due to the peculiar difficulty of labour supervision in agriculture (Nolan 1988). This caused large managerial diseconomies of scale in most aspects of the direct tasks of cultivation. However, there is large scope for benefit from cooperation in the ancillary aspects of the farm process, such as research, irrigation, crop spraying, processing and marketing.

Memories of Private Farming Soviet collective and state farms had, of course, been in operation much longer than those in China, so that there were no direct memories of private farming. However, even in China, by 1989 the epoch of private farming was at least 25 years away. Moreover, no one under the age of around of 45–50 (the vast majority of Chinese farmers) would have had direct experience of running a private farm.

Lumpy Inputs   Soviet reforms failed to devise institutions which would have allowed individual farmers continued access to large, lumpy inputs which dominated the capital stock of collective and state farms (Kiselev 1993). China's rural reform sustained individual farmers' access to lumpy inputs that were beyond the financial and organizational resources of individual farmers. In China the predominantly small-scale mechanical farm inputs (for instance, mechanical threshers, power-tillers, mechanical rice-transplanters) were more expensive relative to average Chinese peasant income in the late 1980s than was a truck or tractor was to the Soviet collective farmer. In the early stages of reform in China most important means of production remained in collective ownership. Only as incomes rose did the share of privately owned assets become more dominant. Most irrigation facilities were beyond the resources of individual farmers. Continued provision by the local and national state apparatus ensured that the irrigation ratio rose from 45 per cent of the arable area in 1978 to 51 per cent in 1992 (Table 1.9).

Quality and Variety of Farm Inputs   In both China and the USSR farm productivity suffered from poor quality and variety of farm inputs, as well as from decisions about farm inputs being taken in offices remote from farmers. A well-devised industrial reform had the potential to enable a large reduction in capital needs per unit of output for the farm sector through the supply of better and more appropriate inputs.

Sale of Farm Output   In both the USSR and China the vast bulk of farm marketings pre-reform was controlled by state compulsory purchases. Increased freedom of choice for farmers about what to produce could have increased efficiency through allowing greater specialization.

Role of the Private Sector   In neither China nor the USSR had rural dwellers lost touch with individual farming. Indeed, private-sector activity was the main source of supply for many of their most important food products. In China the sector was subject to many more vicissitudes than in the USSR, being periodically subject to severe attack. However, as in the USSR for much of the time there was substantial scope for private farming activity (Li 1981: 384; Nolan and White 1983: 252).

Waste of Resources   Far from economizing on labour and capital, the communist approach to agricultural organization resulted in massive waste of resources. In 1980 in the USSR as much as 26 per cent of the workforce was in agriculture compared to under 4 per cent in the USA (Table 1.13). In China 71 per cent of the workforce was employed in agriculture, a similar

Table 1.13 **Comparison of Soviet and US Agriculture, 1974–5**

	USSR	USA
farm workers:		
total no. (m.) (1978)	27	4.1 (annual average)
share of total workforce (%)	26.3	3.7
share of total national investment (1971/5) (%)	26	<5
agriculture's share of GNP (%)	17.6	2.6
sown area (m. ha.)	217	137
fertiliser application (m. tons)	15.0	17.5
stocks of farm machinery:		
tractors: total no. (m.)	2.3	4.4
farm workers/tractor	12	0.9
farm trucks: total (m.)	1.3	2.9
farm workers/truck	20	1.4
combine harvesters: total no. (m.)	0.7	0.7
farm workers/truck	40	5.9
comparative yields:		
grain output per ha. (centners):		
foodgrain	13	21
feedgrain	16	38

Source: Li 1981: 67; USCJEC 1976: 578, 585

proportion to that in the least developed countries in the world (Table 1.1). In both cases agriculture grew at a moderate pace only through absorbing a large share of investment. In the 1970s in the USSR the farm sector's share of total national investment was over 20 per cent, compared to around 5 per cent in the USA (Table 1.13). In China, agriculture's share of national investment in the late 1970s was around 20 per cent (World Bank 1981c: 49).

Implications

In both cases relatively simple institutional changes had the potential to produce large improvements in farm efficiency, and to release labour and investment for other sectors. Improvements in farm performance could have had beneficial effects on light industrial growth and exports through the supply of industrial inputs, as well as cementing support for system reform through improving an essential element in people's livelihood.

The most important and simplest institutional change was contracting farmland to individual households. This 'land reform' alone would have reversed the profound managerial diseconomies of scale and radically improved peasant incentives. Profit-seeking farm households would have become more demanding in their selection of inputs. The largest problem was lumpy farm inputs. In advanced capitalist countries a large part of lumpy inputs are owned either by non-farmers and hired out by specialist suppliers to individual farmers, or are cooperatively owned alongside individual farm operation. In principle, in China and the USSR the land-contract process could have been combined with a maintenance of a large part of lumpy inputs in the hands of profit-oriented cooperatives or state machinery and irrigation companies. However, this required a state system committed to, and able to implement, such a policy.

In Russia right through to the present day, neither the basis on which farmland was to be operated by individual farmers nor the basis on which they might be able to have access to necessary lumpy inputs had been placed in a clear, credible framework. Indeed, the World Bank (1994: 3) considered that the lack of secure access to machinery services and capital were more important factors in explaining farmers' reluctance to leave collective and state farms even than uncertainty over property rights in land.

Natural Resource Endowment

The former USSR was by far the largest country in the world in terms of land area. Its territory accounted for 29 per cent of the world's total. It had massive reserves of timber (around one-quarter of the world total), coal (around one-half of the world's total), oil and natural gas. It also contained the world's largest gold reserves, one-fifth of the world's diamond reserves, the world's second largest deposits of copper, iron ore, nickel and zinc, as well as an abundance of other rare raw materials.

China also is a huge country. Like the former USSR it has massive coal reserves. However, it has not located large oil and natural gas reserves. China's continued need to depend heavily on coal as the main source of energy was a substantial burden during the reform period, since coal requires such large investments in transport per unit of power produced. Despite large foreign investment in oil exploration in the South China seas in the 1980s, significant reserves were not discovered. It is uncertain whether Chinese central Asia will reveal large oil and natural gas reserves. China's timber reserves are tiny for a country of its size, and its precious metals and minerals do not compare with those of Russia.

The willingness with which international oil companies were prepared to invest in exploration in China during its reforms demonstrates the ease with which the USSR also could have attracted a large amount of foreign investment to modernize natural resource production. The necessary conditions were political stability, secure property rights and a guaranteed share of the income from the investment. This would have provided a relatively easy path with which, through simple institutional reform, to raise export earnings. Unfortunately, despite the huge potential attractiveness to foreign investment the amounts invested have been negligible. This has been due to criminalization and corruption, strong links between the Russian government and the 'private' Russian oil companies, protection of the natural resource sector, and substantial popular hostility to foreign capital. The creation of political chaos by Gorbachev's political reforms destroyed the relatively easy avenue through which a Russian economy undertaking a serious economic reform programme might have enhanced its export earnings and helped modernize its economy through technology embodied in imports.

Population Pressure

In the absence of government measures to control fertility, China in the 1980s and 1990s would have faced the problems of high age-specific fertility rate common to most developing countries. In addition it confronted the special problem of a large age cohort entering the reproductive ages. China's system of basic needs guarantees under Mao left it peculiarly liable to explosively high rates of population growth in the absence of tough state action to control reproduction. In the 1960s death rates fell to low levels but birth rates were high during a period in which the government was too preoccupied with other matters to pay attention to policies to control reproduction. This exceptionally large cohort was moving through into the marriageable age groups in the 1980s and 1990s.

Under the people's communes China was successful in the 1970s in raising the average age of marriage. This, combined with greatly increased availability of contraception and strong sanctions helped to reduce sharply the overall birth rate in the late Maoist years which dropped from 36 to 23 per 1,000 between 1968 and 1975 (SSB, ZGTJNJ 1990: 90). Although the age of marriage and the proportion of the population using birth control remained high throughout the 1980s, the bulge in the proportion of the population in the reproductive ages still presented large difficulties in controlling overall fertility.

If the Chinese reforming government had not been able to take tough measures to control population growth, then China's population might well have been around 200 million larger in the mid-1990s, presenting large problems for the rate and structure of investment, which in turn would have slowed down the rate of growth of income and output. The key to its ability to implement the 'One Child' policy was the continued effectiveness of the communist party.

Inflationary Potential

The rate of inflation in China under reform was higher than was reported in the Maoist years. However, compared to the rate of inflation in Russia, or indeed, in most developing countries under reform, China's inflation rate was modest.[6] Did China have an easier task in controlling inflation than did Russia?

It has been argued that Yeltsin's government inherited a legacy of substantial repressed inflation which was a special difficulty for Russia's reforms. In common with the other communist economies, China inherited repressed inflation from the Stalinist period, not least through the excess demand for many goods and services in short supply under the administered economy. These problems were as severe in China in 1976 as in the USSR in 1985. In the USSR after 1985 the problems of repressed inflation rapidly intensified, but this was a direct result of Gorbachev's political reforms. These were in turn the fundamental element of the 'transition orthodoxy': political democratization was considered to be essential before economic reform could be implemented.

In China also there were large structural pressures associated with reforming the planned economy, such as bottlenecks in infrastructure, which tended to stimulate inflation. Moreover, the bottlenecks intensified with the successful achievement of a rapid rate of growth, with surges in demand for slow-gestating capital goods products.

In a country of China's size, there were peculiarly strong inflationary pressures in the reform period associated with the need to decentralize many economic functions of government. In the absence of a comprehensive reform of the financial system, there was, in a 'prisoner's dilemma' fashion, little incentive for local authorities or banks to control the supply of money in the interests of control over the national rate of inflation.

In sum, China's success in combining a reasonable rate of inflation with rapid growth cannot be interpreted as mainly a matter of good fortune in the inherited inflationary potential. It was a peculiarly difficult feat to accomplish simultaneous accelerated growth, large structural transformation and a reasonably controlled rate of inflation. The maintenance of an effective state apparatus was a necessary condition of sustaining the government's fiscal capacity and combining required financial decentralization with some degree of control over money supply growth.

SOCIAL AND POLITICAL FACTORS

Culture

The fact that many of the Asian Newly Industrializing Countries were Confucian revived theories linking culture and economic development that had been long neglected after Max Weber's attempt to explain the rise of capitalism in Western Europe by the Protestant ethic. Confucianism emphasizes hard work, education, meritocracy and hierarchy, which fits the popular conception of an efficient corporation. It is tempting to add China, the birthplace of Confucianism, to the list of countries whose growth can be explained by this value system. However, 'culture' is not a given factor. It is continually being reconstructed either consciously or unconsciously.[7] It is not clear that any type of Confucianism *per se* promotes economic development, as Morishima (1982) has argued. A long scholarly tradition argued that China's variety of Confucianism constituted a large handicap to economic development, due to long-ingrained habits of familism, nepotism and corruption (for example, Levy 1949). The values of the Chinese, family-oriented variant of Confucianism was long thought to be fundamentally opposed to those of the modern business corporation, due to its emphasis upon 'particularism and functional diffuseness' (Levy 1949: 12). Pessimism about China's economic prospects based on the deep-rooted problems of traditional cultural factors was a persistent theme of writing on China in the 1980s.

Administrative Capacity of the Bureaucracy

Both China and the USSR had a long tradition of centralized bureaucratic rule, though the tradition was of much greater antiquity in China. They each had a huge party apparatus, which was closely interwoven with the system of state administration. The Chinese communist party apparatus was no less corrupt or more professionally effective than that of the USSR in the late 1970s. Indeed, the Chinese Communist Party and administrative apparatus was seriously damaged during the Cultural Revolution. Even more than usual in a communist country, promotions in China during this period had been based on ideological rather than professional criteria. Economics had been virtually killed in China during the decade of the Cultural Revolution. By contrast, Soviet economics was very much alive, despite the constraints on the boundaries of discussion. The Soviet central planning apparatus was vastly more technically sophisticated than its Chinese counterpart. Local authorities in the USSR, while tightly constrained in the range of independence, were charged with vastly more complex administrative tasks than their Chinese counterparts, most of which were administering relatively self-sufficient units producing a narrow range of primitive products.

There is a long tradition of political analysis of China which argues that the main reason for China's failure to build on its great medieval technical break-through and experience an industrial revolution was precisely the inhibiting power of the bureaucracy (for instance, Needham 1969). A consensus of informed opinion both inside and outside China in the 1980s felt that the strength of this stifling bureaucratic tradition would prevent China advancing successfully towards a market economy (for instance, the former head of the Marxism Leninism Institute, Su Shauzhi; Su 1988).

The bureaucracy was regarded by almost all commentators as the major obstacle to the implementation of reform policies in communist countries. Most observers regarded it is as self-evident that the bureaucracy would be deeply opposed to economic reform, since reform would deprive them of power and status. Aslund (1991: 14) summarizes this, the most fundamental tenet of the 'transition orthodoxy', as follows:

> A reform reduces the power of the bureaucracy by definition and most of the administration will inevitably oppose reform. Therefore, a successful reform must break the power of the anti-reform bureaucracy ... *To break the power of the party and state bureaucracy may be seen as the key problem of a reform.* (my emphasis)

However, the possession of an effective, competent state bureaucracy is a central element in explaining the rise of almost every successful industrializing country since Britain. There were two logical possibilities to the problems of the old state apparatus. One was to regard it as hopelessly unreformable, inherently opposed to any kind of reform measure, and to destroy it. A second, reformist approach was to attempt to change its goals and methods of operation. This would involve a gradual process of professionalization, making the organization more youthful, introducing more rationality rather than quasi-religious principles into its ethical foundation, and giving the members of the apparatus a central role in the process of reconstructing the Stalinist economy. In the reformist approach the Party members are less threatened and although their tasks alter greatly over a given period of time, they retain their dignity and status, and remain relatively well rewarded.

The Chinese leadership attempted to follow the second approach and was broadly successful in it. However, the Chinese bureaucratic apparatus had no greater capacity to be transformed successfully in this reformist way than did the Soviet one. Indeed, the reverse may well be the case. Consider Miller's (1993: 77) evaluation of the Soviet bureaucracy which Gorbachev inherited:

> The Party's quasi-military structure and traditions made it an effective and durable instrument in the hands of such a leader. It still produced officials who could serve a transformist cause with energy and selfless loyalty. It contained millions of others who would doggedly carry out orders even if they did not fully understand them – indeed who would accept surgery on the Party provided it was administered by one of their own.

The Soviet approach under Gorbachev was entirely different. In the face of great opposition at the top of the Party, Gorbachev, with the support of small group of advisers (especially those in the think-tanks set up by Andropov in the early 1980s, known collectively as the 'New Thinking'), put into practice the policies of *perestroika* and *glasnost* which led to the rapid disintegration of the entire communist edifice in the USSR and Eastern Europe:

> Gorbachev was unusual in that he saw and accepted the logic of human rights dissent, that it falsified the central assumptions of the regime he commanded. This 'New Thinking' of course... was not his work alone. His contribution was to bring together the isolated and alienated intellectuals who orginated it, *to turn a dissident subculture into a policy and to work out a strategy for realising it* (Miller 1993: 206; my emphasis).

Mass Demands for Political Reform

Political outcomes are far from a matter of choice by governments. One line of argument is that the dramatic contrast in political outcomes in China and the USSR was not at all a matter of policy choice but was, rather, an uncontrollable consequence of the fundamental difference in political environment. The most important of such propositions relate to mass demands for democracy on the one hand and the propensity for the respective countries to split into separate political units (their 'fissiparous' tendencies).

Mass Demands for Democracy

The Soviet Union in the late 1970s was a much more highly urbanized society than was China. Its intellectuals had a much stronger interest in

Western values. In the 1970s there was a more widespread hope in the USSR than in China that Western democratic institutions might be put into place.

However, the Soviet political system seemed stable. It had survived relatively intact since the 1920s without fundamental disruptions. Even in the post-Stalin and post-Khrushchev period it still was highly repressive. China's political system had only recently been through the huge upheaval of the Cultural Revolution, which had deeply damaged the communist party, unleashing a period of widespread anarchy. There is no counterpart in Soviet history.

In the Soviet Union, expectations of fundamental political change were low. It was the policy decisions of Gorbachev, namely *glasnost* and *perestroika*, that turned distant hopes into ardent expectations. In the sharpest contrast there was a near consensus among the Chinese leadership that political democratization was not a part of the political agenda in the near future in China. A series of campaigns against 'bourgeois' values ('spiritual pollution') attempted to reduce expectations of change among the politically active population.

Fissiparous Tendencies

In the 1970s both China and the USSR were huge multinational empires. However, the relative size of the 'national minority' population is a major difference between the two countries. The non-Russian population accounted for around one-half of the total Soviet population, whereas the non-Han population in China accounted for well under 10 per cent of the total population. Once the minority nationalities began to pursue their demands for independence in a serious fashion in the USSR the situation was more difficult to control than would have been the case in China.

Successful market and income growth is the most powerful force leading to the disintegration of ethnic differences. Stalinism kept nationalism intact in a 'deep-freeze' beneath a veneer of new 'socialist man'. The national leadership of both countries perpetuated a public propaganda myth that the 'nationality' question belonged to the past. In both cases the 'national minorities' were disproportionately concentrated in more sparsely populated, remote, resource-rich regions. In both cases national liberation movements had been brutally suppressed. However, the severity of these struggles in recent times had been much greater in China than in the USSR. China fought major battles against the Uighur 'national minority' in Xinjiang province in central Asia over a long period, and conducted a protracted and violent guerrilla war against the Tibetan independence movement.

In the 1970s, the expectation of national minority groups was not high in either country. However, the policies pursued by the national leadership were strikingly different. In the Soviet case the policy of political *perestroika* and *glasnost* greatly raised the expectation of national minority groups. In China, national policymakers repeatedly made it clear that attempts to break away from rule by Beijing would be brutally repressed.

Effective central rule in a country may not be undermined only by nationalism. China's long history has been dominated by regular cycles of national disintegration and reunification, even among the Han people. No theme is stronger in Chinese political history than the need to maintain national unity in the face of a high intrinsic propensity for the 'sheet of loose sand' to spin apart into 'great turmoil' (*da luan*). China is not an inherently unified state. National unity has only been maintained over substantial periods through effective government. Its modern history shows only too clearly the high propensity for central rule to fall apart.

CONCLUSION

This chapter has identified many important differences between the economic and political inheritance bequeathed to the leaders of the respective countries at the start of their reform programme. These included China's much lower level of farmland per capita, of per capita income, of urbanization, of industrialization, and of scientific skills. In China small-scale industrial enterprises were much more important than in the USSR. China had a much more important role played by poorly located areas in its structure of industrial assets. China had a much higher rate of population growth, and a more ancient tradition of entrepreneurship. National minority populations occupied a much smaller share of total population in China than in the USSR. China possessed much larger concentrations of capital in the hands of overseas citizens. Some of these differences tended to work to the advantage of accelerated post-Stalinist growth in China, but many of them did not. It is not apparent that on balance the inherited system differences made it likely that well-chosen political and economic policies would lead to faster growth in China than in the USSR.

However, there were also important similarities. Both countries had a high potentiality for fissure into political anarchy and separate nation states. Both countries had large reservoirs of entrepreneurial skill. They each possessed relatively well-educated populations for their level of income, and in both cases there was massive underfulfilment of human productive capabilities. The basic 'planning' methods of the command economy were the same. The key features of both farm and the non-farm institutions were the same. Both systems had relatively large amounts of technical skill and capital stock locked up in the military sector. In each case the economic system was massively underperforming in comparison to the productive potential achievable with existing physical and human capital. In each case, relatively simple system changes were capable of generating an initial large improvement in system performance which could act as the springboard to further, more fundamental change and improvement. In other words, despite important differences, both the former USSR and China possessed large catch-up possibilities, as did most of the former Stalinist countries.

If the analysis in this chapter is correct, then the main cause of the difference in outcome between China and Russia under system reform must be the differences in policy choice. The contrast in policies chosen was itself the result of complex historical factors leading to fundamentally different approaches towards the task of transforming the Stalinist system (for a more comprehensive discussion, see Nolan 1995). The contrast in policy choice applies both to narrowly economic policy and to the wider question of the relationship between political and economic reform.

The Soviet disaster stems primarily from the wholehearted embrace of the 'transition orthodoxy', policies of political reform (*perestroika* and *glasnost*) and subsequent economic change ('shock therapy') advocated by foreign advisers and commentators such as Kornai (1990), Sachs (for instance, Lipton and Sachs 1990), Prybyla (1991) and Aslund (1990, 1991) and their domestic counterparts in the USSR and the Russian Federation.[8] China's reform success stems primarily from its refusal to implement the 'transition orthodoxy' policies which in the 1980s were increasingly urged upon the leaders by both domestic and foreign 'reformers'. It released the growth potentialities embedded within the Stalinist system. It did so through maintaining an authoritarian political system which allowed the gradual unfolding of market forces, remained reasonably fiscally effective, provided a stable environment to encourage foreign direct investment and was able to intervene in a wide array of areas in which markets might be expected to 'fail' in such a turbulent period of system transformation (for further argument, see Nolan 1995).

This chapter contains two implicit counterfactual propositions. The selection of different policies in Russia could have produced rapid growth of output and a large improvement in popular living standards. The selection of a different set of policies in China could easily have produced a political and economic disaster, with a large decline in popular living standards.

Notes

1   I am grateful to Trevor Buck of the University of Nottingham for discussions which led me to write this chapter. I am grateful also to Geoff Harcourt and Michael Ellman

for their perceptive and lengthy comments on an earlier draft, and to Albert Schweinberger, Ajit Singh and Norman Stockman for inviting me to present seminars, based on the chapter, at the Universities of Konstanz, Cambridge and Aberdeen respectively.

2 Due to labour hoarding by managers and the slow workpace among workers.

3 In addition to its large pool of highly qualified scientists, the USSR possessed a large stock of moderately trained scientific workers – larger than the USA's, in fact (USCJEC 1979: 745).

4 In 1979 over 75 per cent of Soviet families had TV sets and refrigerators and 70 per cent had a washing machine (Schroeder 1983: 313).

5 The Chinese data in this paragraph are all from SSB, ZGTJNJ (1983: 81, 97–8, 115).

6 The rate of inflation from 1980 to 1989 was reported to be 5.8 per cent per annum (Word Bank, World Development Report 1991). Russia's inflation rate in the early 1990s accelerated to over 1000 per cent.

7 For example, the Japanese 'culture' of industrial harmony did not emerge spontaneously, but was deliberately invented (Hobsbawm and Ranger 1985).

8 Such as the authors of the '500 Day Plan' for the transformation of the Soviet economy, and subsequently, Chubais and Sobchak.

References

Note: USCJEC = United States Congress, Joint Economic Committee SSB = [Chinese] State Statistical Bureau

Abramowitz, M., 1986, 'Catching up, forging ahead, falling behind'. *Journal of Economic History*, 46(2): 385–406.

Acs, Z. and D.B. Audretsch, 1993, 'Has the role of small firms changed in the US?' in Z. Acs and D. Audretsch (eds), *Small Firms and Entrepreneurship*. Cambridge: Cambridge University Press.

Arnot, B., 1981, 'Soviet labour productivity and the failure of the Shchekino experiment'. *Critique*, 15: 31–56.

Aslund, A., 1989, 'Soviet and Chinese reforms: why they must be different'. *World Today*, 45(11).

Aslund, A., 1991, *Gorbachev's Struggle for Economic Reform*. London: Pinter.

Aslund, A., 1990, 'Gorbachev, perestroika, and economic crisis'. *Problems of Communism*, January–April, 13–41.

Banister, J., 1987, *China's Changing Population*. Stanford: Stanford University Press.

Banister, J., 1992, 'Demographic aspects of poverty in China'. *Working Paper*, The World Bank.

Bergere, M-C., 1981, *The Golden Age of the Chinese Bourgeoisie*. Cambridge: Cambridge University Press.

Berliner, J., 1983, 'Planning and management' in A. Bergson and D. Levine (eds), *The Soviet Economy: Towards the Year 2000*. London: Allen and Unwin.

Blackwell, W., 1983, 'The Russian entrepreneur in the Tsarist period: an overview' in G. Guroff and F.V. Kasterson (eds), *Entrepreneurship in Imperial Russia and the Soviet Union*. Princeton: Princeton University Press.

Brown, A. and M. Kaser, (eds), *The Soviet Union since Khrushchev*. London: Macmillan.

Chen, K., G. Jefferson and I. Singh, 1992, 'Lessons from China's reform'. *Journal of Comparative Economics*, 16: 201–25.

Dobb, M., 1966, *Studies in the Development of Capitalism*. London: Routledge and Kegan Paul.

Donnithorne, A., 1972, *China's Economic System*. London: George Allen and Unwin.

Eberstadt, N., 1986, 'Material poverty in the People's Republic of China in international perspective' in USCJEC, *China's Economy Looks Towards the Year 2000*, Vol. 1. Washington, DC: US Government Printing Office.

Ellman, M., 1994, 'The increase in death and disease under *katastroika*'. *Cambridge Journal of Economics*, 18(4).

Erlich, E., 1985, 'The size and structure of manufacturing establishments and enterprises: an international comparison'. *Journal of Comparative Economics*, 9: 267–95.

Feshbach, M., 1983, 'Population and labour force' in A. Bergson and D. Levine (eds), *The Soviet Economy: Towards the Year 2000*. London: Allen and Unwin.

Gatrell, P., 1986, *The Tsarist Economy, 1850–1917*. London: Batsford.

Goldman, M., 1994, *Lost Opportunity: Why Economic Reforms in Russia Have Not Worked*. London: W.W. Norton.

Gomulka, S., 1991, *The Theory of Technological Change and Economic Growth*. London: Routledge.

Granick, D., 1967, *Soviet Metal-Fabricating*. Madison: University of Wisconsin Press.

Grossman, G., 1979, 'Notes on the illegal economy and corruption' in USCJEC, *Soviet Economy in a Time of Change*, 2 vols. Washington, DC: US Government Printing Office.

Hanson, P., 1978, 'The import of Western technology' in A. Brown and M. Kaser (eds), *The Soviet Union since Krushchev*. London: Macmillan.

Hobsbawm, E. and T. Ranger, (eds) (1985), *The Invention of Tradition*. Cambridge: Cambridge University Press.

Kiselev, S., 1994, 'The state and the farmer'. *Problems of Economic Transition*, 36(10): 67–81.

Kornai, J., 1990, *The Road to a Free Economy*. New York: Norton.

Levy, M. and K.H. Shih, 1949, *The Rise of the Modern Chinese Business Class*. New York: Institute of Pacific Relations.

Li, R., 1981, *Statistical Materials on Soviet Agriculture* (Sulian nongye tongji huibian). Beijing: Nongye Chubanshe.

Little, I., 1979, 'An economic reconnaissance' in W. Galenson (ed.), *Taiwan*. Ithaca: Cornell University Press.

Liu, N., Y. Chen and C. Zhang, 1988, *Seventy Years of Soviet Economic Growth* (Sulian guomin jingji fazhan qishi nian). Beijing: Jijie Chubanshe.

Macmillan, J. and B. Naughton, 1992, 'How to reform a planned economy'. *Oxford Review of Economic Policy*, 8(1): 130–43.

Macpherson, W.J., 1987, *The Economic Development of Japan, 1868–1941*. London: Macmillan.

Miller, J., 1993, *Mikhail Gorbachev and the End of Soviet Power*. London: Macmillan.

Ministry of Agriculture, 1982, *Outline of China's Agriculture* (Zhongguo nongye jingji gaiyao). Beijing: Nongye Chubanshe.

Ministry of Agriculture, 1988, *Statistical Abstract of China's Xiangzhen Enterprises* (Quanguo xiangzhen qiye tongji zhaiyao). Beijing: Xiangzhen Qiye Bu.

Morishima, M., 1982, *Why Has Japan Succeeded?* Cambridge: Cambridge University Press.

Needham, J., 1969, *The Grand Titration*. London: Allen and Unwin.

Nolan, P., 1983, *Growth Processes and Distributional Change in a South Chinese Province: The Case of Guangdong*. London: Contemporary China Institute.

Nolan, P., 1988, *The Political Economy of Collective Farms*. Cambridge: Polity Press.

Nolan, P., 1994, 'Democratisation, human rights and economic reform: the case of China and Russia'. *Democratisation*, 1(1).

Nolan, P., 1995, *China's Rise, Russia's Fall: Politics, Economics and Planning in the Transition from Stalinism*. London: Macmillan.

Nove, A., 1983, *The Economics of Feasible Socialism*. London: George Allen and Unwin.

Perkins, D.H., (ed.) 1977, *China: Rural Small Scale Industry in the People's Republic of China*. Berkeley and Los Angeles: University of California Press.

Prybyla, J., 1991, 'The road from socialism: why, where, what and how'. *Problems of Communism*, XL.

Rawski, T.G., 1989, *Economic Growth in Pre-war China*. Berkeley and Los Angeles: University of California Press.

Sachs, J. and W.T. Woo, 1994, 'Structural factors in the economic reforms of China, Eastern Europe and the former Soviet Union. *Economic Policy*, 18.

Schroeder, G., 1983, 'Consumption' in A. Bergson and D. Levine (eds), *The Soviet Economy: Towards the Year 2000*. London: Allen and Unwin.

Shmelyev, N. and V. Popov, 1990, *The Turning Point: Revitalising the Soviet Economy*. London: I.B. Tauris.

Spechler, M.C., 1979, 'Regional developments in the USSR, 1958–1978', in USJEC, *Soviet Economy in a Time of Change*, 2 Vols. Washington, DC: US Government Printing Office.

State Statistical Bureau (SSB), *Statistical Yearbook of China (SYC)*. Hong Kong: Economic Information Agency.

State Statistical Bureau (SSB), ZGTJNJ, 1984–93, *Chinese Economic Yearbook* (Zhongguo tongji nianjian). Beijing: Zhongguo Tongji Chubanshe.

State Statistical Bureau (SSB), ZGNCTJNJ, 1985–93, *Chinese Rural Statistical Yearbook* (Zhongguo nongcun tongji nianjian). Beijing: Zhongguo Tongji Chubanshe.

State Statistical Bureau (SSB), ZGGYJJTJNJ, 1986–93, *Economic Statistics on Chinese Industry* (Zhongguo gongye jingji tongji nianjian). Beijing: Tongji Chubanshe.

State Statistical Bureau (SSB), ZGGYJJTJZL, 1985, *Statistical Materials on China's Industrial Economy* (Zhongguo gongye jingji tongji ziliao). Beijing: Zhongguo Tongji Chubanshe.

State Statistical Bureau (SSB), ZGGXHZSTJZY, 1989, *Statistical Materials on China's Supply and Marketing Co-operatives, 1949–1988* (Zhongguo gongxiao hezuoshe tongji ziliao). Beijing: Zhongguo Tongji Chubanshe.

State Statistical Bureau (SSB), ZGTJZY, 1984–94, *Statistical Survey of China* (Zhongguo tongji zhaiyao). Beijing: Zhongguo Tongji Chubanshe.

State Statistical Bureau (SSB), ZGRKTJNJ, 1989, *Statistical Yearbook of Chinese Population* (Zhongguo renkou tongji nianjian). Beijing: Kexue Jishu Wenxian Chubanshe.

Su, S., 1988, *Democratisation and Reform*. Nottingham: Spokesman Books.

United Nations Development Programme (UNDP), 1990, *Human Development Report*. New York: Oxford University Press.

USCJEC, 1975, *China: A Reassessment of the Economy*. Washington, DC: US Government Printing Office.

USCJEC, 1976, *Soviet Economy in a New Perspective*. Washington, DC: US Government Printing Office.

USCJEC, 1979, *Soviet Economy in a Time of Change*, 2 vols. Washington, DC: US Government Printing Office.

USCJEC, 1978, *Chinese Economy Post-Mao*. Washington, DC: US Government Printing Office.

USCJEC, 1982, *Soviet Economy in the 1980s: Problems and Prospects*. Washington, DC: US Government Printing Office.

USCJEC, 1986, *China's Economy Looks Towards the Year 2000*, Vol. 1. Washington, DC: US Government Printing Office.

Walker, K., 1965, *Planning in Chinese Agriculture*. London: Frank Cass.

World Bank, 1981a, *China: Socialist Development*. Washington, DC: World Bank.

World Bank, 1981b, *China: Socialist Development, Annex D, Challenges and Achievements in Industry*. Washington, DC: World Bank.

World Bank, 1981c, *China: Socialist Development, Annex C, Agricultural Development*. Washington, DC: World Bank.

World Bank, 1992a, *China: Strategies for Reducing Poverty in the 1990s*. Washington, DC: World Bank.

World Bank, 1992b, *Russian Economic Reforms at the Threshold*. Washington, DC: World Bank.

World Bank, 1979–94, *World Development Report*. New York: Oxford University Press.

World Bank, 1994, *Land Reform and Farm Re-structuring in Russia*. Washington, DC: World Bank.

Xu, D. and C. Wu, (eds) 1985, *China's Capitalist Sprouts* (Zhongguo zibenzhuyi mengya). Beijing: Renmin Chubanshe.

Yanowitch, M., 1977, *Social and Economic Inequality in the Soviet Union*. London: Martin Robertson.

Yeh, K.C., 1984, 'Macroeconomic changes in the Chinese economy during the readjustment'. *China Quarterly*, 100.

Yu, G., (ed.) 1984, *China's Socialist Modernisation*. Beijing: Foreign Languages Press.

2

CHINA'S NEW DEVELOPMENT PATH: TOWARDS CAPITALIST MARKETS, MARKET SOCIALISM OR BUREAUCRATIC MARKET MUDDLE?*

Introduction

System reform is on the agenda across the whole socialist bloc. It promises to reshape international relations and to influence a vast number of people's conception of a desirable form of socioeconomic system. Many Western defenders of the free-market system are delighted at the admissions of system failure in the 'socialist' countries. In fact, Stalinism is almost the only form which 'actually existing socialism' has taken where a whole country has been declared socialist, and it is this which free marketeers wish to see as the only alternative to unrestrained capitalism. Many Western socialists accept this analysis, arguing that Deng Xiaoping and Gorbachev are 'restoring capitalism'. Outside these extreme reactions, a large number of ordinary people in the advanced capitalist economies feel that the reforms in the socialist countries signal defeat for the socialist ideal.

These developments provoke deep reflection on the meaning of 'capitalism' and 'socialism', and their relevance to developing countries such as China. 'Capitalism' is easier to define in an agreed way than 'socialism'. The principal elements of capitalism are a system in which most goods and services are commodities traded in markets, in which labour power itself is a commodity, in which resource allocation is controlled by the pursuit of profit, which in turn is shaped by market-determined prices, and in which the means of production are privately owned. In its pure form, capitalism's direction of movement is determined by the logic of competition in the marketplace, the 'invisible hand', rather than by conscious social control. It is unequal. Society is divided into a mass class of propertyless workers and a small minority class of capitalists in whose hands the ownership and control of capital is concentrated. However, in its pure form, capitalism existed at the most for only a short period in one country, namely nineteenth-century Britain. Thereafter, the governments of virtually all 'capitalist' countries intervened in markets, and these countries experienced a certain amount of redistribution of ownership and control over capital away from a tiny 'capitalist' class as well as enormous increases in political rights for the mass of the population. These economies cannot be called 'capitalist' without qualification. Socialist elements developed within them, and in this author's view the advanced 'capitalist' economies are more socialist than the self-styled 'socialist' countries.

It is much more difficult to find an agreed definition of 'socialism' than of 'capitalism'. The simplest approach is that of Stalinism. It identifies the chief shortcomings of capitalism as the anarchy of free markets together with class inequality based on unequal ownership of the means of production; it conceives of socialism as the obverse of this, substituting the administrative plan for competitive markets and 'abolishing' class inequality by nationalization of the means of production. This vision of socialism remains influential even within the advanced capitalist countries.

If 'socialism' is not comprehensible to ordinary people it will not be supported. Its broad aim should be to improve the quality of life of the whole population of a particular country and, indeed, of all members of the human race. Socialism's distinguishing characteristics are commitment to the equal worth of all human beings (from which follows a concern with inequality and citizens' rights) and a belief that collective action is often necessary to improve the quality of life (from which follows a concern with citizens' duties). Neither Stalinism nor free-market capitalism can be enduring political-economic philosophies because both will be, or already have come to be, seen by the mass of the population in different countries to be inadequate in providing them with a better quality of life. Some form of market socialism is the only viable long-term basis for meeting most people's aspirations. In different countries, and at different stages of development, some elements of quality of life are more important than others.

What does this mean for understanding socialism in developing countries? Socialist development is a long-term incremental process, not a single act of seizure of power. Much of it does not occur through action by political rulers, but rather comes from forces emerging independently among the mass of the population. The full flowering of socialism cannot be constructed by rulers for the people. The advanced economies have already developed the productive forces far beyond the poor countries, with corresponding advances in culture, education and leisure which lay the foundation for democratic life. In contrast, in developing countries the principal objective is transparently simple and one with respect to which people of widely different political persuasions can agree, i.e. improving mass living standards as rapidly as possible. Without this, the most straightforward human needs cannot be met. For poor people all considerations pale before those of improved diet, clothing, housing, education, health and increased availability of consumer durables. The most desirable policy for a poor country is that which advances mass living standards most rapidly, providing the basis in the long run for individual self-fulfilment and democratic life. This generally requires much collective action to interfere with the free market to stimulate growth and to redistribute to groups which lose out in the marketplace.

In this chapter it is argued that capitalist forces of competition and profit-seeking are necessary for successful growth of the productive forces in a developing country and for producing many of the prerequisites of a free democratic society. In the next section it is suggested that China needs these forces and that this is more or less explicitly acknowledged by China's present leaders. However, after years of isolation from the outside world, after the disappointments of Stalinism, and under the influence of an oversimplistic interpretation of the causes of growth in neighbouring East Asian countries and of the relevance of their experience to China, some Chinese economists have an excessively positive view of the virtues of the market. In the third section it is argued that China's policymakers need to be aware of the great variety of ways in which markets fail with respect to both growth and creating a just distribution of the benefits of growth. In the fourth section it is suggested that Stalinism has served China badly. It is in its death throes as a credible political-economic philosophy in China as it is in almost all the other 'socialist' countries. Stalinism emerged as the antithesis of the system which Marx criticized in *Das Kapital*. Having experienced the shortcomings of Stalinism, it would be a great error for the 'socialist' countries to return to a naive trust in the 'invisible hand'. It is argued in the fifth section that the state has an enormous range of tasks to undertake in a country such as China. China does not need the economics of Milton Friedman, but rather a relevant form of market socialism. An optimistic view would suggest that this is broadly the model towards which China is evolving. However, it would be foolish to underestimate the difficulties of a transition out of Stalinism, especially in an extremely poor country like China. I am convinced that China will not return to such a system, but it is difficult to predict whether it will end up closer to capitalist markets, market socialism or even plain market muddle, since this depends on complex political processes rather than the choice of a model from a menu.

Traditional arguments about socialism and capitalism have been conducted principally with respect to the issues of economic growth, political liberties and distribution of power, goods and services. However, two issues stand above all these, namely international military conflict and the environment. If they are not handled well, there will not be much of a world left to argue about. Examination of these would take this chapter into an unacceptable length and beyond the framework of this book. However, their importance overshadows all other considerations, and both capitalism and Stalinism have serious problems in these respects.

The Benefits of Capitalism

Capitalist Dynamism

Capitalism's emergence from feudalism in Europe was characterized by a progressive removal of restraints on competition, by a growing tendency for capital and labour to migrate to activities with higher returns, and by increasing enterprise independence to determine resource allocation, with penalties for failure and rewards for success. This process was associated with widening markets, deepening division of labour, and a growing system of property rights which helped to bring private and social costs and benefits closer together by ensuring that risk-takers and innovators reaped the main part of the reward for their enterprise. Without a well-defined and enforceable system of property rights, third parties can receive some of the benefits from economic transactions. Consequently, socially desirable investments and innovations may not be undertaken because private costs exceed private benefits.

Some of the sternest critics of capitalism's inequalities, notably Marx, recognized the stimulus it provided to economic growth. The late medieval expansion of accumulation, technical progress and market widening were possible because of the emerging capitalist setting. In addition to praising the dynamism of capitalism over feudalism, its critics emphasized its unstable character and an apparent tendency towards concentration of asset ownership alongside the growth of a propertyless class. Unsurprisingly, faced with the growth of monopoly capitalism and the collapse of capitalist production in the early 1930s as opposed to the USSR's dynamism, the generation of socialists whose formative years were between the wars stressed an apparent tendency to stagnation in advanced monopoly capitalism compared with its earlier dynamism. Moreover, capitalist neocolonialism was considered to be incompatible with economic progress in the Third World.

Things turned out differently. Despite continued capitalist instability, with enormous periodic waste from unemployment, socialist economists had massively underestimated capitalism's long-term dynamism. The advanced capitalist economies are, indeed, oligopolistic. However, the fierceness of the global struggle for markets ensures that Schumpeterian rivalry exists among huge firms, powerfully spurring on cost reduction and technical progress. Moreover, instead of stagnation, since the 1950s the Third World has seen a massive, albeit uneven, growth of the productive forces in areas in which capitalism has taken root. The success of the newly industrializing countries (NICs) powerfully challenged traditional socialist interpretations of the relative merits of capitalism and socialism as vehicles for economic progress.

Capitalism is not alien to China. From at least the Song dynasty (AD 960–1275) farmers and petty industrialists producing for the market formed increasingly important 'capitalist sprouts' within the existing mode of production, propelling forward the productive forces. Under extremely adverse political conditions, Chinese capitalism made rapid progress in eastern seaboard cities (especially in and around Shanghai) in the early twentieth century. In the early 1950s, and at any later point when controls were relaxed, petty capitalist forces sprang to life. After almost three decades of administrative planning in China the post-1978 period saw a powerful increase in the impact of the capitalist forces of inter-enterprise competition, independent enterprise decision-making and migration of capital and labour in search of profits, especially in small-scale non-state enterprises and in agriculture, though even here capitalist forces still operated in a far from unconstrained fashion. Overall, the economy performed exceptionally well in this period, with rapid growth of output in the sectors most affected by capitalist forces. The most important results were a sustained growth in the living standards of the Chinese people and a remarkably rapid decline in the number of poor. Naturally, such an exceptionally rapid growth of living standards could not be maintained over the long term, because in part it represented a taking in of the previous 'slack' in resource utilization. However, the period was one of outstanding economic success.

Capitalist Freedoms

Capitalism contrasts strikingly with other political-economic formations in the scope that it provides for individual freedom. Capitalism's essence is freedom of choice in the marketplace, and it is unsurprising that individual freedom is the moral basis of capitalism. This concept was useful to merchants and industrialists struggling to emerge from feudal oppression. However, it also became important for ordinary people. The right to make choices without interference from other individuals and groups or from the state is deeply embedded in the psychology of the citizens of the advanced capitalist countries.

As characteristic as the demand for individual freedom has been the emergence under capitalism of demands for political rights, as individuals' sense of self-worth and rights to choose develop with the emerging market economy.

The relationship between capitalist development and political democracy is complex. The early phases of capitalist development have rarely been associated with extensive political freedoms and rights. However, successful capitalist development has generally, after a certain point, witnessed mass demands for democracy. Successful capitalist development brings an increased sense of individual self-worth, reinforced by a growing sense of membership of an interdependent national community, and by increasing levels of education and, eventually, leisure time in which the mass of the population is able to participate in democratic activities extending beyond the important right to choose periodically local or national rulers. Moreover, there is an international 'demonstration effect' of political concepts spilling over from the advanced to the less developed economies.

In the areas of China affected by modern capitalism pre-1949 there was a ferment of new ideas among, in particular, urban workers and intellectuals, bringing new concepts of freedom and demands for democratic rights. How far can the reintroduction of capitalist forces post-Mao be expected to affect popular consciousness in China? In the 1980s the Chinese leadership made tentative steps to establish a concept of individual freedoms with rights to appeal to an independent judiciary, although the base from which this process set out was extremely low. This was attributable in no small degree to the Cultural Revolution, when the rights and freedoms of so many individuals were trampled upon. The most striking examples of increased individual freedoms were in the cultural sphere, where a real New Economic Policy (NEP) atmosphere prevailed in the 1980s. This new cultural freedom, although still within state-controlled limits, contributed enormously to the improved quality of life.

Will the new areas of freedom and independence accompanying the increased role of market forces be compatible with the continuation of a system of Communist Party control, in which ordinary people have no rights to determine their rulers? The recent history of South Korea and Taiwan might suggest a negative answer, but this is too simplistic. Average incomes and levels of urbanization in these countries are much above those in China. Moreover, 'capitalist' elements still penetrate only part of China's political economy. While important changes in mass consciousness are under way in China, most people still live in relatively isolated rural communities and are mainly concerned with raising personal incomes beyond their still desperately low level. During the USSR's own transition from War Communism's highly centralized economic system to the NEP, relaxation of economic control existed alongside the elimination of the political rights of opposition parties, imposition of centralized control within the Party and a ruthless campaign against left-wing opposition both inside and outside the Party. Moreover,

Hong Kong is a striking example of the fact that it is possible to combine an almost complete absence of citizens' democratic political rights with a high degree of individual economic freedom and rapid growth of living standards. However, there is in China an important minority, mainly urban and intellectual, whose concepts are rapidly becoming internationalized, whose concern for political liberties is strong and who will strongly influence China's future political evolution. The impact of China's growing market forces upon the political set-up can be compared with that of the same force upon the power of feudal rule in late medieval Europe. However, the pace and pattern of change are hard to predict.

Some people have suggested that economic reform of the Stalinist system is impossible without fundamental political reform. The veracity of this depends on time and place. By late 1988 the attempts to reform the Soviet economy had made little headway. Gorbachev's special Party Congress of 1988 was an acknowledgement that fundamental political changes were necessary before serious economic reform could begin. However, in China considerable economic reform occurred with little political change. China's more rapid progress was due firstly to the fact that it is easier to reform 'socialist' agriculture and small-scale enterprise than large-scale industry. In the former activities the producers are given direct access or access within a small group to the income from the means of production. Moreover, the long-term suppression of small-scale non-farm enterprises in the Stalinist system opens up immediate opportunities for a rapid expansion of employment. In contrast, reform of large-scale industry carries far more risks for both workers and managers, who fear unemployment and/or income loss. Indeed, some analysts believe that if working practices are changed, up to a third of the workforce in China's large-scale state enterprises could be shed with no decline in output. Moreover, agricultural and small non-farm enterprises are much more flexible than large state enterprises. Under the Stalinist system, large imbalances between supply and demand develop, so that the introduction of market forces is likely to cause large shifts in production structure. It is much easier for agriculture and small enterprises than for large industrial concerns to shift to new activities (in the former case capital is closer to putty and in the latter case it is closer to clay). The relative importance of agriculture and small-scale enterprises is much greater in China, and the potential for expansion of small-scale enterprises was much greater at the start of China's reform than in the USSR because of the much larger relative importance of surplus labour in China. Once tentatively begun in the late 1970s, China's rural reforms snowballed, releasing tremendous pressure from peasants at each stage to push the reforms further. Unsurprisingly, this was not the case with large-scale enterprises.

A second reason for the fast pace of economic reform in China prior to political reform was China's relatively short experience with the Stalinist-administered economy. The USSR has operated an administered economy for almost twice as long as China. Moreover, markets were further advanced in pre-1949 China than in pre-1917 Russia, albeit that they mostly connected petty-commodity producers to the market. Bringing the habits of market activity to life was not hard in China. Large numbers of peasants, industrialists and traders had direct personal memories of how markets work and needed to be taught little. A third factor distinguishing China from the USSR is the rapid growth which has taken place around it, often in Chinese-dominated societies or in societies in which the Chinese play a strong economic role – Hong Kong, Taiwan, South Korea, Singapore, Malaysia and Thailand. China's leadership is acutely aware of lost time and lost opportunity. By the mid-1930s the lower Yangtze Valley and other areas in coastal Southeast China had already made considerable strides towards modernization, building on earlier 'capitalist sprouts'. While the East Asian NICs grew explosively after the 1950s, comparable parts of China, cut off from international and domestic markets, and with tight controls over the small-scale labour-intensive manufacturing sector which fuelled much of the early growth in the East Asian NICs, grew far less rapidly. The dimensions of the lost opportunity were brought home vividly once reform began in the 1980s. Industrial output, especially in the small-scale labour-intensive sector, grew explosively in favourably situated parts of East and Southeast China, quite reasonably prompting the Chinese leadership to look upon these areas as 'growth poles'.

Problems of Capitalism

Capitalism and Growth

Economists know little more about why output per person grows more rapidly in one country or epoch than in another than that it is because of the provision of more and better capital, and/or better use of capital. Analysis of growth requires both macroeconomics and microeconomics, but combining these levels of analysis is difficult, especially when the vast range of both economic and non-economic factors is included. However, some general points can be made on the subject. While the emergence of capitalist forces of competition and market expansion are, indeed, essential to understanding why growth accelerated in the modern world, unfettered capitalist free markets are not usually the way in which rapid growth rates are achieved. Unconstrained capitalism normally fails with respect to economic growth at both the macrolevel and the microlevel.

Even with considerable national and international intervention in markets, growth in the advanced capitalist countries has been erratic, with episodes of extremely slow and sometimes even negative growth. Many economists in Stalinist countries, used to decades of direct administrative planning, underestimate the difficulties of regulation through macroeconomic levers to produce sustained growth. It is both difficult technically and involves complex non-technical problems. Once labour markets move away from comprehensive state administration and workers begin to bargain for pay, sociopolitical factors affect the macroeconomy. Moreover, the greater the degree of integration into the international economy, the less independence in macromanagement an economy tends to have.

At the microlevel also there are fundamental problems with pure competitive capitalism. Many forms of microeconomic market failure are recognized in standard Western textbooks. These include competition failure, where barriers to entry exist because of increasing returns to scale (the extreme case is a natural monopoly); public goods, where there is zero marginal cost to additional supply and/or it is impossible to exclude others from using the good; externalities, where the actions of an individual or firm impose costs upon or provide benefits to others for which they are not respectively charged or paid; incomplete markets, where a good or service is not provided even though the cost of doing so is less than people are prepared to pay; and finally goods and services which are not provided because too little information is available. Many examples of static market failure also have growth implications, but in a dynamic setting it is difficult to reach firm conclusions. Markets can fail in different ways at the microlevel with respect to growth, size, culture, level of development, location, conjuncture relative to world economic cycles and many other factors affecting both the nature and degree of market failure and the capacity of a given society to resolve it. Successful growth normally depends on devising institutions to overcome market failure, and countries differ enormously in their capacity to construct such institutions, either through voluntary cooperation within and between groups, or through state action to impose the common interest on economic agents.

The reappearance of open inflation in China in the 1980s provides an example of the difficulty of moving away from Stalinist administrative planning towards indirect methods. Inflation in the prices of some important items is inevitable as the economy moves towards a more market-determined system of pricing. Prices of food, transport, housing and energy were all kept artificially low pre-1978, and economic reform was bound to produce pressure for some of these to rise. However, profit rates on some types of products (especially consumer durables) were extremely high prior to reform and a greater role for market forces could lead to a fall in their price.

Moreover, a greater role for market forces produces increased pressure to lower costs of production and accelerate technical progress. It is not inevitable that general inflation should result from economic reform. Large state enterprises responded to increases in the prices of formerly underpriced material inputs not by cutting costs but, in classic oligopolistic fashion, by raising prices for those parts of their output outside direct state control. China had, to some degree, entered the spiral of Western-type cost-push inflation. However, the rate of inflation is closely connected to the relationship between the growth of the money supply and the growth of real output. Enormous sociopolitical influences bear upon the money supply and, to a considerable degree, China's inflation represented a capitulation to those influences. The annual rate of growth of money supply (M1) in China roughly doubled from around 9 per cent in the period 1952–78 to 19 per cent in 1979–86 compared with a reported annual growth rate of real GDP of around 10 per cent in 1980–6. The problem was temporarily exacerbated in 1988 by people's fears about future inflation leading them to reduce their savings and panic buy. Reforms in the price of basic consumer goods, notably food, in the 1980s were followed closely, in order to maintain political stability, by huge unplanned increases in subsidies to urban workers. Moreover, a relatively large proportion of state enterprises made losses, but the state was not prepared to face up to the political cost of bankruptcy and unemployment. Consequently, huge amounts of state funds at different levels were disbursed to cover these enterprises' losses, further fuelling the growth of money supply. Another political element in inflation was the major decentralization in investment allocation in the 1980s. At the enterprise level there was much unplanned diversion of funds towards consumption, and in the absence of full market criteria for state enterprises, local authorities and especially banks, over which local authorities had considerable influence, there occurred an explosion of unplanned investment with little consideration of the social costs or benefits of projects. China in the late 1980s appeared to be one large construction site. These projects sucked in scarce resources and contributed to inflation of wholesale prices in the semi-reformed dual price market for material supplies, as well as feeding the growth of consumers' purchasing power via payments to the huge number of construction site workers. China's inflation of the 1980s could not be attributed simplistically to 'capitalist elements'. Rather, its main cause lay in the politics of reform, working particularly through the money supply which made possible the rise in the general price level. Most East Asian capitalist countries have low inflation rates and low rates of growth of the money supply, while most of the capitalist countries in South America have high inflation rates and high rates of growth of the money supply. Reforming Stalinist economies like China and Hungary also tend to have quite high inflation rates. The reason for these differences is not capitalism *per se*, but rather the political-economic struggles which capitalist forces unleash and which can be resolved in a variety of ways, some more inflationary than others.

Post-1978, many problems emerged to remind the Chinese leadership that, while excessive state administrative control brings microeconomic problems for growth, so too do free markets. One virtue of the people's communes was their capacity to ensure that key cooperative activities were performed. After China's rural reforms of the early 1980s, it proved difficult in poorer areas to mobilize resources for collective health, education and irrigation. Richer areas could finance these directly from the collective non-farm economy, but in poor areas the funds now had to come from individual levies. Although much of the collective expenditure appeared to be useful for the whole village, and had positive externalities for the whole economy (e.g. by helping to bring down birth rates), it proved difficult in many poor areas to obtain the requisite contributions to collective resources. In poor areas the social returns for the local community to more than minimal education may be low because of the simple range of tasks available, so that, left to themselves, it is unsurprising that peasants in those areas opted for lower levels of education than pre-1978. Also, in many areas the marginal returns to irrigation were low after three decades of labour mobilization to expand the irrigated area. Further improvement in poor semi-arid areas often required major irrigation schemes beyond the reach of local cooperation, so that mobilizing labour for village projects might gain prestige for local cadres in the eyes of higher authorities at a high economic cost for villagers. In each of these cases, neither free markets nor even state-led cooperation can solve the problem. Action by regional or national authorities is necessary.

A second example of the dangers of unconstrained markets was the explosive growth of small-scale enterprises in the 1980s. While much of this was beneficial, rapidly absorbing rural surplus labour, much waste occurred. In part this was due to the still unreformed nature of much of large-scale industry, which resulted, for example, in the expansion of small-scale industries into activities in which a reformed large-scale industry would be more efficient. However, in part, the difficulties also reflected classic problems of uncoordinated competitive markets. Short-run returns in many small-scale activities were sufficiently high to bid labour and materials away from activities which would yield higher long-term social returns for the whole economy. To have had such phenomenal all-round growth of small-scale enterprises at a time of acute shortage in energy, appalling deficiencies in the transport system and shortcomings in the educational system, suggests fundamental failure in microeconomic coordination.

Less serious are the microeconomic mistakes which simply reflect the process of becoming reacquainted with markets. For decades Chinese industry had operated in a seller's market. In the 1980s many producers, especially of light industrial products, rushed too rapidly into expanding production in high profit lines. Within a short time many markets became saturated, especially those for low-quality products, and huge stockpiles of unwanted goods built up.

Capitalism and Inequality

The concepts of individual freedom and rights associated with capitalism are extremely important. Most people in the capitalist countries value them highly, and they contribute substantially to their quality of life. They should form a core part of socialist values but too often have failed to do so, tending to be set aside in favour of the pursuit of an alleged 'common good'. These freedoms and rights apply equally to all citizens, but under capitalism equal rights produce unequal outcomes, which are transmitted between generations. At the heart of capitalism is a competitive economic struggle, from which all citizens may gain in the long term as the whole system moves upwards. However, unequal distribution of the gains from competition means that equal rights and freedoms are of different value to different social groups. Freedom to purchase an education or to migrate have a different meaning for an unemployed worker than for a rich company director. Freedom of speech will mean different things for an international media tycoon than for an ordinary citizen. Equality before the law has little meaning for a poor person confronted with the risk and payments required to go to law. Freedom to organize politically becomes a right of inequality if one social group has more resources to organize and influence opinion than another. Freedom can only have the same meaning for all citizens if the state intervenes with the market and redistributes resources.

Reintroduction of the elements of a capitalist economy in China in the 1980s was accompanied by the development of wide inequalities compared with those of pre-1976 which deeply worried many socialists outside China. Under Mao remuneration had been kept within narrow boundaries and the key slogan was 'serve the people'. The appearance in the 1980s of the slogan 'take the lead in getting rich' shocked people after years of Maoist egalitarianism. The impact of the new policies on inequalities was strongest in the countryside. A rapid widening of the range of income within a given village occurred and a small number of relatively very rich ('10000 yuan') rural households quickly emerged, relying on superior skills and better balances between labour power and dependents, and often using better connections in a rural economy which was still not fully marketized. Moreover, in many parts of China concentration of land use began to emerge, encouraged by government policy favouring cultivation by 'farming experts'. Income from renting farmland, hiring labour and usury all reappeared. Intravillage political power began to be affected by the economic inequalities which re-emerged in the villages.

In the 1980s a minority of well-endowed regions (e.g. Southern Jiangsu and the Pearl River Delta in Guangdong province) raised their incomes by relatively large amounts. Under Mao they had been held back both through controls on resource allocation and the level of income allowed to the local population. When these constraints weakened, output and income grew rapidly. The main beneficiaries were eastern seaboard areas close to large cities. By the late 1980s some of these had average incomes many times higher than those in poorly endowed areas. The gap in income between the richest households in these areas and the average income in backward areas was enormous. For example, by the mid-1980s, the richest households in the Wenzhou district of Zhejiang province, which specialized in button manu-facture and trade mainly in private enterprises, had annual incomes of over 150,000 yuan, while in poor areas there were still many villages with annual household incomes as low as 150 yuan – a range of rural incomes of 1,000:1! These differentials were large even by the standards of advanced capitalist countries. Many critics asked what could be 'socialist' about a country with such wide inequalities?

The Problems of Stalinism

Lack of Dynamism of Stalinism

The Stalinist economic model pre-dates Stalin's rise to power. The main-stream of European socialism in the late nineteenth and early twentieth century constructed its vision of a socialist economy using Marx's fragmentary writings on post-capitalist society and his critique of capitalism as a negative model. For such late-nineteenth-century socialist economists as Kautsky, the socialist economy meant eliminating the anarchic, crisis-ridden and wasteful character of capitalism by public ownership, direct administration and elimin-ation of the profit motive. Under socialism the whole economy would be administered as a single enterprise. The Stalinist model found clear expression in Bukharin and Preobrazhensky's *ABC of Communism*, published in the USSR in 1920, and was put into effect during War Communism between 1918 and 1921 in the USSR, supported by most of the Bolshevik leadership. In essence, the post-1929 Stalinist economy was War Communism reintroduced. The international appeal of comprehensive planning was increased greatly by high unemployment between the wars and post-war frustration at widespread Third World poverty. A state-directed 'big push' for rapid growth provided the attraction of an apparently simple solution to the problem of economic backwardness.

For a long time it was possible to attribute the economic problems of the Stalinist model to special factors, such as hostility from the Western capitalist economies or growing complexity of the economy. However, it became increasingly clear that there existed fundamental systemic problems with the model at all stages of economic development. It is no longer tenable to argue that an economy in which the state attempts to administer the details of economic activity is likely to be satisfactory in relation to technical progress and growth of living standards or in minimizing waste, let alone with respect to its impact upon the environment. Among the many problems which have been identified in a system which tries to substitute entirely administrative targets for market coordination are the following. There are insurmountable problems for planners in trying to obtain accurate information and equally large problems in trying to process the information into a complete operational plan. In such a non-market system, if the plan is to come anywhere near balancing inputs and outputs, the key enterprise target must be some synthetic indicator of output. Other goals (e.g. product mix, quality, cost reduction, technical progress) tend to be downgraded in the interests of achieving this objective. The major driving force for capitalist enterprises to reduce costs and innovate, which stems from the incentive of profit and the fear of bankruptcy, is absent. Economic decisions are frequently taken by technically incompetent political cadres. The dynamic effects stemming from the direct connection of enterprises with world markets are missing. Labour motivation for urban workers is dampened by shortages of wage goods, labour hoarding, irregular work patterns due to shortages of inputs and absence of the threat of unemployment. Rural labour motivation is severely impaired by managerial diseconomies of scale in collective forms.

The economic results of such a system are well known. What appeared to an earlier generation of socialist economists to be the major advantage of such a system, namely the ability to 'mobilize resources' on a grand scale, can now be seen to be a reflection of system failure. The system has a pervasive drive to overinvest, and, indeed, the Stalinist economies have all been characterized by very high rates of investment for their level of development.

In relatively closed economies such inefficiency in investment use is necessarily reflected in the high proportion of output allocated to capital goods production. This sector itself is a high consumer of capital goods, leading to a vicious circle of capital goods expansion. Rapid expansion of the capital goods sector began as a conscious system goal, but priority for this sector over the long term reflects system failure: Kruschev's 'steel blinkers' proved easier to put on than to remove. Moreover, such problems are not offset by technical dynamism once the first great infusion of foreign technology has been made in the early periods of planning. On the contrary, a key problem is the system's inability to generate indigenous technical progress. The net result is high rates of investment and overall growth of gross value of output, but poor performance of final consumption growth.

The highly centralized Stalinist model which operated in China from the mid-1950s to the early 1980s blended well with China's centralist political traditions. There were important differences between the approaches of Stalin and Mao to political economy, but in the fundamentals of economic organization and attitudes towards market forces the two remained close. Even during the Great Leap Forward (1958–9) and at the height of the Cultural Revolution (1966–8), China's economy remained firmly Stalinist in its key features (e.g. commitment to administrative planning, absence of markets for capital or labour, collective farms, bias towards the large scale and relative isolation from the international economy).

The highly centralized one-party system provided the opportunity for a single individual to have a major influence on economic development, with extremely detrimental consequences. This system allowed Mao to stifle economic debate for a long period. At the end of the First Five Year Plan (1953–7), a powerful critique of the monolithic administrative planning system was emerging, but its ideas were suppressed, reappearing briefly in the early 1960s. Consequently, for over 20 years economics in China was narrowly dogmatic and methods of economic management were virtually unchanged. The Stalinist political system enabled this to happen. The Stalinist economic system persisted because of a political form which allowed a high degree of central control which could crush the expression of ideas different from those of one person or a small group of people at the top.

China's overall long-term growth rate was impressive. Like other Stalinist economies China rapidly attained self-sufficiency in a wide range of products. However, growth was unbalanced with the growth rate of heavy industry much above that of light industry, which was, in turn, much above that of agriculture. Because of Mao's initial opposition to population control and later diversion of attention away from work to control population growth during the Cultural Revolution, population continued to increase rapidly up until the 1970s. Despite enormous growth in total product, there was little scope for growth of the most important indicator, living standards. Output per person of a narrow range of poor-quality industrial consumer goods grew quite fast, but from a negligible base, so that at the end of the Maoist period stocks of these goods per family were still extremely low. Housing availability per person deteriorated over the long term. Consumption per person of the main agricultural products hardly altered, leaving no reported long-term change at all in the average daily calorie intake. In the early 1980s it became clear that the Maoist period had bequeathed a legacy of dire material poverty for perhaps one-third of the Chinese population. Not only had progress of average material consumption at best been slow, but the variety of cultural life had been greatly restricted. As in all the Stalinist systems only a narrow range of cultural products was permitted, which strongly affected the quality of people's lives.

Not only does the Stalinist political-economic system produce long-term problems, but it is also able to make serious short-term errors. Nothing illustrates this better than the Chinese Great Leap Forward (1958–9). Against tremendous opposition from economists and most of China's leaders, Mao was able to use his position of supreme political power to launch an extraordinarily utopian movement. With his confidence boosted by false reports from grass-roots cadres of the achievements under new social relationships, Mao intended China to leap directly into the realm of 'communism'. He considered it possible to build new forms of social consciousness which would pre-empt the need for bourgeois management and payment systems in town and countryside alike. Never before or since (even in the Cultural Revolution) has such a challenge been made to the capitalist system. Many foreign commentators, including those in the USSR, considered the whole project to be madness. Combined with detailed, and frequently questionable, economic directives (e.g. mass construction of irrigation works, reduced acreage sown to grain and a national campaign to build 'backyard' iron and steel works) went a belief that it was possible in a mass campaign to change social consciousness away from individualism towards collectivism and patriotism, and that this would liberate people's creative energies in a way that would produce rapid economic progress. The implicit criticism of capitalism's constraints on the creativity of the masses was correct, but the results were disastrous.

There was initially a great deal of popular enthusiasm amidst a national holiday atmosphere, with the mass excitement which accompanies an extraordinary event. However, such an atmosphere is hard to sustain when difficulties are encountered. New agricultural institutions (the gigantic 'rural people's communes') multiplied the problems experienced on collective farms. Scarce peak-period farm labour was transferred to activities with low or negative returns. Egalitarian payment systems caused serious urban and rural motivation problems. Invaluable technical expertise was lost as those with scarce skills were transferred for much of the time to mundane tasks. In the heady politicized campaign atmosphere planning collapsed and greater, more irrational, degrees of local self-sufficiency emerged as enterprises and localities desperately sought to produce for themselves products whose supply could not be relied upon through the planning system.

The economic collapse was catastrophic. The full extent of the agricultural decline was initially hidden by widespread misreporting. Its implications for the consumption levels of large numbers of people were much greater than need have been the case owing to the tight control exercised by the Party over information. Local officials sometimes tried to seal off their areas to prevent the news of mass starvation from leaking out. In more open political systems information of severe localized food shortages would have become national news. Instead, in parts of China large numbers of people died of malnutrition – mainly those in the most vulnerable age groups (i.e. the very old and the very young). The concepts of 'excess deaths' and 'deaths through famine' are extremely problematic, and there will never be a clear answer to the numbers of those whose deaths are attributable to the famine of 1959–61. What is certain is that famine did indeed occur on a scale that dwarfs any other famine of the twentieth century. Its origins lie in the closed centralized system of Stalinist political economy. It is not a coincidence that India has not experienced a major famine since 1947, despite regular widespread malnutrition.

Inequality and Restrictions on Liberty under Stalinism

Whatever the political system, substitution of the market-determined allocation of goods and services with bureaucratic allocation introduces dangers of inequalities and restrictions on individual liberties. It establishes a generalized inequality between those who allocate and those who are the recipients of the decisions of bureaucratic allocators. This danger applies even to uncorrupt, honest administrators. There are great possibilities for corrupt behaviour in such situations in terms of bureaucrats selling items illegally on black markets, economically stronger people and regions bribing officials, and bonds of dependence being created between ordinary people and bureaucrats, to the extent that present-giving to and favour-doing for bureaucrats becomes a regular part of daily life. Constant mass vigilance and a high level of public participation is necessary to ensure that the independence of bureaucrats is minimized. This is difficult to achieve even in advanced capitalist countries with high levels of education, plenty of leisure time and strong democratic traditions. The Stalinist system is the obverse of this.

The main features of the Stalinist political system were established during War Communism in the USSR (1917–21) in the face of a desperate civil war and serious opposition from within the domestic socialist movement. Hammered out in wartime, the Party rules of the Stalinist states bear more resemblance to those of an army than to a Western political party. In a memorable phrase, one leading Soviet economist recently described the system as 'barracks socialism'. The structure over which Stalin seized control in the USSR in the late 1920s already had a system of rules which made possible the concentration of power in the hands of one person. Commentators on both Chinese and Soviet post-revolutionary politics have argued that the centralist elements can be explained largely by each country's specific history, without reference to Stalinism. While not disputing the importance of historical influences, the Stalinist system of political economy, in whatever setting it is applied, provides a favourable environment for centralist elements inherited from the country's history to be put into effect, as well as creating new forms of political centralization.

China's post-revolutionary practice was affected powerfully by pre-revolutionary experience. China has unusual, historically bequeathed problems in establishing democratic political rights and individual liberties. No other part of the world of comparable size has such a long tradition of centralized rule by a powerful state. A second factor influencing post-1949 politics was the evolution of the Chinese Communist Party (CCP) pre-1949. Not only was it affected powerfully by the Soviet Stalinist approach towards the Party, but the CCP was involved in a military campaign over more than two decades. Tight inner-Party discipline and limitations on the liberties of non-Party citizens of the Communist Base Areas developed ineluctably during the course of the protracted military struggle. Compared with other Stalinist societies, the 'mass line', which was developed in the Base Areas, did indeed constitute a uniquely close relationship between the Party and the masses, but this was essentially a difference in work style rather than a difference in approach towards political rights. The military-bureaucratic approach towards both inner-Party discipline and the Party's relationship to society developed and was continued after the Chinese revolution of 1949. Stalinist Party organization permits control by one person or a group of people who are able to suppress inner-Party opposition to their views and to shape the very membership of the Communist Party in a way that helps support them. Despite strong inner-Party opposition to collectivization, the Great Leap Forward and the Cultural Revolution, Mao was able to use his power as the head of a highly centralized system to push through unpopular policies.

The Party tightly controlled socioeconomic life throughout the Maoist period. A Party which evolved out of military struggle justified restrictions on liberty in the interests of further struggles: against landlords and capitalists in the 1950s, against massive external opposition, and against those within China who opposed egalitarian socioeconomic policies after 1957. Huge restrictions on personal liberty were put into effect by a tiny group of people during the Cultural Revolution, in the teeth of strong high-level political opposition, in the interests of an egalitarian socioeconomic ethic. Perhaps only North Korea has cut off its citizens so completely from international contacts or imposed such restrictions on cultural output as China's leaders did during the Cultural Revolution. Few modern societies have had such restrictions on freedom of movement as China did then. Even freedom to reproduce was tightly controlled in the latter stages of the Cultural Revolution through the detailed birth plan sent down to production units. Moreover, the mass mobilization led by a small minority with great power, and the absence of an independent judiciary to appeal to, permitted the persecution of groups and individuals in the name of support for the leadership (i.e. Mao) against the 'enemies of the revolution'. Such dangers exist under any situation of mobilization against real or imagined enemies, but were developed to a high degree in the Cultural Revolution. Economic freedom was, of course, confined only to small areas of 'free-market' activity, although even these tiny 'capitalist sprouts' were monitored tightly by state personnel. It is true that large numbers of Party members (perhaps even the great majority) were idealistic and tried to serve their communities well. However, their conception of how their communities would be best served came not from democratic decisions by the community, but rather from their superiors and ultimately from the political leadership. Such fundamental issues as winter-time mobilization of vast amounts of rural labour, the method of income distribution and of factory management were decided within a centrally determined framework, given concrete form in editorials in the *People's Daily*, the *People's Liberation Army Daily* and the *Red Flag*, all controlled by the central Party apparatus.

Under Mao, and especially during the Cultural Revolution, China paradoxically had a system attempting to reduce socioeconomic inequality, but doing so with mass restriction of individual liberties, with little acknowledgement of mass democratic political rights, exercising a highly centralized and concentrated form of political power by a tiny number of central leaders over the mass of the population, allowing the regular exercise of power by local Party members over the mass of the population and opening the door to widespread abuse of that power. These problems, which reached their peak in the Cultural Revolution, cannot be attributed to the shortcomings of certain individuals. The Cultural Revolution simply exhibited in extreme form defects inherent in the Stalinist system combined with features inherited from Chinese history. Individuals matter greatly in history. Had Mao died in 1956 or 1966, rather than in 1976, China's history would have been very different. However, the potential for the creation of political inequality and restrictions on liberty is embedded deeply in the Stalinist political system, whose basic features were established as early as 1921. Both the current Soviet and the current Chinese leadership believe that the Stalinist political system can be reformed from above without altering the leading role of the CCP. This is an optimistic view for which history provides little support.

The Need for State Intervention

State Intervention and Growth

Conventional wisdom in development economics has shifted against the state. A series of criticisms of state intervention in mixed economies buttressed by system reform in the 'socialist' countries has produced a major shift in thinking. Such a strong swing against state intervention and in favour of free markets is highly problematic. However, it must be acknowledged that socialist economists have tended to be too simplistic in their approach to these problems, assuming that a common model of state intervention can solve problems of market failure. In practice, the necessary level and desirable form of state intervention varies enormously. The experience of a wide range of successfully industrializing countries, from France, Germany and Japan in the nineteenth century through to Singapore, Taiwan and South Korea since the 1950s, demonstrates that a key element in rapid growth is devising appropriate ways in which the state can supplement for market failure so as to bring the decisions of profit-seeking enterprises in line with those that are desirable for the overall economy. Only in exceptional cases, such as Hong Kong, have countries relied on the free market during industrialization. Indeed, even in the case of Hong Kong, with unusual supply-side advantages, the state has done much more to supplement for market failure than is commonly supposed (its role in housing and education, for example, has been vital). The idea that the Asian NICs relied on the free market to attain their striking success is a myth. The key to their success lies in the nature of the state. With the exception of Hong Kong, each of the Asian NICs was extremely vulnerable at the start of their take-off, threatened by larger neighbouring countries. Growth was vital if Singapore, Taiwan and South Korea were even to survive as independent countries. In each case the state was able to take decisions beneficial to economic growth without compromising these actions by placating special interest groups. The package of state actions taken in each case was different, and included intervention in labour markets, land reform, state ownership of key industries, protection, subsidies and rewards to exporters, provision of credit, public housing, education, transport facilities, power supplies and agricultural extension services, construction of strategic plans, direct instructions to different enterprises and state finance for research and development. Not all these interventions were successful. Of course, the extraordinary growth of these economies was helped by the boom in world trade and the inward-looking strategies of their potential competitors, especially China and India. However, much of their success is attributable to the way in which these 'developmental states' constructed a strategy which used the dynamism of market forces but identified the many different ways in which free markets would fail to produce acceptable growth. There is a wide variety of relationships between states and sectional interests. It must be recognized that in some cases, although market failure is considerable and economic performance could be greatly improved by effective state action, the state is so corrupted by the influence of sectional interests and/or by the pursuit of power and privilege for bureaucrats rather than the pursuit of growth, that state intervention could produce worse results for growth than those obtaining with market failure and an absence of state intervention. While there is no reason to accept the extreme pro-free-market view that state failure is always worse than market failure, one should not ignore the fact that some states are more successful than others in overcoming market failure, and that in the last instance there is, indeed, the possibility of state failure's being worse than market failure.

Despite considerable economic reform in the late 1980s the Chinese state still had great influence over economic activity, with a much more comprehensive array of controls than, for example, in any of the East Asian NICs. China was moving away from Stalinist economic management, and the role of market forces had increased enormously. The leadership was attempting to strike a new balance between plan and market, relying heavily on indirect methods, mainly macroeconomic levers, to guide the economy. However, the model towards which the system was moving was unclear. The final balance between plan and market was still uncertain, as was the pace and manner in which reform should proceed.

It was argued above that an important characteristic of the East Asian NICs is the relative autonomy of the state which leaves it free to pursue developmental goals with less need to placate sectional interests than in other countries. The present Chinese state in some respects possesses this characteristic. Firstly, unlike the Indian state for example, the Chinese state does not have to placate the interests of landlords or powerful oligopolistic groups in private industry, or indeed to make deals with any socioeconomic group to seek electoral support. Even industrial labour is unable to exert as much organized political pressure as in most developing countries. Secondly, China has been through a long period of turmoil. This began in late Qing and lasted through to 1949. However, the turmoil did not end there. Unlike, say, the USSR, which has had a long period of political stability since the 1920s, China since the late 1950s has endured immense sociopolitical upheavals. The Chinese people feel deeply aware of the development opportunities that have been lost. This attitude is given added force by their strong awareness of China's rich history and of the long period in which it led world historical progress. There would therefore be popular support for a leadership which pursued developmental goals successfully. The traumatic nature of this background is similar in some respects to the political crises which helped provide popular support for the 'developmental elites' in Taiwan, South Korea, Singapore and Hong Kong. However, China still possesses a vast Party (around 47 million members in the late 1980s) and government apparatus. They are closely intertwined, have inherited the country's long habit of bureaucratic rule and have traditions closer to those of India's bureaucracy in recent times than to those of China's East Asian neighbours. Moreover, they benefited in many ways from the semi-reformed state of China's economy in the late 1980s. This apparatus has a strong desire to retain power and privilege. Moreover, the sheer fact of its vast size means that, like India, problems arise from the difficulty of running such a large administrative machine and from the difficulty of attaining unity of purpose when there are conflicting regional interests. To turn China's bureaucracy from an administrative into a developmental state is an enormous task which has hardly begun. It presents a major barrier to continued economic reform. Whenever a problem appears in the course of reform, its instinct is to attempt direct control rather than allow the market to solve the problem. Transformation of the state apparatus is the most crucial and difficult task facing China's leadership for the 1990s. It is extremely difficult to predict the path that China's political economy will take if this is not accomplished.

Despite the need for better functioning markets the economic tasks for the state in China are still enormous, although, of course, the methods and the degree of state activity need to alter dramatically. It is a serious misconception to imagine that macroeconomic levers (e.g. money supply, rate of interest, taxation) alone will suffice to guide the Chinese economy effectively along a high growth path. For example, the market is likely to do a poor job in meeting the Chinese economy's needs for education, health, power supply and transport. Up to a certain point, the social benefits to investment in education and health are likely to be inadequately reflected in the private profits to be made supplying these services. Training and retraining the labour force are vital to economic growth, yet in this area the gap between private and social returns is often wide. State activity is vital. Power supply is notoriously problematic if left entirely to the market. Investments are often enormous and long-term coordination between different forms of energy supply is necessary. The free market might produce inadequate levels of power supply from oligopolistic companies at high prices. Construction of communications networks is also uneven and often beyond the reach of individual businesses.

Moreover, many of the benefits to improved communications come in the form of externalities that cannot be captured in the profits of the individual supplier. The precise institutional form in which these needs are met by the state should be carefully investigated and the crude simplicity of Stalinist methods of provision avoided. Indeed, in these areas the state may often usefully operate in tandem with private or cooperative provision. A serious problem from the Chinese economy in the late 1980s in these types of activities was not that the state was doing too much but rather that it was not doing enough. Indeed, a serious crisis had developed in power supply and transport. It makes poor economic sense to have such rapid expansion of light industry while these sectors languish. Although the form of provision may (and should) alter, the state needs to play a considerable role in these activities: the free-market solution will produce slower growth of national output, and macro-economic levers alone will be inadequate to meet needs.

Mistakes made with respect to agriculture in a developing country are costly. Dismantling the old system of collective labour and income distribution was necessary for the achievement of faster rates of growth of farm output in China, for using farm resources more effectively and for raising national living standards. Agriculture, especially under labour-intensive conditions, is characterized by powerful managerial diseconomies of scale with respect to the direct cultivation of the soil, arising principally from difficulties with labour supervision. However, experience in a wide range of settings from Japan to Denmark has demonstrated the necessity of action above the level of the individual farmer. This can take the form of voluntary cooperation or state action, either direct or through state-organized cooperation. Many activities are frequently beyond the range of the individual farmer, including credit provision, insurance, veterinary facilities, research, quality control, processing, marketing and purchasing large equipment for ploughing, harvesting or spraying. Especially important in large parts of China is the construction and maintenance of drainage and irrigation works. To some degree in China these needs will be met by voluntary cooperation. However, experience in pre-1949 China and in comparable parts of Asia shows how important it is for state action (both central and local) to supplement where voluntary cooperation fails. Many new problems appeared in these respects in China in the 1980s, especially in poor areas where only limited resources were available to the local state apparatus. However, compared with many other parts of Asia, China, despite new problems, still possessed a relatively effective local state structure and there was a strong national policy commitment to supplement for market failure in these vital respects. The historical evidence from pre-1955 Japan, Taiwan and China suggests that full-scale collective farms are not the only way in which these needs can be met.

The state needs to do a great deal to affect the environment in which industry operates: educate, train and retrain its workers; provide direct or indirect support for investment in technical progress; protect selected industries; assist selected industries to compete in world markets; provide assistance for industries which are desirable for the national economy (e.g. due to externalities, lumpiness or long gestation periods) but which the private sector would not set up; support suitable infrastructural construction where the private sector fails to do so. Moreover, the Stalinist system showed the dangers of an economy in which industrial enterprises did not need to compete with each other, and an important function for the state is to ensure that competitive conditions exist.

A key issue is the degree to which direct state ownership is desirable. In China in the late 1980s, virtually all industrial output was produced in 'state' enterprises – even rural 'collective' enterprises were often effectively local state enterprises. Whether or not enterprises are formally owned by the state is less important than the way in which they operate. An enterprise formally 'owned' by the state may be permitted to retain all or none of its profits, to sell freely all or none of its output, to bid freely for and take over other enterprises or to have no such rights. Moreover, the idea that state enterprises cannot in principle operate in a competitive profitable fashion has been belied by many practical examples. None of these is more striking than the turnaround in performance of a succession of British nationalized industries in the 1980s prior to privatization. Much the most important goal for Chinese industry in the 1990s is to devise methods by which the competitive vigour which has already penetrated the small-scale 'collective' industrial sector also enters the large-scale industrial sector. This requires that enterprise management has real independence in the sense possessed in the capitalist countries by those who run (but do not necessarily own) large-scale private capitalist enterprises or the many successful large-scale state enterprises. Operational independence and competition rather than ownership *per se* are the key. However, the issue cannot be dealt with in the abstract. It must be examined with China's situation in mind. China has a long tradition of Party and government intervention in enterprise affairs (e.g. the late Qing system of *guandu shangban* – bureaucratic supervision and merchant operation), so that it is extremely difficult to prise enterprises away from their control. Given this background it is possible that only some form of privatization may break the stranglehold in which large enterprises find themselves. Thus, in China today a substantial amount of privatization of large state enterprises may be necessary, not because it is the only way in principle to provide autonomy, but because it is the only way given China's history. Such action will only be successful in alliance with the substantial array of state actions outlined above.

State Intervention and Inequality

Free markets provide an unequal value of freedom to different social groups. Capitalism can, after a certain point, produce some narrowing of inequalities through the workings of the market. However, the main force tending to produce greater equality in the value of freedom is state intervention to tax, redistribute and provide equal access to facilities that enable people to utilize more fully their human potential. A crucial question for any community to decide, especially a poor one, is the degree to which there is a trade-off between growth and equality, and the appropriate balance to be struck in any given circumstance. All communities have to make decisions about the degree to which they are prepared to interfere with individual liberty in order to redistribute and support collective facilities which provide a more equal value of freedom.

Maoist China was characterized by extreme political inequalities and greatly restricted individual freedom. However, intense state action produced an unusually high degree of equality. Maoist policies sprang from a deep socialist conviction that citizens are of equal value and should be given equal opportunities for self-fulfilment. The Maoist critique of 'bourgeois rights', under which equal rights permit unequal outcomes, was simple and coherent. Defenders of free-market values and its inequalities outside China mention Mao only to ridicule him. This is inadequate. For all the fluctuations in policy, for all the trampling on individual rights and for all the undesirable results for the economy, the Maoist years in China can only be properly assessed if we take seriously the sustained efforts to try to ensure that Chinese citizens shared equally in the development process.

Maoist China did not eliminate socioeconomic inequality. Even under Mao there was an awareness that 'absolute egalitarianism' could have disastrous consequences. In the 1970s one was still better off as a man than as a woman, as an urban worker than as a peasant, as a state worker than as a collective worker, as a peasant near a large city than as one in a remote area, or as a peasant with many able-bodied adults in the household than as one with several young children. However, one of the most sustained attempts in modern history was made to reduce inequality and to ensure maximum poverty relief from given resources. This produced certain advances. For example, the disastrous loss of life after the Great Leap Forward has to be set against the fact that prior to 1978 China's food distribution system and provision of basic health care contributed to a more rapid fall in death rates in normal times than was achieved in most developing countries, so that by the mid-1970s the average life expectancy was very high for a country at its level of income. However, the attempt to make substantial reductions in inequality was a factor contributing to the extremely slow growth of average living standards by reducing the effectiveness with which people made use of productive resources. Greater poverty relief could have been achieved through a less severely redistributive strategy which provided greater incentives to the workforce to use resources well and which did not attempt such radical transformations of the division of labour. For example, other parts of the world and, indeed, China itself pre-1955, have done a great deal to meet basic needs without attempting such radical transformations of relations of production as China carried out with its collective farms. Redistribution *per se* can only go so far in alleviating mass poverty. Growth is essential to take mass living standards beyond a certain level and it is this which must be the overriding goal for a country still at China's low level of development. Equality in poverty, albeit somewhat reduced poverty, is not the most desirable condition.

After Mao's death major changes occurred in all these respects. Logic and China's experience before 1949, as well as that in a wide range of developing countries, all suggest that if market forces are left to work freely in China, inequality will increase. Many people outside China think that this is desirable – a welcome and inevitable corollary of China's move down the path towards capitalism. Others consider that this did, indeed, happen in the 1980s but feel that in permitting it China's leaders are betraying socialism. In fact, there appeared to be a substantial measure of agreement among Chinese leaders that, while growth is vital to China's national pride and power, and to the relief of poverty, control of inequality matters greatly. The seriousness with which this was taken separated China from most developing countries and constituted a genuinely 'socialist' element in its development strategy. There was, of course, considerable debate about the appropriate degree of inequality and along which dimensions, about the degree of trade-off with growth goals, and about the methods to be used to influence inequality and relieve poverty.

At the most fundamental levels of human capital formation and culture important changes occurred in the direction of increased inequality. However, mainly through state action at different levels, China still allocated a larger proportion of national resources to health and education than most poor countries and made them available at prices that enabled a high proportion of the population to have access to them. Problems in poor areas partly reflected the fact that, left to themselves, many peasants decided that long years of education were inappropriate to their work needs. Also, to a considerable degree they reflected a new openness in reporting poor conditions rather than an actual deterioration. China's recent record in national and local (including village) state resource mobilization to provide mass access to the basics of human capital formation is still impressive compared with other developing countries. Moreover, the most dramatic cultural change in the

1980s was mass access to international television programmes which had a homogenizing rather than a differentiating impact on culture.

Under free-market conditions inequalities in asset ownership are important in explaining inequalities in income, power and life chances. In China in the late 1980s, only a tiny fraction of industrial assets was owned by individuals, and the private sector produced a small proportion of industrial output. The 'collective' industrial sector embraced a wide variety of different ownership forms and made a major contribution to China's growth in the 1980s, and there was a strong official ideological preference for 'collective' rather than private enterprise, despite the fact that the latter was legal. A wide variety of options was being mooted in relation to industrial share ownership schemes in order to improve the functioning of state-owned enterprises by separating ownership rights from control over enterprise management. Although no single model had emerged as dominant, there appeared to be a strong awareness of the need to devise share-ownership systems that prevent the concentration of share ownership in the hands of a small number of individuals or private institutions such as is the case under Western capitalism.

In agriculture, the key asset is land. China's land redistribution in the 1980s was extremely egalitarian, with locally equal allocations per person being the principal method adopted. This provided an egalitarian basis to the whole rural reform programme. While land operation was becoming more concentrated through forms of rental arrangement, land remained publicly owned. It could not be bought and sold. It seems impossible that there could emerge a minority landlord class, with land ownership concentrated in its hands, which absorbs a large share of the benefit of farm modernization or, indeed, inhibits such modernization.

While major changes in asset ownership had occurred, China's policies in the 1980s separated it from 'capitalist' developing countries. For example, if China is compared with India, where industrial ownership is concentrated in the hands of only a few families and there is still considerable inequality in ownership of farmland, the difference is striking.

A major criterion in assessing the social characteristics of any state is its approach towards regional inequality, which is particularly important in the case of economies the size of China or India. A notorious deficiency of the Indian state has been its lack of a coherent regional policy and, apart from famine relief, the national government has strikingly failed to mobilize resources to assist backward areas. Much understandable concern was expressed outside China at the fact that there were still a large number of people living in poverty in poorly located areas while well-located areas on the east coast, such as Southern Jiangsu province and the Pearl River Delta in Guangdong province, experienced explosive growth of output and income in the 1980s. Unlike most poor countries, in China in the 1980s there was much research and publication about regional inequalities. Under Mao, the fact that huge numbers of peasants lived in abysmal unchanging conditions was simply not referred to in public discussion. Policies in the 1980s were based on an explicit recognition that there are gains for the national economy in allowing some areas with economic advantages to grow more rapidly than others. The 1980s (and, indeed, the 1930s) demonstrated just how fast growth could be in key areas on the eastern seaboard, and it would be foolish to hold them back. Some trickle-down effects benefited poorer areas. However, policymakers recognized that part of the benefits from growth along the eastern seaboard should be taxed or diverted through the banking system (levels of savings in these areas were high) to assist poverty stricken regions. While more could, undoubtedly, have been done to help disadvantaged areas, the relative level of state assistance for such areas was much greater than in most large 'capitalist' developing countries, such as Brazil or India. While richer areas obtained much larger income growth per person in the 1980s, the combination of rural institutional reforms, a certain amount of trickle-down (e.g. via remittances from migrants) plus state assistance (national and provincial) led to massive reductions in the numbers of Chinese in poverty. This was not inconsistent with the fact that tens of millions still lived in wretched poverty.

Methods of remuneration altered considerably after 1978 within industry, and inter-enterprise inequality in average incomes was wider than pre-1978 as state enterprises were allowed to retain a portion of their profits with which to remunerate their workers. However, there were still many controls, both on the way in which enterprises allocated retained profits and on the proportion of profits enterprises were allowed to retain. In part, this was because incomplete reform in enterprises' environment, notably the price system, meant that profits reflected many factors besides efficiency. Partly, too, it was because there still existed a strong ethos of what consistuted a just (gong ping) differential in average incomes. Within state enterprises, differentials widened, with increased incentives to acquire scarce skills and to work hard. However, differentials were still narrow compared with other developing countries, and there was still a strong sense that differentials beyond a certain level were unjust. Equally, in 'collective' industrial enterprises remuneration was far from being on a free-market basis. For example, rural 'collective' industrial enterprises usually operated under an umbrella body of the local state apparatus, which affected local earnings differentials both directly (e.g. via decisions on wage rates) and indirectly (e.g. via taxation). Again, the concept of a 'just' differential was at the centre of policy.

The new policy of 'take the lead in getting rich' had the most dramatic impact in agriculture. After years of 'serve the people' and 'studying Dazhai' it suddenly became legitimate to seek profits and earn high incomes. The appearance of a group of relatively rich '10,000 yuan' households was taken by many foreign observers as an indication that 'capitalism' had been 'restored' in the Chinese countryside. In fact, this was far from the case. The most striking aspect of the change in rural income distribution was the great increase in the range of regional incomes. It is true that the permitted range of intravillage income differentials widened considerably, but important influences limited their extent. First and foremost was the egalitarian land distribution under the contract system. Second, a wide range of collective services to which poor households had access still operated in most of rural China. Third, the huge expansion of employment in the rural non-farm labour-intensive sector in the 1980s tended to benefit a wide range of villagers in a given area. These same factors helped control income differentials in Taiwan in the 1960s and 1970s. The main source of exceptionally high rural incomes was the private non-farm sector. However, purely private non-farm rural enterprises (as opposed to collective non-farm assets contracted out under various arrangements) still accounted for a small share of the rural non-farm output. Moreover, although tax collection from this sector was far from perfect, the sector was subject to steep progressive taxation.

Large changes in China's income distribution occurred in the 1980s, but although people's positions in the income structure altered and the range of incomes widened, the overall inequality in income distribution was still low compared with other developing countries of similar size and income level. This is not surprising when the range of state influences upon that distribution is taken into consideration. Far from having moved towards free-market principles of income determination, China in the late 1980s was striking in the degree to which state action still limited income inequality. It is possible that permitting greater income inequality (especially at the inter- and intra-industrial enterprise level) than existed in China in the late 1980s could stimulate growth. However, it is essential that such additional income relates to an extra economic contribution and not to exploitation of loopholes in the half-reformed economy. A considerable part of the highest incomes in China in the late 1980s derived from the latter source, reducing popular confidence in the reforms.

The socialist characteristics of the post-Mao Chinese state were evident not only in its continued concern with 'justice' (*gong ping*) in income distribution, but also with its desire to provide for the basic needs of the poorest people. This was reflected in the relatively high level of state provision of education and health facilities. It was also reflected in many of the difficulties that the state faced in trying to reform the price structure and dismantle the system of direct state allocation of items of consumption. The state was moving only slowly towards bringing the price of housing, personal transport, domestic power and food into closer line with costs (whether they should fully cover costs in all cases is, anyway, highly debatable). Most urban housing was still administratively allocated. A large part of urban grain supply was rationed (as well as some other food items), and price control over food supplies was still important. This partly reflected continued political pressure from the urban population as a whole, but it also reflected the continued concern of the state with guaranteeing 'basic needs'. Although crude, the surest way to do this is to guarantee supplies to the whole population, although this is far from ideal (a targeted programme would be more suitable). In the countryside also, the 'basic needs' philosophy was still reflected in the system of grain supply to poor or disaster-struck areas and in the continuation, over much of rural China, of collective support for locally poor households.

Conclusion

It is possible to visualize a feasible form of market socialism for China in the 1990s. It is necessary to continue to move away from Stalinist administrative planning in order to achieve an acceptable long-term pace of growth of output and living standards. However, the desired economic growth cannot be provided by free markets or simply by market regulation via indirect levers such as interest rates, taxes and subsidies, important as these are in guiding the economy. Indeed, a great deal of direct state action is necessary at China's current stage of development to supplement for the many different ways in which markets do, and are likely to, fail as market forces grow. China has much to learn in these respects from East Asian 'developmental states'. Countries which grow fast are those which have devised sensitive institutional solutions to market failure. This requires something different from the Stalinist approach. Open-mindedness and flexibility are the key. Rigid adherence to certain formulae (whether state, private or cooperative ownership, whether large or small scale) is likely to cause problems, since the degree of market failure with respect to growth is likely to be different in different countries and at different stages of development.

However, improving the quality of life for the whole population of a given country is about more than the attainment of fast and efficient growth of output and average living standards, vital as these are. China's experience under Mao demonstrated the dangers of a static redistributive approach towards poverty resolution and the damage to growth that can result from ultra-egalitarianism. However, because ultra-egalitarianism caused great difficulties does not mean that its obverse is desirable. There is no reason in principle why China cannot improve her already relatively advanced system of provision of the 'basic needs' of human self-realization to all her people in a way that is compatible with the maintenance of incentives.

Some elements of a market socialist system began to be put in place in the 1980s as China moved away from the Stalinist command economy, to which system it seems unlikely that it will return. However, strong elements of the Stalinist economy still remained in the late 1980s. Moreover, no clear model of the new system had been provided to the Chinese people, suggesting considerable uncertainty among the leadership. Politics is essential to the outcome of the reform process. Some argue that without political democracy China's economic reforms will not succeed, nor, they argue, if they did succeed, could China be called a socialist country. Neither of these propositions is correct. It is possible that continued tight political control might be compatible with continued economic reform. Indeed, in China, it may even be a condition of such progress. All socialist goals cannot be achieved simultaneously in a poor country. Attempting to do so may prevent the successful achievement of any of them. The main goal for China in the 1990s is to devise a set of institutions and policies which achieves reasonable growth of output and living standards, and enables all its citizens to move out of poverty, albeit at different rates. The achievement of political democracy is a less important goal for most Chinese people at present, and one which, anyway, is extremely difficult to attain in a mainly peasant low-income country. Moreover, by the late 1980s the economic reform, especially the reform of large-scale state enterprises and agricultural prices, had already involved great social tension, with some social groups gaining more than others, sometimes at the expense of these latter groups, and would result in further tension in the future. Immediate granting of full democratic rights might produce uncontrollable social upheaval, with no benefit to the mass of the population. Moreover, a great advance in democracy might reduce the autonomy of the state, increasing the impact of the groups best able to take advantage of political rights, notably urban workers, bureaucrats and intellectuals, at the expense of less well-placed groups, notably peasants. Under these circumstances, such key reforms as a hard budget constraint on state enterprises, removing subsidies on urban foodstuffs, shifting relative prices in favour of agriculture and controlling growth of the money supply might all be more difficult to accomplish.

The second main political issue in the reforms is the question of whether China's vast Party and bureaucracy can be transformed into a genuinely 'developmental state', intervening only where it is necessary to meet social goals, and being pragmatically prepared to work through the market where that produces the best results and to withdraw if the goal of intervention has been accomplished. This is a huge change from the present situation, in which administrators feel that they have the right to intervene directly in almost any economic activity. This form of political reform is, indeed, essential. With respect to the relationship of the Party and bureaucracy to the economy, China's reform may end up anywhere on a continuum from post-Independence India to Hong Kong under British rule. China has to contend with 2,000 years of bureaucratic rule as well as 40 years of Stalinist administration superimposed upon that. However, there have been periods in China's history, usually early in the life of a new dynasty under the impact of the shock of the collapse of the preceding ones, when the bureaucracy worked uncorruptly and effectively. Moreover, the 'development states' of Taiwan and Singapore came from fundamentally the same Chinese tradition. Will the 1980s come to be seen as the dawn of a new Golden Age for China, analogous to that of the early Qing (1644–1911) emperors Kang Xi and Qian Long, with capable leaders and effective administrators, backed by able advisors, running a form of market socialism which inspires other large Third World countries in the post-Stalinist epoch and lays the foundation for a high-income democratic socialism? Will the 1980s be seen instead as a time of enormous short-term gains from the release of the system from the inefficiencies of Stalinism, but a false dawn, being merely the prelude to slow long-term growth and market muddle as self-seeking bureaucrats and an authoritarian Party ensure that neither plan nor market works well? Or will the 1980s be viewed as a temporary resting place for the Chinese economy in its transition out of Stalinism to unconstrained capitalism alongside the collapse of both the Party and effective planning? One can only pose the questions and hope that the answer is the first one.

Notes

* 　I am extremely grateful to the following people for their detailed comments on a long early draft of this chapter: Chris Bramall, Michael Landesmann, Liu Minquan, Bruce McFarlane, Ashwani Saith and Zhang Xunhai. I have also benefited from discussion with Carl Riskin, Bob Rowthorn, John Sender, Ajit Singh and Ravi Srivastava. None of these agrees fully with the views expressed in it.

3

POLITICS, PLANNING, AND THE TRANSITION FROM STALINISM: THE CASE OF CHINA*

The way out of the present problems lies not in giving up planning but in giving it new content (Chakravarty 1987: vii).

INTRODUCTION

After the collapse of communism in Eastern Europe and subsequently in the USSR, the conventional wisdom about economic and political reform was initially simplistic. Political democratization and economic liberalization were widely regarded as recipes for prosperity. This reflected the mainstream, neo-liberal political and economic thinking in the West in the 1980s.

The leading international institutions, especially the IMF, drew on their experience in 'stabilization' and associated 'liberalization' programmes to argue for rapid moves towards a market economy and a greatly reduced role for the state in the economy. Moreover, in large areas of the developing world, the condition for economic aid had come to include political democratization. The attitudes of Western governments were not homogeneous. However, domestic political pressures meant that mostly they were not interested in assisting the former communist countries to turn themselves into competitor industrial powerhouses. The advanced economies in the late 1980s faced large problems in coping with the structural adjustment consequent upon the explosive growth in newly industrializing countries, especially, but not exclusively, those of capitalist East Asia. It was unrealistic to imagine that the OECD countries could make their goal in assisting reform of the Centrally Planned Economies (CPEs) the creation of a powerful state which would lead the industrialization process in the fashion of the Meiji Japanese government, or subsequently, the government of Taiwan, South Korea or Singapore. Their goal was a more neutral one: to assist the former CPEs to create a framework of property rights and accompanying law, producing an environment in which private enterprise could flourish, and from which their own economies also might benefit through increased trade and capital flows.

Of course, many Western experts did indeed believe that a free market environment with a minimal role for the state would produce the most rapid pace of economic advance.

The leaders of the former communist countries were extremely hostile to the notion of 'planning', which they identified with their own experiences under the Stalinist 'administered' economy. Leadership attitudes in these countries arose from a deep-rooted hostility to the politics of a strong state and from a shattering crisis of intellectual confidence, which led the policy-makers to turn to 'Western' expertise for advice and intellectual inspiration. This was expressed dramatically by Janos Kornai:

> [My approach to reform is that of] liberal thought (using the term 'liberal' in accordance with its European tradition). Respect for autonomy and self-determination, for the rights of the individual, is its focus … [I]t advocates a narrowed scope for state activities. It recommends that citizens stand on their own feet, and rely on their own power and initiative. Perhaps the role of the government will be reconsidered at a later stage. *But right now, in the beginning of the transformation process … it is time to take great steps away in the direction of a minimal state.* Perhaps later generations will be able to envisage a more moderate midway.' (Kornai 1990: 22) (My emphasis, PN)

The experience of China (and, indeed, that of almost all the Asian former Stalinist countries) calls into question these initial crude propositions about the transformation from Stalinist political economy. The Communist Party has remained in power. This authoritarian, nationalist state may well have provided a better opportunity successfully to build a powerful economy than the overthrow of the Communist Party would have done. The contrast between China's experience and that of Eastern Europe and the former USSR raises profound ethical and philosophical issues about the relationship between the rights of individuals and their duties towards enabling the attainment of common goals of the community or nation.

This chapter analyses the striking economic success that China has achieved since the mid-1970s. It argues that this is, in part, due to special factors that cannot be replicated elsewhere. However, to a considerable degree it is due to a comprehensive, experimental approach to political economy in a time of rapid structural change that does indeed have lessons for the other former CPEs. This chapter argues that the reforming former Stalinist economies need to re-understand the economic function of the state, shifting from the crude formulations of Stalinist 'planning' (in reality 'administration' rather than true planning) towards a renewed vision of planning which views its economic function as a creative interaction with the market to produce instrumental interference towards goals which cannot be precisely predicted because they release the creative power of markets, but shape and guide the setting within which market forces operate. The former Stalinist economies should be reflecting on the reasons why some economies are so much better than others at instrumental intervention. They should seek to understand why state intervention is often corrupt and wasteful, but is sometimes strikingly successful.

The careful analysis in recent years of the reasons for rapid growth in the Asian Newly Industrializing Countries has contributed to a rethinking of the role of the state in economic development. The huge contrast between the outcomes in Eastern Europe and Russia on the one hand, and the Asian CPEs, China in particular, will provide further large impetus to this process. It is likely that economics will become much more sensitive to the importance and complexities of the role of the state.

1. POLICY ENVIRONMENT

1.1. Politics

From Totalitarianism to Authoritarianism

Despite maintaining a monopoly of control over political life, and tightly controlling the boundaries of freedom, a large range of socio-economic decisions was removed from the direct control of Party administrators. China's development strategy moved closer to that of Taiwan and South Korea in the 1960s and 1970s, than to China under Mao or the USSR pre-Gorbachev. The 1980s saw a clash between two different forms of 'new authoritarianism' in Chinese politics. One branch saw this as the vehicle to lead forward towards a rapid transition to a free enterprise economy based on privatization of assets, the 'hard state' being necessary to enable the beneficiaries from this process to control mass discontent at the uncertainty, unemployment and inequality it produced. However, the view of the most powerful of China's leaders was that authoritarianism enabled the government to have a controlled move towards a market economy: economic change and popular consciousness could move forward in some sort of balance, with 'social tolerance' for change given a high weight; 'fairness' (gongping) and maintenance of living standards for the bottom segments of society could be sustained.

Political Stability

Economic life disintegrates without political stability. Neither foreign nor domestic investors have confidence. If politics is unstable, the state apparatus

Table 3.1 **Alternative Scenarios for China's Politics in the 1990s**

Possibilities	Desirability (rank)	Likelihood (rank)
(1) Overthrow of the CCP		
(*a*) Great turmoil (*da luan*)	Extremely undesirable (4)	Quite likely (2)
(*b*) Populist indecision	Very undesirable (3)	Quite likely (2)
(*c*) Purposive, reforming, democratically elected government	Extremely desirable (1)	Very unlikely (4)
(2) CCP remains in power		
(*a*) Indefinite quasi-Stalinism	Very undesirable (3)	Unlikely (3)
(*b*) Rational, secular, reforming authoritarianism	Desirable (2)	Very likely (1)

will be less able to guide economic development. The Chinese pro-democracy movement in the 1980s disagreed that a rapid move towards democratic institutions might produce *da luan* – great disorder. Table 3.1 suggests the different paths that China's politics might have taken in the late 1980s and early 1990s, their relative likelihood and desirability. The risks attached to pushing for rapid growth of democracy in China are high. Even though option 1(*c*) is much the most desirable this is not a likely outcome. The initial post-communist experience of the advanced Eastern European countries suggests that the likely outcome of an attempt to establish a Western-style democracy in China is much more likely to be 1(*b*) than 1(*c*). Indeed, for China, 1(*a*) is at least as likely an outcome as 1(*b*), with a sustained period of political turmoil, which one might loosely call the 'South-Eastern European' path to post-Stalinist political evolution. With successful economic development, it is inconceivable that widespread popular pressure would not in time push the system towards a firmly rooted democracy based upon high levels of income and all the associated cultural attributes.

In the 1980s, despite growing international and domestic pressure from liberal reformers, the Communist Party retained a firm grip on its monopoly of political power. He Xin's comments reflect the dominant view among China's leaders: 'Is it feasible to transplant [American-style democracy] into China? ... If practised in China, this type of system would result in the creation of a politically weak, lax government, unable to unite the nation. Can such a "feeble" government resolve the current complicated and tough social problems in China? Can it prevent internal strife and the country from dividing? ... If the [Chinese Communist] Party was terminated now, China would be thrown into serious political chaos and there would be no unity of the people. This would bring certain disaster to China' (He 1990). China's elderly leaders consistently talked of China as analogous to a 'sheet of loose sand', which had a high propensity to lapse into the kind of political anarchy that had existed over much of the country for most of the late nineteenth and early twentieth centuries.

Professionalization of the Bureaucracy

The attempt to modernize the bureaucracy began early in the post-Mao period, spearheaded by Deng Xiaoping,[1] to create a professional bureaucracy. The intention was to dismiss into retirement the old guard of party officials in the government administration who did not possess high technical qualifications. This effort parallels those of Bismarckian Germany and Meiji Japan in the late nineteenth century, or Taiwan and South Korea in the 1950s, in which a key point of the modernization drive was the creation of a professional government administration which was responsible to an unelected executive authority rather than to an elected parliament. Slow, but important progress was made in the 1980s: '[T]he speed of organizational turnover, and the relative ease with which it has occurred, has been impressive … [T]he Chinese bureaucracy now has a greater ability and willingness to bring technical competence to bear on competing policy alternatives' (Harding 1987: 208–9).[2] However, China in the 1980s remained a one party state, with the CCP (Chinese Communist Party) firmly in control of political life. The challenge to its authority in Tiananmen Square was repressed brutally.

Decentralization

China is a huge country, and there are large problems in trying to coordinate planning decisions from a central authority. The decentralization of important aspects of economic decision-making to lower levels of government has made a large contribution to improved economic performance. Self-evidently, local governments have much closer knowledge of local conditions than do central planners. Under appropriate revenue-sharing arrangements, they have a strong incentive to improve the performance of the economy over which they have responsibility. China's reforms in this sphere were broadly successful: 'Local government objectives are to enhance their revenue base and to develop an investment strategy that will foster growth. Both can be met by developing profitable industries' (World Bank 1990: 95).

1.2. Economics

Economic Ideology

In the 1980s China's policymakers shifted decisively away from the Stalinist model. However, the Chinese leadership insisted upon a powerful role for the state in guiding market forces. Unlike their Eastern European counterparts in the wake of the anti-Stalinist revolutions of 1989, the Chinese leadership in the 1980s was deeply interested both in investigating the ways in which market forces could improve the functioning of their economy as well as in learning from the planning experience of Japan and the East Asian Newly Industrializing Countries. Few people in China, even among its leaders, now believe that a non-market economy is a feasible way to bring prosperity to any society.

Price Reform

By the mid-1980s, the Chinese government came to the conclusion that price reform was 'the key to the reform of the entire economic structure' (Central Committee 1984: 684). However, social stability was given a high priority. The government resolved to proceed cautiously since 'the reform of the price system affects every household and the national economy' (Central Committee 1984: 684).[3] Moreover, it was regarded as dangerous to conduct sweeping price reform before enterprises were accustomed to operating in a competitive market environment. The two reforms had to be synchronized.

After much internal debate and considerable advice to reform prices rapidly, the government decided to do so only gradually and in a controlled fashion. The method adopted to move relative prices towards market-determined prices was the dual-track system, with the proportion sold at free or floating prices gradually expanding in relation to those sold at state-fixed prices, and with the latter gradually moving towards the former. In the late 1970s virtually all prices were directly controlled by the state. By the mid-1980s there had been a large growth in the role of free markets, but even by 1990 it was still the case that no more than around one-half of the value of marketed goods was sold at free market prices (Table 3.2).

Agriculture

The institutional structure of post-Mao agriculture in China strongly resembled the modern 'Japanese' path in its balance between activities undertaken by individual households and those undertaken by the collective or the state. The Chinese government, through the Communist Party, remained substan-

Table 3.2 **Proportion of Products Sold at Different Types of Prices (%)**

	1978	1986	1990
Share of total retail sales sold at:			
state-controlled prices	97	n.a.	29.7
state-guided prices	0	n.a.	17.2
market-regulated prices	3	n.a.	53.1
Share of total sales of agricultural products sold by farmers at:			
state-controlled prices	94.4	37	25.2
state-guided prices	0	n.a.	22.6
market-regulated prices	5.6	n.a.	52.2
Share of ex-factory means of production for industrial use sold at:			
state-controlled prices	100	64	44.4
state-guided prices	0	23	18.8
market-regulated prices	0	13	36.8

Source: Li 1992: 17, and Tian 1990: 143.

tially in control of the de-collectivization of farmland in the early 1980s. Equity considerations were paramount, with locally equal per capita distribution of land use as the dominant form. This egalitarian land reform tended greatly to increase socio-economic stability. It provided an asset which gave security to the weakest members of the village. It made public action easier to organize, since villagers shared a common relationship to the principal means of production. It provided a hugely egalitarian underpinning to rural, and indeed national, income distribution. Land ownership remained firmly in the hands of the village government, despite urgings from many economists that land ownership should be truly privatized. Community land provided an important basis of local government power. The terms on which land is used is determined by the community's government, and it is within the community's power to obtain more or less of the rental income for itself to be used for community purposes, whereas under a private-ownership, free-market system the rental income would accrue to private landlords. In so far as the need for land concentration develops, this should be realizable with the community acting as the landlord.

There were only small risks for Chinese peasants in de-collectivization. The managerial aspects of the new arrangements were simply an extension of the work already undertaken on the private plot: most farm work was unmechanized.

Despite rapid growth in the role of individual households, collective and local state activity remained a fundamentally important component of rural capital accumulation. Indeed, alongside the growth of individual households' accumulation went a large absolute growth in input provision by village (*cun*), township (*xiangzhen*), and co-operating households, providing inputs that were beyond the capacity of individual households.[4]

In most poor countries a large part of the rural population relies on informal, high-interest credit, thereby inhibiting the level of investment, especially among poorer but potentially efficient farmers, as well as making poor people dependent upon traditional money lenders. In the 1980s Chinese peasants saved roughly 13–15 per cent of their current income (ZGT JNJ 1990: 312), which resulted in a rapid increase in accumulated savings. This was deposited mainly in official institutions, notably the credit co-operatives and the Agricultural Bank. These institutions provided security, and 'usury' was still discouraged. A massive growth of institutional credit occurred in rural China in the 1980s with outstanding loans per peasant from the two institutions together increasing fourfold in real terms from 1980 to 1988 (ZGNCT JNJ 1989: 293–5).[5]

China feeds around 24 per cent of the world's population from just 7 per cent of the world's arable land. In the long term there is little doubt that it will be to China's advantage to import much larger amounts of land-intensive farm produce than it does at present. However, there are large risks involved in greater integration with world food markets, especially for a country of China's size and income level. If China was much more dependent upon world markets for its food supplies and some exogenous shock sharply reduced its ability to import foodstuffs, the results would be catastrophic. Until China can be confident of access to the main markets for its manufactured exports and of the state of world grain markets, it would be unwise to progress too far towards organizing its international food trade along the lines of comparative advantage.

Although in the 1980s private trade in farm produce was legalized, an important part of farm produce remained under compulsory procurement, notably a large share of grain, cotton and edible oil marketings. Moreover, the state and the quasi-state 'supply and marketing co-ops' remained the dominant channel for the sale of farm inputs, which provided an important channel of control through which rural cadres could exercise sanctions over peasants in order to induce compliance with policies which were in the interests of the wider local or national community.

State Industry

China's reforms of state industry in the 1980s were cautious and experimental. A large body of informed opinion considered that in the early 1980s China should have liberalized industrial prices, eliminated the industrial material balance planning system, opened the industrial economy to the forces of international competition, and rapidly privatized state industry.

In the post-Mao period China went to great lengths to attract foreign capital, being able to assure foreign investors of the 'good investment environment with 'stable social order and cheap labour' (*Beijing Review* (1991) 33/44). Local governments pushed central government regulations to the limit in order to attract foreign investment. Around three-quarters of the total inflow of capital in the 1980s came from Taiwan and Hong Kong, and was strongly concentrated in the coastal provinces of Southeast China, especially Guangdong and Fujian. In addition to direct foreign investment, much overseas capital went into loans to indigenous factories to help them to upgrade their technical level through the import of new machinery (Sung 1991). These factories then undertook processing and assembly operations for the overseas Chinese capitalists. China's export growth was assisted greatly by Hong Kong capitalists' marketing activities on behalf of Mainland enterprises. China's political stability and booming economy, especially in the face of the world economic downturn in the late 1980s/early 1990s, made China an attractive haven for foreign, and especially Far Eastern, investment, soaking up the large capital surpluses that several of the region's economies had accumulated in the 1980s, with a further positive effect on China's growth.

China's instrumental attitude towards international trade in the 1980s had a lot in common with that of South Korea: 'In foreign trade our principle is to encourage exports and organize imports according to needs' (*Beijing Review* (1990) 33/44). A wide array of measures was adopted to promote exports, including foreign exchange retention rights for priority export sectors, tax rebates and direct rewards to exporters. At least a part of China's manufactured exports in the 1980s was being produced with zero or even negative net value-added at world market prices (Hughes 1991; Vogel 1989). China maintained a battery of import controls, including state allocation of much foreign exchange and a wide array of quantitative restrictions (Vogel 1989). Priority was given in allocating rights to import to those products that it was judged would most rapidly raise China's labour productivity.

A superficial view of Chinese state industry in the late 1980s might conclude that nothing had changed in the nature of property rights compared to pre-1976, since the 'state' was still the 'owner' of the bulk of the industrial capital stock. However, property rights do not simply provide an alternative

between 'state' and 'private' ownership. Rather, there is a whole gradation of
property rights from comprehensively unrestrained individual property rights
through a wide gradation of controls on the rights to sell assets, produce and
market output, employ labour, and dispose of the income from assets. Within
the texture of apparently unchanged 'state' ownership, important changes did
in fact occur in the 1980s.

Following extensive experiments, the government widely introduced profit
retention schemes in the early 1980s. By the mid-1980s, over two-fifths of
fixed investment undertaken by state enterprises was financed from the enterprises' self-raised funds, so that a growing share of 'state' enterprises' capital
stock was its 'own', since nominal ownership of fixed and working capital was
assigned to the party which was the source of the initial investment (World
Bank 1990: 149). By 1989, 21 per cent of fixed investment by 'state-owned'
units was financed by domestic loans (ZGT JNJ 1990: 154), mainly from
banks. Indeed, it was possible to perceive in embryo similarities between the
Chinese system and that of Korea and Japan, in which industrial corporations
maintain close ties, cemented by equity holdings with the principal banks
(World Bank 1990: 149).

In the second half of the 1980s, a number of industrial enterprise groups
began to emerge. The state began to push important parts of state industry
along Japanese and South Korean lines, with a succession of mergers, acquisitions, and joint ventures encouraged by the central and local governments
(*Far Eastern Economic Review*, 5 Sept. 1990; Yi 1992). These changes were
intended to overcome the narrow product range and limited capacity for
technical progress in single enterprise companies. The attempt to create in a
planned way the corporate structure of advanced monopoly capitalism, based
around huge conglomerates, stands in stark contrast to the *laissez-faire*
approach adopted for enterprise privatization in Russia and Eastern Europe.

For example, in electrical appliance industry in the early 1980s China did
not have any modern large-scale producers. The government began to build
large combines out of related industries, giving them priority in the import of
foreign technology, which grew very rapidly due to China's export success,
importing numerous complete production lines from different countries.
Through mergers, acquisitions and joint ventures, several large industrial
conglomerates were established.[6] For example by the late 1980s the Wanbao
Group had several dozen enterprises with a total of 10,000 employees, annual
output of over one-million refrigerators (among other products), and had
become the eighth largest manufacturer of refrigerators in the world. In 1990
China's electrical appliance industry exported 200 million US dollars worth
of goods, and the scope of its exports had broadened to include increasingly
sophisticated products. China had begun to penetrate some of the world's

most competitive markets. In 1988, for example, China exported 800,000 electric fans to the USA.[7]

China in the 1980s had an exceptionally high savings rate: China's households saved no less than 23 per cent of their disposable income in 1981–7, compared to 18 per cent in Taiwan (1965–81), 21 per cent in Japan (1976–82), and just 8 per cent in the USA (1976–82) (World Bank 1990: 126). The main channel through which these reached industry was via banks and government bonds rather than shares. Share ownership systems developed only slowly, confined to an experimental role.

The right of state enterprises to determine their product mix was extended gradually. By the late 1980s only about one-fifth of industrial products was allocated directly by the State Planning Commission (Dong 1990: 66).

State enterprise managers became selected increasingly for their business skills since this would increase the likelihood of the enterprise earning profits for the government unit to which it was subordinate. In the absence of welfare benefits provided by the state, as opposed to the enterprise, the establishment of competitive labour markets would have been socially explosive. In the 1980s, the Chinese government began to reform the system of welfare and housing provision in the state sector but it was a complex process.[8]

The rate of growth of money wages in state enterprises in the 1980s was rapid in relation to China's history since 1940[9] but was well below the rate in most Latin American countries over the same period. China's workforce still lacked an independent, defensive trade union movement, and was unable to bargain for wage increases in the way that occurs in countries with democratic institutions.

Rural Non-Farm Enterprises

In former communist countries the IMF/World Bank recommends 'the rapid privatisation of small enterprises through outright sales to individuals, co-operatives and others' with the assets sold 'as quickly as possible' (IMF 1990: 2 and 27). China followed a different path. In the 1980s it once again became legal to set up and run small businesses, and the private sector grew extremely rapidly. None the less, within the overall structure of the rural non-farm sector, the 'collectively'-owned sector, i.e. *xiang* (township) and *cun* (village)-run enterprises, remained massively dominant (ZGJ JNJ 1985: v, 19 and 1989: v, 15).

China's 'collectively'-owned enterprises are not co-operatives in the normal sense of the word. Rather, they resemble national state-owned enterprises, with the 'state' being the local community (*xiang* or *cun*). The 'rural enterprises department' of the local government monitors the enterprises' operation.

Poor transport in rural China provided a large degree of protection to rural enterprises from competition from the urban enterprises. Moreover, the rural non-farm sector, like the urban sector, benefited from substantial protection from other countries' potentially competitive labour-intensive industries. The rural non-farm sector was more flexible than partially reformed state industry in adjusting its product-mix to rapidly changing markets.

In the rural non-farm sector in the 1980s competitive factor and product markets were quickly established. Trade unions hardly existed and the large reserve army of surplus labour placed considerable downward pressure on rural wages. Whereas in the state sector the workforce was long established and used to a low pace of work, the workforce in rural non-farm enterprises was mainly first generation, lacking the privileges or organizational capacity of the state sector worker. Most workers in this sector were recruited on a contract basis, which made it possible to dismiss workers or terminate a contract for individual shortcomings, as well as to cut back staff in response to changing market conditions. In 1986, 70 per cent of the main material inputs of the rural non-farm enterprises were obtained from the market (Economics Research Institute 1987: 11). In the same year over two-thirds of rural non-farm enterprises' marketings were sold at prices determined by the enterprises themselves (Economics Research Institute 1987: 13).

The incentive structure for the management of the rural 'collectively owned' non-farm sector changed dramatically. The most important institutional innovation was the contract between the enterprise and local government. The most important part of the contract was the profits target.

Rural collectively-owned enterprises became the key to prosperity for Chinese local governments in the 1980s. While agriculture grew rapidly over the decade, the explosive growth of the non-farm sector meant that its share of total rural output rose quickly (from 31% of the gross value of rural output in 1980 to 55% in 1989 (ZGT JNJ 1990: 33)). Their capacity to absorb surplus labour was high, and the greater its success in this respect, the more approval local leaders won from their community, or from the governments at higher levels. Non-farm enterprises were vitally important, too, as the most dynamic contributors to local government revenue. It was strongly in the interest of local governments to ensure the expansion of profits from enterprises within their jurisdiction.

Local governments played a large role in the growth of the rural community enterprises. The most important decisions in local capital markets were taken either directly by the local government or, typically, by them in collaboration with the local managers of financial organizations (Byrd 1990: ch. 9). The local government's rural non-farm enterprises department identified new opportunities for profitable investment and took the risks involved in setting up new enterprises. They also made the final decision to close down collective enterprises and transfer the human and physical resources to other uses within the community. The World Bank's own study concludes: 'Without the deep involvement of community governments, China's rural non-farm sector could not have grown as rapidly as it did in the late 1970s and early 1980s' (Byrd 1990: 358).

An important consequence of the rapid growth of competitive small business, especially in the countryside, was that it provided a spur to the state sector. Markets were truly becoming contestable. This affected all markets, not just that for final products. Labour and capital were increasingly attracted towards the sector with higher returns, which frequently was the non-state sector. In the labour market, for example, the structure began to resemble the traditional Japanese pattern of a dual labour market. Employment in the modern large-scale sector, with *de facto* lifetime employment for most employees, expanded relatively slowly (from 36 million in 1984 to 45 million in 1991), while employment in industry outside this sector, where market forces operated much more powerfully in the labour market, grew explosively (employment in rural industry grew from 10 million in 1984 to 33 million in 1991) (ZGT JZY 1985: 26, and ZGT JZY 1992: 17).[10]

2. CRITICISM

2.1. Politics

The view that democratic politics in poor countries is positively and causally related to economic growth has gained widespread currency in recent years. Dasgupta's influential article (Dasgupta 1990: 4 and 27–8) argues: 'The choice between fast growth in income and negative liberties is a phoney choice ... Political liberties are *positively* and significantly correlated with per capita income and its growth. Nations whose citizens enjoy greater political liberties and civil liberties also perform better in terms of ... improvements in life expectancy at birth, per capita income, and infant survival rates.' This is most gratifying, because one can kill two birds with one stone, and feel virtuous in one's support for greater 'democracy' because this will not only not harm growth but will improve it. Supported by 'reasoning' and 'statistical analysis'[11] such as Dasgupta's, the IMF began to make 'democratization' of political institutions a third aspect of conditionality alongside 'stabilization' and privatization.

This approach was supported strongly by the apparent inability of East European communist countries to make progress in their economic reform

beyond a certain point. The notion that gradual reform of the planned economy was infeasible due to the authoritarian nature of the Communist Party
was a central plank of Kornai's extremely influential criticism of the 'Third
Way', Kornai (1986) is scathing in his criticism of the 'naive reformers' who
believe that a Communist Party can preside over a process that the considers
will inevitably lead to its own demise.

A chorus of trenchant criticisms was made of the Chinese Communist
Party in the 1980s, arguing in the same fashion as Kornai that the introduction of a market economy was impossible under communist rule: 'To survive
and successfully evolve as a living social organism, the system of free markets,
private property, and contractual buyer-seller transactions must operate within a legal order and in a politically democratic environment' (Prybyla 1990:
188). It was widely felt that the CCP could not itself make the transition to
secular rational rule. It had the double burden of highly centralized traditions
of Leninism plus millennia of centralized rule in China. The conventional
wisdom, espoused in article after article and conference after conference, was
that the CCP had to be removed from its monopoly of political power if the
move to a market economy was to be put into effect:

> Deng Xiaoping tried to restart China's economy without affecting the
> dictatorship of its entrenched vanguards ... Although the term had not
> yet been invented, Deng sought *perestroika* without *glasnost*. This is not a
> particularly unusual project. There are innumerable examples of similar-
> ly placed monopolists of political power who wanted economic modern-
> isation without political reform ... It does not work ... instead of dupli-
> cating South Korea and Taiwan, China seemed to have taken as its
> model Ferdinand Marcos's Philippines. (Johnson 1990: viii–x)

In the euphoria of post-communism, it was very hard to believe that such a
brutal, undemocratic regime as China's could perform well economically. In
the wake of Tiananmen it was felt to be morally repugnant to dare to suggest
that such a brutal regime as the Chinese could possibly lead the economy forward successfully, let alone attract wide popular support. In fact, such violent
repression of protest movements as that at Tiananmen is normal rather than
exceptional in developing countries. Similar actions in recent years include
that in Thailand in 1976 (Thammassat University), in South Korea in 1980
(Kwangju), and in India in 1990 (Srinagar). None of these received remotely
as much publicity in the West as the Chinese massacre, despite their great
ferocity, and none of them had any lasting negative impact on the respective
countries' economic performance.

2.2. Economics

In the post-Mao period, China put into practice a form of market socialism and, indeed, by 1992 the term 'socialist market economy' had become the official description of the system. A fundamental tenet of the advice received by East European reformers after the 1989 revolution, and subsequently by Russian reformers, was that the Third Way of 'market socialism' with a combination of strong planning and market, and a gradual reform of the Stalinist system, cannot work.

An important part was played in this argument by the apparent failure of China's reforms, which it was argued fitted the same pattern as the 'failed' reforms of Eastern Europe: 'In Hungary, and also in a number of the other socialist countries, the principle of "market socialism" has become a guiding idea of the reform process ... Under this principle, state firms should remain in state ownership, but by creating appropriate conditions, these firms should be made to act as if they were a part of a market ... I wish to use strong words here, without any adornment: the basic idea of market socialism simply fizzled out. Yugoslavia, Hungary, China, the Soviet Union, and Poland bear witness to its fiasco. The time has come to look this fact in the face and abandon the principle of market socialism.' (Kornai 1990: 58)

Jan Prybyla was one of the most articulate critics of China's incremental reform strategy (Prybyla 1990 and 1991): 'To make the socialist system economic and modern at least three comprehensive measures have to be taken simultaneously. First, all market – for consumer goods and factors of production – must be freed ... Second the bulk of property must be privatised ... [Third] the bureaucratic class must be *denomenklaturised*. Its allocative prerogatives must be abolished' (Prybyla 1990: 190). He, in common with a large body of analysts, argued that China's post-Mao reforms had 'failed'. Writing after Tiananmen he called the Chinese economy a 'broken system, which had crucial negative lessons to teach Eastern Europe: *The sad chronicle of China's post-Mao attempt to introduce a modern economic system contains a useful lesson which others, notably the East Europeans are taking to heart.* The lesson is that to address the economic problem in a modern way in the context of a low calibre, inefficient, slothful, wasteful, cronified socialist system, one must go all the way to the market system, do it quickly, and not stop anywhere on the way. To go part of the way slowly, "crossing the river while groping for the stones" as the Dengists put it, is to end up the creek to nowhere.' (Prybyla 1990: 194; emphasis added)

There was a remarkable degree of unanimity among advisers to the ex-communist governments of East Europe and Russia in the aftermath of the defeat of communism. The idea that China's reforms had 'failed', powerfully reinforced by the Tiananmen massacre, played an important role in bolstering their view of the necessary requirements of successful reform. The common view was that the pace of the transition from central planning should be rapid.[12] Anders Aslund, a close adviser to the Yeltsin government, argued: 'Common sense suggests that if you are sliding into a chasm, you should jump quickly to the other side ... and not tread cautiously. There is no theory supporting a gradual switch of system' (Aslund 1990: 37).

The IMF/World Bank/EBRD (European Bank for Reconstruction and Development)/OECD combined view of reform in Russia best reflects the Western conventional wisdom about reform in the former communist countries. Their view was that enterprises would not respond in desirable ways to market signals unless private property rights were established: 'Stabilisation and price reform together will only set the scene for a meaningful supply response if they are accompanied by the establishment of private ownership rights and the elimination of the panoply of controls which currently prevent competition and discourage the efficient use of resources' (IMF 1990: 2). They argued that enterprises' attempts to make profits produce undesirable outcomes unless prices were determined by market forces: 'Markets cannot begin to develop until prices are free to move in response to shifts in demand and supply, both domestic and external ... Price decontrol is essential to end the shortages that ... afflict the economy' (IMF 1990: 17). They argued that economic progress would be greatly inhibited unless there was full integration into the world economy: 'It is ... essential to move as rapidly as possible to a transparent and decentralised trade and exchange rate system, in order to hasten the integration ... into the world economy ... The exchange rate [needs] to be moved to market clearing levels. [Only] a few sectors [need to be shielded] for a short time from intense competition of international markets' (IMF 1990: 17). They put their combined weight of opinion behind a rapid transition towards a market economy, despite explicitly acknowledging the risks involved: 'The prospect of a sharp fall in output and rapid increase in prices in the early stage of a radical reform is daunting ... *In advocating the more radical approach we are well aware of the concerns of those who recommend caution*' (IMF 1990: 16–19) (my emphasis, PN).

3. RESULTS

The most important criterion by which governments in all settings, but especially in poor countries, are judged by their own populations is their success in economic affairs, and particularly in providing employment and raising incomes. In the former communist countries in Eastern Europe and in

Table 3.3 **Comparative Economic Performance of the Chinese Economy in the 1980s**

	China	India	Low income countries[a]	Middle income countries
Av. annual growth rate, 1980–9 (%):				
GDP	9.7	5.3	3.4	2.9
Agriculture	6.3	2.9	2.5	2.6
Industry	12.6	6.9	3.1	3.0
Services	9.3	6.5	4.4	2.8
Av. annual real growth rate of exports, 1980–9 (%)	11.5	5.8	0.8	5.5
Av. annual growth rate of population, 1980–9 (%)	1.4	2.1	2.7	2.1
Av. annual rate of inflation, 1980–9 (%)	5.8	7.7	14.9	73.0
Debt service as % of exports of goods and services: 1980	4.6	9.1	11.4	26.1
: 1989	9.8	26.4	27.4	23.1
Index of av. p.c.[b] food consumption, 1987–9 (1979–81 = 100)	128	113	103	101
Daily calorie intake p.c.[b]: 1965	1,931	2,103	1,960	2,482
: 1988	2,632	2,104	2,182	2,834
Crude death rate (no/1000)				
: 1965	10	20	21	13
: 1989	7	11	13	8
Infant mortality rate (no/1000)				
: 1981	71	121	124	81
: 1989	30	95	94	51
Life expectancy at birth (years)				
: 1981	67	52	50	60
: 1989	70	59	55	66

Notes

[a] excluding India and China.

[b] p.c. = per capita.

Source: World Bank 1983 and 1991.

Russia, the reforms since 1989 have produced desperately poor short-term economic results.

A detailed consideration of the performance of the Chinese economy in the reform period is beyond the scope of this paper. However, the broad outlines of this are provided in Tables 3.3–3.5. China's incremental path produced outstanding economic advance over the course of a decade and a half.[13] In the first decade or so of economic reform China outperformed almost all developing countries in terms of output growth and export performance (Table 3.3). Moreover, compared both to most developing countries and to most of the reforming former Stalinist economies, it remained relatively unburdened by foreign debt and had achieved fast growth with relatively low inflation. China's system of authoritarian political control enabled her, in contrast to most other developing countries, to be able to control population growth, despite the bulge in the reproducing age cohorts in the 1980s. The improvement in economic performance was achieved through a sharp improvement in overall economic efficiency, reflected in the fact that the growth of output was accompanied by an extraordinary surge in popular living standards

Table 3.4 **Changes in the Standard of Living in China, 1978–89**

	1978	1989
Index of real p.c.[a] consumption	100	210
Consumption p.c. of:		
grain (kgs)	196	242
edible oil (kgs)	1.6	5.4
pork (kgs)	7.7	15.6
fresh eggs (kgs)	2.0	6.0
sugar (kgs)	3.4	5.4
cloth (metres)	8.0	11.6
Ownership of consumer durables (no/100 people):		
sewing machines	3.5	12.2
watches	8.5	50.1
bicycles	7.7	32.8
radios	7.8	23.6
TVs	0.3	14.9
Housing space p.c. (sq metres)		
cities	3.6	6.6
villages	8.1	17.2
Doctors per 10,000 people	10.7	15.4

Note: [a] per capita.

Source: ZGT JZY 1990: 40–2.

(Table 3.4) and remarkable reduction in absolute poverty (Table 3.5). China's economic performance in the 1980s was much better than that in the most relevant comparator country, namely India, and was vastly better than virtually anyone in the late 1970s could have hoped. Were Eastern Europe and the former USSR to achieve comparable advances (beginning from a much higher base, of course) in the 1990s, their reforms would be regarded as immensely successful.

4. A CHINESE PUZZLE

The fact that the Chinese system of political economy in the 1980s was 'market socialist' and yet was one of the most dynamic in terms both of output and income growth that the modern world has seen, presents economists with a puzzle: why did it perform so well in the first decade and a half of reform,

Table 3.5 **Poverty in China, 1978–1990**

	1978	1985	1990
Total population (m.)	963	1,059	1,143
Urban	172 (17.9%)	251 (23.7%)	302 (26.4%)
Rural	790 (82.1%)	808 (76.3%)	841 (73.6%)
Average per capita income (1978 yuan)			
Urban	–	557	685
Rural	134	324	319
Poverty line (current yuan/year)			
Urban	–	215	19
Rural	98	190	275
Incidence of poverty (million)			
Total	270 (28.0%)	97 (9.2%)	98 (8.6%)
Urban	10 (4.4%)	1 (0.4%)	1 (0.4%)
Rural	260 (33.0%)	96 (11.9%)	97 (11.5%)

Notes

After three years of apparent stagnation in real rural per capita consumption, a substantial further growth occurred in 1991 (State Statistical Burean, ZGT JZY 1992: 42). Had the 1991 data been made available to the World Bank, it is likely that there would have been some further reduction reported in rural poverty.

The poverty line used in this table was calculated by revaluing for each year at current prices a constant 'poverty line' bundle of goods and services.

Source: World Bank 1992, v.

despite the fact that the economic institutions and policies were gravely inadequate in relation to mainstream Western economic theory and policy? There are a number of possibilities, of different orders of difficulty for mainstream Western economics to digest.

The 'easy' answer for economists reflecting on the shambles of post-Stalinism in Eastern Europe and the former USSR is that China entered its reform programme with important advantages compared to Eastern Europe and Russia. These include China's low level of international debt, the special role of Hong Kong (and, increasingly, Taiwan), and the fact that China enjoys a strong 'capitalist' tradition stretching back at least a thousand years. It may be argued also that it is easier to reform a low income, predominantly rural CPE.

A more worrying possibility is that China's incrementalist approach to economic reform may have been correct and the attempt in most of Eastern Europe and in the former USSR to move rapidly towards a market economy may have been a serious mistake.[14] The correct economic advice to the former Stalinist economies may have been to stress that their structural transformation would require a lengthy period of extensive state intervention to cope with probable large areas of market failure. The enthusiasm of post-communist 'capitalist triumphalism' among advisers to Eastern Europe and the former USSR may have caused a major mistake in assessing not only the required speed of the transition but also the desirable economic functions of the state over an extended period. The huge tasks of structural transformation in an atmosphere of great uncertainty in the reforming CPEs is precisely a situation in which it is likely in principle that market failure will be especially large, with private agents tending, more than under other circumstances, to look towards the short term and speculation rather than towards longer-term investment, so that the gap between private and social benefits may be especially wide.[15] The early stage of development economics in the 1940s and 1950s, and indeed, the practical experience of the Newly Industrializing Countries of East Asia,[16] may have been more relevant to the enormous tasks of transition that these economies now face than mainstream economics of the 1970 and 1980s which stressed the shortcomings of the state as a vehicle for achieving socially desirable goals.[17]

An even more worrying possibility for mainstream economics is that a main part of the reason for the contrast may lie in the realm of politics. A successful reform strategy may require a comprehensive perspective of political economy. A more successful transition away from a communist economy may be easier to achieve with a strong state which is able to place the overall national interest above that of powerful vested interest groups. A self-reforming Communist Party may be the least bad vehicle available to accomplish this. The causes for China's success may lie above all in the set of historical factors which allowed the Communist Party to survive in China whereas it was overthrown in Eastern Europe and Russia, and to preside over the introduction of an increasingly competitive economy.

The most worrying thought of all is the possibility that China's explosive growth (and, increasingly, a wider growth process in former Stalinist South-East Asia) since the 1970s reflects a huge inherent catch-up and overtaking possibility which may have been latent in all the former Stalinist economies on account of the vast under-performance in relation to their huge physical and human capital inheritance. The reform of the Stalinist economies may be seen by history to have been a knife-edge situation in which correct choices in political economy could produce explosive growth and incorrect ones could send the system spinning backwards at high speed for an extended period.

CONCLUSION

The Stalinist vision of a development path without markets and competition is dead. After 1989 there was extraordinary unanimity among Western economists as to the desirable path that the former Stalinist systems should take, and great optimism about the results that might be achieved. The revolutions in East Europe were widely felt to offer the possibility of a swift construction in those countries of free market capitalism under the auspices of liberal democratic institutions. In the wake of the Tiananmen massacre, China's communist leadership was felt to be close to collapse. China's post-Mao reforms were widely felt to be cosmetic and ultimately to have achieved little. China was argued to demonstrate to the USSR and East Europe the danger of taking the halfway house path of incremental reform. Now it is time to take stock and consider soberly the lessons that may be learned about reforming Stalinist systems. Ultimately, this involves reflection on the nature of economics itself. This period has revealed how little the subject typically has to offer in considering grand questions of systemic change. Far too often, economic advice has been little more than slogans. Too rarely has it consisted of careful, pragmatic political economy.

Throughout the 1980s critics both inside and outside China argued that meaningful economic reform required a prior political revolution, involving the overthrow of the Communist Party, as occurred in Eastern Europe in 1989 and in the USSR in 1991. The argument that rapid political change in China might lead to chaos (*da luan*) which would prevent any serious economic strategy being followed, and would therefore be harmful to the interests of most Chinese people, was regarded widely as an immoral attempt to defend a 'fascist' regime. The creation of a stable, effective political system following the collapse of communism is a long process. Economic life atrophies without stable politics. The counterfactual question which must be posed is: would China's economy have advanced as rapidly as it did in the 1980s if the Chinese Communist Party in the late 1970s had been overthrown as those in Eastern Europe and the USSR were in 1989–91? Is it likely that a stable political system would have emerged quickly, under the guidance of which the Chinese economy could have prospered? Rather, is it not the case that the descent into political turbulence in the USSR and in much of Eastern Europe, especially the impoverished Southeast shows the possible path that China might have followed? It is extremely difficult to organize a careful release of the political 'safety valve', with a controlled transition from Stalinist to democratic politics.

Throughout the 1980s China's incremental economic reform strategy came under fierce criticism from foreign economists and increasingly from China's own economists, who were allowed greater freedom to speak out until 1989. The implicit counterfactual proposition at the heart of much of the criticism is that China could have grown more successfully if she had early on taken a risk and dared to reform with 'one cut of the knife'. Whether one's hope is that China will have unrestrained capitalism or, as this essay has argued is desirable, that it will establish some form of market socialism, the dangers of trying to cross the river in one leap can now be seen with much greater clarity. The collapse of national output in the former GDR and USSR, and the serious decline in much of Eastern Europe, has produced great social tension. However, few people are likely to starve to death as a result. The same would not be true for China. The Great Leap Forward and the Soviet collectivization drive during the First Five-Year Plan showed vividly the price that could be paid in a populous poor country for a misguided attempt to leap into a new socio-economic order that would allegedly solve a vast array of problems at a stroke. The construction of a post-Stalinist economy is a long and complex process. The experience of the former GDR and Poland illustrate the risks involved in too rapid an attempt to move away from the Stalinist economy.

China's experience with incremental reform since 1978 confirms that this path brings great tensions, not least those associated with corruption. However, it shows that large gains in economic performance can be made even by a communist government which is determined to cling to power, and with extensive state ownership. For this to be so, the government must have recognized that the Stalinist system of economic organization had failed to improve people's living standards in a satisfactory way. It must be committed to forcing former Stalinist institutions to operate in a truly competitive environment. In the USSR in the 1920s the market socialist model of NEP was indeed overthrown. However, in the modern world once the process has gone beyond a certain point it is virtually impossible that the economy can revert to Stalinism. China had gone well beyond that point by 1991. A striking characteristic of the Chinese economy in the wake of the Tiananmen massacre was the fact that the move towards a market economy continued powerfully.

With hindsight, it seems most unlikely that some form of radical political democratization and associated 'big bang' programme of economic reform could have produced as successful an economic performance as China achieved since the late 1970s. Almost all China's citizens now have gained experience of markets, but unlike in the USSR and East Europe, the concept of a large state, working in the national interest to harness the market for common goals, remains a respected concept in the popular mind.

China still faces obstacles in progressing towards a market economy, not least those arising from pressure of population upon natural resources. It is conceivable that a combination of pressure from the collapse of the Communist Parties in the USSR and Eastern Europe, and the disruption stemming from the death of Deng Xiaoping might yet lead to a loss of nerve by the Party in the face of a mass popular demonstration in the capital and to the overthrow of the Communist Party of China. It is still an open question whether the Party can make further progress towards transforming itself from a totalitarian into a 'rational authoritarian' party, which legitimates its tenure of office for the period of transition towards a more prosperous society in non-'Marxist', non-quasi-religious terms. Accepting the need for and managing political change may yet prove to be more of a stumbling block for the post-Mao regime than the management of a programme of incremental economic reform towards a market economy.

A simple homogeneous policy package of political economy cannot be recommended to all reforming socialist countries regardless of their size, location, income level and historically bequeathed political conditions. The slogans 'free market' and 'democracy' do not provide a panacea for the complex problems of transition out of Stalinism. Nor is it possible to recommend China's politically authoritarian, economically incremental path of transition from Stalinism to other former socialist countries. The dangers of a wild attempt to leap out of a Stalinist and into a capitalist economy ought now to be clear enough. However, an incremental path of economic reform may be much more difficult to effect in countries which lack as strong a political leadership as China possessed in the 1980s. Faced with the desperate economic collapse in large parts of the former communist world in Eastern Europe and the former USSR, a new authoritarian, political leadership based upon cultural and economic nationalism becomes increasingly probable. This is perhaps the most likely in Russia, the first socialist country and the once proud leader of the world socialist movement, in which the sense of national humiliation is the most intense.

Notes

* I am grateful to Ha-Joon Chang and Bob Rowthorn, as well as to my colleague Geoff Harcourt, for their comments.

1 The need to professionalize, reduce in size, and make more youthful China's government bureaucracy was a central theme of Deng's speeches in the early 1980s (Deng 1984).

2 Harding (Harding 1987: 204–11) provides a careful account of the large increase in the proportion of technically qualified bureaucrats and the substantial decline in their average age during the early to mid-1980s.

3 'There is much confusion in our present system of pricing … This irrational price system has to be reformed … otherwise it will be impossible to assess correctly the performance of enterprises … As the reform of the price system affects every household and the national economy as a whole, we must be extremely prudent, formulate a well-conceived, feasible programme based on the growth of production and capability of the state's finances and on the premise that the people's real income will gradually be increased, and then carry it out in a planned and systematic way' (Central Committee 1984: 683).

4 Still in 1990 individual households were supplying only an estimated 23% of machine ploughing, 30% of drainage and irrigation services, 15% of plant protection, 48% of seed supply and just 3% of veterinary services (Department of Agriculture 1991).

5 Figures in current prices deflated by the national retail price index.

6 These included the Wanbao (in Guangdong), Jinxing (in Shanghai), the Panda Group (in Jiangsu province) and the Peony Group (in Beijing).

7 The information in this paragraph is from *Beijing Review*, 34/23 (10–16 June) 1991.

8 The most important sign of movement towards a competitive labour market in the state sector in the 1980s was the rapid rise in the number (10 million in 1978 to 24 million in 1988) and proportion of 'non-fixed' workers (from 14% in 1978 to 24% in 1988) (ZGLDGZT JZL, 1949–85 (1987: 28 and 33) and ZGLDGZT JNJ (1989: 203)), who had less rights and lower average wages than did existing state enterprise employees (on wage differentials, see ZGLDGZT JZL 1949–85 (1987: 171)).

9 Around 11% per annum in state enterprises from 1978 to 1989 (ZGT JZY 1990: 41).

10 In the collectively owned segment of rural industry, it would be incorrect to describe the labour market as precisely analogous to that in the traditional small-scale sector in Japan. While the security of employment might be less than in the modern, large-scale sector, in advanced areas there is a well-developed system of community welfare and commitment to retraining workers rather than simply declaring them redundant as businesses cease to be competitive.

11 In fact, Dasgupta's selection of developing countries is bizarre, omitting a large number of fast growing authoritarian ones (e.g. Chile, Peru, Brazil, Singapore, Hong Kong, Mexico and Taiwan are all excluded) as well as most of the communist countries (North Korea, Algeria, Mozambique, Angola, Cuba, Vietnam, Burma and Cambodia are all excluded). Moreover, his 'statistical analysis' consists of a series of rank correla-

tion coefficients between pairs of variables, among which much the weakest relationship is that between growth and political freedom.

12 One could add a very long bibliography of economists who advocated high speed as the only 'logical' way to achieve a successful transition. Kornai's account (Kornai 1986) of the 'failure' of Hungarian reform was deeply influential in the early days of thinking about reform in the post-communist countries.

13 The reforms began the moment Mao Tsetung died in 1976.

14 This kind of 'Great Leap Forward' into a new socio-economic system which, allegedly, will bring great benefits was exactly that, paradoxically, against which Popper warned in the late 1950s in respect to the communist experiment: 'Every version of historicism expresses the feeling of being swept into the future by irresistible forces ... Contrasting their "dynamic" thinking with the static thinking of all previous generations, [the historicists] believe that their own advance has been made possible by the fact that we are now 'living in a revolution' which has so much accelerated the speed of our development that social change can now be directly experienced within a single lifetime. This story is, of course, sheer mythology' (Popper 1957: 160).

15 This applies *a fortiori* in so far as the reforms are accompanied by socio-economic instability to which they may have themselves contributed.

16 See especially, Amsden 1989; Wade 1990.

17 Writing in respect of the economics profession's view of the role of the state in development economics, Stern comments: 'The apparent swing in the profession from wholehearted espousal of extensive government intervention to its rubbishing seems to be an example of unbalanced intellectual growth ... There are problems and virtues with both state intervention and the free market' (Stern 1989: 621–2).

References

Amsden, A., 1989, *Asia's Next Giant: South Korea and Late Industrialization*. Oxford: Oxford University Press.

Aslund, A., 1990, 'Gorbachev, Perastroika, and Economic Crisis', *Problems of Communism* (Jan.–Apr.), 13–41.

Byrd, W., 1990, 'Entrepreneurship, Capital, and Ownership', in W. Byrd and Q. Lin (eds.), *China's Rural Industry*. Washington, DC: World Bank.

Chakravarty, S., 1987, *Development Planning: The Indian Experience*. Oxford: Oxford University Press.

Central Committee of the CCP, 1984, 'Decision on Reform of the Economic Structure', reprinted in S. N. Liu and Q. Wy (eds.), *China's Socialist Economy*. Beijing: Foreign Languages Press.

Dasgupta, P., 1990, 'Well-being and the Extent of its Realisation in Poor Countries', *Economic Journal*, 100: 1–32.

Deng, X.P., 1984, *Selected Works of Deng Xiaoping. (1975–1982)*. Beijing: Foreign Languages Press.

Department of Agriculture, 1991, 'China's Land Contract Management System and the Operation of Co-operative Organisations in China in 1990', *Problems of Agricultural Economics ['Nongye jingü wenti']*, 8 and 9.

Dong, F., 1990, 'Reform of the Economic Operating Mechanism and Reform of Ownership', in Nolan and Dong (eds.).

Economics Research Institute, 1987, *Report on the Organisation and Growth of China's Township Enterprises, Economic Research Materials*, 7.

Hicks, G., (ed.) 1990, *The Broken Mirror*. Harlow: Longman.

Harding, H., 1987, *China's Second Revolution*. Washington, DC: The Brookings Institution.

He, X., 1990, 'Scholar Discusses Democracy and Other Issues', *Beijing Review*, 33/4 (20–26 Aug.).

Hughes, H., 1991, 'Constraints on Export Growth: Foreign or Domestic?', unpublished ms.

IMF, World Bank, OECD and EBRD, 1990, *The Economy of the USSR: Summary and Recommendations*. Washington, DC: World Bank.

Johnson, C., 1990, 'Forward', in Hicks (ed.).

Kornai, J., 1986, 'The Hungarian Reform Process: Visions, Hopes, and Reality', *Journal of Economic Literature*, 24: 1687–737.

—, 1990, *The Road to a Free Economy*. London: Norton.

Li, P., 1992, 'Price Reform the Progressive Way', *Beijing Review*, 35/18, 4–10, May.

Nolan, P. and F.R. Dong, (eds.) 1990, *The Chinese Economy and its Future*. Cambridge: Polity Press.

Popper, K.R., 1960, *The Poverty of Historicism*. London: Routledge and Kegan Paul.

Prybyla, J., 1990, 'A Broken System', in Hicks (ed.).

—, 1991, The Road from Socialism: Why, Where, What and How', *Problems of Communism*, 40 (Jan.–Apr.).

Stern, N., 1989, 'The Economics of Development: A Survey', *Economic Journal*, 99 (Sept.): 597–685.

Sung, Y., 1991, 'The Reintegration of Southeast China', unpublished ms.

Tian, Y., 1990, 'Prices', in Nolan and Dong (eds.).

Wade, R., 1990, *Governing the Market*. Princeton: Princeton University Press.

Vogel, E., 1989, *One Step Ahead in China*. London: Harvard University Press.

World Bank, 1983, 1985, 1987, 1991, *World Development Report*, Washington, DC: World Bank, and New York: Oxford University Press.

World Bank, 1990, *China: Mecroeconomic Stability and Industrial Growth under Decentralised Socialism*, Washington, DC: World Bank.

World Bank, 1992, *China: Strategies for Reducing Poverty in the 1990s*. Washington, DC: World Bank.

ZGJ JNJ, 1985, 1989, *Chinese Economic Yearbook [Zhongguo jingii nianiian]*. Beijing: Economic Management Magazine.

ZGLDGZT JZL, 1985, *Statistical Materials on Chinese Labour and Wages 1949–1985 [Zhongguo laodong gongzi tongji ziliao]*. Beijing: Zhongguo tongji chubanshe.

ZGLDGZT JNJ, 1989, *Chinese Yearbook of Labour and Wages [Zhongguo laodong gongzi tongji nianjian]*. Beijing: Zhonguo tongji chubanshe.

ZGNCT JNJ, 1989, *Chinese Rural Statistical Yearbook [Zhongguo nongcun tongjinianjian]*. Beijing: Zhongguo tongji chubanshe.

ZGNYJ JGY, 1982, *Chinese Agricultural Outline [Zhongguo nongye jingii gaiyao]*. Beijing: Ministry of Agriculture.

ZGT JNJ, 1990, *Chinese statistical Yearbook [Zhonuo tongji nianjian]*.

ZGT JZY, 1985, 1986, 1990, 1991, 1992, *Chinese Statistical Outline [Zhongguo tongji zhaiyao]*. Beijing: Zhongguo tongji chubanshe.

4

DEMOCRATIZATION, HUMAN RIGHTS AND ECONOMIC REFORM: THE CASE OF CHINA AND RUSSIA

Introduction

The dramatic contrast in outcomes from the reform process in China and Russia is one of the great phenomena of our age, with enormous consequences for the citizens of those countries as well as great implications for international political economy. It sheds new light on the old debate about the relationship between political institutions, economic progress and human rights.

The contrast in outcome stems from many factors. Both China and Russia possessed enormous possibilities for 'catch-up' inherent in the massive unrealised potentialities of the communist economic system. It is not at all obvious that these catch-up possibilities were greater in China than in Russia. Self-evidently, the contrasting conception and practice of economic reform was an extremely important influence. However, this chapter will not discuss either of these issues.[1] Instead, it explores the arguments of principle involved in the debate about democratization in the communist countries (section 1), and the political setting within which the economic reforms were enacted in China and Russia (section 2). It argues that political choices made by the respective leaders were critical in determining the respective economic outcomes, and the consequent impact upon a range of human rights. These are examined in section 3. The contrast in choices of political strategy was determined in part by some accidents of history and in part by the different degree to which the respective leaders responded to arguments made by the international community of politicians, scholars and advisers.

The dramatic contrast in outcomes from the very different patterns of reform pursued in the two countries raises profound questions about democratization as a policy prescription for developing and/or reforming communist countries. Democratic political rights are just one of a spectrum of human rights. Others include the right to personal safety, employment, food, shelter, clothing, education, health services and social security. I argue that, at least in large reforming communist countries, democratization of politics may harm economic performance and hence set back the improvement or even damage the level of achievement of human rights other than the right to vote. It argues that it was irresponsible for Western social scientists and policy-makers to hold out high hopes for the functional usefulness of political democ-ratization in achieving other human rights, which may be more important in such countries at this juncture.

1. Political Democratization and Economic Reform in the Communist Countries

Mainstream Western social scientists and politicians have provided a chorus of encouragement and approval for Soviet political 'democratization' under Gorbachev and Yeltsin. A wide variety of arguments has been advanced which suggested that rapid 'democratization' was the correct path for the Stalinist countries. These arguments were part of a wider movement towards encouraging and even imposing 'democracy' (in the form of International Monetary Fund conditionality) upon developing countries as well as the for-mer Stalinist countries. There was a virtual orgy of political correctness and self-righteousness in the advanced capitalist countries. China was the whip-ping boy. Attitudes from Western social scientists and politicians towards China's sustained communist authoritarianism descended from tolerance and disapproval to virtual pariah status after the Tiananmen massacre and the Velvet Revolution of 1989. When Gorbachev visited China during the Tiananmen demonstration in 1989 he was seen almost universally outside China to symbolize the progressive, successful leader visiting a backward, politically bankrupt regime.

A number of arguments combined in Western social science and policy-making to produce these attitudes.

Arguments in Favour of a Revolutionary Approach to Political Institutions in Communist Countries

(a) **The benefits of creating the institutions of political economy** *de nove*: There has been a greatly increased interest in the relationship between institutions and economic performance.[2] One approach to the reform of the former communist countries has been to argue that the end of communism provides the opportunity to construct the economic and political institutions of these countries from scratch, learning from the accumulated wisdom of Western social science research, and avoiding the mistakes that many countries have made. This can be called in simple terms the institutional 'advantages of the latecomer':

Big leaps can only occur in the aftermath of destruction of an ossifed and non-performing system ... In history, major dynamic rebirths have only occurred after catastrophic destructions ... Like Western Europe after World War II, Eastern and Central European Countries now have the historic opportunity to create *ex novo* optimal economic and social institutions and thereby free their latent energies.[3]

(b) The desirability of maintaining a small role for the state: It is not hard to understand why the generation of rulers who immediately followed old-style communist rule should have had a strong desire for a 'small state' in both politics and economics. All societies have to confront the balance between individual rights and an individual's duties to the wider social interest. In the immediate post-communist period, it was not surprising that the rights of the individual were strongly emphasized over the necessity for the observation of wider duties in order to achieve common goals. This was expressed powerfully in the writings of Janos Kornai:

[My approach to reform is that of] liberal thought (using the term 'liberal' in accordance with its European tradition). Respect for autonomy and self-determination, for the rights of the individual, is its focus ... [I]t advocates a narrowed scope for state activities. It recommends that citizens stand on their own feet, and rely on their own power and initiative. Perhaps the role of the government will be reconsidered at a later stage. *But right now, in the beginning of the transformation process ... it is time to take great steps away in the direction of a minimal state.* Perhaps later generations will be able to envisage a more moderate midway.[4] (my emphasis added)

(c) Democracy is foremost among the fundamental human rights: Many commentators have argued that, irrespective of the context, democracy is at least as important a component of welfare as material aspects. So deeply has concern over 'human rights' penetrated the international institutions that in many instances in recent years, the World Bank and the International Monetary Fund have attached political democratization as a condition of development assistance.

(d) Democracy is inextricably linked with individual property rights: For markets to function effectively, the necessity of clearly delineating property rights is frequently argued.[5] The emergence of stable property rights from their insecure position under feudalism was a central element in

European capitalist development.[6] This was strongly associated with the growing demands of the newly emerging bourgeois class for political representation in Parliamentary institutions. Many critics argued that the introduction of a market economy in communist countries required the transition to a democratic politics: 'to survive and successfully evolve as a living social organism, the system of free markets, private property, and contractual buyer-seller transactions must operate within a legal order and in a politically democratic environment'.[7]

(e) A totalitarian party cannot preside over the transition to a market economy: There was wide disbelief among Western political economists that a totalitarian communist party could lead a movement towards a market economy sufficiently far to cross a minimum 'threshold' level of market activity. Kornai deeply criticized the 'naive reformers' who believed the party could itself bring about a successful reform:

> The reform is a movement from 'above', a voluntary change of behaviour on the side of the controllers and not an uprising from 'below' on the side of those who are controlled. There is, therefore, a stubborn contradiction in the whole reform process: how to get the active participation of the very people who will lose a part of their power if the process is successful.[8]

He urged other reforming socialist countries to learn from the Hungarian experience which showed the apparent logical impossibility of a communist party leading from 'above' a successful reform which retained a substantial economic role for the state in an economy which combined the virtues of plan and market. In other words, a political revolution which overthrew the communist party was an essential precondition of successful transition away from the Stalinist system of political economy.

(f) Democracy at the very least appears not to harm growth and may well assist in its achievement: An important strand of academic research also supports the proposition that greater democracy will not harm and may even accelerate the rate of growth of income in poor countries. The work associated with the World Institute for Development Economics Research (WIDER) has been important in this debate, of which Dasgupta (1990) has been especially influential. This chapter analyses recent cross-sectional data from a large number of developing countries, and presents the extremely important empirical finding that greater democracy in developing countries does not appear to harm growth performance: '[The] choice ...

between fast growth in income and ... negative liberties ... is a phoney ... choice ... statistically speaking societies are not faced with this dilemma .... Political liberties ... are positively and significantly correlated with *per capita* income growth.'[9] It is but a short step to the argument that democracy *benefits* growth of per capita income and this view rapidly entered the mainstream of development studies in the early 1990s as if it were a proven fact.

Problems with Political Democratization in Reforming Communist Countries

(a) Problems with a 'Big Leap' in the system of political economy: The system of political economy is an integrated fabric of politics, economics, ideology and social relationships. Karl Popper long ago identified the dangers of attempting to make great leaps in the whole system of political economy:

> Every version of historicism expresses the feeling of being swept into the future by irresistible forces ... Contrasting their 'dynamic' thinking with the static thinking of all previous generations, they believe that their own advance has been made possible by the fact that we are now 'living in a revolution' which has so much accelerated the speed of our development that social change can now be directly experienced within a single lifetime. This story is, of course, sheer mythology.[10]

Popper argued strongly against communist revolutions precisely because they ignored a fundamental scientific principle, namely the benefit of trying to improve the functioning of a system by experimentation with small segments rather than taking risks and trying to leap to a potentially superior situation but with great uncertainty about the outcome.

Support for Popperian caution is provided by an important strand of the new institutional economics: the evolutionary approach, which emphasizes the role of knowledge in economic life. Ultimately, economic activity is undertaken by individuals with limited information. An economic system is a complex network of knowledge lodged in individuals' minds. Destroying existing institutions has a high cost in that it takes time for individuals to reconstruct their knowledge about the workings of the economy.[11]

(b) The arguments for a strong role for the state in the transition period: It is precisely during a complex process of transition from one kind of socio-economic system to another that 'market failure' might be expected to be especially large. This is likely to be a time of great uncertainty. Hence, it is likely that investors' time preferences are strongly oriented towards the short term. Consequently, it may be especially important for the state to intervene in capital markets to ensure that investments which yield their returns over the long term are undertaken at a desirable level.

Economists almost all concede the case for state intervention in favour of infant industries. The Stalinist economies present an extreme form of the 'infant industry' argument. In the Stalinist economies in most sectors, not only the technical level, but also the whole institutional organization, involving labour markets, capital markets and the ownership structure, placed these economies at a disadvantage compared to competitor countries. Extensive state action was needed to construct a competitive industrial sector.

As the economy moves away from Stalinism, great personal uncertainties arise. There are certain to be huge changes in the system of pricing and consumer goods supply, in the system of welfare provision, and in the ownership and organization of housing. If the state simply steps out of these areas, great social dislocation will result. Whatever system the country ends up with there is a strong argument for extensive state action in these areas during a substantial transition period to reduce the shock of the transition process and guarantee a social safety net for all citizens. Since the absence of a social safety net will mean large suffering for the most disadvantaged groups in society, there is a strong case for incrementalism and extensive state action in this area above all.

Ownership rights over huge amounts of assets are certain to be altered greatly. The manner in which the reallocation of property rights occurs is bound to have a huge impact on the future class structure of the country concerned. If the state abdicates control over the process, then it is very likely that a highly unequal structure of asset ownership will emerge, with the outcome strongly related to initial inequalities in power and access to information.

(c) The historical evidence: mass democracy typically followed rather than preceded or accompanied industrialization. Hardly a single country has grown from low to high income in a democratic framework. Contrary to popular belief, none of the advanced economies had mass democracy in the early stage of modern economic growth.[12] During the take-off phase virtually all of them were governed by liberal principles which granted political rights to property holders, but did not mostly allow political power to be granted to the urban or rural proletariat, to impoverished racial minorities, or to women. The development of mass democracy followed rather than preceded the take-off. This has been the case too in successful industrializers in the late twentieth century.

Democratic institutions have not been associated with rapid economic growth in the developing countries. India is by far the most striking example in the developing world of long-term commitment to democratic institutions. The need to maintain the political support of vested interest groups whose voice could be expressed through the ballot box and whose financial support enabled elections to be fought, has been a factor in explaining the maintenance of policies which have damaged the growth performance of the Indian economy. It explains the retention of protectionist barriers in many sectors much longer than was economically useful, the setting of artificially high exchange rates which have damaged exports, the failure to impose hard budget constraints on state enterprises in many cases where this would have helped better use of scarce resources, the failure to carry out effective land reform, and the allocation of much expenditure on projects whose main purpose has been to placate regional or class interests rather stimulate national growth.

(d) Quantitative studies of democracy and growth have some serious problems: Careful scrutiny of the data upon which Dasgupta's widely quoted result is based show that much more cautious conclusions are in order, especially if these are applied to the reforming communist countries. Dasgupta provides correlation coefficients for the relationship between several pairs of 'development' variables (political liberties, civil liberties, level of income, growth of income, infant mortality and life expectancy). Several of the correlation coefficients are indeed high. Thus, there is a strong or fairly strong correlation between, respectively, civil rights and political democracy, falls in infant mortality and growth of income, rise in life expectancy and income growth, and falls in infant mortality and rise in life expectancy. None of these is surprising. However, the correlation coefficient between democracy and income growth is much weaker (and that between civil rights and income growth is even more so), while the correlations tell one nothing about the direction of causation. In so far as there is a correlation between income growth and democracy, it is more likely on a priori grounds that the line of causation runs from rising incomes to demands for democracy than the other way round.[13] This could then lead to a very different line of reasoning for policy, namely, that the best way to establish firmly-rooted democratic rights is to first ensure development of the productive forces.

Cross-sectional studies that appear to show that there is no negative relationship between the level of democracy and economic growth are a poor guide to the impact upon growth of the process of democratization in authoritarian countries, whether developing non-communist or industrialized former communist. The countries analysed in studies such as Dasgupta's fail to differentiate between countries which have a stable level of democracy, and countries which are in the middle of transition from one level of democracy to another. However, policies which advocate democratization of authoritarian countries ought to carefully investigate the *process* of democratization, in order to see whether those countries which have democratized authoritarian systems grow more or less rapidly.

Moreover, there is little precedent for the dramatic rupture of political institutions involved in the democratization of communist regimes, and it is deeply problematic to apply results drawn from very different situations. The best way to analyse such a phenomenon may have been simply to think carefully about historical evidence and the logic of the process. It was not possible to investigate quantitatively a process which had not yet occurred.

(e) The proposition that communist parties cannot allow the development of a market economy is questionable: In principle, it ought to be possible to devise a process of transition in the tasks of a communist system so as to obtain support from the communist party for a transition, provided the bulk of the party's members are given useful functions under the changing arrangements, and are provided with satisfactory financial and psychological rewards under the new system. Moreover, if the leadership is able successfully to build a prosperous economy under communist party leadership, then there is no reason why eventually the communist party might not end up as the dominant political party under a system of democratic elections.

Indeed, there are important historical examples that support the proposition that under certain circumstances it may be possible for a Stalinist totalitarian communist party to make the transition to a rational authoritarian party. In the early 1920s in the Soviet Union, following a period of highly centralized rule in both the economy and politics during War Communism, the Soviet Communist Party was able to maintain its tight hold over the country's political life while recognizing the need for the country's economic success of a greatly increased role for market forces.

In China in 1949 the Communist Party emerged from the civil war as a highly centralized and disciplined organization. It had exercised tight control on all aspects of social and economic life in the Base Areas. In the immediate post-Liberation period, up until the High Tide of collectivization in 1955–6, alongside the tight control it exercised over political and cultural affairs, it operated a mixed economy, with guidance rather than directive planning in many spheres of the economy.

In the post-Stalinist period since the late 1970s, both China and the communist parties of Burma, Vietnam, and Laos have led the transition towards a market economy.

(f) National unity may be hard to sustain under democratic post-communist systems: Self-evidently, nationalism is an extremely powerful political force, but its connection with 'democracy' is complex.

National unity in many of the advanced capitalist countries did not come about peacefully. In the nineteenth century, both German and Italian unification were achieved through violence. Despite the mythology, even the unity of the USA was far from maintained through democratic procedures. The fundamental issue in the American Civil War was not slavery but national unity. In modern-day India, far and away the greatest violence by the national state has been undertaken in order to maintain national unity, with substantial violence directed by the central government against separatist movements, with significant loss of life, most notably in Kashmir and Punjab.

In large formerly Stalinist countries the forces of nationalism are especially difficult to deal with. Under Stalinism, national minorities' consciousness within the overall nation state was supposed to have evaporated with the creation of a new communist identity. Paradoxically, capitalism proved much better at eroding nationalism than the non-market Stalinist economy, with its constraints on the movement of peoples and its isolation of the population from homogenizing forces in international culture, embodied by internationally traded goods and services. National minorities' consciousness was kept in the deep-freeze by Stalinism. Once the tight constraints of Stalinism were relaxed, these forces erupted.

A rapid change in national boundaries in a large communist country with a highly integrated regional structure of production can cause particular problems. It makes it very unlikely that a gradual solution could be attempted to reforming the system of directive planning. New bases of product exchange have to be created alongside the difficulties of renegotiating international political relationships and reforming the system of planning. The uncertainty alone could be expected to have a large negative effect on output. Where assets in a newly independent country were formerly owned by the central authorities immediate uncertainty arises in respect to property rights, which may take time to be resolved and/or be resolved in a way that is not beneficial to growth. The position of much of the workforce is rendered highly uncertain since many of them will now be living in a 'foreign country'. The rupture of the country into a series of new national units is an extreme case of the problems stemming from radical reforms in forcing individuals to discard their old basis of knowledge and learn a complete new set of information about the economic process.

(g) Political stability is an important condition of economic advance: There was a high probability that post-Stalinist societies would experience great difficulty in establishing stable political order in the wake of the Communist Party's demise. It takes time for a stable set of political parties to emerge that can construct a clear set of policy choices to present to the electorate. The possibility of political disorder is accentuated by the likelihood that a rapid political transition would lead to hasty decisions being taken about the nature of political institutions and rules, such as the method of voting at elections.

Economic life disintegrates without political stability. Neither foreign or domestic investors have confidence. If politics is unstable, it almost certainly means that the state apparatus, whatever its wishes, will be less able to guide economic development. Its ability to raise taxes, provide a framework that can guarantee property rights and encourage investment will be reduced. The huge success of China in attracting international investment and the failure of most of Eastern Europe and the former USSR to do so is intimately related to the contrast in political conditions. The existence of a rich diaspora is far from sufficient a condition for attracting foreign investment, as demonstrated by the signal failure of India to attract investment from its huge diaspora.

(h) 'Democracy' in the labour market is an ambiguous concept: The concept of 'democracy' in the labour market is complex and ambiguous.[14] There is a dangerous tendency to confuse the rights of one segment of society, namely the organized working class, with the whole of society. In fact they are far from identical. It is not at all obvious that the rights of an aristocracy of mainly male labour, the industrial working class, have a morally superior claim to organize themselves at the potential expense of other social groups, which include not just capitalists, but also much larger numbers of women without wage employment, retired people, farm workers and the huge numbers working in the 'informal' sector. Protecting the rights of the 'aristocacy of labour' over other social groups may harm the growth process in all sorts of ways, and damage the employment prospects of non-organized workers through raising the real price of labour in the industrial sector.

Reforming communist countries face great difficulties in moving away from a system of privilege for the urban 'aristocracy of labour' towards a system of competitive labour markets. The political cost of establishing competitive labour markets may be too high in a democratic setting. A large part of the national budget may end up being spent not in retraining and restructuring but in subsidies to keep politically dangerous workers quiet in their former occupations.

In a Stalinist economy moving toward a form of market economy, price liberalization is certain to create demands for compensating increases in money wages. Without some form of incomes policy there is large danger of a spiral of cost-push inflation developing. Moreover, the habits of trade unions and government responses can quickly become ingrained so that systems of political economy find it hard to break out of the wage-price-money supply spiral once the process has been set in motion. Particularly instructive is the contrast between the Latin American (high inflation) and East Asian countries (low inflation) in this respect in recent decades. Evidence from a number of developing countries in the process of transition from an authoritarian to a political democracy shows them to have a poor record in controlling inflation. Such regimes characteristically are less able to tax effectively, and find it harder to control government spending and the growth of the money supply.[15]

(i) 'Free and fair elections' are far from a sufficient condition of establishing democratic societies: The ability of people to take advantage of political rights depends on their level of culture and on the amount of energy they have to devote to political activity. Encouraging elections in countries or enforcing elections upon countries may do little to really democratize political life. Like other 'bourgeois rights', the capacity to take advantage of the rights depends on one's position in the country's class structure. In any 'democracy', the capacity to benefit from the right to freely organize political parties and contest elections is strongly related to the possession of wealth, and the post-Stalinist regimes will be no different. If the post-Stalinist reforms are accompanied by rapid changes in the distribution of wealth and by new concentrations of administrative power emerging from the old communist power structures, then it is very questionable how much genuine increase in democracy there will actually be.

The 'right to vote' in a 'free and fair election' is only as meaningful as the choices which the electors are given. In elections in the advanced capitalist countries, electoral platforms almost always involve incremental changes whose effects are reasonably predictable. The most radical changes in modern developed-country democratic politics may well have been those which occurred in the 1980s under Mrs Thatcher in Britain. The programme of successive Conservative governments was undoubtedly 'radical', but it was still incremental and fairly predictable. The main planks of the programme were trade union legislation and privatization of clearly identified sections of the nationalized industries. The outcomes have been reasonably close to those predicted in the manifestos.

However, if the electorate of a reforming communist country is offered much wider choices involving comprehensive changes of system then the outcomes are far more unpredictable. It is not possible for the full effects of revolutionary programmes upon either the country or upon individuals to be calculated by the voters. Moreover, the more revolutionary the reforming programme, the less reversible will be the policies by the time the next election occurs. Therefore the electorate is deprived of meaningful choice and simply votes in the dark, with vague sentiments governing the choices they make. Whether this amounts to more 'democracy' is debatable.

2. The Political Setting in China and Russia

The Chinese leadership after 1976 and the Soviet leadership under Gorbachev differed hugely in their conception both of the desirable path of economic reform and the desirable relationship between economic and political reform.

USSR

The Soviet leadership had experienced a lifetime of political stability. They could not imagine that their country could be plunged into political turmoil by over-rapid political reform. Writing at the beginning of the Soviet reform process, Gorbachev expressed his hopes as follows:

> The main idea of the January [1986] Plenary Meeting – as regards ways of accomplishing the tasks of *perestroika* and protecting society from a repetition of errors of the past – was the development of democracy. It is the principal guarantee of the irreversibility of *perestroika*. The more socialist democracy there is, the more socialism we will have. This is our firm conviction, and we will not abandon it. We will promote democracy in the economy, in politics and within the Party itself. The creativity of the masses is the decisive force in *perestroika*. There is no other more powerful force.[16]

From as early as July 1986 Gorbachev had determined that a successful economic reform needed to proceed much more rapidly than the pace at which Soviet reforms were proceeding. He decided that this required a prior radical political reform:

> In the summer of 1986, it became clear that Gorbachev had changed his strategy ... [H]e turned to 'perestroika' of the political system' and his language was radicalised ... Apparently, Gorbachev had concluded that he could not implement a viable economic reform without breaking the

entrenched political resistance and for that he needed a political reform, raising the pressure from below.[17]

Almost without exception Western commentators and advisors believed this to be a correct evaluation of the logic of the reform process. There was a chorus of praise from the West for Gorbachev's far-sighted vision and daring in moving the USSR rapidly towards political democracy (the monopoly of political power held by the Communist Party was formally ended just four years after Gorbachev began the programme of political *perestroika*). Aslund's view is representative of a large number of Western writers: 'to break the power of the party and state bureaucracy might be seen as the key problem of a reform. It is difficult to perceive any other solution than a far-reaching democratisation with a strong popular pressure and openness balancing the bureaucracy'.[18]

Only in hindsight did some writers begin to acknowledge the dangers of the path that had been followed, and even then in the most equivocal terms: '[t]o be effective, far-reaching economic reform must ultimately be accompanied by political reform. Admittedly, there is a danger that the political reforms may come too fast and lead to anarchy, but a refusal to relax politically is an equally serious threat to the overall success of any reform effort'.[19] In fact, the tentative, experimental economic reforms of the late 1980s, which did not initially look too different from China's reforms, were completely swamped by the effects of political *perestroika*. The Communist Party collapsed. The nation state disintegrated and a feeble, populist government was brought into being. The budgetary situation quickly became hopeless. The money supply ran wildly out of control. A disastrous spiral of withdrawal from the market was set in motion at every level from the republics down to the enterprise, and large parts of the system relapsed into a virtual barter economy. From having a relatively low level of indebtedness, the USSR rapidly moved towards becoming one of the world's most indebted countries, as the foreign trade situation careered out of control.

China

The aged Chinese leadership which returned to power in the post-Mao period had personally experienced the anarchy of political life for much of the 'Republican' period. Under the Republic, the hopes of the more Western-oriented Chinese intellectuals for the establishment of a stable democratic system in China after the 1911 Revolution were dashed as China entered the prolonged turmoil of the warlord period. In addition, the same leaders had more recently been through the searing experience of the Cultural

Revolution. They had seen the damage to economic life, the threat to ordinary citizens' safety and sense of security, brought about by the destruction of the Party during the high years of the Cultural Revolution. Self-interest in clinging to power was, of course, extremely important in determining their approach towards political reform. However, an important, though indeterminable, part of their approach was also based on an extremely realistic appraisal of the options facing China. Writing early in China's reform process Deng Xiaoping in 1979 presented the Chinese leadership's view of the relationship between different aspects of the reform process as follows:

> At present, when we are confronted with manifold difficulties in our economic life which can be overcome only by a series of readjustments and by consolidation and reorganisation, it is particularly necessary to stress publicly the importance of subordinating personal interests to collective ones, interests of the part to those of the whole, and immediate to long-term interests … [T]alk about democracy in the abstract will inevitably lead to the unchecked spread of ultra-democracy and anarchism, to the complete disruption of political stability and unity, and to the total failure of our modernisation programme. If this happens then the decade of struggle against Lin Biao and the Gang of Four will have been in vain, China will once again be plunge into chaos, division, retrogression and darkness, and the Chinese people will be deprived of all hope.[20]

The Chinese leadership was determined not to allow any semblance of national disintegration. The national government fought a harsh campaign against the separatist movement in Tibet and it made the reintegration of Hong Kong and Taiwan into the Mainland a central focus of foreign policy. While the regime moved away from the depths of totalitarian intervention in social life, it remained an authoritarian one-party state. Serious political opposition was dealt with brutally, most notably in the case of the Tiananmen massacre of 1989.

The government believed that political democratization was a diversion from the most important task, namely that of improving the performance of the economic system in order to raise living standards and make China a more powerful and respected country. Its position was made starkly clear by Deng Xiaoping in his key speeches in the late 1970s:

> In the China of today we can never dispense with leadership by the Party and extol the spontaneity of the masses … In 1966 the Chinese economy, having gone through a few years of readjustment, was in a position to develop rapidly. But Lin Biao and the Gang of Four did it grave damage.

Only now ... has our economy returned to the road of sound growth. If a handful of people are allowed to kick aside the Party committees and make trouble, the four modernisations will vanish into thin air.[21]

A chorus of trenchant criticism was directed at the Chinese Communist Party (CCP) in the 1980s. Western human rights groups spoke out against the undoubted harshness of the Chinese government (throughout the 1980s and into the 1990s several thousand, often public, executions per year was the norm). It was felt widely that the CCP could not itself make the transition to secular rational rule from a quasi-religious ideological rule. It had the double burden of highly centralized traditions of Leninism plus millennia of centralized rule in China. The conventional wisdom, espoused in article after article and conference after conference, was that the CCP had to be removed from its monopoly of political power if the move to a market economy was to be put into effect:

Deng Xiaoping tried to restart China's economy without affecting the dictatorship of its entrenched vanguards ... Although the term had not yet been invented, Deng sought *perestroika* without *glasnost* ... This is not a particularly unusual project. There are innumerable examples of similarly placed monopolists of political power who wanted economic modernisation without political reform ... It does not work ... Instead of duplicating South Korea and Taiwan, China seemed to have taken as its model Ferdinand Marcos's Philippines.[22]

In fact, this aged leadership has presided over almost two decades of sustained movement towards a market economy. Like other East Asian authoritarian regimes, such as Thailand and South Korea, periodic violent suppression of opposition has gone alongside the maintenance of a basically stable political environment, with very slow change in political institutions. Political stability and government administrative strength has provided a framework in which the potentiality of the market can be gradually unleashed alongside a strong economic role for the state in the 'socialist market economy'. Whatever the future path for China may be it has experienced a sustained period of a 'Third Way' in both politics and economics. It is, of course, possible to argue that China would have performed even better than it had if it had established a democratic system early on. However, the logic of the arguments presented in section 1 suggests that this is improbable. Rather, it seems inescapable that the nature of the political choices made during this period were a major, though indeterminable, factor in the Chinese economic performance under reform.

Table 4.1 **Comparative Economic Performance of the Chinese Economy in the 1980s**

	China	India	Low income countries[a]	Middle income countries
Av. annual growth rate, 1980–9 (%):				
GDP	9.7	5.3	3.4	2.9
Agriculture	6.3	2.9	2.5	2.6
Industry	12.6	6.9	3.1	3.0
Services	9.3	6.5	4.4	2.8
Av. annual real growth rate of exports, 1980–9 (%)	11.5	5.8	0.8	5.5
Av. annual growth rate of population, 1980–9 (%)	1.4	2.1	2.7	2.1
Av. annual rate of inflation, 1980–9 (%)	5.8	7.7	14.9	73.0
Debt service as % of exports of goods and services: 1980	4.6	9.1	11.4	26.1
: 1989	9.8	26.4	27.4	23.1
Index of av. p.c.[b] food consumption, 1987–9 (1979–81 = 100)	128	113	103	101
Daily calorie intake p.c.[b]: 1965	1,931	2,103	1,960	2,482
: 1988	2,632	2,104	2,182	2,834
Crude death rate (no/1000)				
: 1965	10	20	21	13
: 1989	7	11	13	8
Infant mortality rate (no/1000)				
: 1981	71	121	124	81
: 1989	30	95	94	51
Life expectancy at birth (years)				
: 1981	67	52	50	60
: 1989	70	59	55	66

Notes

[a] excluding India and China.

[b] p.c. = per capita.

Source: World Bank 1983 and 1991.

3. Contrasting Results of Reform

China

Output: China's economic growth record under reform policies placed it in the front rank of growth performances during the relevant period. It was arguably the fastest growing economy in the world in the 1980s, and it also attained one of the fastest growth rates of exports, with a real growth rate of almost 12 per cent per annum in the 1980s (Table 4.1). Behind the growth of total output, a massive accumulation process has taken place, with huge additions to the stock of capital goods. China's capital goods industries were expanding in leaps and bounds to feed the appetite of overall economic growth. The leading edge of Chinese industry was being rapidly modernized with imports of high technology products, and the capital goods produced by modernized domestic factories.

Material Consumption: The growth of output was accompanied by an extraordinary surge in popular living standards in the 1980s (Table 4.2). The quantity and quality of food sharply improved, with sustained rises in the consumption of meat, fish and fruit. A massive new clothing industry came into being. Vast new consumer durable industries sprang up in the 1980s, with a 'first wave' of goods such as bicycles, watches, TV sets, fridges and washing machines, followed by a more complex array of goods in the 'second wave', including products such as motor cars, motor cycles and video recorders (Table 4.2).

Welfare Indicators: Despite aspects in which inequality increased sharply in the 1980s, China did well at raising the incomes of the poorest 40 per cent of the population. This is reflected in the improvement in already extremely favourable 'basic needs' indicators (see Table 4.1).

Poverty: A combination of trickle down from poor regions and explicit government policy to assist poor regions produced a remarkable reduction in poverty in China in the post-Mao period. The World Bank estimates that the total number in poverty fell from around 270 million in the late 1970s to around 100 million only one decade later (Table 4.3).

Inequality: Undoubtedly, the growth of market forces produced large new inequalities in China during the reform period. The absolute gap between regions widened. Inequality in respect of some aspects of income distribution certainly increased substantially compared to the Maoist period. However, throughout the reform period China remained deeply committed to full

Table 4.2 **Changes in the Standard of Living in China, 1978–89**

	1978	1989
Index of real p.c.[a] consumption	100	210
Consumption p.c. of:		
grain (kgs)	196	242
edible oil (kgs)	1.6	5.4
pork (kgs)	7.7	15.6
fresh eggs (kgs)	2.0	6.0
sugar (kgs)	3.4	5.4
cloth (metres)	8.0	11.6
Ownership of consumer durables (no/100 people):		
sewing machines	3.5	12.2
watches	8.5	50.1
bicycles	7.7	32.8
radios	7.8	23.6
TVs	0.3	14.9
Housing space p.c. (sq metres)		
cities	3.6	6.6
villages	8.1	17.2
Doctors per 10,000 people	10.7	15.4

Note: [a] per capita.

Source: ZGT JZY 1990: 40–2.

employment. It undertook a massive, egalitarian land reform in the early 1980s, in which land ownership remained in the hands of the local communities. The government at different levels maintained a fairly effective tax system. The vast bulk of assets remained in some form of state ownership, with ownership rights residing in the hands of either the central state, the city, the county, or the village community, thereby severely limiting the possibility for wealth accumulation by private individuals.

Psychology: China experienced around one hundred years of national humiliation, beginning in the 1840s with the Opium Wars, extending through to the chaotic period of the warlords from 1911 to 1927. For a brief interlude of around ten years there was some semblance of national progress under the Guomindang, but the modernization effort was retarded by the Japanese occupation from 1936 to 1945. In 1949, there was enormous popular enthusiasm for the leadership of the CCP, under whom Mao claimed the Chinese people would 'stand up' at last. Despite large achievements, the policies of the CCP produced the disaster of the Great Leap Forward, in which as many as

Table 4.3 **Poverty in China, 1978–1990**

	1978	1985	1990
Total population (m.)	963	1,059	1,143
Urban	172 (17.9%)	251 (23.7%)	302 (26.4%)
Rural	790 (82.1%)	808 (76.3%)	841 (73.6%)
Average per capita income (1978 yuan)			
Urban	–	557	685
Rural	134	324	319
Poverty line (current yuan/year)			
Urban	–	215	19
Rural	98	190	275
Incidence of poverty (million)			
Total	270 (28.0%)	97 (9.2%)	98 (8.6%)
Urban	10 (4.4%)	1 (0.4%)	1 (0.4%)
Rural	260 (33.0%)	96 (11.9%)	97 (11.5%)

Notes

After three years of apparent stagnation in real rural per capita consumption, a substantial further growth occurred in 1991 (State Statistical Burean, ZGT JZY 1992: 42). Had the 1991 data been made available to the World Bank, it is likely that there would have been some further reduction reported in rural poverty.

The poverty line used in this table was calculated by revaluing for each year at current prices a constant 'poverty line' bundle of goods and services.

Source: World Bank 1992, v.

30 million people may have died from starvation and related illness. The Cultural Revolution in the late 1960s and early 1970s brought anarchy to much of the country, damaged the economy and caused great suffering to a large number of people.

The massive success of the economic reforms has brought a renewed sense of national pride. The fact that the reform programme has been carried out under the aegis of the Communist Party, with only gradual change in ideology, has produced only a limited sense of mass psychological disorientation.

Human Rights: In the 1980s China remained a one-party, authoritarian state throughout the reform period. It also remained a state with an extremely tough legal system, with several thousand executions in an average year. This presents profound ethical and philosophical dilemmas.

If one looks beyond the right to vote in an election, to a wider range of human rights, then the situation in China improved drastically during the reform period. There was an explosion in the provision of a wide range of 'human rights', including improved health, education, freedom to migrate, huge increases in employment opportunities, better food, clothing, housing and a greatly increased range of cultural products. China's system of basic needs provision under Mao had enabled it also to achieve very low death rates for its level of income. By the early 1980s, China's death rate had fallen to an exceptionally low level for a poor country. The decade of economic reform in China saw no trend deterioration in China's exceptionally low death rates. Indeed, Judith Banister, the most respected analyst of China's demography, concludes that between 1981 and 1990, there were 'real improvements in mortality ... especially for females above infancy and for children of both sexes'.[23] She notes: 'it is impressive that the rural population of China has experienced measurably lower mortality in only nine years, especially since the Chinese countryside had already achieved rather advanced mortality conditions for a developing country rural area by 1981'.[24]

USSR

Output: Soviet economic performance under Gorbachev was extremely poor. After the collapse of the communist government a poor performance turned into a disaster (Table 4.4). The disintegration of the USSR in the late 1980s led to a collapse also of proper statistical reporting. Any estimates are of only the roughest magnitude. Table 4.4 provides an extremely crude view of the picture as portrayed by standard sources. It shows a crisis of massive proportions, comparable in scale to the awful downturn in production in China after the Great Leap Forward.[25] Capital accumulation in Russia collapsed in the early 1990s (Table 4.4). Moreover, due to the disastrous foreign trade performance, the capital stock was unable to modernize quickly through the import of foreign technology. While a huge new capital goods industry was growing in China, the capital goods industry in Russia in the early 1990s was simply disappearing.

Material Consumption: Bare statistics fail to capture the massive extent of the dislocation and suffering for a large proportion of the population. Despite the poverty of hard data, no-one seriously disputes the fact that real incomes have fallen drastically for the vast bulk of the population since the late 1980s.

Table 4.4 **Selected Economic Indicators for the Former USSR (all data are at constant prices except where indication is to the contrary)**

	1989	1990	1991	1992	1993*
Net Material product	100	96.0	80.7	64.5*	58.1
Gross industrial output	100	98.9	90.9	77.3*	68.0
Gross agricultural output	100	97.7	87.9	80.0*	75.2
Retail trade turnover	100	110.4	99.4	59.6*	53.6
Gross fixed investment	100	101.0	89.2	49.1	–
Volume of foreign trade:					
Exports	100	86.9	85.2	63.4*	
Imports	100	98.6	90.8	70.8*	
Foreign trade in current US$:					
Exports	100	94.8	71.5	53.5	–
Imports	–	100	64.1	57.5	
Foreign debt (billion $)	60	61	65	76	–
Consumer prices (% change on previous year)	5.0	8.0	150	2,500*	1,000

Note: * estimates, for Russia only

Source: Economist Intelligence Unit, *Country Report CIS* (formerly USSR), no. 4, 1992, and United Nations, Economic Commission for Europe, *Economic Survey for Europe 1992–3* (New York: United Nations, 1993).

Welfare Indicators: One of the most striking consequences of the economic collapse is the disintegration of the health service, which was already experiencing serious problems in the Gorbachev epoch, and a sharp rise in poverty. A recent expert analysis of Russian health, talks of an 'explosion of morbidity'.[26] In 1993 it was revealed that alarming increases were occurring in infectious diseases such as measles, whooping cough, tuberculosis and syphilis (the rise from 1990 to 1993 were 142 per cent, 72 per cent, 34 per cent and 300 per cent respectively).[27] Large rises were reported also in diphtheria, dysentery and typhoid.

Moreover, the breakdown of government was accompanied by large increases in crime. Murders rose by a reported 42 per cent in 1992 and a further 60 per cent in the first half of 1993.[28] Russia's murder rate for the first half of 1993 stood at 25/100,000 people, placing it firmly in the category of 'high homicide' countries, with rates well above most other 'high homicide' countries, countries such as Mexico (20/100,000) and Brazil (15/100,000).

Psychology: The consequences of the collapse are not just economic, but also involve too the deepest sense of national humiliation in this country which for most of the twentieth century was accustomed to consider itself as the leader of the world's socialist nations. The psychological consequences of these massive changes should not be underestimated. The sense of personal uncertainty has greatly increased, especially because the changes since the mid 1980s occurred against a background of extremely high levels of insecurity about most fundamentals, such as employment, personal safety, education, health and housing. The mood of national despondency and humiliation is quite comparable to that of the 'three dark years' in China in the early 1960s.

Poverty: A mass of anecdotal evidence supports the conclusion that for a large fraction of the population, probably well over one-half, the period since the late Gorbachev years has seen a serious deterioration in living standards, alongside a large rise in income for a small fraction of the population. One serious, though extremely rough, estimate has been carried out by the Russian Statistical Office (Goskomstat) together with the World Bank to estimate the current level of poverty in Russia. In these studies, 'poverty' was defined as an income which would allow a level of food consumption adequate to maintain a normal body weight at an average level of activity. It suggests that around 37 per cent of the Russian population is now living in poverty. The situation was worse for children. In 1992, 46–47 per cent of all children below the age of 15 were living in poverty.[29]

An important aspect of the impoverishment is the deterioration in diet. In 1992 alone, according to household budget surveys by Goskomstat, the consumption of meat and meat products fell by 11 per cent, of milk and dairy products by 16 per cent, of fish by 19 per cent, of vegetables by 10 per cent and fruits and berries by 15 per cent. On the other hand, the consumption of bread rose by three per cent and potatoes by nine per cent.[30]

Inequality: Alongside the spiralling collapse has gone a massive redistribution of wealth. In the chaotic economy of the early 1990s Soviet citizens have vastly different capacities, related to age, political position and connections, and initial capital endowments, to benefit from the 'privatization' of assets. The situation is analogous to a famine, in that people are disposing of personal assets, however pathetic these might be, at a high rate in order to survive, leading to a decline in their real price, enabling those who possess capital to accumulate resources at an especially fast rate. A new 'aristocracy', often building on the old positions of power under the Communist Party, is being created at high speed, in a fashion which eerily recalls Hoskins' comments on the dissolution of the monasteries in sixteenth-century Britain:

The spoilation of the Church during the greater part of the sixteenth century is one of the most fundamental divides in English history. Some called it the Great Sacrilege ... more modern historians refer placidly to the Great Transfer; I prefer to label it the Great Plunder, and to see in it that conspiracy of rich men procuring their own fortunes in the name of the commonwealth, whatever brand of the Christian faith they publicly or privately professed, and however they wriggled from one side to the other when the political wind veered round unexpectedly.[31]

Human Rights: While China's economic prosperity and widening process of marketization is steadily leading to the inexorable democratization of daily life under the umbrella of one-party rule, Russia's disastrous economic performance is continuing simultaneously with a slide back into authoritarianism. In the medium term, at least, Russia seems to have obtained a perilous deterioration of economic performance and in the quality of daily life alongside a reappearance, though under much more anarchic conditions, of political authoritarianism.

If one constructs a balance sheet of 'human rights', then one has to offset the fact that Soviet citizens have gained the right to vote and to speak freely, against the huge deterioration in other 'human rights' for most people, including the right to live safely, to employment, to decent food, to a decent education, housing and health service, as well as witnessing a huge rise in unequal capacities to benefit from the new 'negative' freedoms (for example, freedom of speech, freedom to accumulate capital freedom to fight elections), which have been gained since the mid-1980s.

A powerful symbol of the deterioration in human rights under Soviet and post-Soviet reform has been the alarming rise in death rates. In the early 1960s the USSR stood proudly as a country with one of the lowest death rates in the world. By the late 1970s the USSR's death rate had begun to rise ominously, reflecting mainly an increase in death rates among working age males. By the late 1980s, Russia's death rate had risen above the level for middle-income countries. However, the most remarkable development was to occur in the post-Soviet period. By 1993 Russia's death rate had risen about one-quarter above the levels of the late 1980s. Life expectancy certainly still stood above the levels of the low income countries,[32] but by the mid 1990s it is very likely that Soviet life expectancy is beginning to lag behind the middle-income countries, certainly for men, if not also for women, an eloquent testimony to the awful results of the reform process in Russia.

Table 4.5 **Crude Death Rates in China, Russia, and Selected Groups of Countries (No/1000)**

	1960	1970	1982	1991	1993
China	10.0	7.6	6.6	6.7	–
Russia	7.4*	8.7*	10.5*	11.4	14.3
Low income countries**	24	19	16	13	–
Middle income countries	17	11	10	8	–
High income countries	10	10	9	9	–

* RSFSR
** Excluding China and India

Sources:
A. Bergson and D. Levine (eds.), *The Soviet Economy: Towards the Year 2000* (London: Allen & Unwin, 1983).
SSB, *Chinese Statistical Yearbook (ZGT JNJ)* (Beijing: Chinese Statistical Publishing House), p. 78
Ellman
World Bank, 1984 and 1993

Conclusion

The fact that the Chinese system of political economy in the 1980s was 'market socialist' and yet was one of the most dynamic in terms both of output and income growth that the modern world has seen, presents the mainstream social scientists with a puzzle: why did it perform so well in the first decade and a half of reform, despite the fact that both economic and political institutions and policies were gravely inadequate in relation to mainstream Western theory and policy advice? Why did Russia, which democratized quickly and tried to implement Polish-style 'shock therapy' after 1990, perform so disastrously? There are a number of possibilities, of different orders of difficulty for mainstream Western political economy to digest.

The 'easy' answer is that China entered its reform programme with important advantages compared to Russia. However, it is questionable if on balance China did indeed enter its reform programme with any net advantages over the USSR in terms of its capacity to respond to the 'challenge' of de-Stalinization. A more worrying possibility for the mainstream economists who had advocated 'shock therapy' (and in many cases still do so) is that China's incrementalist approach to economic reform may have been correct and the attempt in the former USSR to move rapidly towards a market economy may have been a serious mistake. There seems to be a growing consensus that this was indeed the case.

Table 4.6 **Life Expectancy in Selected Countries and Groups of Countries**

		1970	1982	1991
Low income countries	men	46	50	54
	women	47	52	57
Middle income countries	men	58	58	65
	women	62	62	71
High income countries	men	68	71	73
	women	75	78	80
China	men	61	65	67
	women	63	69	71
Russia	men	61 (1979/80)	62	63
	women	73 (1979/80)	74	74

Source: World Bank, 1984, and 1993, and Ellman

The correct economic advice to the former Stalinist economies may have been to stress that their structural transformation would require a lengthy period of extensive state intervention to cope with probable large areas of market failure. The enthusiasm of post-communist 'capitalist triumphalism' among advisers (domestic and foreign) may have caused a major mistake in assessing not only the required speed of the transition but also the desirable economic functions of the state over an extended period. The early development economics of the 1940s and the 1950s, and indeed, the practical experience of the Newly Industrializing Countries of East Asia,[33] may have been more relevant to the enormous tasks of transition that these economies faced than the mainstream economics of the 1970s and the 1980s, which stressed the shortcomings of the state as a vehicle for achieving socially desirable goals.[34]

The implications of the Russia–China contrast are also extremely worrying for Western political scientists, since there was such wide agreement that 'democratization' in reforming communist countries would produce major benefits for human welfare. This article has argued that an important part of the reason for the difference in outcome lies in the sphere of political choice. A successful transition away from a communist economy may be easier to achieve with a strong state which is able to place the overall national interest above that of powerful vested interest groups and is able to implement a gradual transformation of the whole network of economic institutions. A self-reforming communist party may be the least bad vehicle available to accomplish this.

The conclusion that the differences in economic performance of China and the former USSR largely originate from policy differences, and that an important part of the policy difference lay in the respective strategies of political change, becomes even more disturbing when we consider the possibility that all Stalinist economies possessed a huge inherent catch-up and overtaking possibility, on account of the vast underperformance in relation to their extensive physical and human capital inheritance. The tremendous success of the Chinese economy during the 1980s and into the early 1990s, and the growing evidence of a similar acceleration in other Asian reforming communist countries, suggests that such potential was indeed large.

The reform of the Stalinist economies may be seen by history to have been a knife-edge situation in which correct choices in political economy could produce explosive growth, and incorrect ones could send the system spinning backwards at high speed for an extended period, with high costs in terms of a range of fundamental human rights. The provision of the right to vote periodically in elections may appear as less and less adequate a compensation for the loss of other human rights consequent upon economic failure.

It is hard to avoid the conclusion that in the USSR the leadership's willingness to pursue political democratization played an important role in making most citizens of that country much worse off, while the Chinese leadership's resistance to the pressures to democratize played an important role in making most Chinese people much better off. At least in large, heterogeneous, reforming communist countries the link between political democratization and human welfare seems to have been inverse. This is an extremely important and largely unexpected result which goes strongly against the grain of a large body of Western social science thinking in the recent past.

Notes

1 For more detailed analysis see P. Nolan, *State and Market in the Chinese Economy* (London: Macmillan, 1993); P. Nolan, 'Political Economy and the Reform of Stalinism: The Chinese Puzzle', *Contributions to Political Economy*, vol. 12 (1993); P. Nolan, *China's Rise, Russia's Fall* (London: Macmillan, 1994).

2 See, for example, M. Olson, *The Rise and Decline of Nations* (New Haven, CT and London: Yale University Press, 1982), L.G. Reynolds, *Economic Growth in the Third World* (New Haven, CT: Yale University Press, 1985), and D.C. North, *Institutions, Institutional Change and Economic Performance* (Cambridge: Cambridge University Press, 1990).

3 A Steinherr, 'Essential Ingredients for Reforms in Eastern Europe', *MOCT-MOST* no. 3 (1991), p. 6. Alfred Steinherr is Director of the Financial Research Department of the European Investment Bank, Luxembourg.

4 J. Kornai, *The Road to a Free Economy* (New York and London: W.W. Norton, 1990), p. 22.

5 In fact, China's reform experience calls this proposition into question since for most of the past seventeen years of explosive growth property rights in land and most industrial means of production have been extremely vague.

6 See D.C. North and R.P. Thomas, *The Rise of the Western World* (Cambridge: Cambridge University Press, 1973).

7 J. Prybyla, 'A Broken System', in G. Hicks (ed.), *The Broken Mirror* (Harlow: Longmans, 1990), p. 188.

8 J. Kornai, 'The Hungarian Reform Process: Visions, Hopes and Realities', *Journal of Economic Literature*, vol. 24 (1986), p. 1729.

9 P. Dasgupta, 'Well-Being and the Extent of its Realisation in Poor Countries', *Economic Journal*, vol. 100 (1990 Supplement), pp. 27–8.

10 K. Popper, *The Poverty of Historicism* (London: Routledge & Kegan Paul, 1957), p. 160.

11 See R. Nelson and S. Winter, *An Evolutionary Theory of Economic Change* (Cambridge, MA: Harvard University Press, 1982), P. Murrell, 'Evolutionary and Radical Approaches to Economic Reform', *Economics of Planning*, vol. 25 (1992), pp. 79–95.

12 See Therborn, op. cit.

13 In each of the Asian Newly Industrializing Countries, but most strikingly in Korea and Taiwan, successful development policies resulting in large increases in *per capita* output and income were followed by mass demands for democratization of political life. Moreover, all the advanced capitalist countries followed a similar sequence, which governments eventually found it impossible to resist.

14 H. Phelps Brown, *The Origins of Trade Union Power* (Oxford: Oxford University Press, 1983), Ch. 2.

15 World Bank, *World Development Report* (New York: Oxford University Press, 1991), p. 134. On the 'populist' roots of Latin American inflation, see R. Dornbusch and S. Edwards (eds.), *The Macroeconomics of Populism in Latin America* (Chicago, IL and London: University of Chicago Press, 1991).

16 M. Gorbachev, *Perestroika* (London: Collins, 1987), p. 63.

17 A. Aslund, *Gorbachev's Struggle for Economic Reform* (London: Pinter, 1991), pp. 33–4.

18 Ibid., p. 14.

19 M. Goldman, *What Went Wrong With Perestroika?* (New York: Norton, 1992), p. 65.

20 Deng Xiaoping, 'Uphold the Four Cardinal Principles', in *Major Documents of the People's Republic of China* (Beijing: Foreign Languages Press, 1979), p. 55.

21 Ibid., pp. 48–9.

22 C. Johnson, 'Forward', in Hicks (ed.), *The Broken Mirror*, pp. viii–ix.

23 J. Banister, *Demographic Aspects of Poverty in China*, World Bank Working Paper (Washington, DC: World Bank, 1992), p. 12.

24 Ibid.

25 In fact, unofficial estimates of output suggest that the downturn began before 1989, and there may well have been negative growth of national product over the whole 1985–90 period. See Aslund, op. cit., p. 200.

26 Feshbach, quoted in M. Ellman, 'The Increase in Death and Disease under *Katastroika*' (unpublished ms., 1993).

27 Ellman.

28 Ibid.

29 Ibid.

30 Ibid.
31 W.G. Hoskins, *The Age of Plunder* (Harlow: Longmans, 1976), p. 122.
32 The age structure of these countries is very different from that of an industrialized country like Russia, and therefore direct comparisons of crude, rather than age-specific death rates are meaningless.
33 See especially A. Amsden, *Asia's Next Giant* (Oxford: Oxford University Press, 1989); R. Wade, *Governing the Market* (Princeton: Princeton University Press, 1990); and H.J. Chang, *The Political Economy of Industrial Policy* (London: Macmillan, 1993).
34 Writing in respect of the economists' view of the role of the state in development economics, Stern comments: 'The apparent swing in the profession from whole-hearted espousal of extensive government intervention to its rubbishing seems to be an example of unbalanced intellectual growth ... There are problems and virtues with both state intervention and the free market'. N. Stern, 'The Economics of Development', *Economic Journal*, vol. 99 (1989), pp. 621–2.

5

BEYOND PRIVATIZATION: INSTITUTIONAL INNOVATION AND GROWTH IN CHINA'S LARGE STATE-OWNED ENTERPRISES*
(with Wang Xiaoqiang)

1. FOREWORD

If one takes a journey southward from the center of Shanghai one passes mile after mile of thriving new businesses. They are mainly township and village enterprises (TVEs) mostly housed in new buildings, often Sino-foreign joint ventures, making a vast array of goods, many destined for the world market. The bewildering array of products includes footwear, packaging, luggage, sports goods, electronic goods, clothing, furniture and toys. One could be forgiven for thinking this *was* the new Chinese industrial revolution. After a journey of some 70 kilometres, one has almost reached the edge of greater Shanghai and is at the border with Zhejiang Province. There, on formerly desolate sand flats, stands a vast new petrochemical complex, the huge state-owned Shanghai Petrochemical Company (SPC). Production began at SPC in 1977. It is now the largest petrochemical complex in China, in the process of high-speed expansion. A large fraction of the synthetic fibers, resins and plastics consumed by Shanghai's booming TVEs is provided by SPC. Large-scale upstream industry and downstream industry are the Siamese twins of the new Chinese industrial revolution.

2. INTRODUCTION

It is widely thought that small-scale non-state enterprises, notably the 'township and village enterprises' (TVEs) are the chief source of China's new industrial revolution (e.g., World Bank, 1996a, pp. 71–5). SOEs are widely thought to be a homogenous group that has lagged far behind non-state enterprises, making increasing losses, stagnant and simply waiting to die. The widely held conclusion drawn from this set of stylized facts is that China's industrial reforms confirm the central hypothesis of the 'transition orthodoxy', namely, that only privatization can solve the industrial problems of communist countries. These views receive their latest airing in the World Bank's recent publications, *Bureaucrats in Business* and *From Plan to Market* (World Bank, 1996a, b). It is argued that China's booming non-state enterprises, whose goods flood Western markets, show the way to China's state-owned 'fossils' and all other such 'fossils' in the developing world, trapped in an archaic world of state-owned, inward-looking, heavy-industrial development presided over by 'corrupt' bureaucrats.

This paper demonstrates that the reality of China's industrial reforms is much more complex than this. First, a large share of the assets in non-state industry is owned by the whole of each local community, of which the TVE workers are a small minority, even in the most advanced areas. Local bureaucrats have strong incentives to employ well-paid, dynamic, profit-seeking managers who make money for the whole community. These enterprises are better seen as local state-owned multi-plant firms. This institutional innovation presents a much more severe challenge to conventional approaches toward property rights and economic performance than the World Bank (World Bank, 1996a, p. 131) and many other commentators acknowledge. The lessons from this experience are still to be absorbed by the wider literature in development economics. Although the analysis of them is far from complete, there are now many studies outlining the basic features of their operation. Instead of adding to this literature, this paper instead focuses on large SOEs.

In fact, China's large SOEs have played a vital role in China's explosive industrial growth. The main body of this paper (Section 4) analyses the growth and institutional evolution of these enterprises. Analysis of China's SOEs has focused on aggregate statistical studies of the whole state industrial sector. Rarely is a distinction even made between different branches and sizes of state enterprise, as though the economic characteristics of the production of plastic toys were identical to that of the petrochemical sector which provides the inputs for the toys. Since William Byrd's pioneering work in the mid-1980s (Byrd, 1992) there have been virtually no micro-studies of the institutional evolution of this massive sector.[1] Yet in the long run the evolution of this sector will be much more important for China and for the global economy than the TVEs will be. Moreover, the complex changes in this sector are of deep importance for the theory of the role of property rights and institutions in economic development. Its performance also casts light on the potentialities that were latent in the Soviet Union's large-scale industrial sector, and thereby upon the argument that it was 'necessary' and 'inevitable' for there to be a massive post-Soviet Russian industrial depression.[2]

This article demonstrates that China's large SOEs are not stagnant fossils waiting to die. This sector has already undergone large change due to enhanced enterprise autonomy, the impact of market forces, rapid growth of domestic demand for upstream products, strategic integration with the world economy and the state's policy to promote large businesses. China's large SOEs are developing new institutional forms that do not neatly fit into existing patterns. China is experimentally changing its institutions through a combination of central policy, local initiative and interaction with international investment. This presents a challenge to the 'transitional orthodoxy' and to ideas concerning property rights in development economics. There is not a universal model of property rights and government action that works best in all circumstances. China's experience with the reform of large SOEs shows the diverse possibilities for effective industrial institutions.

However, even the largest and most effective of China's large SOEs are still far short of being 'modern industrial corporations'. The achievement of this goal has nothing to do with privatization, and still less to do with downsizing. It is intimately related to globalization, and the ability to bargain with the multinationals for transfer of technology. It involves going beyond autonomy and requires further state policies to assist the construction of giant corporations that can do business with the multinational corporations on an equal footing.

Such a realistic perspective on the nature of big business and the goal of large SOE reform in former communist countries is absent from *Bureaucrats in Business*, as it is from most 'transitional orthodoxy' writing (e.g. World Bank, 1996b). As the first part of this paper will show, the World Bank's perspective is ahistorical, lacking real world content about the role and nature of big business in the advanced economies, and of the role of the state in supporting big business.[3]

3. THE TRANSITION ORTHODOXY:[4] SYSTEM REVOLUTION, PRIVATIZATION, CLOSURE, GLOBALIZATION

(a) Anti-bureaucratic Revolution

There was widespread disbelief that the communist bureaucracy could lead a movement toward a market economy sufficiently far to cross a minimum 'threshold' level of market activity. The correct 'sequence' of system reform in communist countries was seen to be: first, an anti-communist revolution, second economic liberalization. Anders Aslund, Janos Kornai and Jeffrey Sachs are three of the most influential figures in the 'transition orthodoxy', given wide prominence in World Bank-organized conferences and publications on the 'transition'. They argued passionately for the necessity of a liberal anti-communist revolution in order to allow 'real' economic reform:

> A reform reduces the power of the bureaucracy by definition, and most of the administration will inevitably oppose reform. Therefore, *a successful reform must break the power of the anti-reform bureaucracy ... To break the power of the party and state bureaucracy might be seen as the key problem of a reform* (Aslund, 1991, p. 14, emphasis added).

> There is ... a stubborn contradiction in the whole reform process: how to get the active participation of the very people who will lose a part of their power if the process is successful (Kornai, 1986, p. 1729).

> *The collapse of communist one-party rule was the sine qua non for an effective transition to a market economy.* If one proposition has been tested by history, it is that the communist parties of Eastern Europe would not lead a process of radical reform sufficiently deep to create a real market economy (Lipton and Sachs, 1993, p. 34, emphasis added).

For initiating the revolutionary political change which destroyed the communist bureaucracy, the transition orthodoxy considers that Gorbachev deserves 'undying merit' (Kornai, 1992, p. 574). Deng Xiaoping was a villain who sustained bureaucratic rule to the detriment of democracy and system change. In the late 1980s and early 1990s, it was almost universally thought that the Soviet system reforms had 'succeeded' and China's had 'failed', due to the destruction of the bureaucracy in the one and the sustaining bureaucrats' power in the other.

The transition orthodoxy ridiculed the possibility that a 'gerontocratic', 'hard-line' communist bureaucracy might possess the skills successfully to lead a communist transition along a 'third way' to the market:

> *The bureaucracy provides an extraordinarily important practical argument for radical free market policies,* even in circumstances where 'market failures' exist and pure theory might suggest more nuanced policies. It is naive to think of the existing bureaucracy as equipped, professionally and temperamentally, to implement sophisticated policies based on Western-style theories of the 'second best'. The bureaucracy cannot be relied for efficiency in regulating monopoly prices, promoting infant industries, or implementing industrial policy (Lipton and Sachs, 1993, p. 35, emphasis added).

It was thought that foreign investors would not invest substantially in a country still ruled by communist bureaucrats: 'The low regard in the West for the communist governments, [makes] it impossible for them to mobilise the international financial support vital for the economic transition' (Lipton and Sachs, 1993, p. 34).

(b) Privatization

Privatization was viewed as the 'indispensable process' by which the very institution of private property would be reintroduced in the socialist economies (Borenzstein and Kumar, 1991, p. 230). A rapid transformation of the ownership of the means of production was considered to be necessary 'to ensure a complete break with the old regime' (Borenzstein and Kumar, 1991, p. 231). The Shatalin 500 day program in Russia, the quintessential document of the transition orthodoxy, expressed the populist theme of privatization as follows: '*The [privatisation] programme gives equal chances to everybody* ... practically everyone, even if he does not have any considerable initial capital, will have an opportunity to get his share of the national wealth' (Yavlinsky *et al.*, 1991, p. 217, emphasis added).

For the Bretton Woods orthodoxy 'enterprise reform' was equated with privatization. Autonomous owners and managers must 'take responsibility for the full range of business decisions and for the financial benefits and costs of those decisions'; 'Experience shows that this is most likely to happen when assets are privately owned' (IMF *et al.*, 1990, pp. 16–17). It was thought that private property alone could provide incentives for managers to minimize costs and respond to market signals (Borenzstein and Kumar, 1991, p. 229). Private property was thought to provide the only means for owners to 'monitor, assess, and control the performance of the managers effectively running the enterprises' (Borenzstein and Kumar, 1991, p. 229).

The transition orthodoxy believed that both economic theory and the experience of the 'third way' in communist countries provided conclusive evidence that it was futile to expect that a large SOE could behave as a market-oriented agent:

> It is time to let go of this vain hope once and for all. Never, no more ... [B]ureaucratic co-ordination is as much the spontaneous effect and natural mode of state property's existence as market co-ordination is of private property. Twenty years of Hungarian experience together with the experience of all other reform-minded socialist states demonstrate that this is no longer a debating point, but simply a fact that must be accepted (Kornai, 1990, pp. 58–9).

It was argued that governments find it impossible to resist lobby pressure to allow 'soft budget constraints' and prevent loss-making SOEs going bankrupt.

The 'transition orthodoxy' rejected any option other than transferring property rights from the state to 'truly private hands' (Kornai, 1990, 1992; Lipton
and Sachs, 1991). The goal was thorough privatization of large SOEs. As
Kornai graphically put it:

> It is my firm conviction that history is not like a film reel that can be
> stopped at any moment, or run on fast forward or backward at will.
> Socialist state ownership means the complete, 100% impersonalisation
> of property. We cannot simply reverse this process in an attempt to
> reduce the percentage gradually to 95, 90, 85% and so on. *The reel must be
> fully rewound and played from the beginning* (Kornai, 1990, p. 73, emphasis
> added).

(c) 'Close the Large, Support the Small'

The 'transition orthodoxy' thought that most of the large-scale SOE sector
would need to close down. Attempting to support and reconstruct the large-
scale sector was regarded as a waste of resources. Industrial growth was visualized as coming mainly from new small and medium-sized enterprises:

> For the most part, Eastern Europe's production sector is composed of
> large, inefficient firms. *Many, if not most, of them will have to close,* and others
> will need to shed labour on a large scale. *Growth will come largely from the rest
> of the economy, which exists to-day only in embryonic form.* Badly needed are
> small to medium-scale firms, high-tech manufacturing, and most forms
> of services ... *The challenge of restructuring will be to efficiently close much of the
> old structure and allow for rapid expansion of a new one* (Blanchard *et al.*, 1991,
> pp. 64–5, emphasis added).

(d) Globalization

The transition orthodoxy's vision was that 'close' integration into the international economic system would spontaneously accelerate growth in the reforming economies.[5] No industrial policy was necessary. The privatized businesses
of the reforming economies would simply lock into global markets:

> The vision is of one large inter-linked network of producers and con-
> sumers plugged into an efficiently operating level playing field of the
> open international and globalised economy. International markets
> provide co-ordination in and of themselves, which national strategies
> and policy interventions can merely distort (Hirst and Thompson, 1995,
> p. 59).

It was regarded as essential to quickly remove barriers between the 'distorted' communist prices and world market prices, with only a brief period (two to three years) of protection for a few sectors:

It is ... essential to move as rapidly as possible to a transparent and decentralised trade and exchange rate system, in order to hasten the integration ... into the world economy ... The exchange rate [needs] to be moved to market clearing levels. [*Only*] *a few sectors* [*need to be shielded*] *for a short time from the intense competition of international markets* (IMF *et al.*, 1990, p. 17, emphasis added).

4. THE REALITY

(a) The Complexity of Business Institutions in Advanced Capitalism

(i) Personalization, Impersonalization and Competition

State ownership is the extreme form of property impersonalization. The transition orthodoxy advocated the 'personalization' of property, transferring state-owned assets into the hands of 'real flesh-and-blood persons' (Kornai, 1990, pp. 50, 57, 70, 75, 85). The fiercely competitive institutions of advanced capitalism, however, are far removed from personalized ownership. There have been two major challenges to the control of firms by 'flesh-and-blood persons', namely, the joint-stock company, and the Japanese system of manager-controlled cross-holdings.

In the United Kingdom, in the 1930s, more than two-thirds of the shares of quoted companies were held by individuals. Today, the typical large firm no longer belongs mainly to 'real flesh-and-blood persons'. By 1970 in the UK individual stock holdings had fallen to 45% (Moyle, 1971, pp. 6–7), and are currently less than 20%. In the United States, institutions hold about two-thirds of the equity of the 1,000 largest US public companies (Lorsch, 1991, p. 139).

The joint-stock company was a Schumpeterian force for 'creative destruction' which 'revolutionized' the economic structure from within. It destroyed the 'personal enterprise' through the separation of ownership and control. When several 'real flesh-and-blood persons' put their property together, establishing a joint-stock company, their property becomes a legal person, separate from its owners. In law, the bloodless joint-stock company has equal rights with any flesh-and-blood person, including its owners. If 'real flesh-and-blood persons' do not like the way in which the bloodless legal person employs their assets, they can sell their shares, but they cannot withdraw their property: What shareholders really own are their shares and not the corporation' (Demsetz, 1988, p. 114). Since shareholders spread their shareholdings to avoid risk, a single shareholder, whether an individual or an institution, generally has little interest in personally overseeing the detailed activities of any given firm's operation (Fama, 1980). Even big institutional shareholders generally disperse their shares widely.[6] Shareholders are no longer entrepreneurs who operate firms themselves. They have become monitors or share traders, rather than organizers, operators or managers (Lazonick, 1991, p. 78).

The joint-stock company made it possible for entrepreneurs to run the firm as organizers or managers, rather than as owners and founders. Alongside the decline in owners' control over managers, competition among large firms intensified, acutely so in the recent past with the acceleration of technical progress and liberalization of global markets. Impersonal, institutional ownership in advanced capitalism is compatible with the fierce competition among large firms.

In Japan, most large companies are members of a small number of industrial groups, the *keiretsu*. A *keiretsu* usually owns less than 2% of any other member firm, but it typically has a stake of that size in every firm in the group, so that between 30% and 90% of a firm is owned by other group members (Drucker, 1991, p. 106). Japanese corporations have about 70% of their shares held by other corporations (Aoki, 1994, p. 21; Sheard, 1994, p. 312). Through the cross-holding process, Japanese managers effectively hire friendly owners:

> The seemingly crisp categories of principal and agent become fuzzy as the managers of one firm become the owners of another, and in turn are held by managers of that firm. It is less that management has been separated from control, therefore, than that control had been merged into management (Gerlach, 1992, p. 238).

The system is a kind of 'collective defence to maintain the control by management over ownership' (Suzuki, 1991, pp. 78–9).

Under this system there is only a low level of merger and acquisition. From the managers' point of view, to be taken over by others is to surrender to their enemies. Externally hired managers are rare, reflecting the fact that in Japan competition is a war with no prisoners taken, with a good chance they will lose jobs after a takeover. This life-and-death battle forces Japanese managers to build an alliance with their employees building long-term programs, such as housing, training, lifetime employment and the seniority system. Managers and workers 'may agree to trade wage increases for job security or better opportunities for promotion made possible by the growth of the firm' (Aoki,

1987, p. 273). Hence, the level of strikes in Japan is low. Instead, Japanese labour unions and their members are very interested in having a voice in management (Koike, 1987). Workers in large Japanese firms often endure hardship in order to enable their firm to survive and grow (Hashimoto and Raisian, 1985; Mincer and Higuchi, 1988).

The removal of ownership control means that the unconstrained Japanese managers can afford to ill-treat owners with impunity. In 1990, the total dividend payout of all public corporations in Japan was 30% of profits compared with 50% in Germany, 54% in the US, and 66% in the United Kingdom. Managers in Japan spend more on corporate entertaining than they pay out in dividends (Aoki, 1987, p. 622). Without ownership control, internally oriented and immobile managers tend to reinvest profits rather than distribute them (Boltho, 1975; Lichtenberg and Pushner, 1992, p. 7). Depreciation and corporate savings together have amounted to as much as one-half of total domestic savings, underpinning Japan's high investment rates. Japanese firms acted as if they had 'investment hunger', and often 'over-invested' (Johnson, 1982). Japanese managers can ignore short-term profitability as a measure of their performance and concentrate instead on 'Schumpeterian' competition, such as foreign market penetration, quality control and long-term product development. 'Share price increase' is their least important target and 'market domination' their most important one (Best, 1990, p. 10). Outside Japan it is a common criticism that Japanese companies owe their success to government assistance and the restriction of foreign business in Japan. Within Japan business leaders think the real source of their success is 'fierce domestic competition' (Kanter, 1991, p. 155).

(ii) Institutional Diversity of Powerful Large Firms

There is not a simple institutional explanation for why some firms rather than others emerge as giants. For example, in the steel industry, over the course of the 20th century there have been just two firms, US Steel and New Japan Steel, which have held the top position; a third, Posco, is now about to move into that position. The institutional characteristics of these firms, however, are quite different from each other.

United States Steel (now USX) has always been privately owned. Carnegie Steel prospered as an infant industry behind the high tariff barriers in place in the United States from the mid-19th century onward (Ruigrok and Van Tulder, 1995, pp. 211–12). In 1900, Carnegie merged with Federal Steel to create a 'giant of giants' (Chandler, 1990, p. 130), United States Steel, much the largest steel producer in the world and the world's largest industrial corporation. In 1901 its share of US output was 66% for crude steel, 60% for steel rails, 62% for heavy structural shapes, 65% for plates and sheets and 78% for wire rod output (Chandler, 1990, p. 138).

New Japan Steel (Nippon Steel) is currently the world's biggest steel company. It had its origins in the Yawata Steelworks, founded in 1896 by the Japanese government (Yonekura, 1994, p. 274), producing 62% of Japan's total crude steel output in 1926 (Yonekura, 1994, p. 97). In the early 1930s, the government 'rationalized' the steel industry, establishing Japan Steel, composed of Yawata and several smaller producers. Technically, the new firm was a private company, but the government owned more than 50% of the company's stock, and retained many other rights to intervene in the firm's operations (Yonekura, 1994, p. 143). By 1945 it produced almost 90% of Japan's pig iron output, and over one-half of crude steel output (Yonekura, 1994, p. 210). The Allied forces demanded that Japan Steel be split into two companies, Fuji and Yawata, but in 1970, the New Japan Steel (Nippon Steel) was established out of the re-merger of these two companies. The new 'Japan Steel' accounted for around two-fifths of total Japanese steel output (Yonekura, 1994, p. 210). The merger, 'the largest in Japanese industrial history', was supported strongly by MITI who 'faced the liberalisation of foreign trade and investment in Japan and felt the necessity of fostering world class companies to compete internationally' (Yonekura, 1994, p. 235).

Posco (South Korea) is widely acknowledged to be the world's most successful steel firm. It is currently the world's second largest steel-producing firm, and will soon take over the top slot. It was founded by the South Korean government in 1968 as a calculated planning move to enable South Korea to supply domestically the steel needed for its fast-growing shipbuilding, automobile, electronics and construction industries (Amsden, 1989, Chapter 12). Famously, the World Bank advised against building the plant, arguing that it was 'premature' for the country to have a large steel plant (Hogan, 1994, p. 40). The firm is still owned and controlled by the state.[7] Posco has had a near-monopoly within domestic supply.[8]

(b) The Centrality of Big Business in the World Economy

The large-scale 'modern' industrial enterprise emerged in the advanced capitalist economies at the end of the nineteenth century, alongside rapid changes in production technology, and has remained at its core ever since:

> The modern industrial enterprise played a central role in creating the most technologically advanced, fastest growing industries of their day. These industries, in turn, were the pace-setters of the industrial sector of their economies ... [They] provided an underlying dynamic in the development of modern industrial capitalism (Chandler, 1990, p. 593).

It is playing a central role also in the late industrializing economies. Even in Taiwan, an economy with a reputation for small scale enterprise, the large-size firm (often a government enterprise) spearheaded industrialization in the early stages of growth. In Korea, the modern industrial enterprise takes the form of diversified business groups, or *chaebol*, whose size and diversity are similar to those of the *zaibatsu*, Japan's postwar big business groups (Amsden, 1989, pp. 8–9).

The large multi-plant firm has been a central force in cost reduction and technical progress. It often benefits from economies of scale, associated with reduction in unit costs from large plant size. In many sectors plants of less than a certain scale face substantial unit cost disadvantages (Scherer and Ross, 1990, pp. 115 and 140). Large firms often benefit from economies of 'scope' from product diversification associated with reduced transaction costs involved in multi-plant operation (Chandler, 1990). Large, multi-plant firms may benefit from reduced transport costs, superior research and development,[9] reduced risk, lower capital costs, the capacity to create a brand name, credit provision to customers and after-sales service (Chandler, 1990, p. 200). In many sectors firms which do not operate several plants are at a competitive disadvantage (Scherer and Ross, 1990, pp. 115 and 140).

Large firms are found disproportionately (though not exclusively) in capital intensive, 'upstream' industries, in which economies of scale and scope tend to be relatively strong. Chandler's analysis of the 401 giant companies with more than 20,000 workers found that in the mid-1970s, 72% of them were clustered in a narrow range of industries, namely, chemicals, petroleum, primary metals, the three machinery groups (non-electrical and electrical machinery, transportation equipment), and food (Chandler, 1990, p. 19). These are 'precisely the industries where income elasticity of demand is high, technological progress is rapid, and labour productivity rises fast' (OECD, 1972, p. 15, quoted in Wade, 1990, p. 25).

An important influence upon the 'transition orthodoxy' was the increased role of small and medium-sized firms in the advanced capitalist countries. Using computer numerically controlled machine tools, firms frequently replace conventional automated production with flexible manufacturing systems. A large increase has occurred in outsourcing of components and service activities by large firms. A clear move towards a 'Toyotist' pattern of industrial organization is occurring across the capitalist world, as core firms become connected with 'second tier' and 'third tier' suppliers (Ruigrok and Van Tulder, 1995). The early 1990s saw a considerable 'downsizing' in employment in large firms associated with the cyclical downturn in demand in the OECD countries: total employment in the firms included in the Fortune 500 list fell from over 16 million in 1990 to under 12 million in 1994

(Ruigrok and Van Tulder, 1995, p. 155). This process was assisted by the large increase in the intensity of labor as managers took advantage of the huge rise in the 'reserve army of labor' and changes in labor laws to radically alter traditional working practices. A sea change took place in management philosophy, with a pronounced shift of emphasis in large firms away from the 'top line', growth in revenues and diversification toward profitability, 'downsizing', 'bottom line' and focus on 'core business'.

Despite these large changes, however, big businesses still occupy centre stage in the advanced capitalist economies. Huge corporations with tens or even hundreds of thousands of employees stand at the centre of the capitalist system. In the United States, the share of the 100 largest manufacturing companies fell from 29.1% of GNP in 1978 to 24%, still a very large share, and their share of employment remained steady, at 43.3% in 1978 and 42.3% in 1990. Over the same period in Japan the share of the top 100 manufacturing firms rose from 22.1% of GNP to 29.7% and their share of employment rose from 17.4% to 22.4%, while in Europe the share of the top 100 manufacturing firms in GNP rose from 18.1% to 19.5% and the share of employment rose from 25.1% to 28.2% (Ruigrok and Van Tulder, 1995, p. 155).

Around 37,000 transnational corporations (TNCs) worldwide directly employ around 73 million people, or around 20% of the employment of the advanced capitalist countries. Such firms, however, increasingly stand at the center of an industrial 'web' of suppliers who depend on them for their existence and prosperity, in a new global form of the late medieval 'putting out system'. These account for at least as many 'indirect employees' as are directly employed by the giant firms. The TNCs' total share of employment in the advanced economies may be around 40%:

> There is dire need for new statistical techniques to assess the influence of 'transnationals' on indirect employment ... and to cope with the paradox that core firms with a Toyotist concept of control have increased their structural influence over the economy, because they have lowered their number of directly employed workers (Ruigrok and Van Tulder, 1995, p. 155).

The 'core' of the world's most powerful firms is growing fast, despite outsourcing and disposal of 'non-core' business. In the 1990s the rapid liberalization of world markets has led to a powerful tendency toward concentration of ownership. In industry after industry there has occurred a rise in the global market share, accounted for by a small number of firms expanding through organic growth, merger and acquisition within their core competence as the size of competitive global markets has massively increased. Hardly a sector has not seen this process, with a powerful trend towards concentration in activities as diverse as automobile components, aerospace, defence equipment, power equipment, farm machinery, pharmaceuticals, soft drinks, snack foods, household goods (from detergents to shampoo and toothpaste), telecommunications, chemical fertilizers, advertising, power generation, investment finance and legal practices.

For example, in the power equipment industry, there are large economies of scale and scope. The main elements of power stations, boilers and turbines are of enormous size. Moreover, their size has steadily risen as technical progress has brought down costs of electricity generation, in part through ever bigger units of production, but also through a wide range of other aspects of technical progress. A major advantage for a giant such as General Electric in establishing its technical lead in turbine technology has been the spillover from its aero engine division (*Financial Times*, May 16, 1995). Power generation equipment firms must be able to guarantee the quality of their hugely expensive products and have the resources to be able to rectify problems if they arise. Bidding for projects requires the investment of large sums with uncertain outcomes. Increasingly, power equipment makers have to be able to provide capital for project construction. A firm such as General Electric has a huge advantage in winning orders in that it is supported by GE Capital, the financial services division of the parent company. A sharply increasing share of power equipment companies' profits are generated by after-sales service, so power equipment firms need to have large service divisions. Increasingly, long-term service contracts form part of the package provided by the major producers.

The industry was already highly concentrated at a global level by the 1980s and has become more so since then. There are now just five main integrated producers of power plants worldwide. In the gas turbine sector in 1990–5, General Electric accounted for 50%, Westinghouse (in alliance with Mitsubishi Heavy Industry) for 18%, Siemens for 14% and ABB for 14%, while in steam turbines GE accounted for 20%, Westinghouse/Mitsubishi for 14%, GEC-Alsthom for 11%, and ABB for 10% (Wagstyl, 1996). It is likely that the already small number of firms will grow even smaller alongside growing world demands for power-generating equipment:

> The all-round skills needed to compete simultaneously in building, alliance making, financial investment and servicing gives enormous advantage to the big integrated companies. The time when this battle of the giants is resolved is fast approaching (Wagstyl, 1996).

(c) The Centrality of State Action: the 'End of History is not yet in Sight'

(i) The Importance, Still, of the Nation State

The activities of the national government have been central to the explanation of successful growth in developing countries. Lloyd Reynolds concludes his magisterial survey of 'growth' in the Third World since the mid-nineteenth century as follows:

> Even though we know that growth of agricultural output, growth and diversification of exports, and a high rate of investment seems to be important, the sources of sustained growth remain mysterious ... Some of the most important variables excluded from economic models can be labelled as political. *Government matters ... For good or ill, government is central to economic growth* (Reynolds, 1985, pp. 413–14, emphasis added).

The way in which 'government matters' is elusive, however.

> When we ask in precisely what ways government matters, the answer seems to include the following: strength of nationhood; the degree of continuity in political leadership; degree of interest in economic growth by the governing group; administrative competence of government; and general stance of economic policy (Reynolds, 1985, p. 44).

From the mid-nineteenth to the mid-twentieth century, China, for so long the world's leading economic region, failed conspicuously to 'catch up'. While Japan and other East Asian countries did 'catch up', China was mired initially by massive internal turmoil, and later by Mao's inward-looking, commandist policies. It is now making up for lost time, catching up at high speed. China's rise is challenging the dominant economic position of the OECD and the world hegemony of the United States. It is in this epoch that the philosophy of the 'borderless', stateless world (Ohmae, 1996) and the 'end of history' (Fukuyama, 1992) has developed.

It is unlikely that the end of US hegemony will indeed coincide neatly with the end of the nation state. The world is increasingly integrated in terms of the mobility of goods and capital. The migration of capital, however, is not random. It is strongly related to the policies pursued by different national governments. Moreover, for people, it is farcical to talk of a 'borderless' world. There is still a vast, and arguably growing, difference in income and life chances for citizens in different countries. Even measured in terms of PPP dollars, the average output per person in developing countries, which contain almost three-fifths of the world's total population, still stands at only $2,700, and at just $900 in the least developed, compared to over $15,000 in the industrialized economies (UNDP, 1996, pp. 135–7). Behind these figures stands a world of difference in terms of well-being and the opportunities to realize human potential.

Between 1870 and 1920 around 18 million Europeans migrated to the United States, mainly to escape poverty in Europe (Foreman-Peck, 1983, p. 146). In the past decade the rich countries have experienced relentless competitive pressure, businesses have downsized, and either US-style adjustment of falling real wages, or 'European'-style adjustment of rising unemployment and falling welfare spending, have taken place (Wood, 1994). In the face of these pressures, controls on international migration are tightening:

[D]espite the rhetoric of globalisation, the bulk of the world's population lives in closed worlds, trapped by the lottery of their birth. For the average worker or farmer with a family, one's nation state is a community of fate. Wealth and income are not global, but are nationally and regionally distributed between poorer and richer states and localities (Hirst and Thompson, 1995, pp. 181–3).

Indeed, far from becoming less important, nationality may become ever more important:

As the advanced economies seek to police the movements of the world's poor and exclude them, the capriciousness of the notions of citizenship and of political community will become ever more evident (Hirst and Thompson, 1995, pp. 181–3).

In these circumstances, the national governments of poor countries have a duty to employ every means at their disposal to promote the industrial advance of their countries and thereby lift their citizens out of poverty. There is no 'ethical' duty for poor country governments to obey the laws of the international 'level playing field' established by the rich countries.[10] Rather, it is their 'duty' to manipulate these arrangements so as to benefit the growth of output and income in their own country.

(ii) The State and Big Business

The state has been central to the rise of most of the world's giant corporations. Far from simply emerging from the free market, the normal path through which the world's leading corporations developed was through extensive government support:

> Virtually all of the world's largest core firms have experienced a decisive influence from government policies and/or trade barriers on their strategy and competitive position. History matters! There has never been a 'level playing field' in international competition, and it is doubtful whether there ever will be one (Ruigrok and Van Tulder, 1995, p. 221).

Britain's Industrial Revolution took place under an explicitly Mercantilist philosophy of high protection and export promotion. Its infant industries were heavily protected, denying the massive textile industries of China and India access to the British market (Smith, 1776, Vol. 1, Book iv, Chapter 2), and gave Britain's infant textile industries the chance to mature. Moreover, while Britain's authoritarian state had no laws to prohibit capitalists from combining to lower the price of labor, it had 'many [laws] against [workmen] combining to raise it' (Smith, Vol. 1, Chapter viii, pp. 74–5). By the mid-19th century Britain's 'big business' (compared to the rest of the world) was able to prosper with free trade.

The United States in the nineteenth century unashamedly industrialized behind high protectionist barriers, 'free riding on free trade' (Lake, 1988, Chapter 3). As early as 1791, Alexander Hamilton argued for US industrialization behind tariff barriers (Ruigrok and Van Tulder, 1995, p. 211), and for almost two centuries, US tariffs rarely were below 30%, and often much higher (Ruigrok and Van Tulder, 1995, pp. 211–12). Despite the passage of antitrust laws, huge oligopolistic firms were allowed to grow. By the interwar period, US firms dominated big business globally, with around two-thirds of the world's top 50 companies (Schmitz, 1993, p. 31). Government procurement spending has been a continuing strong influence on US big business, with an especially powerful effect upon the aircraft, computer, semiconductor and electronics industries (Ruigrok and Van Tulder, 1995, p. 221).

There is a common current of economic thinking which stretched from Meiji Japan through to Sun Yatsen and the Kuomintang (initially on mainland China, and subsequently in Taiwan), through to South Korea and Singapore since the 1950s. This approach pragmatically regarded the best arrangement as that which would more rapidly produce national prosperity in a world of hostile international competition. The free market and the Stalinist command system were regarded as equally irrelevant. The broad approach owed much to that of Friedrich List. Chiang Kaishek, the leader of the Kuomintang, in the midst of his party's struggle with the Chinese Communist Party, wrote in 1947:

China cannot compete with the advanced industrial nations. She must therefore adopt a protectionist policy with regard to foreign trade, and a policy of economic planning with respect to her industrial development. Private capital alone will not be sufficient to operate on a large scale, or to compete with the trusts and government operated enterprises of foreign nations. *This is the great weakness of laissez-faire economic theory and makes it unsuitable for China* (Chiang Kaishek, 1947, p. 279, emphasis added).

Within Asia, a distinction can be made between the 'developmental state', notably in Japan, and the 'entrepreneurial state', notably in Taiwan and South Korea (Blecher, 1991). In Japan the catch-up process after World War II was facilitated by the Japanese government, MITI in particular, through a wide array of trade and industrial policies that went counter to mainstream economic theory (Johnson, 1982). As one of the key bureaucrats in MITI said: '[w]e did the opposite of what the American economist told us to do. We violated all the normal concepts' (quoted in Ruigrok and Van Tulder, 1995, p. 214). Only in the 1980s, after the catch-up had largely been completed, did Japan begin to join the ranks of the supporters of an international free trade regime. It was in this environment of close indirect support from the state that the giant Japanese firms that today lie at the heart of the Japanese economy developed. Japan currently has no less than 12 firms among the top 50 firms in the Fortune index of the world's largest companies (Ruigrok and Van Tulder, 1995, Table 9A).

The history of the Japanese motor car industry illustrates the big business–government relationship well. In the 1920s and 1930s car production in Japan was dominated by Ford and General Motors, who occupied around 90% of the total market. Under strong pressure from the army, the government licensed just two domestic firms, Toyota and Nissan, to make automobiles, and simultaneously outlawed car imports and foreign car production in Japan. Toyota and Nissan grew rapidly under the impact of huge government procurement demand. In the early 1950s the domestic car industry faced certain destruction as imports flooded the market. The government responded by erecting a 'barrage of import barriers', including outright prohibition of most types of car imports and high tariffs. The share of imports fell from 45% in 1951 to just 1% in 1960 (Nestor, 1991, p. 103). MITI played a key role in upgrading motor industry technology in the 1950s by bargaining with foreign producers to establish short period joint ventures during which technology was transferred over a few years and the joint venture was then terminated (Nestor, 1991, pp. 104–5).[11] MITI supported the growth of a small number of oligopolistic 'national champions': by 1970 Toyota and Nissan between them accounted for over 65% of national vehicle sales (Nestor, 1991, p. 107). Huge firms were established, gaining massively from economies of scale, with a comprehensive program of government indirect support, and based mainly on the domestic market. Only then did Japan's car producers attempt to conquer world markets[12] and there were moves to liberalize imports (Nestor, 1991, p. 113). Right through into the 1990s there was 'a bewildering web of non-tariff barriers' (Nestor, 1991, p. 108).

In Taiwan and South Korea the state went far beyond influencing the environment within which big business operated. In both cases the state played an important role in the construction of large-scale business through the direct operation of upstream, heavy industry, which the private sector was unable or unwilling to undertake. Posco in South Korea is the most famous example, but in Taiwan the extent of direct state ownership of large-scale heavy industry was even wider (Wade, 1990 Chapter 4, 'State-led industrialization'). The state in Taiwan concentrated its influence upon the relatively large-scale firms (over 300 employees), which account for around 60% of the total value of industrial output, 'leaving the downstream smaller-scale firms much freer' (Wade, 1990, pp. 73 and 110). State control and leadership focused on upstream industries such as synthetic fibers, plastics and metals (Wade, 1990, p. 109), including the highly effective state-run China Steel. Even in sectors where public enterprises did not dominate, such as plastics and textiles, the state 'aggressively led private producers in the early years' (Wade, 1990 p. 110). Through its extensive ownership and operation of vital upstream industries, as well as numerous other measures, such as import controls, tariffs, entry requirements, domestic content requirements, and concessional credit, the Taiwanese state has strongly influenced the operation of the private sector (Wade, 1990).

The South Korean government actively encouraged the growth of powerful, large-scale private businesses, the *chaebols*, by providing them with a protected domestic market, and supplying them with tightly controlled, but low-interest credit from the state-owned banking system (Chang, 1994). The South Korean 'entrepreneurial state' instigated 'every major industrial diversification of the decades of the 1960s and 1970s' (Amsden, 1989, p. 80):

> The state masterminded the early import-substituting projects ... The transformation from light to heavy industry came at the state's behest ... The government played the part of visionary in the case of Korea's first colossal shipyard ... and it was responsible for the Big Push into heavy machinery and chemicals in the late 1970s. It also laid the ground-work for the new wave of import substitution that followed heavy industrialization and that carried the electronics and automobile industry beyond the simple stage of assembly. The government enacted the automobile

protection law as far back as 1962, as part of its five-year economic development plan. In conjunction with this decision, it promoted the oil-refining industry (Amsden, 1989, pp. 80–1).

Uniquely among developing countries, by 1993 South Korea had no less than four companies in the Fortune 100 list of the world's largest companies, namely Samsung, Daewoo, Sangyong and Sankyong (Ruigrok and Van Tulder, 1995, Table 9A). In the mid-1990s Samsung and Daewoo were each in course of a massive plan to hugely expand their production capabilities abroad, especially in Europe.[13]

(d) The Difficulties of Privatizing Large Enterprises in Former Communist Countries

The transition orthodoxy's original vision of privatization was to privatize large SOEs by selling them case by case as going concerns, an approach based especially on the UK's experience (World Bank, 1996b, p. 53). In fact, as the World Bank now acknowledges, privatizing large and medium-size enterprises proved to be far more difficult than originally thought' (World Bank, 1996b, p. 50). Sales to outsiders proved to be 'too costly and slow, far more difficult to implement than anticipated, and most important, few in number' (World Bank, 1996b, p. 53). Giving enterprises free to managers and employees (or in the World Bank's inaccurate language, 'management-employee buyouts') naturally was 'relatively fast and easy to implement' (World Bank, 1996b, p. 54). But, the subsequent problems were huge: 'The [Russian program] well illustrates the drawbacks of management-employee buyouts' (World Bank, 1996b, p. 55). The behavior of Russian privatized firms is 'hard to distinguish from that of state firms' (World Bank, 1996b, p. 55). Moreover, in the 'give away', the 19% of adult Russians employed in privatized firms received 56% of the equity 'sold' up until June 1994, while the remaining 81% ended up with 15% of the divested assets (World Bank, 1996b, p. 55). Moreover, transactions since then 'have almost certainly added to the disparity' (World Bank, 1996b, p. 55). The third form of privatization, equal access vouchers to the whole population also can be executed rapidly, but 'they raise no revenue for the government and they have uncertain implications for corporate governance' (World Bank, 1996b, p. 56).

The experience of the first six years of post-communist rule shows that there is no satisfactory way to privatize large SOEs. Still in the mid-1990s, in countries such as Hungary and Poland over one-half of large SOEs remain in the public sector. The ones that have tried rapid privatizations of large SOEs have encountered big difficulties, now explicitly acknowledged by the World Bank.

(e) Implications for Policy in China's Reforms of the Large Enterprise Sector

(i) Experimentalism and Caution

If the tasks of privatization of large SOEs are so complex, if it is practically difficult to do so without implementing schemes that are likely to damage the construction of large powerful firms, if, as this article argues, this sector holds the key to the future prosperity of a large segment of the economy, then the logical answer is to proceed experimentally with their reform. Once wild changes have been implemented, constructing a powerful large-firms sector may take a long time. The only alternative is to try cautiously to devise schemes that can improve the performance of large SOEs for the long period that they *must* remain predominantly in public ownership: 'It seems therefore that most of China's state enterprises must continue to remain publicly owned for some considerable period of time, and that the main issue is how to reconcile this with improving their efficiency' (Wood, 1994, pp. 38–9).

(ii) Privatization or Managerial Autonomy?

Instead of making the goal of large SOE reform that of 'turning back the reel' to the 'primitive capitalism' of 'real flesh-and-blood persons', such as happened in Russia's Bretton Woods-inspired voucher privatization, a more logical path is to learn from the business structure of advanced capitalism. This would attempt to move toward modern impersonalization, in which large firms mainly are owned either by institutions or by other firms. The institutional 'distance' to be travelled is much less if the goal of reform is the latter rather than the former, since the large SOE is much closer to the modern impersonalized firm than it is to the privatized firm owned by 'flesh-and-blood persons'.[14]

If one approaches the reform task from this perspective, then the main goals of reform become autonomy and competition rather than privatization. Indeed, in the most important recent example of extensive privatization in an advanced capitalist country, namely in the United Kingdom under Margaret Thatcher, the strategy followed was precisely 'improvement before privatization'. A series of 'changes in the internal environment' was carried out before privatization, including changes in the organizational structure, objectives, management, labor relations, communication and reporting systems, and the nature and location of the business (Parker, 1993; Bishop and Kay, 1989; Rowthorn, 1990; Veljanovski, 1992). Indeed, one of the architects of British privatization, Alan Walters, was scathing about the illogicality of proposals for privatization of large enterprises in the former communist countries:

The naive belief in the emerging market economies, encouraged on occasion by enthusiasts from the West, is that, with the large-scale state-owned enterprises, all that is needed is to change the ownership from the state to private persons ... But this conclusion is a misleading and dangerous simplification ... There was thought to be no point in trying to reform the existing state-owned enterprises while they remained in state ownership ... *Under Mrs. Thatcher reform of the nationalised corporations was carried through while they were in the public sector* (Walters, 1992, pp. 102–104, emphasis added).

(iii) Building Large Firms

We have seen that large firms are central to the prosperity of the advanced economies and have a key role to play also in fast-growing, late industrializing ones. A central goal for the governments in transition economies ought to have been supporting the emergence of 'modern industrial corporations', often in heavy industry, which could have formed the basis for prosperity in other parts of the economy. This task would have been greatly facilitated by policies that enabled incomes and demand to grow steadily.

Encouraging the growth of large firms in transition economies was complicated by the fact that the communist economies destroyed the central idea of capitalist industry, namely the competitive *firm*. They attempted to run the whole economy as a single factory, based on administrative orders rather than competitive struggle between rival firms. The transitional economies needed actively to construct competitive *firms* rather than passively privatizing individual *plants* (or even segments of plants), but this goal received scant attention (if any) in the transition orthodoxy. This is ironic, since it is the *firm* rather than the *plant* that is the key location of decision-making and competition within the capitalist economies. Privatization of individual plants/enterprises leaves a transition economy with few, if any, large indigenous firms. An important part of the reform process was to establish a sequence of *large multiplant firms* which could take advantage of economies of scope as well as simply plant-level economies of scale. This typically meant reorganization of a number of plants simultaneously within a given ministry. The best policy was not passively to sell off, or, more typically, to give away, individual plants to private owners, attempting to construct a textbook form of perfect competition. After such a privatization, as the case of Russia demonstrates, it would take a long time for large indigenous firms to emerge through the spontaneous play of market forces in the face of open competition from globalized big business.

5. CHINA'S INSTITUTIONAL INNOVATIONS

(a) Building Modern Big Business under New Circumstances

In sharp contrast to the transition orthodoxy the Chinese government has attempted to support the growth of powerful, autonomous big businesses that can compete with the global giants: 'The goal is to form competitive and independently managed industrial giants ... The fact is that mass production is desperately needed by modern society' (Yao Jianguo, 1992). Large SOEs maintained their leading role throughout the reform process (see below). In this strategy, China's planners have proceeded experimentally. In the course of its industrial reforms, China has made important institutional innovations in respect to the large-scale sector, no less than in respect to TVEs.

China's situation is in many ways different from that of other East Asian countries. China is reforming a comprehensively state-administered industrial system. It is widely thought that China under Maoist planning was an economy in which small firms dominated the industrial structure and that this facilitated the transition task. This is typically contrasted with the 'over-industrialized' Soviet economy dominated by large SOEs (Sachs and Woo, 1994). In fact the large-scale state sector was at the center of China's industrial structure under the Maoist system: in 1987 establishments with over 1000 employees occupied 64% of the total value of fixed assets, and produced 48% of the total value of industrial output (SSB, ZGGYJJNTJNJ, 1988 p. 7, 293).

China is vastly larger than any of its East Asian neighbours. This makes it more difficult for the Chinese state to control economic activity as closely as in these countries. It makes the Chinese market and production level potentially vastly more important. Today there are much larger pools of mobile capital than even a decade ago. If a developing country wishes to have access to the markets and capital of the advanced economies, then it must accept greater international regulation of the rules under which its economy operates than was the case for previous late-comers. This applies *a fortiori* to China because of its vast size: its trade surplus with the United States is already larger than Japan's. China's size and the fact that it is still ruled by the communist party mean that it faces much greater possibilities for economic and political issues to be interlinked than was the case for other East Asian countries.

(b) Protecting and Supporting Emerging Big Businesses

The Chinese economy had been isolated from the world economy since the 1940s. In the reform period the Chinese leadership realized that deeper integration with the world economy was essential for modernization. They were acutely aware, however, of the possibility that hasty, unplanned integration could lead to large problems: 'Reforming the economic structure and opening to the outside world is our unswerving principle, but it must be executed with great care so as to ensure success' (Central Committee of the Chinese Communist Party and the State Council, 1985, p. 441). Instead of the 'close' integration[15] recommended by the reform orthodoxy with free trade and free movement of capital, the government's intention was planned, 'strategic' integration.[16] An important component of this was a policy of support for emerging indigenous big business while simultaneously attempting to benefit from capital and technology transfer from multinational companies (MNCs).

(i) Foreign Investment

After cautious growth of foreign direct investment (FDI) in the early 1980s, and a hiatus after the Tiananmen massacre, the pace accelerated remarkably in the early 1990s, with China far and away the most important transition economy destination for FDI. Paradoxically, it was the transition economy with arguably the tightest government control over the conditions under which foreign investors operated, and about which MNCs complained constantly. Still in the mid-1990s, the central government directs large foreign investments in accordance with its plan priorities:

We shall guide the orientation of foreign investment in accordance with the state's industrial policies, directing foreign investment towards infrastructure and basic industry construction, key projects and upgrading technology in existing enterprises, in particular towards projects to increase the export of foreign currency earning projects (Chen Jihua, 1994).

The Chinese government repeatedly used the lure of foreign investment opportunities in China's huge potential market in order to secure technical transfer from multinational companies. A good example of this is the program of technical upgrading at China's two leading power equipment companies, Harbin Power Equipment Company (HPEC) and Shanghai Electrical Company (SEC), which between them account for around 50–60% of the domestic market (Nolan and Wang Xiaoqiang, 1998). Their technical level advanced very fast after 1980. A key part of this was the Fifteen Year (1981–96) Programme for Technical Transfer to the Chinese power equipment industry, organized by the State Council and the Ministry of Machine Building, with the intermediation of the China National Import/Export Corporation, which negotiated the technical transfer program with Combustion Engineering (later ABB) and Westinghouse. The program raised the two domestic firms' unit capability to design and produce thermal power generating sets. During the 1980s the technical transfer program raised the unit production capability at Shanghai from 125 to 300 MW and at HPEC from 200 to 600 MW. The program was a calculated risk for the MNCs. They felt that if they assisted the upgrading of the Chinese power equipment industry, then they might be able to use this as leverage with the Chinese government to gain access to the potentially vast Chinese market.

China's development strategy after 1978 contrasted sharply with that pursued by South Korea and by Japan at comparable phases in their economic growth, when they severely limited direct foreign investment. The Chinese government was confident that it would be able to control the conditions under which foreign investment occurred, and that the economy was so large that no individual foreign investor could exercise a large influence on the state: 'Our socialist economic base is so huge that it can absorb billions of foreign funds without shaking the socialist foundation' (Deng Xiaoping, 1984, p. 5). In the early 1990s the share of China in many MNCs' worldwide total assets, sales and employment was rising rapidly. Moreover, mainland Chinese capital invested in joint ventures was growing fast. At some point China may become a larger market for many of these companies than their nominal 'home' market. Moreover, their ownership structure may become 'Sinicized' as Chinese institutions and individuals increasingly acquire shares in these companies.[17]

(ii) Foreign Trade

China's attitude toward international trade altered radically after Mao's death. In sharp contrast to the prevailing conventional wisdom in the Bretton Woods institutions, China's attitude toward international trade was instrumental: 'In foreign trade our principle is to encourage exports and organise imports according to needs' (*Beijing Review*, 1990, 33(44)).

In the late 1970s, the whole of the Chinese large-scale state sector resembled an 'infant industry'. It was an 'infant' in that it was technically backward, had not yet developed modern managerial skills, was burdened with huge social security obligations, and had not yet progressed from the 'no-firm', command economy structure based on state-commanded *plants* to a multi-plant large firm structure. Nor had the price and material balance system for large upstream SOEs been reformed substantially until the early 1990s. Under these circumstances, China's large enterprises could not possibly compete on a 'level playing field' with the world's leading MNCs. From the late 1970s to the mid-1990s, the Chinese government maintained a battery of protective measures.

The government employed a wide array of quantitative import restrictions. High tariffs were maintained right through until the mid 1990s. Despite some decline in the early 1990s as China attempted to gain access to the General Agreement for Tariffs and Trade (GATT), in 1995 the simple average tariff on China's imports still stood at 36%. In addition, China adopted such non-tariff barriers (NTBs) as requiring rigorous inspection procedures for selected imports. Government procurement policy, especially for infrastructure investment, also constituted an important form of protection for emerging indigenous large businesses. For example, in the power equipment sector until the mid 1990s, most new large power plants were funded directly by the central government, and all these contracts were awarded automatically to one of the three leading domestic producers.

In the mid 1990s the situation began apparently to change, as China sought to gain admission to the World Trade Organisation (WTO), and as pressure for reduced protection increased from the United States especially due to the large size of its trade deficit with China. In 1996 the government agreed to a larger eduction in tariffs, the simple average falling to 23%. Moreover, in 1994, China and the United States signed a Memorandum of Understanding (MOU) in which China committed itself to phase out import licensing by 1997 (Dickson, 1996, p. 8). But, the overall impact of these changes on the degree of protection for China's large firms is unclear.

In the case of the steel industry, although the simple average tariff on imported iron and steel had fallen to just 9.1% in 1996, and the licensing system was ended, powerful new non-tariff barriers were erected in the mid 1990s (Dickson, 1996, p. 23). These included import 'registration', which could be withheld if there was felt to be a 'market need', and 'canalisation' of steel imports through selected state importing companies (Dickson, 1996, pp. 98–9). China's barriers to steel imports have been 'strengthened and reformulated' since 1993, despite apparent liberalization (Dickson, 1996, p. 22):

Very strong national aspirations exist in China for the development of domestic, import-substituting industries, iron and steel being no exception. China's steel industry, despite being a behemoth, is still an *infant industry*. Instead of binding quota constraints, China seems to have designed a system which is discretionary in nature. The government gives itself the administrative leeway to impose control if necessary, for example, where 'market disruption' is perceived. *The threshold for 'disruption' would be anything threatening the viability of domestic iron and steel enterprises, so essentially the motivation is protection of industry* (Dickson, 1996, pp. 21–2).

(c) Redrawing the Boundaries between the State and the Non-state Sector: 'Grasp the Large, Let Go of the Small'

(i) Size Structure

During the reform period, the government began gradually to 'give up' the myriad of small SOEs, contracting them out, leasing or selling them, and, increasingly, allowing them to go bankrupt (Project Group, 1996, pp. 18–19). Individually run small businesses were allowed freely to start up. In 'socialist China' in the mid-1990s, 99% of total industrial enterprises were *not* owned by the state, and 78% of the total number of industrial enterprises were owned by 'real flesh-and-blood persons' (SSB, 1983, ZGTJNJ, p. 207 and 1994, p. 373). During the reforms the share of industrial output produced by SOEs plummeted from 78% (GVIO, at current prices) in 1978 to 48% in 1992 (SSB, 1993 ZGTJNJ, p. 412). In 'capitalist' Taiwan in 1952, public corporations accounted for 56% of total industrial output (Amsden, 1979, p. 367). SOEs, which once dominated the centrally planned economy had been slowly turned into 'islands in a sea of thriving and dynamic non-state enterprises' (Singh and Jefferson, 1993, p. 10).

Within the state sector the central government increasingly focused its planning efforts on the relatively small number of large firms. Its policy was: 'grasp the large and let go of the small (*zhua da, fang xiao*) … The dominant role of the state-owned enterprises should be brought into play mainly through … the large and super-large enterprises' (Project Group, 1996, pp. 16–17). The share of small scale SOEs in total industrial output value collapsed from around 36% in 1980 to less than 10% in the early 1990s.[18] But large SOEs actually *raised* their share of total industrial output from 25% in 1980 to over 28% in 1991 (GVIO at current prices); (SSB, CEY, 1981, p. 212) and (SSB, 1992, ZGTJZY, p. 70). Within the 'formal' sector (i.e. township level and above), their share of industrial output value rose from around one-quarter in 1980 to over 38% in the mid 1990s.[19] Within the state sector, large SOEs almost doubled their share of gross output value from 32% in 1980 to 60% in 1994 (SSB, ZGTJNJ, 1986, p. 276, and 1995, pp. 392–3)[20] and in the mid 1990s, the 500 largest enterprises accounted for 37% of total assets, 46% of sales value and 63% of total profits (Project Group, 1996, p. 17). Around three-fifths of the top 500 enterprises were in six, mainly heavy, industrial sectors,[21] following the familiar pattern observed by Chandler (1990) in the advanced capitalist economies.

(ii) Sectoral Structure

The state increasingly focused upon activities which could not be fulfilled by other ownership forms. These included natural monopolies; industries related to energy resources and basic raw materials, including the exploitation and processing of petroleum and natural gas, and the production of iron and steel, non-ferrous metals and basic raw materials; 'pillar' industries that play a leading role in the national economy, such as the petrochemical and heavy machinery industries, electricity generating equipment, automobiles and construction; and industries 'playing an important role in national defence and national strength', including defence, space and atomic energy, as well as other industries related to high and new technology (Project Group, 1996, pp. 16–17). State industry increasingly concentrated on large-scale 'upstream' activities, with a sharply declining share of output originating in 'downstream' activities such as printing, furniture, wood and straw products, leather products, plastic products, food products, metal products, building materials and drink.

During 1978–92 light industrial growth (real GVIO) accelerated to almost 15% per annum (SSB, ZGTJNJ, 1993 p. 58). In China's highly protected economy such growth required simultaneous rapid growth of output from 'upstream' heavy industry (Table 5.1): during 1978–92 the real average annual growth rate of GVIO in heavy industry was almost 11% (SSB, ZGTJNJ, 1993 p. 58). SOEs were hugely dominant in these sectors. During 1978–94 China's place in the world's ranking in coal output rose from third to first, in steel it rose from fifth to second, in electricity from seventh to fourth, in cement from fourth to first, in chemical fertilizer from third to second, and in chemical fibers from seventh to second (SSB, ZGTJNJ, 1995, p. 779). Heavy industrial products typically require much larger amounts of capital per unit of output, need larger plant sizes, rely much more on technical skills than pure entrepreneurship (e.g., marketing, product choice, skills in distribution), and have much longer gestation periods than does light industry. In the uncertain environment of a transitional economy, it was essential that the state played a central role in the expansion of these sectors. The inter-sectoral relationship shifted from unbalanced heavy industry growth to a balanced growth path, rather than to light industry emphasis to the neglect of heavy industry.[22]

(iii) Distribution of Profit and Loss-makers

It is widely thought that the Chinese SOEs have 'specialized' in loss-making enterprises. Indeed, officially reported SOE losses rose from 5.3% of total

Table 5.1 **Output of Selected Heavy Industrial Products in China**

Item	Unit	1980	1994
Chemical fibres	m. tons	0.45	2.80
Plastics	m. tons	0.90	4.01
Mining equipment	'000 tons	160	480
Petroleum equipment	'000 tons	60	190
Chemical industry equipment	'000 tons	70	292
Power generating equipment	m. kwh	4.19	16.74
Computer numerically controlled (CNC) machine tools	number	1613 (1984)	6223
Internal combustion engines	m. h.p.	25.4	165.5
Crude steel	m. tons	37.1	92.6
Cement	m. tons	79.9	308.2
Plate glass	m. standard cases	27.7	119.3
Sulphuric acid	m. tons	7.6	15.4
Coal	m. tons	620	1240
Electric power	billion kwh	301	928

Sources: SSB, ZGTJNJ (1995), section 12 (1986): section 15, and SSB, CEY (1981): section IV.

SOE pre-tax profits in 1978 to 23.2% in 1990 (SSB, ZGTJNJ, 1995, p. 403), and the government subsidy to loss-makers in 1991 reached 17% of total government expenditure (SSB, ZGTJNJ, 1991 pp. 408, 209, 212). The following considerations, however, need to be kept in mind.

First, as state industry became increasingly oriented toward the 'upstream' sectors, so it became increasingly liable to the impact of the 'accelerator' principle, namely, fluctuations in demand for capital goods changes disproportionately with demand for 'downstream' products. SOE losses fell from 23% of total SOE pre-tax profits in 1990 to 17% in 1994 (SSB, ZGTJNJ, 1995, p. 403). Second, many SOEs 'cut away' the most profitable segments of the business and put them into a joint venture, leaving behind the weakest workers and the oldest equipment. Third, large SOEs are rarely loss-makers: in 1992 just 42 of the top 500 enterprises reported losses (Development Research Centre, 1993, pp. 2–11). Large SOEs have a profit rate two or three times as large as for smaller-scale enterprises (Table 5.2). It was the huge number of small and medium state enterprises, frequently producing down-

Table 5.2 **Pre-tax Profits in Chinese SOEs for Different Enterprise Sizes, 1994**

Size class of SOE	No. of enterprises	Share of total SOE GVIO (%)	Share of total SOE value-added (%)	Share of total SOE pre-tax profits (%)	Pre-tax profits as a % of size class's GVIO
Large	4,009	59.5	63.6	75.9	14.5
Medium	10,508	21.9	19.3	15.0	7.8
Small	65,214	18.6	17.1	9.1	5.6
Total	79,731	100.0	100.0	100.0	–

Source: SSB, ZGTJNJ (1995), 392–5

stream products, that mainly bore the brunt of the impact of competition from the non-state sector, rather than the large-scale upstream sector, which typically produced goods that were beyond the technical capability of the TVEs.

Fourth, a large share of SOE losses is concentrated in a small number of sectors (SSB, 1991 ZGTJNJ, pp. 394–417). In 1990 machinery and textiles, third and fourth largest SOE loss-makers respectively in absolute terms, accounted for 18% of total SOE losses. Their prices were almost completely liberalized by the early 1990s. In these sectors small and medium-sized SOEs faced severe competition from TVEs, and were the main cause of SOE loss-making in these sectors. The only sectors in which there were substantial reported losses across all SOE enterprise sizes were coal, and the petroleum and natural gas extraction industries, which accounted for over 34% of total SOE losses in 1990. In 1992 no less than 32 of the 42 loss-makers among the top 500 enterprises were in these two sectors (Development Research Centre, 1993 pp. 2–11). A main reason for such widespread losses was the fact that their output, distribution and prices still were substantially controlled by the state even in the mid-1990s.

Fifth, loss-making is not always inimical to economic development (Chang and Singh, 1993). We have seen that the main loss-making industries are upstream ones, of which those in the fuel sector are the most important. These provide cheap inputs for other profit-making industries. For example, steel uses a huge amount of cheap coal and electricity. Rail transport and electricity production, both of which in turn provide subsidized inputs for other sectors, each relies heavily on coal.[23]

Sixth, SOEs are not unique in making losses. In 1993, around 40–50% of joint ventures in China were reported to be loss-makers (RGCER, 1994, p. 23), compared to around 30% for state enterprises (SSB, 1994, ZGTJNJ, p. 85). There were, however, several differences between SOE and joint venture loss-makers. Large SOEs bear a high tax burden, with profit tax and other levies taking 50–75% of an enterprise's net earnings (Gescher, 1990). In 1993 the tax burden of large SOEs was more than twice that of joint ventures. Moreover, as we have noted, the state sector supplies underpriced industrial inputs to the rest of the economy (Wang, 1993; Koo et al., 1993). Moreover, large SOEs bear heavy social responsibilities, in terms of pensions, housing, education and medical care (Perkins, 1988; Minami, 1994).[24]

(d) Managerial Autonomy

China's large SOEs have not been viewed by the Chinese government as objects to be closed down, but, rather, as institutions with 'great strength and potential' (Project Group, 1996, p. 6), whose performance can be improved with careful, experimental reform. The central focus of reform of large SOEs has been to grope toward ways of enlarging managerial autonomy, in other words toward the 'separation of ownership from control', a concept which preoccupied Chinese discussion of large SOE reform.

(i) Decline of the Material Supply System

Over the course of the reform years, the central authorities engineered a gradual decline in resource allocation through the material balance planning system: by 1989, around two-thirds of SOEs' output was through the market (Jefferson and Rawski, 1994, p. 51). In the early 1990s this process accelerated, with just 7% of total industrial output value directly controlled by planners in 1993 (Jefferson and Rawski, 1994, p. 63). Large-scale upstream industry was the slowest to be liberalized, but even for these enterprises, by the mid-1990s, allocation and prices had been substantially liberalized.

By the mid-1990s, even in the largest of upstream industries, managers decided all key issues. They needed to co-ordinate input supplies through the market. They were forced to evaluate the capability of different suppliers and had to learn to bargain about price and delivery. They had to decide the product mix and product price. They had to compete for markets. Accountancy and marketing departments grew rapidly. In large SOEs producing complex engineering products such as power equipment, product reliability and after-sales service became significant elements in inter-firm competition.

(ii) Contract Responsibility System

The contract system was experimented with from the late 1970s, and became generalized in the mid-1980s, with innumerable local variations (Byrd, 1992; Gao, 1996). Enterprises were required to hand over agreed amounts of profits and taxes to the state, in return for which the management was given extensive autonomy and significant responsibility for raising investment funds from retained profits, bank loans and, eventually, other sources (e.g., joint ventures, stock market flotations, bonds). By the late 1980s, over two-fifths of fixed investment undertaken by state enterprises was financed from enterprises' 'self-raised funds'.

The contract system established a strong link between the performance of the firm and the prosperity of the local government or other 'principal' to which the 'hand-overs' were made, either in whole or in part. A substantial share of contracted profit and tax 'hand-overs', even for large SOEs, typically were handed over to the local authorities. In some cases the main principal could be more distant from the SOE,[25] though even these firms must typically make tax payments to the local authorities. For example, under the contract system, Shougang accounted for around one-half of the 'hand-overs' of industrial sector profits to the Beijing government, and around one-third of 1% of Beijing's total budgetary revenue (Nolan, 1995, p. 9). Even in the most unlikely parts of the Chinese state bureaucracy, the contract system produced large changes in behavior. For example, China's leading pharmaceutical firm, Sanjiu in Shenzhen, grew from nothing in 1987 into a powerful business, among China's top 100 firms by value of sales by 1992, while 100% owned by the General Logistics Department (GLD) of the People's Liberation Army (PLA). The GLD in Beijing allowed the dynamic management team a high degree of autonomy in return for a contracted share of the profits (Xiaoqiang, 1998).

The 'contract responsibility system' turned large SOEs toward profit (Perkins, 1988; Jefferson and Rawski, 1994). It established a strong link between profits and both retained earnings and capacity expansion (Jefferson and Rawski, 1994, pp. 52–5). Simultaneously, there was 'a considerable reduction' in the softness of the budget constraint (Jefferson and Rawski, 1994, p. 52). Workers at poorly-performing SOEs faced an increasing prospect of low wage growth, deterioration of bonuses, erosion of health benefits, layoffs, compulsory transfers to ancillary units, and recently, even dismissal (Jefferson and Rawski, 1994). Moreover, in the 1990s some large SOEs began to downsize. In 1992, China's coal industry cut its total employment by 4% (Jefferson and Rawski, 1994, p. 62). Large SOEs began transferring redundant workers to newly established service companies, which over time may attenuate their connection with the parent company.

Many fast-growing and fast-modernizing large SOEs emerged under the contract system, with strong managers allowing a high degree of autonomy in return for fulfilment of the contracted 'hand-overs' (Byrd, 1992; Nolan, 1995). For example, at Shougang, Zhou Guanwu led a massive expansion and modernization drive designed to thrust the firm into the number one slot in China's booming steel industry (see above) (Nolan, 1995). Under his 'military-style' leadership Shougang made large purchases of low-price second-hand equipment from Europe and the United States. It bought Mesta (Pittsburgh), one of the world's leading steel technology firms, and rapidly advanced the firms' automatic control capabilities.

In one variant or another, the contract system was the dominant form of relationship between large SOEs and their administrative superiors until at least the mid-1990s. It was technically ended in 1994. The goal was to replace it with a system of joint-stock companies (see below) with 'hand-overs' decided by a combination of dividends from share ownership and a new structure of corporation tax and value-added tax. In practice, there were substantial continuities, with negotiation of both sorts of 'hand-overs' between 'principal' and 'agent'. Moreover, for some key large SOEs, such as in the iron and steel industry, a form of contracting did survive *de jure*. This group of enterprises was not permitted to diversify its ownership, but remained wholly state owned firms', still handing over an agreed share of profits and taxes to higher authorities. For this category of firm, the reforms of the operating system under way in the mid-1990s continued to focus on the provision of greater autonomy for managers with clear identification of the assets for which they were responsible. But the core firm within such large SOEs, as an independent 'legal person', was permitted to wholly own subsidiary enterprises, invest in other enterprises as well as to diversify into joint ventures with both foreign and other domestic institutions.[26] It thereby participated in the complex process of 'ownership diversification' (see below).

(iii) The Joint-stock Company Again

As early as 1985, Wood argued for the need to 'rearrange the pattern of state ownership rights ...' Instead of having particular enterprises belonging to particular ministries or local governments, the ownership of each enterprise would be spread among several different public institutions interested mainly in its profits (1994, p. 28; also see World Bank, 1985).

By the mid-1990s, in China, the joint-stock company had once more become a powerful weapon to transcend the limits of the previous form of ownership and operation, in this case the government as the sole owner and operator of SOEs.

The introduction of this form of ownership was welcomed by SOEs, partly because of the flexibility provided by the corporate shareholding structure, but more importantly because it gave a separate identity to the secured corporation: 'The board of directors and shareholders could cushion the enterprise against government intervention, which has always been the biggest problem of state-owned firms' (Hu Yebi, 1993, p. 11).

Foreign direct investment   The joint venture, by introducing foreign investors, signalled the start of ownership reform. By 1993 there were over 20,000 foreign-invested industrial firms with 2.9 million employees, which produced over 9% of total industrial output (SSB, ZGTJNJ, 1994; pp. 98, 378). Most of these were small-value joint ventures with downstream firms. A smaller number, however, were large investments with large SOEs, the main purpose of which, from the Chinese side, was to assist large-scale technology transfer, and from the side of the joint venture partner, was to gain access to China's booming market. The Chinese government specified that 'when large and extra-large enterprises are transformed into Sino-foreign joint-stock companies, the stock rights on the Chinese side must be above 50%' (Project Group, 1996, 11, 12–13). The following are some leading examples of joint ventures with large SOEs:

– *Iron and steel*. By 1994 Shougang Iron and Steel Corporation, China's second largest steel producer, had established 39 Sino-Foreign joint ventures (Nolan, 1995). One of the most important of these was with NEC (Japan), with a total investment of over $300 million by 1996. This new business quickly became the largest manufacturer of semiconductors in China, and was the only one to manufacture value-added semiconductors, as opposed to mere assembly (*Financial Times*, January 24, 1996). A major goal was to assist technology transfer so that Shougang could enter 'downstream' production of such products as computers, faxmachines, video recorders, TVs and video cameras using the products of the joint venture (Nolan, 1995).

– *Petrochemicals*. In the petrochemical industry there were many small-scale joint ventures, but in 1996 two large scale joint venture investments to construct ethylene crackers (each of which was around 600,000 tons) were announced (*Financial Times*, October 22, 1996): one was for $2.5 billion, between Shanghai Petrochemical Company, China's largest petrochemical producer, and BP; the other was between BASF and Nanjing Petrochemical Corporation.

– *Power equipment manufacture.* Two of the three largest power equipment manufacturers in China either have, or are negotiating, major joint ventures with multinational partners. SEC has a joint venture with Westinghouse[27] and Dongfang (Sichuan) is negotiating one joint venture between its hydro generator plant and GE (Canada), and another between its thermal generator plant and Siemens (Germany). In each case, the Chinese partner is contributing all its productive assets (70% of the share value of the new joint venture) and the foreign partner injected cash to purchase a 30% ownership share.

International flotation   Beginning in 1993, the Chinese government allowed selected large SOEs to issue shares on 'foreign' stock markets, the vast majority of which were in Hong Kong, and a small number in New York. By 1995 there were 17 on the Hong Kong market alone, with more planned for 1996. The companies allowed to list abroad are mostly at the forefront in terms of performance and prospects, and mainly from key upstream sectors, including firms from the petrochemical (there were five from this sector alone), power generation equipment, iron and steel, glass, heavy machinery and shipbuilding sectors. Prior to their flotation on the foreign markets these companies went through a thorough process of institutional restructuring. In each case, the original SOE separate off the social service component from the main company, to which fees were to be paid, and established a new joint stock company, in which the original SOE was a majority shareholder, with a minority share-ownership floated abroad. The main purchasers of the shares in these flotations were institutions (e.g., in 1995, three Hong Kong institutions held 69% of the shares in Harbin Power Equipment Company traded in Hong Kong). The flotation provided an important source of capital. At least as important, it helped greatly to promote the idea of the joint stock company as a suitable path for large SOEs to follow.

The plan for joint stock companies   In 1994, the government unveiled a plan to transform SOEs, other than those 'producing special products and military industrial enterprises', into joint-stock companies with managerial independence from government control. The majority of large and medium-sized SOEs were to become limited liability companies (Project Group, 1996, p. 12). Consistent with the policy of 'grasping the big and letting go of the small', after the reorganization of large and medium-sized SOEs, the state intends through state holding companies to maintain a controlling share ownership in the 'pillar industries' and 'key enterprises in the basic industries'. As for general enterprises where non state-owned capital will be absorbed as much as possible, the state will have equity participation, not a controlling interest (Project Group, 1996, p. 12).

One hundred large SOEs were selected as the first batch formally to put into practice the 'modern enterprise system' with joint-stock companies as the basis.[28] Behind each of the emerging large joint-stock SOEs lay a multiplicity of institutions, large and small, each of which had an interest in the firm's performance, mainly, but not exclusively, attributable to their share in the firm's ownership. These might include:

— the local authority who benefited from dividend payments to the state holding company and tax handovers, as well as from the income and employment generated by the firm;

— the relevant central ministry or quasi-ministerial body (e.g., Sinopec) which benefited from either the forwarding of some portion of the contracted profit payment or from the direct handover of contracted profits;

— other domestic institutional shareholders, including giant, quasi-governmental investment institutions, such as CITIC or Everbright Holdings, as well as smaller ones, such as other local authorities;

— a foreign joint venture partner, which benefited from the dividend payments from the joint venture;

— foreign shareholders (mainly institutions) which received dividend payments.

This was a potentially powerful network of institutions, each of which had some common interest in promoting the firm's performance, none of which had the interest or capability to run it directly, all of which perceived that their best interest was served by having a strong management team running the firm. The joint-stock company route to property rights transformation is highly flexible: 'There could be any desired mix of public and private ownership, including ownership by various kinds of financial intermediaries. The mixture could also be quite easily changed in the light of experience and the development of China's financial sector' (Wood, 1994, p. 39).[29]

(iv) From State Factories to Large Multi-plant Firms

The emergence of the multi-plant firm formed another avenue for the development of independence of managers relative to state owners.

Enterprise groups Support for the idea of industrial groups became a central plank of government policy for enterprise reform. The concept helped to legitimate a widespread process of expansion of large SOEs into multi-plant firms, in which the core firm was 'connected through capital' with a network of smaller firms. At the center of most of them was a large SOE 'core company'. A typical large SOE by the mid-1990s would have investments in numerous 'second tier' companies, mainly supplier firms, sometimes owning a controlling interest, often a minority interest. The core firm typically had an incentive to upgrade the technology and control the quality of supplies from 'second tier' companies. It typically appointed the managers of the subsidiary company, reorganized their production structure, might shift workers and equipment to other locations, and set contract targets for profits to be achieved and for 'handovers' to the core firm.

For example, Dongfeng Automobile Group was based at the former giant No.2 Automobile Plant in Hubei Province. By the early 1980s it had expanded to include around 300 smaller automobile plants. The constituent plants reoriented production under the guidance of the parent company, which was also the conduit for channelling new technology. They were re-specialized into a variety of processes, such as assembly, special purpose car production and the production of specialized inputs (Yao Jianguo, 1992). In 1978 Shougang was a traditional large SOE at a single site in Beijing with around 110,000 employees. By the early 1990s it had expanded into a huge multi-plant firm, with around 160 'second tier' companies and a total of around 280,000 employees. Sanjiu Enterprise Group only began production in 1987, established by the Guangzhou branch of the GLD (see above). By the early 1990s it had become a large multi-plant pharmaceutical producer. In addition, however, it had around 100 'second tier' companies, including China's largest hotel chain (operating over 30 hotels), a construction company that employed several tens of thousands of laborers, and several large food and drink plants across China.

Mergers and acquisitions   A large process of mergers and acquisitions developed in China during the transitional process, in the absence of privatiz-ation and a developed stock market, but typically with the state acting as the mediator. There were three main channels through which this occurred.

First, it was due to the state requiring large SOEs to absorb and reorganize loss-making enterprises, change their management methods and advance their technology. To this extent it was a 'top-down' process. A leading ex-ample of this was the merger of Shougang in 1988 with 13 large loss-making military enterprises, employing around 60,000 workers. These were mainly remote, inland 'Third Front' enterprises, with little prospect of turning their position around on their own. Loss-making enterprises with which Shougang merged were given strict performance targets. If they failed to meet these tar-gets, they could be returned to their original administrative authority and cast out of the Shougang system.

Second, mergers were due to 'bottom-up' pressure from a successful, emerging large firm. The initiative for such mergers often came from the more powerful firm, but it always required state mediation and sanction. An important element in the merger movement in China was the acquisition by strong, fast-growing firms of weaker, loss-making firms. Frequently, the superior authority of loss-making firms sought out more powerful firms in order to initiate a takeover, in the hope that they would be relieved of the burden of the loss-making enterprise. The taking-over firm typically participated in the takeover in the belief that under new management, 'hidden value' might be 'dug out' by the taking-over company. This concept is used routinely by taking-over firms in China to describe the economic logic behind their takeover.

A typical large-scale administrative merger undertaken by the initiative of a powerful firm was the takeover by Shougang in 1983 of 17 large steel local works, with around 30,000 employees. The merger enabled Shougang to gain access to the more profitable 'downstream' segments of steel production in which these firms specialized (Nolan, 1995). The enterprises being taken over were transferred to Shougang at a stroke.

A large number of 'mergers' were essentially 'takeovers' involving careful calculation of the prospects for turning around the performance of the firm being taken over, with tough insistence on the conditions necessary to bring about this goal. A typical example of this is the takeover in 1995 by the Sanjiu Group (see above) of the Shijiazhuang Beer Factory (Hebei). This was one of many takeovers undertaken by Sanjiu in its rise to a powerful position in pharmaceuticals and allied industries. The Shijiazhuang Beer Factory had around 2,000–3,000 employees. This loss-making firm was administered by the local City government. In the takeover deal Sanjiu was assigned an option to take a 51% controlling share ownership in the firm, in recognition of Sanjiu's good image, marketing network, trademark and capital that it would inject into the business. Sanjiu took a five-year contract on the business. If, at the end of the five year period, the firm was making sufficiently large profits, Sanjiu could exercise the right to purchase the shares that had been reserved for this purpose, and could become the majority owner of the business. Sanjiu was given a high degree of autonomy in management. In the case of the Shijiazhuang plant, as in other Sanjiu takeovers, the company head was appointed by Sanjiu headquarters. In this case Sanjiu advertised for an expert in the beer industry and replaced the existing manager. Sanjiu cannot simply dismiss 'surplus' workers. It developed the idea of providing surplus workers with the incentive of a lump-sum severance payment. A condition of receiving this was that the worker concerned had to sign a contract formally severing his connection with the factory, though this did not necessarily mean he would forfeit his right to company housing or a pension: 'in all things in China one has to go carefully'.

Third, the merger movement is due to opportunism by large SOEs. They use their bargaining power with local governments to enhance the number of firms owned by them, in order to be able to increase the size of their business empire as property rights became more formalized and ownership became more tangible. To some degree,[30] this can be seen as a 'positioning' process, in anticipation of a possible future move toward more concrete private property rights being permitted over former SOEs. Through merger, a large state firm can acquire potential future assets of great value, including the land on which the firm is located. In principle, a merger between two SOEs today could bring considerable personal gain for employees at some future point.

Merger may be an especially powerful process of advancing business capabilities in a transitional economy, since business and technical skills are not so widely available as in an advanced economy. The merger process, led by capable firms with advanced technological and management skills, can have a powerful positive externality effect, spreading business capability more rapidly than would be the case in the absence of merger. Moreover, the pressure for mergers is reinforced in a poor transitional economy such as China. This provides especially large incentives for merger consequent upon the undeveloped state of market institutions, which inhibits the capacity to obtain needed inputs easily and reliably through contracts mediated by the market mechanism.

(v) Privatization or Pluralized Institutional Ownership?

Is China's reform of large SOEs essentially a process of privatization? In fact, as ownership reform went progressively deeper, it could not be said that the main direction was a change from public to private ownership. Only a tiny fraction of ownership rights of large firms in China was in the hands of individuals. It was also hard to see that the newly diversified owners were, indeed, controlling management. Ownership reform in China was altering the role of the government as the sole owner and operator of enterprises. Diversification did not enhance the power of owners, but, rather, augmented managerial autonomy. In terms of Kornai's theory of 'turning back the reel to the beginning', ownership reform in China failed to turn the reel back very far. Indeed, China's newly diversified ownership structures in large SOEs hardly even began to 'turn back' in the direction of 'real flesh-and-blood persons'. Indeed, from the point of view of property rights, the ownership reforms in large SOEs, as in TVEs, were producing a 'vaguely defined ownership maze' (Singh and Jefferson, 1993, p. 9). By contrast, from the perspective of managerial autonomy, the picture became gradually clearer. As ownership reform went deeper in large SOEs, they evolved progressively from state-administered plants toward pluralized institutional ownership and *de facto* management control.

The ownership of each of China's large SOEs has spread gradually among a variety of public institutions, each of which has an interest in the firm's performance. This has led bureaucrats to have a vested interest in assisting the firms to do business more effectively. This phenomenon has been most studied and is most transparently visible at the local level, especially in the operation of the TVEs: 'Local officials have assumed new roles as entrepreneurs, selectively allocating scarce resources to shape patterns of local economic growth ... In the process local governments have taken on many characteristics of a business corporation, with officials acting as the equivalent of a board of directors' (Oi, 1992, p. 124).[31] This phenomenon can be seen also, however, in the behavior of municipal officials, under whose tutelage there often are large SOEs upon whom the city's prosperity more or less substantially depends, both in terms of direct revenue and indirect benefits that prosperous large firms brings (ask Atlanta, Seattle, Pittsburgh or Detroit): Yulin City's future is intimately bound up with the performance of Yuchai Diesel Engine Company; the future of Harbin, 'City power of equipment generation', is intimately related to the performance of HPEC;[32] Beijing's future is linked closely with that of Shougang, and Shanghai's is linked closely with that of SPC.

Even at the national level, however, there are strong bureaucratic interests in the performance of large SOEs under the tutelage of the central ministries or quasi-ministerial bodies, such as Sinopec, which are increasingly sharing the ownership rights of large SOEs with other institutions. These institutions bargain with multinationals for technical transfer, attempt to attract large-scale investment away from contending Third World locations, and lobby the central authorities to protect 'their' firms from unsustainable international competition. The different institutions which own the large SOEs share a common interest in having the firms run by effective managers. Neither the term 'developmental state' nor 'entrepreneurial state' is adequate to capture the complex web of interests that now connect government and emerging big businesses in China. Whatever the name one chooses to give it, it is clear that a new institutional form is being born.

Based on the 'ownership maze' and vaguely defined property rights, the powerful growth of China's large-scale upstream SOEs has already lasted for 16 years and seems set to continue. This growth has shown that 'there is no inherent reason why secure property rights will be an effective incentive only if they are assigned to individuals' (Oi, 1992, p. 100). China's bureaucrats have no individual ownership stake in China's large firms. It is the bureaucrats, however, who are restructuring state industry, withdrawing the state from downstream areas of competitive light and processing industries, concentrating instead on upstream areas of natural monopolies and capital intensive industries. It is the bureaucrats who are restructuring SOEs, by allowing small SOEs to shrink, and expanding large SOEs' autonomy through careful, persistent, institutional experimentation. It is bureaucrats at both the local and national level who mobilize resources that the market would be unable to organize, such as technical transfer from multinational firms. A principal reason why China's large SOEs have grown so powerfully is that the bureaucrats have been so active in the areas where China's emerging big businesses need help.

(e) A Level Playing Field? How Big is Chinese 'Big Business'?

We have seen that during China's reforms a powerful group of large SOEs emerged which are gradually becoming genuinely autonomous competitive firms. The 'merger' boom has involved large SOEs 'merging' with small ones, or small ones merging among themselves. But, up to the time of writing (early 1997) *not one merger of a large SOE with another has occurred*. The local authorities jealously protect their right to the stream of revenue from 'their' large SOE. The increasingly autonomous large SOEs are jealous of their hard-won independence from the state. Nor does it appear that the Chinese government has given much thought to the possibility of merging one large enterprise with another to create firms that can challenge the world's largest. Therefore, in the mid-1990s, despite large changes in their behavior, with powerful growth and modernization, even the largest of China's large SOEs was still small compared to the global giants in all aspects other than employment.

For example, despite large changes in its operational methods and its growth in size, in 1996 HPEC was still far from being able to compete directly with the leading multinational power equipment makers. It remained very small indeed compared to the giants of world power equipment generation (Table 5.3). If the Chinese 'playing field' in the power equipment market were made truly 'level', the competitors standing on the field would be of grotesquely unequal size.

HPEC cannot compete with the multinationals in new technology. It has mainly to concentrate on catching up through acquiring existing technology from the world's leading multinational firms. How can this be done? HPEC cannot afford to purchase the technology. It has, therefore, to be acquired through some form of co-operation with the multinational giants in the industry. A major advantage for Chinese power equipment firms is that the potential market is so huge that they can bargain for excellent terms for technical

Table 5.3 Size of HPEC and Leading Firms in the World's Power Equipment Industry, 1995

	Employees ('000)	Turnover (m.$)	Assets (m.$)	Profits (m. $)	R and D (m.$)
HPEC	27,000	310	898	14	3
General Electric	216,000	59,316	252,000 ('93)	5,915	1,280
of which: Power Division	25,000 ('94)	5,900 ('94)	–	1,200 ('94)	–
Westinghouse	84,400	8,848	10,398 ('92)	77	–
of which: Power Division	–	3,000	–	–	–
GEC Alsthom	–	11,108	–	–	444
of which: Power Division	–	4,000	–	–	–
Siemens	393,900	57,948	58,400 ('94)	1,445	5,008
ABB	207,557	29,718	24,900 ('94)	1,447	2,589
of which: Power Division	–	–	–	870	

Sources: HPEC (1995), *Financial Times*, January 1, 1996; June 27, 1996; May 15, 1996, UNCTD (1995), 20–21, AND DRC (1993), 478–479.

transfer. Moreover, the leading international firms in the power equipment sector are intensely competitive. Thus a bargaining agency in China would be in a strong position to play one leading firm off against the other. Moreover, this possibility is increased by the close identification of these huge firms with a given country (or two in the case of ABB and GEC-Alsthom). This makes it possible to involve closely the government of that country (or countries in the case of ABB and GEC-Alsthom) in the negotiation and bargaining process.

There is a danger that, in their fight with each other, the increasingly autonomous Chinese firms may be prepared to improve their own firm's short-term position through joint ventures that do not extract the maximum possible technical transfer from the multinationals. This may leave them in the position of dependent subcontractors for the multinational firm, but technically a 'domestic firm' as far as the supply of equipment is concerned, even though the technology is mainly developed elsewhere. Large Chinese SOEs may then find that having struggled to gain autonomy from the Chinese state, they give it up to multinational firms.

In the mid 1990s HPEC was at a crossroads. It had made the 'first jump' from a state-administered plant to a relatively autonomous competitive firm, with diversified institutional ownership. It had developed institutional and technical capabilities that could form the basis for a further development to challenge the existing multinationals and themselves join the ranks of the leading world producers. Moreover, there was a huge domestic demand potential that could underpin this effort. The Chinese domestic power equipment market is the fastest growing and potentially the world's largest. In order to capitalize on the large gains so far made in the Chinese power equipment industry and to enable HPEC to make the 'second jump' to a firm that is truly competitive with the giants of the world's leading power equipment manufacturers, it is necessary that important interventions are by the state. The technical and institutional gap is still too large for the leeway to be made up under free competition in capital and product markets. Just as the leading firms of the advanced capitalist economies were strongly supported in their formation by their respective national governments, so too at this critical juncture, if China wishes to build up firms of comparable size, considerable state intervention is required. To some degree this requires a continuation of policy, such as in the allocation of procurement contracts. In some other respects, however, such as merging the leading firms and coordinating the bargaining with leading international firms in order to secure technical transfer, it requires much more extensive state action.

(f) Government Reform is Another Core

China's 'bloated' bureaucracy grew even more 'bloated' during the reform period: the numbers of full-time government and Party employees rose from 4.7 million in 1978 to 10.3 million in 1994 (SSB, ZGTJNJ, 1995: Table 4.3),[33] while the total number of Party members grew from 35 million in the mid 1970s to over 50 million in the early 1990s.

In 1994, China's courts convicted over 20,000 people of corruption, including a Vice Minister, 28 bureau directors and 202 branch directors (*Beijing Review*, March 27–April 2, 1995, p. 6). The level of high corruption makes China's future both economically and politically uncertain. Even collapse of the Communist regime cannot be ruled out.

Ownership reform in China goes steadily deeper. But the 'ownership maze' leaves a huge space for the state to intervene. Formerly, the state was giving commands to state firms. Today, the newly autonomous large SOEs need a variety of state interventions to help them to grow and compete on the world stage. In this situation it is essential that enterprise reform is combined with the reform of the state itself.

In the 1980s almost all experts considered that China's leadership was irredeemably 'hardline' in its opposition to fundamental system reform, its interests irreconcilable with the market economy. Its members were thought to be incapable of turning toward the market and competitive behavior. The evidence from the reform years shows that contrary to this view, the CCP and the PLA possessed a rich legacy of organizational and motivational skills. Even old Party cadres and army officers were able to make the transition to the market economy given the correct incentive structure. Indeed, their lifetime experience of thinking strategically and mobilizing people in complex institutions was an invaluable weapon for the construction of an effective market-oriented business organization. Many of them were to lead the modernization of China's prominent SOEs during these years.[34] Moreover, the Cultural Revolution generation of Party members, steeled by the complexity and ferocity of that struggle, often also proved highly effective heads of fast-growing large SOEs.[35]

After 16 years of reforms and growth, the Chinese government has not only transformed the economic structure. It has also been transformed by it.[36] Many different government agents, used to being components of the command system, have been reformed into a new mixed system. Some of them have been downgraded;[37] some of them have been commercialized as companies;[38] some of them have been changed into professional social organizations;[39] some of them have been combined with others;[40] some new agents have been established.[41] There is a mushrooming of 'quasi-state institutions' which are 'most often in the form of companies or corporations, designed to act as an intermediary between enterprises and state agencies proper', inhabiting 'a new hybrid institutional world which is neither fully state nor enterprise but a fusion of both' (White, 1991 p. 12).[42] Meanwhile, there has been a huge increase in the technical competence of Chinese officials at all levels. In short, China's outstanding growth since the 1970s has relied not only on enterprise reform but also reform of the government itself.

Both transition and growth in China are continuing. During this dynamic process, it is difficult to conclude which government agency ought to be closed, and which ought to be strengthened. It is a progressive process corresponding to the progressive process of enterprise reform. Typically the function of many 'quasi-state institutions' cannot be defined precisely or copied from a textbook. The combination of enterprise reform and government reform also is a process of 'groping for stones to cross the river'. Since 'turning back the reel to the beginning' is not an option, China must explore a new way to survive. In other words, China needs a new theoretical interpretation transcending conventional theory, in order to understand both the relatively successful past and the uncertain future.

6. CONCLUSION

The World Bank (and the transition orthodoxy in general) conceived of only one feasible path for large SOEs in all former command economies: privatization. It was *completely* disinterested in the construction of big businesses as a policy goal. It *totally* failed to distinguish between the privatization of former command-run *plants* as opposed to the building of multi-plant *firms*. It visualized only four possible ways for the performance of large SOEs in former command economies to be improved, each of which put privatization at the forefront: 'sales to outsiders', 'management-employee buyouts', 'equal-access voucher privatization' and 'spontaneous privatization' (World Bank, 1996b, pp. 50–6). Each of these is now acknowledged, even by the World Bank, to have large problems, which were not anticipated when it confidently gave its advice in the early phase of the 'transition'.[43]

China has not followed this path. It has adopted none of the methods recommended by the transition orthodoxy for the improvement of large SOEs. Despite following an unorthodox path, Chinese big business has grown rapidly, modernized at speed and substantially changed its operational methods. Despite large remaining problems, however, China's large SOEs have played a central and essential part in China's new industrial revolution. China's bureaucrats have played an active role in the institutional reconstruction and modernization of large SOEs. This contrast between the World Bank's advice and the results of the reform process in China's large SOEs calls into serious question the wisdom of the 'transition orthodoxy' which the Bank represented. It raises the counterfactual question: What would China's large SOEs look like today if they had followed the 'transition orthodoxy' of an anti-bureaucratic revolution, 'close' integration with the world economy and privatization?

It is tempting to say that China is so large that its experience is irrelevant to other developing countries. Even small countries, however, need big business in order to be prosperous. Many of the potentially powerful firms of the future could emerge from today's large SOEs in developing countries. These plants contain large reserves of human skills and technical capabilities. Simply privatizing them and forcing them immediately into open competition with the world's giant firms, as has happened in Russia, will result in their demise or, at best, in their becoming branch plants of globalized big business. China has shown that a different path is possible: instead of allowing the destruction of large SOEs, it has attempted the long, slow path of institutional and technical reconstruction. Such a path means accepting that there must be a large role for bureaucrats: hence, improving the bureaucracy, rather than destroying it, becomes a central policy task. It involves accepting that the institutional solutions are often awkward and muddy, specific to the country and sector concerned rather than following an idealized universal form of business organization, which rarely existed anyway except in the early days of capitalism.

Notes

* This paper is written by Peter Nolan and Wang Xiaoqiang, based on research carried out by them in China between December 1994 and December 1996, supported by a grant from the British Economic and Social Research Council (Grant number R 000235525). The research project which this grant supports is entitled 'The emergence of the modern industrial corporation in China'. It is administered by the Department of Applied Economics, University of Cambridge.

1 The authors of this paper are engaged in a research project to closely examine this issue. Publications from this project so far include Nolan (1995, 1998); Xiaoqiang (1998).

2 See Nolan (1995) for a deeper exploration of this issue.

3 The issue of why this is so is explored in depth in Chang and Singh (1993).

4 For a more comprehensive discussion, see Nolan (1995).

5 See Singh (1993) for a critical discussion.

6 Among the 50 largest US companies, only eight have shareholders who hold 5% or more of the equity. The California Public Employees Retirement System holds equity in 1,300 US corporations plus 300 international ones. (*Economist*, 1996, p. 6).

7 Thirty per cent is owned by the government directly, 40% by the Korea Development Bank (government owned) and 30% by private commercial banks, themselves government-controlled (Amsden (1989) p. 315).

8 This monopoly was only recently broken, with the permission granted by the Korean government to Hyundai to set up a 10-million-ton plant. This was said to be a reward to Hyundai for the 'the group's efforts in winning Seoul co-hosting rights to the 2002 World Cup'. Mr Chung Mong-joon, a son of Hyundai's founder, and head of Hyundai shipbuilding business, is also the president of the Korea Football Association and FIFA vice president (*Financial Times*, July 4, 1996).

9 In 1994 the world's top 300 companies (in terms of research and development expenditure) allocated a total of over £124 billion to R & D, amounting to 4.3% of their total sales value. Among these was an elite 'club' of around 30 firms which spent over £1 billion each on R & D. Within these was a tiny elite of just nine firms which spent over £2 billion each on R & D. Hitachi, Siemens and AT & T each spent £3 billion, and General Motors spent more than £5 billion on R & D (*Financial Times*, June 27, 1996).

10 This is not to say that it may not be politic for the poor countries to sometimes obey these rules, nor to deny that aspects of the international rules may sometimes work to the advantage of a given poor country. It is simply to suggest that these rules should be looked at pragmatically, in relation to the degree to which obeying them or not contributes to the growth of any given poor country at a given juncture.

11 MITI skilfully played off one firm against another by promoting the fear that if they did not sell out the Japanese would simply buy from another foreign firm at this point (Nestor (1991), p. 104).

12 During 1973–80 Japan's global market share rose from 18% to 30%. By 1996, Japanese producers occupied 24% of the US market for automobiles and light trucks.

13 Daewoo's purchase of Thomson Multimedia has turned it into the world's biggest manufacturer of TV sets, with 15% of the global market (*Financial Times*, October 22, 1996). Samsung has manufacturing sites in seven European countries, producing TVs, microwaves, computer moniters, excavators, microchips, cameras, TV tubes, TV glass and refrigerators (*Financial Times*, October 21, 1996).

14 Andreff has expressed a similar view: 'Should we introduce into [transition economies] the "purest" form of private ownership, that of the "boss-owner" who supervises, monitors, controls the exercise of all property rights, when in capitalist market economies a number of medium-size and big firms have adopted more "socialized" forms of corporation, e.g., social capital spread among millions of shareowners, employee ownership plans, outsider control by pension funds, managerial insider control' (Andreff (1996), p. 76).

15 For an extensive evaluation of the Chinese government's approach toward integration with the world economy in terms of 'close' versus 'strategic' integration see Singh (1993).

16 'Our aim in expanding economic and technological exchange with foreign countries is to enhance our ability to be self-reliant and to promote the development of the national economy' (Hu (1982), p. 287).

17 It is not too fanciful to imagine that at some point global companies which today are 'based' in Europe or the United States may become 'based' in China with Chinese directors and managers of these companies more influential than those from other parts of the world.

18 Derived from SSB, CEY (1981, p. 212) and SSB, ZGTJZY (1992, p. 70).

19 The share of large enterprises in gross industrial output value (at current price) of enterprises at *xiang* level and above rose from 25.1% in 1980 to 38.0% in 1994. SSB, CEY (1981, p. 212) and SSB, ZGTJNJ (1996, p. 388).

20 The figure for 1980 is at constant 1970s prices and that for 1990 is at current prices. It was not possible to obtain a comparison at a completely consistent set of prices.

21 Ferrous metals, 85; tobacco processing, 50; transport equipment, 47; machinery, 46; chemicals, 38; coal mining, 31. Development Research Centre (1993, pp. 2–3). Among the top 100 enterprises (by value of sales), 34 were in petroleum and petrochemicals, 29 in ferrous metals, 11 in motor vehicles, and eight in tobacco processing Development Research Centre (1993, pp. 2–3).

22 Indeed, during 1978, China's ranking in total world output shifted from fifth to fourth largest in steel, third to first place in coal, eighth to fifth in crude oil, seventh to fourth in electricity, and fourth to first in cement. SSB, ZGTJNJ (1993, p. 901).

23 It has been estimated that in 1990 the total subsidy provided for coal-using industries on account of the low price of coal relative to international prices was 3.3 billion yuan, Albouy (1991, pp. 10–12), equivalent to 66% of total losses in state coal mines in the same year. SSB, ZGTJNJ (1990, p. 442).

24 In 1991, for example, the expenditure on employment insurance alone in the state sector reached 91.3 billion yuan, which was equivalent to 33% of total wage bill of the state sector, and was twice the size of the total losses of SOEs. SSB, ZGTJNJ (1992, pp. 806, 424). It is questionable how many Chinese SOEs would be loss-makers if their accounts were constructed according to Western practice, and if such services as housing, health and education were provided at market prices. These are typically provided at a nominal price, even in the mid-1990s, constituting a huge subsidy to SOE employees, and a correspondingly large drain on profits.

25 For example, most tobacco companies contracted directly with the central authorities in Beijing. The main producers of petrochemicals, such as Shanghai Petrochemical Company, from the mid-1980s contracted directly with Sinopec in Beijing, a quasi-ministerial holding company, under which are 38 large petrochemical plants, producing more than 80% of China's petrochemical output. Sinopec in turn contracts to hand over an agreed amount of profits to the central government each year. One of the most prosperous businesses under the General Logistics Department (GLD) of the PLA, Sanjiu Enterprise Group, after an initial period of contract with the local branch of the GLD in Guangzhou, shifted to contracting directly with the GLD headquarters in Beijing.

26 A huge company such as Shougang continued to have a 'wholly state owned' core firm, with around 58,000 employees, dealing directly with the state, with formalized ownership rights over subsidiary branch companies employing over 200,000 people as well as investments in around 70 joint ventures with either domestic or foreign capital.

27 Westinghouse has committed itself to invest $100 million in modernizing the plants in Shanghai (*Financial Times* September 16, 1996).

28 By 1996, they had 'established 348 fully capitalized subsidiary companies, 437 subsidiary holding companies, 310 subcompanies, and 619 shareholding companies'. Li Rongxia (1996, p. 15).

29 For example, interviewed by us in March 1996, the head of the Shanghai Petrochemical Company, Wu Yixin, said he could easily foresee the day when the state's ownership share in the firm could fall from its present majority position, to around 30%, as other sources of capital were invested in the business. But he found it hard to imagine in the foreseeable future that it would be allowed to fall below this level.

30 This is a highly sensitive issue, which it is not possible to directly investigate. It involves also complex psychological issues.

31 Oi labels this new institutional development 'local state corporatism'. Oi (1992, p. 100).

32 For example, Yulin Yuchai in Guangxi Province is the largest medium-duty diesel engine manufacturer in China. Yulin City obtains around 80% of its tax revenue from Yuchai, and the local Yulin City's Assets Management Bureau obtains 40% of the dividends handed over to the state holding company. Similarly, Harbin City in Heilongjiang Province is heavily dependent on HPEC. Dividends from HPEC are handed over to the majority owner, the state holding company, and help to directly sustain the life of the city. In addition, tax payments from HPEC account for around 60% of the total industrial tax revenue of Harbin City.

33 A wider definition would put the number of government bureaucrats at a considerably larger figure.

34 On the importance of continuity of leadership at Erqi, see Byrd (1992) and at Shougang, see Nolan (1995). On the role of the Army's motivational and strategic skills see Nolan (forthcoming).

35 For example, the head of one of China's most powerful, fast-growing heavy engineering firms in the mid-1990s, Yuchai, had been a Red Guard leader in the Cultural Revolution. Nolan and Wang Xiaoqiang (1998).

36 For an account of the same process in Taiwan at an earlier stage see Amsden (1985, p. 101).

37 E.g., in 1994, the State Bureau of Price Management and the Ministry of Materials, extremely important agents of the planning regime, were incorporated separately into

the State Planning Commission and the Ministry of Domestic Trade.

38 E.g., the former material and commerce distribution systems and most former industrial ministries have become companies.

39 E.g., the Ministry of Electronic Industry has given up all administrative control of enterprises and become an industrial association.

40 E.g., with 'quota purchases' dramatically reduced, the Ministry of Grain, the Ministry of Trade and the General Commune of Supply and Sales have been merged into the new Ministry of Domestic Trade.

41 E.g., the Commission for Security Supervision with authority over the newly established stock and future markets.

42 Prominent examples are many labor service companies attached to local labor bureaux, six newly established investment companies attached to the Planning Commission, and many industrial trade companies established under the Ministry of Foreign Economic Co-operation and Trade.

43 For example, to the former USSR and to the successor government of the Russian Federation, and helped inspire Mr. Chubais's mass privatization program, 'the fastest privatisation in human history', in the words of British advisor Richard Layard.

References

Albouy, Y., 1991, Coal pricing in China: Issues and reform strategy. *World Bank Discussion Papers*, no. 138, World Bank, Washington DC.

Amsden, Alice A., 1979, Taiwan's economic history: A case of Etatisme and a challenge to dependency theory. *Modern China* 5(3), 341–79.

Amsden, Alice A., 1985, The state and Taiwan's economic development. In *Bringing the State Back In*, eds. Peter B. Evans, Dietrich Rueschemeyer and Theda Skocpol, pp. 78–106. Cambridge University Press, Cambridge.

Amsden, Alice A., 1989, *Asias Next Giant: South Korea and Late Industrialization*. Oxford University Press, New York and Oxford.

Andreff, W., 1996, Corporate governance of privatised enterprises in transforming economies: A theoretical discussion. *MOCT-MOST* 6, 59–80.

Aoki, Masahiko, 1987, The Japanese firm in transition. In *The Political Economy of Japan*, eds. Kozo Yamamura and Yasukichi Yasuba, 1, 263–288.

Stanford University Press, Stanford. Aoki, Masahiko, 1990, Toward an economic model of the Japanese firm. *Journal of Economic Literature*, 28, 1–27.

Aoki, Masahiko, 1994, The Japanese firm as a system of attributes: A survey and research agenda. In *The Japanese Firm: The Sources of Competitive Strength*, eds. Masahiko Aoki and Ronald Dore, pp. 11–40. Oxford University Press, London.

Aslund, A., 1991, *Gorbachev's Struggle for Economic Reform*. Pinter, London. Berle, Adolf A. and Means Gardiner C. (1967) [1932] *The Modern Corporation and Private Property*, revised edition. Harcourt, Brace and World Inc., New York.

Best, Michael H., 1990, *The New Competition: Institutions of Industrial Restructuring*. Polity Press, Cambridge.

Bishop, Matthew R. and A. Kay John, 1989, Privatisation in the United Kingdom: Lessons from experience. *World Development* 17(5), 643–57.

Blanchard, Olivier, Dornbusch Rudiger, Krugman Paul, Layard Richard and Summers Lawrence, 1991, *Reform in Eastern Europe*. MIT Press, London.

Blecher, Marc, 1991, Developmental state, entrepreneurial state: The political economy of socialist reform in Xinju Municipality and Guanghan County. In *The Chinese State in the Era of Economic Reform: The Road to a Crisis*, ed. Gordon White, pp. 265–91. Macmillan, Basingstoke.

Boltho, Andrea, 1975, *Japan: An Economic Survey, 1953–73*. Oxford University Press, Oxford.

Borenzstein, E. and M. Kumar, 1991, Proposals for privatization in Eastern Europe, IMF Staff Papers, 38, IMF, Washington DC.

Byrd, William A., 1992, ed., *Chinese Industrial Firms Under Reform*. Oxford University Press, Oxford.

Byrd, William A. and Lin Qingsong, 1990, eds. *China's Rural Industry: Structure, Development, and Reform*. Oxford University Press, Oxford and New York.

Central Committee of the Chinese Communist Party and the State Council, 1985. Summary of the forum on the Changjiang Delta, Zhujiang Delta and Xiamen-Quanzhou Triangle, February 18, in Major Documents.

Chandler, Alfred D. Jr., 1977, *The Visible Hand: The Managerial Revolution in American Business*. Harvard University Press, Cambridge, MA.

Chandler, Alfred D., Jr. 1990, *Scale and Scope*. Harvard University Press, Cambridge, MA.

Chandler, Alfred D. Jr., 1992, What is a firm? A historical perspective. *European Economic Review*, 36, 483–92.

Chang, Ha-Joon and Ajit Singh, 1993, Public enterprises in developing countries and economic efficiency – A critical examination of analytical, empirical, and policy issues. UNCTAD *Review* 1993 (4), United Nations Conference on Trade and Development, Geneva.

Chang, Ha-Joon, 1994, *The Political Economy of Industrial Policy*. Macmillan, Basingstoke.

Chen Jihua, 1994, Report on the implementation of the 1993 plan for national economic and social development. *Beijing Review* 37(15), 11–17.

Chiang Kaishek, 1947, *China's Destiny*. Dennis Dobson, London.

Clague, C. and G.C. Rausser, 1992, eds., *The Emergence of Market Economies in Eastern Europe*. Blackwell, Oxford.

Demsetz, Harold, 1988, *Ownership, Control, and the Firm: The Organisation of Economic Activity*, 1. Basil Blackwell, Oxford.

Deng Xiaoping, 1984, *Selected Works of Deng Xiaoping*. Beijing, Foreign Languages Press.

Development Research Centre, 1993, *Listing of China's Largest Enterprises*. Management World Editorial Dept., Beijing.

Dickson, I., 1996, China's steel imports: An outline of recent trade barriers. University of Adelaide, Chinese Economy Research Unit.

Dore, Ronald, 1987, *Taking Japan Seriously: A Confucian Perspective on Leading Economic Issues*. Stanford University Press, Stanford.

Drucker, Peter F., 1991, Reckoning with the pension fund revolution. *Harvard Business Review* 69(2), 106–14.

Evans, Peter B., Rueschemeyer Dietrich and Skocpol Theda, eds. 1988, *Bringing the State Back in*. Cambridge University Press, Cambridge.

Fama, Eugene, 1980, Agency problems and the theory of the firm. *Journal of Political Economy*, 88, 288–307.

Forman-Peck, J., 1983, *A History of the World Economy*. Harvester Press, Brighton.

Fukuyama, F., 1992, *The End of History and the Last Man*. Penguin Books, Harmondsworth.

Gao, Shangquan, 1996, *China's Economic Reform*. Macmillan, Basingstoke.

Gerlach, Michael L., 1992, *Alliance Capitalism: The Social Organisation of Japanese Business*. University of California Press, Berkeley, Los Angeles and Oxford.

Gescher, Jeanne-Marie C., 1990, A legal opinion. *China Trade Report*, 28, 6–7.

Hart, Oliver D. and Moore John, 1990, Property rights and the nature of the firm. *Journal of Political Economy* 98(4), 1119–58.

Hashimoto, Masanori and Raisian John, 1985, Employment tenure and earnings profiles in Japan and the United States. *American Economic Review* 75(4), 721–35.

Hay, Donald, Morris Derek, Liu Guy and Yao Shujie, 1994, *Economic Reform and State-owned Enterprises in China, 1979–1987*. Clarendon Press, Oxford.

Hirst, P. and G. Thompson, 1995, *Globalisation in Question*. Routledge, London.

Hogan, W.T., 1994, *Steel in the 21st Century*. Lexington Press, New York.

Hu, Yaobang, 1982, Create a new situation in modernisation, *Major Documents*.

Hu Yebi, 1993, *China's capital market*. Chinese University of Hong Kong, Hong Kong.

Huang Yasheng, 1990, Web of interests and patterns of behaviour of Chinese local economic bureaucracies and enterprises during reforms. *China Quarterly*, No. 123, 431–58.

Hughes, Alan and Ajit Singh, 1983, *Mergers, concentration, and competition in advanced capitalist economies: An international perspective*. Department of Applied Economics, Cambridge University, Cambridge.

IMF, World Bank, OECD and EBRD, 1990, *The Economy of the USSR – Summary and recommendations*. World Bank, Washington, DC.

Jefferson, Gary H. and G. Rawski Thomas, 1994, Enterprise reform in Chinese industry. *Journal of Economic Perspectives*, 8(2), 47–70.

Johnson, Chalmers A., 1982, *MITI and the Japanese Miracle*. Stanford University Press, Stanford.

Kanter, Rosabeth Moss, 1991, Transcending business boundaries: 12,000 world managers view change. *Harvard Business Review* 69(3), 151–64.

Kennett, D. and M. Lieberman, eds. 1993, *The Road to Capitalism*. Dryden Press, Orlando, FL.

Koike, Kazuo, 1987, Human resource development and labour-management relations. In *The Political Economy of Japan*, eds. Kozo Yamamura and Yasukuchi Yasuba, 1, 289–330. Stanford University Press, Stanford, CA.

Komiya, Ryutaro, 1987, Japanese firms, Chinese firms: Problems for economic reform in China, Part II. *Journal of the Japanese and International Economics* 1(2), 229–247.

Koo, Anthony Y.C., Hon-Ming Li Elizabeth and Peng Zhaoping, 1993, State-owned enterprise in transition, in *China's Economic Reform*, ed. Walter Galenson 1990 Institute, San Francisco.

Kornai, J., 1986, Hungarian economic reform: Hopes, visions and reality. *Journal of Economic Literature*.

Kornai, Janos, 1990, *The Road to a Free Economy*. W.W. Norton and Company, New York.

Kornai, Janos, 1992, *The Socialist System: The Political Economy of Communism*. Clarendon Press, Oxford.

Lake, D., 1988, *Power, Politics and Trade*. Cornell University Press, London.

Lazonick, William, 1991, *Business Organisation and the Myth of the Market Economy*. Cambridge University Press, Cambridge.

Li Rongxia, 1996, Progress in reform of state-owned enterprises. *Beijing Review* 39(25), 17–23.

Lichtenberg, F.R. and G.M. Pushner, 1992, *Ownership structure and corporate performance in*

Japan. NBER Working Papers Series, no. 4092, National Bureau of Economic Research, Cambridge, MA.

Lipton, David and Sachs Jeffrey, 1991, Privatisation in Eastern Europe: The case of Poland. In *Reforming Central and Eastern European Economies: Initial Results and Challenges*, eds. Vittorio Corbo, Fabrizio Coricelli and Jan Bossak, pp. 231–51. World Bank, Washington, DC.

Lipton, David and Sachs Jeffrey, 1993, Creating a market economy in Eastern Europe: The case of Poland. In *The Road to Capitalism*, ed. D. Kennett and M. Lieberman. Dryden Press, Orlands, FL.

Lorsch, Jay W., 1991, Real ownership is impossible. *Harvard Business Review* 69(6), 139–41.

McDonald, Kevin R., 1993, Why privatisation is not enough. *Harvard Business Review* 71(3), 49–59.

Major Documents of the People's Republic of China, 1991, (Major Documents), Foreign Languages Press, Beijing.

Minami, Ryoshin, 1994, *The Economic Development of China: A Comparison with the Japanese Experience*. Macmillan, Basingstoke.

Mincer, Jacob and Higuchi Yoshio, 1988, Wage structures and labour turnover in the United States and Japan. *Journal of the Japanese and International Economies* 2(2), 97–133.

Monsen, Joseph R. and Downs, Anthony, 1965, A theory of large managerial firms. *Journal of Political Economy* 7(3), 221–36.

Monsen, Joseph R., Chiu John S. and E. Cooley Daevid, 1968, The effect of separation of ownership and control on the performance of the large firm. *Quarterly Journal of Economics* 82(3), 435–51.

Moyle, John, 1971, The pattern of ordinary share ownership 1957–1970. Occasional Papers, no. 31, University of Cambridge Department of Applied Economics, Cambridge.

Nee, Victor, 1992, Organisational dynamics of market transition: Hybrid forms, property rights, and mixed economy in China. *Administrative Science Quarterly*, 37, 1–27.

Nestor, W., 1991, *Japanese Neo-Mercantilism*. Macmillan, Basingstoke.

Newbery, David M., 1992, The role of public enterprises in the national economy. *Asian Development Review* 10(2), 1–34.

Newbery, David M., 1991, Sequencing the transition. CEPR Discussion Paper, no. 575, Oxford University, Oxford.

Nolan, P., 1993, *State and Market in the Chinese Economy – Essays on Controversial Issues*. Macmillan, Basingstoke.

Nolan, P., 1995, From state factory to modern corporation? China's Shougang iron and steel corporation under economic reform. Department of Applied Economics, Working Paper, Amalgamated Series, no. 9621, Cambridge University, Cambridge, UK.

Nolan, P., 1996a, Large firms and industrial reform in former planned economies: The case of China. *Cambridge Journal of Economics*.

Nolan, P., 1996b, Big business with Chinese characteristics. Department of Applied Economics, DAE Working Papers, Amalgamated Series, no. 9516, Cambridge University, Cambridge, UK.

Nolan, P., 1998, *Indigenous Large Firms in China's Economic Reform*. Contemporary China Institute, University of London.

Nolan, P. and Wang Xiaoqiang, 1998, Harbin Power Equipment Company: and the battle for the Chinese market. *Competition and Change*.

Nolan, P., Wang Xiaoqiang, Gao Shiqi and Liu Yan, (forthcoming) *The evolution of a state-owned enterprise*: The Shanghai Petrochemical Company.

OECD, 1972, *The Industrial Policy of Japan*. OECD, Paris.

Oi, Jean C., 1992, Fiscal reform and the economic foundations of local state corporatism in China. *World Politics* 45(1), 99–126.

Ohmae, K., 1996, *The End of the Nation State*. Harper Collins, London.

Parker, David, 1993, Ownership, organisational changes and performance. In *The Political Economy of Privatisation*, ed. Thomas Clarke and Christos Pitelis, pp. 31–53. Routledge, London.

Perkins, Dwight H., 1988, Reforming China's economic system. *Journal of Economic Literature* 26, 601–45.

Project Group for the Establishment of a Modern Enterprise System under the Chinese Academy of Social Sciences, 1996. A research report on planning for the reform of state-owned enterprises before 2010. *Social Sciences in China* 17(40), 5–18.

Research Group of the Centre of Economic Research, Planning Commission (RGCER), 1994. Research report on foreign direct investment in China, mimeo [in Chinese].

Reynolds, Bruce L., 1987, and the staff of the Chinese Economic System Reform Research Institute (CESRRI-a) (1987) *Reform in China: Challenges and Choices*. M.E. Sharpe, Armonk, New York.

Reynolds, Bruce L., 1985, *Economic Growth in the Third World*. Yale University Press, New Haven, CT.

Rowthorn, Bob, 1990, Privatisation in the UK, Mimeo, Faculty of Economics and Politics, University of Cambridge, Cambridge, UK.

Rowthorn, Bob and Ha-Joon Chang, 1993, Public ownership and the theory of the state. In *The Political Economy of Privatisation*, eds. Thomas Clarke and Christos Pitelis, pp. 54–69. Routledge, London.

Ruigrok, W. and Van Tulder R., 1995, *The Logic of International Restructuring*. Routledge, London.

Sachs, Jeffrey and David Lipton, 1990, Poland's economic reform. *Foreign Affairs* 69(3), 47–66.

Sachs, Jeffrey and W.T. Woo, 1994, Structural factors in the economic reforms of China, Eastern Europe and the former Soviet Union. *Economic Policy* 9(18).

Scherer, F.M. and D. Ross, 1990, *Industrial Market Structure and Performance*. Houghton Mifflin, Boston.

Schmitz, H., 1993, *The Growth of Big Business in the United States and Western Europe, 1850–1939*. Macmillan, Basingstoke.

Schumpeter, Joseph, 1950 [1942], *Capitalism, Socialism and Democracy*. 3rd edn. Harper, New York.

Sheard, Paul, 1994, Interlocking share-holdings and corporate governance. In *The Japanese Firm: The Sources of Competitive Strength*, eds. Masahiko Aoki and Ronald Dore, pp. 310–49, Oxford University Press, London.

Singh, Ajit, 1990, The stock-market in a socialist economy. In *The Chinese Economy and its Future: Achievements and Problems of Post-Mao Reform*, eds. Peter Nolan and Dong Fujeng, pp. 161–78. Polity Press, Cambridge.

Singh, Inderjit, 1992, China: Industrial policies for an economy in transition. *World Bank Discussion Papers*, no. 143, World Bank, Washington DC.

Singh, A., 1993, 'Close' versus 'Strategic' integration with the world economy and the 'market friendly approach to development' versus an 'industrial policy' Paper presented to the UN University/World Bank Symposium on Economic Reform in Developing Countries, Washington DC.

Singh, Inderjit J. and Gary H. Jefferson, 1993, State enterprises in China: Down to earth from commanding heights. *Transition* 4(8), 8–10.

Smith, Adam, 1937 [1776], *The Wealth of Nations*. Cannan Edition, Modern Library, New York.

State Statistical Bureau (SSB), 1983, *Statistical Yearbook of China, 1981*. Economic Information Agency, Hong Kong.

State Statistical Bureau (SSB), (various years). *Chinese Statistical Yearbook*, State Statistical Bureau, Beijing [in Chinese].

State Statistical Bureau (SSB), (various years). *Chinese Statistical Outline*, State Statistical Bureau, Beijing [in Chinese].

Steinherr, Alfred, 1991, Essential ingredients for reforms in Eastern Europe. *Moct – Most* (3), 3–28.

Stepanek, James B., 1991, China's enduring state factories: Why ten years of reform have left China's big state factories unchanged. In *China's Economic Dilemmas in the 1990s: The Problems of Reforms, Modernisation, and Interdependence*, ed. Joint Economic Committee at US Congress, 2, 440–54.

Study Group to Japan, Chinese Economic System Reform Research Institute, 1988, *The Enlightenment of Japanese Model: The Firms, Government, and Middle Organisations*. Sichuan People Press, Chengdu [in Chinese].

Suzuki, Yoshitaka, 1991, *Japanese Management Structures, 1920–80*. Macmillan, Basingstoke.

Tsuru, Shigeto, 1993, *Japan's Capitalism: Creative Defeat and Beyond*. Cambridge University Press, Cambridge.

UNDP, 1996, *Human Development Report*. Oxford University Press, New York.

Veljanovski, Cento, ed. 1992, *Privatisation and Competition: A Market Prospectus*. Institute of Economic Affairs, London.

Vernon-Wortzel Heidi and H. Wortzel Lawrence, 1989, Privatisation: Not the only answer. *World Development* 17(5), 633–41.

Wade, Robert, 1990, *Governing the Market: Economic Theory and the Role of Government in East Asian Industrialisation*. Princeton University Press, Princeton.

Wagstyl, S., 1996, Intense competition squeezes margins. *Financial Times*, June 26.

Walters, A., 1992, Misapprehensions on privatisation. In The Emergence of Market Economics in Eastern Europe, ed. Clague and Rausser, Blackwell, Oxford.

Wang Xiaoqiang and Ji Xiaoming, 1988, [1985] Thoughts on the model of non-stock enterprise *Chinese Economic Studies* 22(2) 38–46 (Original Chinese version: *Economic Development and Reform*, no. 1, 1985, 13–26).

Wang Xiaoqiang, 1989, Transcending the logic of private ownership. Chinese Economic Studies 23(1), 43–56 (Original Chinese version: *Economic Development and Reform*, no. 4, 1988, 27–48).

Wang Xiaoqiang, 1993, Groping for stones to cross the river: Chinese price reform against 'big bang'. *Discussion Papers on Economic Transition*, DEPT 9305, Department of Applied Economics, University of Cambridge.

White, Gordon, 1991, The road to crisis: The Chinese state in the era of economic reform. In *Chinese State in the Era of Economic Reform: The Road to a Crisis*, ed. Gordon White, pp. 1–20. Macmillan, Basingstoke.

Williamson, Oliver E., 1975, *Market and Hierarchies: Analysis and Antitrust Implications*. Free Press, New York.

Williamson, Oliver E., 1985, *The Economic Institutions of Capitalism: Firms, Markets, Relational Contracting*. Free Press, New York.

Wood, Adrian, 1991, Joint stock companies with rearranged public ownership: invigoration of China's state enterprises further considered. Mimeo, Programme of Research into the Reform of Pricing and Market Structure in China, London School of Economics, CP no. 11.

Wood, Adrian, 1994, China's economic system: A brief description, with some suggestions for further reform. Mimeograph, Programme of Research into the Reform of Pricing and Market, London School of Economics, CP No.12, revised and republished in P. Nolan and Fan Qimiao, eds. (1994), *China's Economic Reforms: Achievements and Problems*, Macmillan, Basingstoke.

World Bank, 1985, *China: Long-Term Development Issues and Options*. Johns Hopkins University Press, Baltimore and London.

World Bank, 1991, *China: Macroeconomic Stability and Industrial Growth Under Decentralised Socialism*. World Bank, Washington, D.C.

World Bank, 1996a, *Bureaucrats in Business*. Oxford University Press, New York.

World Bank, 1996b, *From Plan to Market*. Oxford University Press, Washington D.C.

Yao Jianguo, 1992, Experimenting with enterprise groups. *Beijing Review* 35(19), 14–19.

Yonekura, S., 1994, *The Japanese Iron and Steel Industry*. Macmillan, Basingstoke.

Yavlinsky, G., *et al.* 1991, *500 days: Transition to Market*. St Martins Press, New York.

6

CHINA, AND THE GLOBAL BUSINESS REVOLUTION[1]

Introduction

It is likely that China will enter the WTO in the second half of the year 2001. This will be an event of historic significance, comparable in importance to the country's opening up after the Opium Wars. China's impending entry to the WTO raises many issues. One of the most important of these is the potential impact upon its large-scale state-owned enterprises. This poses deep policy challenges for China's leaders.

For almost two decades the Chinese government experimentally charted its own independently constructed reform programme. With the entry to the WTO under such detailed, internationally set conditions, China has voluntarily given up a wide area of autonomy in charting the complex path of economic reform. The US–China WTO agreement 'in itself constitutes a massive programme of economic system reform' (Cooper, 2000). The WTO agreement with the US is 250 pages long, with a detailed account of the steps that China agrees to take in order to implement the WTO rules. This is not just an 'agreement on paper'. The minute details will be taken very seriously by the high-income countries. It is the most detailed agreement yet signed by any country on its entry to the WTO – far more specific than that signed by India, for example. Under the terms of the WTO agreement, China must cease to provide special support for large state-owned enterprises. Within China, the WTO rules require the whole country to become an internal free trade area. China has been granted only a five-year adjustment period before it must implement in full the rules of the WTO. Many important changes will have effect from the day that China joins the WTO.

Many commentators, both within and outside China, believe that entering the WTO will invigorate Chinese large-scale industry. 'Competition from abroad will help the Chinese to raise their level of efficiency, just like the US auto industry did in the 1980s in the face of Japanese competition'.[2]

In the course of two decades of struggle, China's large enterprises have changed substantially, gradually undertaking evolutionary institutional change in key aspects of their business organization (Nolan and Wang, 1998). During the same period, the world's leading businesses have undergone revolutionary transformation. As the epoch of the 'global level playing field' moves ever closer, it becomes increasingly necessary for China's reforming large enterprises to benchmark themselves realistically against the global giants. China's large firms have made substantial progress in building 'large modern corporations'. However, they have failed to catch up with the world leaders. Indeed, they have fallen further behind than they were just a decade or so ago. China's large-scale industries will face immense difficulties on the 'global level playing field' which is about to arrive in China. This presents China's policymakers with difficult choices.

The growing realization of this brutal reality has been a major reason why China's entry to the WTO was not completed almost two years after the conclusion of the historic agreement with the USA. China's impending entry to the WTO marks a highly important event in the history both of China's relations with the rest of the world. It also marks a watershed in the history of industrial policy.

1. China's Policy Goal

China began liberalizing the post-Mao economy in the late 1970s. The early versions of the contract system in industry were introduced in 1979, of which that at Shougang was the most important and symbolic. Therefore, one can say that China's industrial policy has been in operation for two decades.

A consistently stated goal of China's industrial policy has been to construct globally powerful companies that can compete on the global level playing field:

> In our world today economic competition between nations is in fact between each nation's large enterprises and enterprise groups. A nation's economic might is concentrated and manifested in the economic power and international competitiveness of its large enterprises and groups. International economic confrontations in reality show that if a country has several large enterprises or groups it will be able to maintain a certain market share and hold an assured position in the world economic order … *In the same way now and in the next century our nation's position in the international economic order will be to a large extent determined by the position of our nation's large enterprises and groups.* (Wu Bangguo, Chinese State Council, quoted in *Economic Daily*, 1 August 1998) (emphasis added).

In pursuit of this objective, China's stated goal of industrial policy has been to construct a group of large-scale powerful industrial firms that can challenge the global leaders. These include:

- AVIC in the aerospace industry;
- Sinopec and CNPC in oil and petrochemicals;
- Sanjiu, Dongbei, and Shandong Xinhua in pharmaceuticals;
- Harbin, Shanghai Electrical, and Dongfang in power equipment;
- Yiqi, Erqi, Shanghai Auto and Tianjin in automobiles;
- Shougang, Angang, and Baogang in steel;
- Datong, Yanzhou and Shenhua in coal mining.

China's chosen global giant corporations were supported through a sequence of industrial policies, including:

- tariffs, which fell gradually but still were significant in many sectors at the end of the 1990s;
- a wide range of non-tariff barriers, including limitations on access to domestic marketing channels, requirements for technology transfer and to sub-contract to selected domestic firms as the price for market access;
- government procurement policy;
- government selection of the joint venture partners for major international joint venture projects;
- preferential loans from state banks;
- privileged access to international stock markets with listing in Hong Kong and New York.

2. The Japanese Example

During a similar period in Japan's development, from the 1950s to the 1970s, Japan's industrial planners supported the growth of a series of oligopolistic companies that developed into globally powerful firms. After two decades of industrial policy in Japan, the country possessed a whole corps of globally competitive companies. By the late 1980s, it had twenty of the largest one hundred corporations in the *Fortune* 500 list, including Toyota, Hitachi, Matsushita, Nissan, Toshiba, Honda, Sony, NEC, Fujitsu, Mitsubishi Electric, Mitsubishi Motors, Nippon Steel, Mitsubishi Heavy Industry, Mazda, Nippon Oil, Idemitsu Kosan, Canon, NKK, Bridgestone, and Sumitomo Metal. These companies developed through extensive support from state industrial policy, including tariff and non-tariff barriers, restrictions on foreign direct investment, preferential purchase policy by state-owned utilities, government defence procurement contracts, government-subsidized

R&D, government-sponsored rationalizations of different industries, and a 'flexible', pragmatic competition policy which allowed the growth of oligopolistic competition.

3. China's Success

China's gross domestic product has grown at an officially reported rate of 10.2 per cent per annum from 1980 to 1990, and 11.1 per cent from 1990 to 1998. Industrial value-added grew at an officially reported rate of 11.1 per cent in the 1980s and 15.4 per cent from 1980 to 1998 (World Bank, 1999: 250–251).

After twenty years of industrial policy in China, using many similar measures to those used by Japan, and with a similar explicit policy goal, major changes had taken place in China's large, state-owned enterprises. They had:

- grown rapidly in terms of value of sales;
- absorbed a great deal of modern technology;
- learned how to compete in the marketplace;
- substantially upgraded the technical level of their employees;
- learned wide-ranging new managerial skills;
- gained substantial understanding of international financial markets;
- become sought-after partners for multinational companies.

Under these policies, China's large state-owned enterprises have avoided the industrial collapse of the former USSR. This is not a small achievement, and the possibility of system collapse in China still needs to be taken very seriously indeed.

Under these policies also, China has attracted huge amounts of foreign direct investment. Throughout most of the 1990s, China was the largest recipient of FDI after the USA, regularly accounting for around 10–12% of total world FDI and around one-third of total flows of FDI into developing countries (UNCTAD, 1999). Increasingly, global corporations have viewed China as central to their long-term strategy.

4. Can Large Chinese Firms Compete on the Global Level Playing Field?

The historic agreement of November 15th 1999, between the US and China on China's accession to the WTO, makes the task of benchmarking Chinese large firms against the global leaders even more urgent. Since the signing of this historic agreement, China's entrepreneurs and political leaders have been forced to take a deep look at the degree to which their large corporations have become ready for the intense competition on the 'global level playing field'.

Through an examination of selected cases from the Chinese 'national team', this section evaluates the degree to which China's large corporations are ready for the challenge of that awaits them inside the WTO. *To what extent did twenty years of industrial policy enable China's large firms to close the gap on the global leaders?*

Aerospace: AVIC

In the 1970s there was a wide gap between China's aerospace industry and the world's leading companies. In this, the most 'strategic' of all Chinese industries, the gap between China's 'national champion' and the global giant companies widened drastically after the 1970s.

The extent of the gap is revealed by the fact that the entire Chinese civilian aircraft fleet, with the exception of a small number of domestically made turbo-props, is imported. China's attempt to build its own indigenous large aircraft, the Y-10, failed. China's attempt to partner the multinationals in co-designing and building a large civilian aircraft failed. China's sub-contracting for the multinational giants remains at a pathetically low level compared to the levels of Japan or South Korea. Even China's domestically-made turbo-prop is only able to make a few export sales through the use of key imported components, reflecting the backward nature of its aero-engine and avionics industry.

At least as revealing about the failure to make any inroads on the world's leading corporations is the fact that the Chinese military has been forced to rely more and more heavily on imports, and domestic production under licence, of fighter planes from the former USSR. China's airforce is now almost wholly dependent for advanced fighters on Su27s bought from the former USSR. The number either already produced or on order is now well over one hundred, and rising. Moreover, China is negotiating for the purchase of the more advanced Su30s.

The core aerospace business of AVIC in the late 1990s was extremely small, totalling less than $1 billion annual sales revenue, on a par with a medium-sized company such as Vickers or Cobham (Table 6.1). Moreover, AVIC contained the full range of aerospace activities, including engines and avionics as well as airframes. AVIC had been turned into a vast empire of diversified businesses, totally unable to compete directly with the global giants in aerospace.

The 'reform' of AVIC in 1999 had no immediately comprehensible rationale. Instead of one huge diversified conglomerate with no capability to compete with the multinationals, it created two smaller and even less internationally competitive conglomerates. The reform could have separated the vast civilian business from the aerospace business, but was unable to do so because this would have provoked much opposition from the subordinate entities who

Table 6.1 **Selected Indicators of the Competitive Capability of Leading Chinese Companies Compared with the Global Giants: Aerospace**

Company	Revenues $billion	Post-tax profits $million	Employees '000s	R&D $million
Boeing ('97)	45.8	(178)	239	1,830
Lockheed-Martin ('97)	28.1	1,300	190	1,060
BAe ('97)	10.4	681	44	690
AVIC ('97)	3.1	72	560	n.a.
of which: aerospace	0.7	–	–	–

Note: Figures in brackets indicate losses.

stood to lose many of their most profitable activities. It could have separated engines and avionics from the airframe business, but it didn't. It could have separated military from civilian aerospace, but it didn't. If its main goal was to develop its capability as a sub-contractor, then it might have allowed strong subordinate production units such as Xian, Chengdu and Shenyang to become independent companies that could compete for business with the multinationals, but it didn't. In sum, the prospects for AVIC on the global level playing field are bleak.

Alongside the halting, uncertain reforms in the Chinese aerospace industry, the most revolutionary epoch in the history of the world industry has taken place. By the late 1990s, after an unprecedented epoch of merger and acquisition, only a tiny handful of firms dominated the entire world industry in both civilian and military aircraft. The epoch of 'national champions' had vanished, to be replaced by just two international European-based corporations, EADS and BaeSystems, contesting with the two massive US-based firms, Boeing and Lockheed Martin, for the entire world's market. Moreover, the process was becoming even more internationalized, with the beginning of a possible revolutionary period of massive transatlantic mergers and acquisitions, affecting even the formerly sacrosanct military aerospace sector. These changes placed China's halting efforts at industrial policy at an even greater disadvantage on the global stage.

Pharmaceuticals: Sanjiu

Sanjiu is exceptionally interesting from the point of view of industrial policy and catch-up, since it had the backing of the People's Liberation Army. This provided many difficulties, but also conferred some important advantages,

Table 6.2 **Selected Indicators of the Competitive Capability of Leading Chinese Companies Compared with the Global Giants: Pharmaceuticals**

Company	Revenues $billion	Post-tax profits $million	Employees '000s	R&D $million
Merck ('97)	26.03	8,069	54	2,760
Novartis ('97)	22.34	6,166	87	2,620
Glaxo Wellcome ('97)	17.38	4,626	53	1,870
Sanjiu ('97)	0.67	98*	13	n.a.

Note: * pre-tax profits

such as access to markets and the possibility of taking over other enterprises in the sector. Sanjiu developed a modern business system. It had the benefit of a powerful leadership team, and an outstanding chief executive officer. Sanjiu developed a powerful brand within China. It had an acute sense of the importance of product quality and modern production systems. It had a professional management team, with a deep awareness of global trends in the pharmaceutical industry. It was one of the earliest Chinese firms to develop a modern marketing system.

However, despite these great strengths and business achievements, Sanjiu faces enormous difficulties in competing directly with the multinationals (Table 6.2). China's pharmaceuticals industry is highly fragmented. China has thousands of small-scale pharmaceuticals producers that will face large difficulties on the global level playing field. The largest companies, such as Sanjiu, occupy only a tiny fraction of the national market. Even the leading pharmaceuticals companies, such as Sanjiu, are tiny in scale compared to the global giants. R&D is crucial to the ability to compete with the multinational giants. Even one of China's leading pharmaceutical companies, such as Sanjiu, has a minuscule research capability compared to the global leaders. Zhao Xinxian, Sanjiu's chief executive officer recognizes explicitly that his company cannot contemplate direct competition. The alternative routes within the pharmaceuticals sector are, firstly, to produce out-of-patent, low value-added medicines, with low rates of profit. Several of China's large state-owned enterprises have a considerable capability in this area. However, none of the global giant companies relies on this as their path to growth and high levels of profits.

The second path, and that which Sanjiu has chosen, is to focus on traditional Chinese medicines. Sanjiu's chosen route is especially interesting as it raises the issue of the degree to which Chinese firms can compete with multinationals without engaging in head-to-head competition. This path enabled Sanjiu to expand rapidly within China, rising quickly to become one of the top two pharmaceutical companies. However, Sanjiu has found it very difficult to grow in China apart from its main product, *Sanjiu Weitai*, the stomach medicine. On international markets, despite passing FDA health requirements, it is also difficult for it to grow. The overseas Chinese community is not sufficiently large to provide for sustained long-term growth. The extent of prescription of Chinese traditional medicines by Western doctors is still small. Moreover, lacking a patent, there is nothing to stop Western pharmaceutical companies producing the product and using their massive marketing structure to sell traditional Chinese medicines such as *Sanjiu Weitai*, should they find the market growing more rapidly than at present. Sanjiu would find it hard, or simply impossible, to compete with such a strategy. Moreover, there is nothing to prevent the multinationals from adopting such a strategy even within China, if they find the profit margin sufficiently attractive.

Therefore, Sanjiu's ability to compete directly with the multinationals is virtually non-existent. It is a highly successful business that has performed extremely well in an important niche market, which is essentially a branch of the food industry rather than medicine. However, this market, which avoids head-on competition with the multinational giants, has only limited long-term growth prospects. This fact explains to a large degree, Sanjiu's decision to enter a wide range of businesses other than pharmaceuticals. At one point it had a huge range of largely unrelated businesses, even including automobile production. Even after it had drastically reduced its portfolio's range, it still had a wide range of activities. However, these were mainly in food and drink, which are reasonably closely related to Chinese medicine. Sanjiu's main assets are now its high-quality managerial personnel, its brand and its marketing skills. These may enable the company to remain a moderately successful food and drinks conglomerate for a reasonable period of time. However, they do not suggest that Sanjiu will be able to compete with the multinational giants of the pharmaceuticals industry.

The 1990s saw a revolutionary change in the structure of the world pharmaceuticals industry. The global industry was massively transformed by a sequence of massive de-mergers and mergers. One after the other, the global giants of the chemical industry de-merged their pharmaceuticals businesses. These de-mergers were followed by a sequence of massive mergers. By the late 1990s, a small group of colossal pharmaceuticals companies had emerged. They undertook vast, multi-billion dollar R&D expenditure. They developed a huge capability to develop drugs through clinical trials and to market their portfolio of drugs through common channels. They also had the financial resources to withstand the failure of a large fraction of their R&D investment and the possible disasters of drugs that turned out to be harmful to health. This global revolution made the emerging Chinese 'national champions' appear even more puny by comparison.

Complex Electrical Equipment: Harbin Power Equipment Company

Compared with other developing countries, at the end of the 1970s China had a relatively advanced power equipment industry. It had three major producing units, with around three-quarters of the domestic market between them. At the beginning of the reform process, these three entities were under a single central source of control. Under reform, these enterprises faced two decades of rapidly growing demand, providing an important opportunity for catch-up. Under these circumstances, China's leading producers made considerable progress. Harbin benefited greatly from a government-orchestrated programme of technical transfer, enabling it to upgrade its technical capability significantly. If the three main Chinese producers had been able to effect a merger, they would have formed a genuinely large-scale entity, even in global terms. Not only was the Chinese market one of the world's fastest-growing, but also, a large fraction of Chinese equipment is coal-fired, so that China might have built a considerable capability in this branch of the industry.

However, China's industrial policy did not follow this path. Instead, China's policies of enhancing the independence of subordinate operational units allowed the separate units to become increasingly autonomous. Both Dongfang and Shanghai Electrical Corporation were allowed to establish joint ventures with multinational companies. In addition, many smaller Sino-foreign joint ventures were established. Harbin's own attempt to form a northeast China electrical company, uniting its interests with those of neighbouring electrical equipment producers, foundered on the separate ambitions of the electrical equipment manufacturers. Moreover, even Harbin itself did not constitute a unified modern corporation. It consists of three main separate entities each with their own strong traditions. The 'unification' to form Harbin Power Equipment Company (HPEC), was principally as a vehicle to gain permission for flotation. Even after flotation, the separate entities within HPEC had a wide range of independent functions.

The increasing independence of the power generation sector from the equipment manufacturing sector already changed sharply the competitive landscape of the Chinese power equipment industry from the mid-1990s onwards. Foreign-invested and wholly domestically owned power stations increasingly looked towards buying equipment with the lowest costs, including

Table 6.3 **Selected Indicators of the Competitive Capability of Leading Chinese Companies Compared with the Global Giants: Power Equipment (1998)**

Company	Revenues $billion	Post-tax profits $million	Employees '000s	R&D $million
Siemens	57.95	990	376	5,008
: power division	6.39	n.a.	n.a.	n.a.
ABB	29.72	2,500	208	2,368
General Electric	100.47	9,296	293	1,930
: power division	8.47	1,306	n.a.	n.a.
Harbin (HPEC)	0.35	9	27	3

costs of maintenance, with high levels of reliability and the ability to meet increasingly stringent anti-pollution regulations, irrespective of the country of origin of the manufacturer. In this sector, China still has significant industrial policy measures, including restrictions on foreign investment in both the equipment and the generation sector, limitations on the size of power plant imported, and domestic content requirements. Even with these measures, the share of multinational companies, through import and domestic production in joint ventures, rose sharply, reaching around one-half of annual installed capacity by the mid-1990s. Most significantly, the entire first tranche of equipment for the massive Three Gorges Project, comprising fourteen 700MW units, was awarded to multinational companies.

Despite considerable progress, China's domestic industry in the late 1990s remained institutionally fragmented. The fragmentation even penetrated its leading companies, including the separate sub-units within HPEC. Alongside the growth of autonomy at the enterprise level within China, the global 'battle of the giants' was reaching its endgame, with just three giant companies dominating the world market, emerging from the former diverse structure of separate national champions within each advanced country. As a separate entity, it would be extremely hard for HPEC, China's leading firm, to compete even within China with the global giants on the global level playing field (Table 6.3). China's main producers other than HPEC were increasingly being integrated into the global sub-contracting system of the multinational giant companies. Despite the considerable progress, even in this sector, the institutional and technical gap between China's leading companies and the world leaders has enlarged during the reform period.

Oil and Petrochemicals: CNPC and Sinopec

The Chinese oil, gas and petrochemical industry is highly important in a global perspective. China has risen to become a major player in the world energy economy. During the reform years the Chinese industry has made major technical advances. Large institutional changes have taken place, with a massive reorganization of the two main players into huge vertically integrated companies, combining upstream and downstream assets. The industry has absorbed modern management techniques. It has raised substantial capital on international markets through a series of H-share flotations, carrying out huge internal restructuring of the floated companies, PetroChina (CNPC) and Sinopec, to prepare for flotation. A sequence of massive, multi-billion dollar international joint ventures has been agreed. With greatly increased autonomy for the production units, real competition began to develop among domestic producers.

However, despite these significant advances, important difficulties remained unresolved for the industry, placing it at a considerable disadvantage in the global competition. At the institutional level, the industry remained torn by the tension between trying to create powerful, autonomous enterprises and trying to construct globally competitive, giant multi-plant firms. For most of the reform period, production units gained increasing autonomy. However, the central authorities within the industry placed limits on the degree of autonomy. Powerful subordinate enterprises, such as Daqing and Shanghai Petrochemical Company, were not allowed to undertake large-scale mergers with other domestic enterprises, lest they challenge the authority of the ministry and/or holding company. Belatedly, in the late 1990s, the central government undertook a comprehensive change of direction. They attempted complete reorganization of the industry, integrating the upstream and downstream components of the sector, with the aim of greatly enhancing the authority of the central bodies so as to create two truly integrated, globally competitive firms. This is a huge task, since the embedded vested interests at the level of the production enterprises are very large. It will require a major struggle to truly centralize control within the sector.

Apart from the institutional issue, major technical problems still exist for the industry. China's reserves have not proved as prolific nor as well-located as was once hoped. Offshore oil reserves have proved disappointingly small and are typically located at considerable depths. China's onshore oil reserves are mainly located in relatively distant areas in China's central Asian republics, notably Xinjiang. These are of uncertain amount and typically are at great depth. Both the costs of raising and transporting the products are high. In the downstream part of the industry, China's major companies have a

Table 6.4 **Selected Indicators of the Competitive Capability of Leading Chinese Companies Compared with the Global Giants: Oil and Petrochemicals**

Company	Revenues $billion	Post-tax profits $million	Employees '000s	R&D $million
Exxon/Mobil ('97) (a)	182	11,730	123	720
Royal Dutch/Shell ('97)	128	7,760	105	770
BP Amoco ('97)	123	8,540	123	390
CNPC ('98)	33	107(b)	1,540(c)	n.a.
Sinopec ('98)	34	194(b)	1,190(d)	n.a.

Sources: Nolan, P., Case Studies China Big Business Programme, 1996–99, and Annual Reports

Notes
(a) proforma
(b) pre-tax profits
(c) after restructuring for flotation, the number of employees at PetroChina (CNPC) fell to 480,000.
(d) After restructuring for flotation, the number of employees at Sinopec fell to 511,000.

proliferation of high-cost, small-scale refineries. They have only a relatively small share of petrochemical output from high value-added, high profit margin products. The downstream distribution system is backward compared to the global giants, lacking high value-added products, such as environmentally-friendly varieties of petrol, lacking modern logistics systems and without a high quality global brand. The Chinese industry is still highly protected through tight restrictions on foreign direct investment, with projects typically requiring many years of negotiation before obtaining approval, major restrictions on the openness of bidding for major oil and gas exploration and development projects, and through labyrinthine controls on the distribution system for oil and petrochemical products.

Alongside China's halting, uncertain reforms has gone a revolution in the world's oil and petrochemical industry. A handful of companies in the advanced economies now occupy the commanding heights of the industry (Table 6.4). They possess large, high quality reserves, distributed around the globe. They have integrated oil refineries and petrochemical plants. They have high levels of R&D, and a portfolio of globally leading, high value-added, products in the petrochemical and oil products sectors. They have a sophisticated logistics system and global brand names. China's partially reformed national champions, CNPC and Sinopec, are still far from the completion of a massive process of institutional restructuring. The flotations of CNPC (PetroChina) and Sinopec in 2000 produced only around one-half of the amount originally hoped for. Their flotation was only successful due to the fact that the global giants took a large share of the floated equity in each of the companies. Moreover, in return for this they were granted greatly increased access to the downstream market, especially in the high-margin petrol station business. The global giants were steadily increasing their ownership position within the Chinese companies through a series of giant joint ventures in natural gas, oil production and petrochemical complexes.

Autos and Auto Components: Yuchai

China entered the reform period with a highly fragmented automobile industry. The degree of fragmentation increased in the early years of reform as a large number of domestic new entrants entered the fast growing industry, which was protected from international competition and had a high degree of local protection. In this, as in other sectors, the government built its industrial policy around the attempt to allow the growth of a small number of domestic producers, who were encouraged to compete with each other in the fast-growing domestic market. Three powerful production units within the old planned economy were selected to form the core of the reformed industry, namely Shanghai Auto, Yiqi (Number One Auto) and Erqi (Number Two Auto). Large-scale foreign direct investment in auto assembly was closely guided to these plants. The auto components sector was even more fragmented than the auto assembly sector. In the late 1980s there were more than 1,600 components makers, and more than 200 enterprises manufacturing internal combustion engines. In this sector also the government tried to support the growth of a small number of powerful enterprises that could compete with the global giant companies.

Yuchai began as one of the large number of state engine manufacturers. It grew at high speed, stimulated by the rapid growth in the market for medium-duty trucks. Its growth was due to a number of astute management decisions. These included the purchase of second-hand equipment from abroad, clever product choice and development, a keen sense of the importance of brand and advertising, including a deep understanding of the importance of product reliability and product guarantees, and early development of a sophisticated, national marketing system. Yuchai was a pioneer in all these developments and reaped the benefits of first mover advantage. Yuchai's ambition was to form a pillar of the development of the Chinese components industry. Its chief executive officer hoped to develop Yuchai into a Chinese version of the US

Table 6.5 **Selected Indicators of the Competitive Capability of Leading Chinese Companies Compared with the Global Giants: auto Components**

Company	Revenues $billion	Post-tax profits $million	Employees '000s	R&D $million
Bosch ('98)	28.61	446	n.a.	2,020
Denso ('98)	13.76	461	57	1,350
Caterpillar ('98)	20.98	1,513	86	838
Cummins Diesel Engine ('98)	6.27	(21)	28	255
Detroit Diesel ('98)	2.16	30	7	98
Yuchai ('98)	0.14	15*	9	n.a.

Notes
Figures in brackets indicate losses.
* pre-tax profits

companies Detroit Diesel or Cummins Diesel Engine, both large-scale global diesel engine makers (Table 6.5).

In order to accomplish this goal, Yuchai needed to be able to develop the engine business by taking over other powerful diesel engine makers, and securing a long-term market with the main truck makers, namely Yiqi and Erqi, which between them occupy 90 per cent of the Chinese medium duty truck market. The chief executive officer of Yuchai persistently lobbied the central government to support Yuchai as China's 'national champion' in the diesel engine sector, having already demonstrated its managerial and technical capabilities. However, Yuchai's main consumers, Yiqi and Erqi, decided that they would prefer to retain their own engine-making capability within the company, and internalize the profits from the diesel engine business. They were able to lobby the central government successfully to allow them to retain their independent capability in diesel engines. Indeed, Erqi had established a major joint venture with Cummins Diesel to develop its technical capability. By the late 1990s, despite having demonstrated immense entrepreneurial capability, Yuchai faced a bleak market prospect.

Despite rapid growth and institutional change, the Chinese auto industry remained at a severe disadvantage compared to the global giants at the end of the 1990s (Table 6.6). In the auto assembly sector, even its leading producers remained small scale compared to the global giants. For example, in the late 1990s, Shanghai Auto, the country's largest auto company with around 60

Table 6.6 **Selected Indicators of the Competitive Capability of Leading Chinese Companies Compared with the Global Giants: Autos**

Company	Revenues $billion	Post-tax profits $million	Employees '000s	R&D $million
GM ('98)	161.3	2,960	600	7,800
Ford ('98)	171.2	23,160	364	7,500
Daimler-Chrysler ('98)	154.6	5,660	300	5,800
Yiqi ('98)	4.4	21*	156	n.a.
Erqi ('98)	2.6	(5)	134	n.a.
Shanghai ('98)	4.8	594*	60	n.a.

Notes:
Figures in brackets indicate losses.
* pre-tax profits

per cent of the national market, produced only around 200,000 vehicles per year. This compared with over 5 million vehicles for GM, almost four million for Ford and three and a half million for Toyota. The company's domestic success was entirely due to its joint venture with VW. Shanghai Auto is closely integrated within the VW global system.

The global auto-assembly industry is in the process of high-speed concentration, with large-scale mergers, including the Daimler-Chrysler pathbreaking merger. In the auto components industry, the late 1990s also saw an explosion of mergers and concentration, as well as the de-merger of the auto component giants Delphi (from GM in 1999) and Visteon (from Ford, in 2000). Alongside the continued explosive growth through merger and acquisition of the leading tyre companies (Bridgestone, Goodyear and Michelin) other specialist components makers are merging at high speed in order to meet the globalizing needs of the world's biggest auto assemblers. The world's leading auto components companies, such as Cummins Diesel Engine, have already entered China in force, incorporating local joint venture partners into their global system. The capability even of the most successful of China's independent first-tier auto components makers, such as Yuchai, to compete on the global level playing field is very limited indeed. Had the central government supported Yuchai's bid to be the core national champion for China's diesel engine sector, then there might have been a serious possibility of challenging the global giant diesel engine companies.

Steel: Shougang

China's steel industry boomed during the economic reforms. During this period, Shougang rapidly increased its output. It undertook a wide-ranging programme of modernization, technical upgrading and diversification into activities that might support its further expansion. It developed a significant export capability in both steel and steel plant construction. Its computerization skills developed sufficiently for it to win an important competitive contract to design and install the control systems for a leading US steel maker. Both Shougang's plans for expansion and its management style bore a close resemblance to those of South Korea's Posco steel company.

Despite these important advances in Shougang's institutional and technical capability, Shougang faced severe limitations on its capability to compete on the global level playing field (Table 6.7). In the first place, although its output grew rapidly, a large part of the growth was in low value-added, low quality steel, such as construction steel. In the late 1990s, after two decades of rapid growth, high quality steel still accounted for only 15 per cent of its total output. Shougang's sales value in 1997 amounted to $2.2 billion, compared with $11 billion for British Steel, $12 billion for Usinor and $25 billion for Nippon Steel.

All four of China's top producers together, namely Shougang, Angang, Baogang and Wugang, had a sales revenue of $9.0 billion, still well below that of the main European and East Asian producers, reflecting, to a considerable degree, their high proportion of low quality, low value-added products. Shougang found it hard to extricate itself from a vicious circle. The fact that it principally produced low quality steel meant that it was mainly in competition with small-scale local producers contesting with them for local markets. The low value-added produced low profit margins, which in turn limited Shougang's capacity to modernize through investment in R&D and new products. In the late 1990s Shougang was extremely anxious to develop joint ventures with leading Western companies in order to acquire technology in high quality steels, such as those for large-scale modern buildings.

Shougang's plans to double its capacity by building a completely new steel plant at Qilu in Shandong province were overturned by the central government after the retirement in 1995 of its chief executive officer, Zhou Guanwu. At a stroke, this bureaucratic decision rendered irrational a large part of Shougang's diversified expansion, since many of its acquisitions had been intended to support the construction of Qilu. Without Qilu, these served little purpose for Shougang. Using the modern Kaiser Steel Plant, which Shougang had bought cheaply in California, Shougang might well have been able to make a high level of profits in a new plant with much lower manning

Table 6.7 **Selected Indicators of the Competitive Capability of Leading Chinese Companies Compared with the Global Giants: Steel**

Company	Revenues $billion	Post-tax profits $million	Employees '000s	R&D $million
Nippon Steel ('98)	21.59	90	28 ('95)	n.a.
Posco ('98)	9.72	680	23 ('94)	n.a.
NKK ('98)	14.15	849	18 ('95)	190
Usinor ('98)	10.65	373	58 ('95)	180
Shougang ('98)	2.16	25*	218 ('97)	n.a.
Baogang ('98)	3.12	265*	35 ('97)	n.a.

Note: * pre-tax profits

levels than at the main site. This might have formed the basis for a serious challenge to the multinational giant companies.

Alongside the blockage placed on Shougang's expansion, the global industry began to enter a period of large-scale institutional and technical change. In the US, a new form of large steel firm based around mini-mills began to develop, of which Nucor is the leading example. A truly global steel company, Ispat, based in London, with a collection of steel plants across the world, rapidly came to prominence. Within Europe a series of large-scale cross-border mergers transformed the industry. By the year 2000, a small group of 'European champions' had emerged in the industry, led by Arbed, Thyssen-Krupps, Usinor and Corus (the merger of British Steel and Hoogovens). In February 2001, Usinor announced that it was to merge with Arbed (Luxembourg) and Aceralia (Spain). The new entity would leap in to first place in the world steel industry. It would have a combined physical output of 45 million tons. It would occupy leading positions in several areas of high quality, high value-added steels, and possess a formidable marketing and research capability. It would have a level of sales revenue, at around $20 billion, and a level of profits that would put it far beyond any rival. One analyst commented: 'This completely changes the shape of the steel industry in Europe and globally'. The *Financial Times* commented: 'This shows all the signs of being a seminal moment in the history of European manufacturing' (*Financial Times*, 17 February 2001). Even in the unglamorous steel industry, globalization's high-speed advance poses deep challenges for China's large corporations.

Each of these firms had global reach, with plants across the world, and a high capability in specialist, high quality, high value-added steel. They were able to supply the global needs of large firms in such industries as packaging, automobiles, complex machinery, high quality construction and white goods. The leading companies established close ties with their customers in order to met their global needs for high quality steel.

Baogang (Shanghai) is the only large Chinese steel company that, by the late 1990s, had established a capability to compete on the global level playing field with the world's fast-transforming steel companies. Its greenfield site, strongly supported by the local Shanghai government, without a large body of existing employees and with the benefit of a booming local market for high quality steels, had developed into a potentially competitive firm able to compete on the global level playing field. In contrast, other leading steel firms in China remained heavily dominated by low quality products. As import controls were reduced in the 1990s, China's imports of steel rose substantially. These principally consisted of high quality products, reflecting the weakness of domestic firms in these areas. For example, in 1996, China still imported one-half of consumption of car sheets, 70 per cent of its tin sheets, and 80 per cent of its cold rolled stainless steel sheets.

China's leading steel firms may well be able to compete at the low value-added end of the market. However, the steel market is becoming increasingly segmented. In the high value-added and high profit part of the industry, which is closely linked with the needs of globalizing large firms, only Baogang can feel some degree of confidence that it is able to directly compete with the emerging global giants of Europe and the established giants of Asia in Japan and Korea. Shougang, like other large traditional Chinese steel firms, will find it difficult to compete directly on the global level playing field in high quality steel. Moreover, as China's international markets for steel are further liberalized, Shougang will face intensified competition from other countries' producers of low value-added steel, such as the former USSR.

Mining: Shenhua

In the midst of a vast sea of coal producers, the Chinese government has supported the construction of a potentially globally competitive large coal company. The government has used powerful measures of industrial policy to help support the growth of a large modern 'high-quality coal company'. A primary objective is that this company can supply Chinese power stations with high quality coal that can reduce the environmental damage of burning coal to generate electricity. A subsidiary, but also important, goal is to create a firm that can compete with the global giant corporations in this sector, especially in supplying the fast-growing markets of northeast Asia, but also in supplying large modern coal-fired power stations on the Chinese coast. It has supported Shenhua's development through the grant of property rights to the vast coal reserves under the Ordos Plateau, as well as through the direction of large preferential loans. Following closely the model of the world's leading coal producers, Shenhua is building a dedicated railway line to ship coal 800 kilometres from Shenhua to a dedicated port facility on the coast. Starting from scratch, Shenhua has very low manning levels compared to old established state-owned mines, which gives it a large advantage compared to domestic competitors in relation to wage costs, welfare burden and ability to organize a highly qualified and highly motivated workforce.

Despite these positive aspects of Shenhua's development, it confronts many difficulties in battling with the global giant companies. Shenhua's property rights over the associated railway and port facilities are ambiguous. It is uncertain how secure will be Shenhua's long-term right to use the facilities exclusively. Nor is it clear how the long-term charge for using the facilities will be set. Shenhua operates in a fundamentally different environment from that of the multinational coal companies. The main source of domestic and international competition for the latter is other modern coal companies. However, Shenhua faces a fierce battle with other domestic producers as well as an increasing battle with the multinationals. Shenhua must compete with small-scale local producers that pay subsistence wages to workers in conditions that have not been seen for over 100 years in the advanced economies. The small producers are heavily supported by their local governments in their battle for survival with the large coal companies. Shenhua must compete also with heavily subsidized state-owned enterprises. Not only does Shenhua face severe domestic competition it has also had to accept a major reorganization of its business structure, being forcibly merged by the central government with five large state-owned enterprises. This drastically altered Shenhua's character. Three of the mines are in a terminal state of decline and heavily loss-making. Instead of being a company with 7,000 employees, Shenhua became a company with 80,000 employees overnight.

Alongside the rise of the Chinese coal industry has gone a powerful re-shaping of the coal industry in the outside world. The world coal industry is becoming rapidly segmented. A large part of the industry is still producing with traditional methods within developing countries. In Europe, the industry has rapidly declined, as power stations have shifted heavily to oil and gas. However, a powerful group of modern, high quality coal companies has emerged. They are supplying the modern coal-fired power stations in the US and East Asia. Increasingly, they are supplying the power stations of developing countries, as the power generation industry is privatized, and operators seek the lowest-cost source of high quality coal. The emerging global giants, such as RWE, Billiton, BHP and Rio Tinto, are able to compete successfully in these markets by benefiting from having large deposits of high quality, mainly open-cast mines, through the provision of coal that is washed and graded, through centrally purchasing large amounts of modern large-scale equipment, and through supplying coal reliably through a tightly integrated transport system. Shenhua's capability to compete with these companies is weakened greatly by the problems it faces in domestic competition and by the enforced merger with the five state-owned mines.

The world's leading firms in metals and mining have entered a period of intense consolidation. The latest example of this process was the announced merger in early 2001 of BHP and Billiton, to produce a giant with almost $20 billion annual revenue. Like the other metals and mining giants, BHP-Billiton will have leading global positions in a range of mining industries, including not only coal, but also iron ore, aluminium, copper, titanium, and nickel. This provides the opportunity for powerful economies of scope applicable across a range of mining products, including finance, branding, marketing, human resources, and procurement, as well as diversification providing greater resistance to price fluctuations of any given metal or mineral product.

Conclusion: China's Industrial Policy Failure

By the end of the 1990s, none of China's leading enterprises had become a globally competitive giant corporation, with a global market, a global brand, and a global procurement system:
- China had just five companies in the *Fortune* 500 (*Fortune*, August 2 1999);
- China did not have one company in the world's top 300 companies by R&D expenditure (DTI, 1999);
- China did not have a single company in the *Financial Times* 500 companies ranked by market capitalization (*Financial Times*, 28 January 1999);
- China did not have any representatives in MSDW's list of the world's top 250 'competitive edge' companies (MSDW, 1999).

The competitive capability of China's large firms after two decades of reform was still extremely weak in relation to the global giants. This was extremely marked in the high-technology sectors, such as aerospace, complex equipment such as power plants, pharmaceuticals, as well as in 'mid-technology' sectors such as integrated oil and petrochemicals and auto components. However, even in sectors with apparently less advanced technology, such as steel and coal, there was a significant gap with leading global companies in the high value-added segments of the market. By the simplest of measures of sales revenue, profits and R&D, China's vanguard of leading firms that are intended to 'compete on the global level playing field' were still far behind the global leaders.

If the leading firms in each sector are compared with the global leaders, then it must be acknowledged that, despite significant progress, *China's leading firms were further behind the global leaders than they were when the industrial policies began almost two decades ago.*

In these fundamental senses, China's industrial policy of the past two decades must be judged a failure. The reasons for the failure of China's industrial policy are partially internal and partially external.

5. Internal Reasons for China's Failure

On the internal front, China's industrial policy encountered a number of peculiar problems which substantially differentiate the Chinese policy environment from that which faced Japan and Korea during their comparable period of catch-up at the level of the large firm:

Where is the firm?   China's industrial policy suffered from a lack of consistency in identification of the 'firm'. A great deal of China's economic reform process focused on increasing the autonomy of large 'enterprises', ultimately granting them rights as legal persons. This path of reform viewed the large plant as the core of enterprise reform. Based on the foundations of the contract system, the reform period witnessed an evolving struggle by former state-owned enterprises to increase their autonomy from the central authorities in Beijing. They did this through the following methods:
- independently using their retained profits to modernize and grow;
- struggling to become joint venture partners of the major multinationals and acquire modern technology;
- struggling to list on international markets and raise capital for modernization;
- taking over or investing in second and third tier enterprises.

This path of reform led to a situation in which it was almost impossible for strong state-owned enterprises to merge with other strong enterprises. Whereas in the world outside China, 'strong' were merging with 'strong' at high speed, in China the strong enterprises remained substantially independent of each other. When the state turned its attention towards attempting to merge large strong enterprises into large multi-plant companies, it proved extremely difficult to rebuild central control over the large subordinate companies.

Impoverished economy   China's attempts to construct large modern firms took place within the confines of an economy that was still extremely poor. China's income level and level of urbanization was far below that of Japan in the 1950s or 1960s, or Korea in the 1970s and 1980s, during the comparable periods of their industrial policies. This meant that China's aspiring globally competitive firms had to face a 'struggle on two fronts':

- A large fraction of domestic demand is still for relatively simple, low value-added products. In this market, China's aspiring large firms had to confront a sea of domestic small and medium-sized competitors, competing on price, often protected by local government policy and by a poorly developed transport system.
- In the relatively small market for high value-added products, China's aspiring large firms increasingly had to confront severe competition from imports and local production by multinationals. China's aspiring global giants were basically unable to compete in global markets, and remained confined to producing for the domestic market, caught in a vicious circle of limited scale in high value-added production, further restricting their capability to invest and grow in these areas of the market.

Local protectionism China's huge size and strong traditions of relatively autonomous local government created a strong basis of regional support for emerging large firms. This is advantageous for firm growth in some senses. However, in an epoch of explosive globalization, it is not feasible for a single country, even one of China's size, to support several major players in each sector. In Europe, the governments of France, Italy and Germany have been extremely reluctant to allow the process of cross-border merger to grow rapidly. However, it has been hard for them to resist this process in areas where the government does not have an ownership share. A major fear has been the possibility that a given country may be the main loser in downsizing and rationalization. This issue is even more acute in China, given the massive over-manning. Consequently, local governments have strongly resisted the merger of large local firms with large firms based elsewhere in the country.

Inheritance from the planned economy China's reforms began from an existing body of large-scale state-owned enterprises, with large numbers of employees. As in the former USSR, the core of China's industry was a small number of large-scale plants. Under the Maoist system, and possibly influenced also by a distinctive East Asian cultural approach, China's large firms were constructed as a 'large family', with cradle-to-grave social support and a deep sense of social commitment to employees and their families. Only after two decades of reform were China's large enterprises seriously attempting to downsize their workforce.

The retention of such a large number of employees on the payroll not only affected costs. It also drastically affected the possibility of creating a modern, competitive system of labour organization. A combination of government policy and the huge numbers of employees placed severe constraints on the growth of real wages. Moreover, the surrounding sea of poverty has meant that it is politically extremely difficult to implement such remuneration measures as stock options. Instead, the most successful large enterprises have allocated a large fraction of their disposable income to expanding welfare facilities which are provided reasonably equally for all employees, rather than reinforcing material incentive-based remuneration. This has stimulated a large number of highly qualified personnel to leave large state enterprises to work in better-rewarded jobs.

Incentive to diversify   Several factors interacted to cause a powerful incentive to diversify:
- limited capability to compete in export markets;
- constraints on mergers and acquisitions among large firms;
- commitment to the 'large family';
- high transaction costs consequent upon the undeveloped nature of the infrastructure.

These forces created a powerful incentive for diversification into unrelated businesses in order to provide channels for growth, profits and employment. This approach was legitimated by the central government's support for the idea of a 'business group' with a core firm at its centre. In an even more extreme way than in Korea or Japan, the typical large Chinese firm constructed a wide network of diversified second and third tier businesses in which it invested. Only a small fraction of these were able to benefit from economies of scale.

Failures in China's bureaucracy   The bureaucratic apparatus with which China was attempting to implement industrial policy was very different from that in Japan or South Korea. The vast communist party that is still at China's core, with over 50 million members, has been a source both of strength and weakness in the country's attempt to develop large competitive firms. Japan relied on relatively small professional civil services. It was powerfully imbued with a commitment to achieve economic advance following a massive military defeat. China's bureaucracy is vastly greater in absolute terms and even larger in relative terms. It lacks the intense commitment to national development of its neighbours in northeast Asia, for which national economic advance was a matter of life or death for the country. Despite great advances in its technical capabilities and important successes in aspects of industrial policy, China's bureaucracy has been unable to truly separate itself from the operations of the leading enterprises.

Moreover, after twenty years of reform alongside extensive state intervention, the Party had become deeply imbued with corruption, which seriously inhibited its efforts to implement a consistent, effective industrial policy. In 2000–1, as China prepared to join the WTO, a series of central government investigations up and down the country revealed massive levels of corruption that reached deep into the Party hierarchy. In one of the most prominent of these investigations, in Guangdong province, the state sentenced seven people to death for their part in a tax fraud that 'may rank as the country's biggest corruption scandal since the Communist era began in 1949 … The scandal reinforces a sense that corruption is withering the root and branch of China's ruling communist hierarchy' (*Financial Times*, 3 March 2001). In March 2001, Beijing's highest leaders pledged last week to the National People's Congress (NPC), or parliament, to combat rampant corruption in all its forms. Officials highlighted grave problems with China's legal system, including corrupt and incompetent judges. Last year authorities investigated more than 45,000 cases of corruption – up 15 per cent from 1999. The number of bribery cases climbed 28 per cent while counterfeiting smuggling, and tax evasion cases rose 45 per cent, according to figures released at the NPC (*Financial Times*, 20 March 2001).

Li Peng, NPC chairman, reportedly told the Beijing meeting that corruption had 'become so serious that it threatened to topple the ruling Communist party' (*Financial Times*, 20 March 2001). Li Lanqing, a vice-premier, reportedly warned in January that unless current trends were reversed it would 'ruin the party and the state' (*Financial Times*, 3 March 2001).

Ideological commitment to state ownership   In sharp contrast with Japan and South Korea, China's policymakers remained committed throughout to maintaining the commanding heights of large-scale industry in state ownership. Large state enterprises were allowed gradually to expand the absorption of capital from non-state sources, including Sino-foreign joint ventures, and flotation on domestic and international stock markets. However, even after two decades of enterprise reform, the government remained committed to substantial public ownership of large enterprises, providing a continued channel for bureaucratic intervention in large firms' management, despite persistent attempts to 'separate ownership from management'. This was in sharp contrast with Japan and South Korea during their catch-up.

This approach also ran counter to the trend in the advanced economies in which a string of global leading firms evolved out of privatized state enterprises. These included Usinor, Arbed, Corus (formerly British Steel), Posco and China Steel (Taiwan) in the steel sector, Elf Aquitaine, ENI, Repson/YPF and BP Amoco in oil and petrochemicals, Rolls Royce, British

Aerospace and Aerospatiale-Matra in aerospace, and British Telecom, Deutsche Telecom, France Telecom and Telecom Italia in telecoms. By the year 2000, not one of the world's top 300 firms by R&D spending, and only a tiny handful of the world's top 500 companies by value of sales, was in the public sector.

Whereas Japan and South Korea had a relatively simple non-ideological goal of building globally competitive giant corporations, China's industrial policy remained suffused with ideology intertwined with the objective of building global giant corporations. The ideological objective provided a justification for central bureaucratic intervention to limit the expansion of ambitious and increasingly autonomous large enterprises such as Shougang, SPC and Daqing, and for the persistence of bureaucratic interference in the management of technically autonomous large enterprises.

6. External Reasons for the Failure of China's Industrial Policy

At least as important as the special difficulties that confronted China on the internal front in implementing a successful industrial policy, is the fact that China's attempt to build large globally competitive firms coincided with the most revolutionary epoch in world business history, possibly even including the Industrial Revolution. The period during which Japan and South Korea were putting into place their industrial policy to build global giant corporations was a far less dynamic one, albeit that the international economy grew strongly. China's efforts to support the growth of competitive global corporations has taken place at a time of unprecedented change in the international business system and in technical progress. There were a number of aspects to the *global business revolution:*

Liberalization of world trade and capital markets   The period since the late 1980s has witnessed for the first time the opening up of a *truly global market place* in goods, services, capital and skilled labour. The only market which still remains bound firmly by nationality is the vast sea of unskilled labour. The integration of the global market place has been facilitated by the dramatic transformation in *information technology*. It has been facilitated also by the comprehensive change in the impact of the international institutions. It is no longer practically feasible to benefit fully from trade with and investment from the developed countries without agreeing to extensive economic liberalization of international economic relations, especially those implemented by the WTO (including TRIPs and World Telecoms Agreement).

Explosive M & A   This period has witnessed by the world's most explosive period of *mergers and acquisitions*. Global M&A rose from $156 billion in 1992 to around $3,300 billion in 1999. This process seems to be far from over, and already massively exceeds, in real terms and in terms of its significance, previous merger booms. Instead of an epoch of national champions and conglomerates, the advanced economies' business structures have been revolutionized. In almost every sector (including such diverse sectors as aerospace, IT, pharmaceuticals, autos, auto components, petrochemicals, complex equipment, fast-moving consumer goods, packaging and power equipment – see Table 6.8 – a small number of focused global producers dominates the world market. It is not only the core businesses that have experienced this explosive process of concentration. The deepening interaction between core companies and supplier companies has created an explosive 'cascade' effect that is rapidly leading to concentration and focus among the first tier suppliers and even spilling over into second and third tier suppliers.

Dramatic growth of business capabilities of leading global firms
The leading firms are able to benefit from large expenditures on focused R&D. The resulting technical progress has been comprehensively dominated by the global giant corporations. In 1998, the world's top 300 corporations spent around $250 billion on R&D, providing an explosive propulsion to the world's stock of applicable knowledge: 'MNCs *are the world's chief repositories of economically useful knowledge and skills. All the screaming in the world will not change this*' (Martin Wolf, *Financial Times*, 17 November 1999). The leading firms are able also to benefit from massive expenditure on *marketing and brand-building*, of which advertising is just one component. The leading firms are able to attract the world's most able workers. They are able to benefit also from massive cost savings consequent upon *global procurement* systems and large benefits from deep, constant interaction with supplier companies, facilitated by the revolution in information technology.

A veritable '*external firm*' of global dimensions is being created in sector after sector. Increasingly, leading firms in all sectors are being distinguished by their capability to undertake *systems integration* stretching across the value chain. The most dramatic recent illustration of this process is the announcement by Ford, GM and Daimler-Chrysler that they are to establish a joint internet procurement network (*Financial Times*, 27 March 2000). A large fraction of the world's auto components procurement will therefore flow through this unified system. The world's total auto components procurement amounts to $1,780 billion. The central coordination of a large fraction of the world's auto components makers through a single system represents a highly significant step in the growth of the 'external firm' that stretches across the entire value chain.

Table 6.8 **Global Oligipoly in the Business Revolution**

Company name	Sector	Global market share (%)	Source
AEROSPACE			
Boeing	Commercial aircraft orders over 100 seats	70	*MSDW, '98*
Airbus	Commercial aircraft orders over 100 seats	30	*MSDW, '98*
Rolls-Royce	aero-engine orders	34	*FT, 6 Mar. '98*
GE	aero-engine orders	53	*FT, 6 Mar. '98*
Pratt & Whitney	aero-engine orders	13	*FT, 6 Mar. '98*
IT			
Lucent	internet and telecoms equipment	17	*FT, 27 Oct. '99*
Intel	micro-processors	85	*MSDW, '98*
Microsoft	computer systems	90+	*MSDW, '98*
Cisco	computer routers	66	*MSDW, '98*
	: high end routers	80	
Corning	optical fibres	50	*FT, 15 Nov. '99*
Hyundai Electronics	DRAMS	21	*FT, 15 Oct. '99*
Samsung Electronics	DRAMS	20	*FT, 15 Oct. '99*
Sony	electronic games	67	*FT, 29 Mar. '00*
Nintendo	electronic games	29	*FT, 29 Mar. '00*
Ericsson	mobile phones	15	*FT, 8 Feb. '99*
Nokia	mobile phones	23	
Motorola	mobile phones	20	
PHARMACEUTICALS			
Glaxo-Wellcome/ SKB	prescription drugs	7	*FT, 18 Jan. '00*
	: central nervous system	12	
	: anti-infection	17	*Glaxo-Wellcome,*
	: respiratory	17	*Annual Report,*
	: anti-asthma	31	*1999*
	: anti-herpes	49	

Table 6.8 **continued**

Company name	Sector	Global market share (%)	Source
	PHARMACEUTICALS *(continued)*		
Merck	prescription drugs	5	*FT, 18 Jan. '00*
	: statin anti-cholesterol	40	*Merck, Annual*
	: angiotension converting enzyme inhibitors	30	*Report, 1998*
Medtronic	Implantable/interventional therapy technologies*	45	*MSDW, '98*
	: pacemakers	50*	*MSDW, '98*
	AUTOS		
Ford/Mazda/Volvo	automobiles	16	*MSDW, '99*
GM	automobiles	15	*MSDW, '99*
Daimler-Chrysler	automobiles	10	*MSDW, '99*
VW	automobiles	9	*MSDW, '99*
Toyota	automobiles	9	*MSDW, '99*
Renault/Nissan	automobiles	9	*MSDW, '99*
	AUTO COMPONENTS		
Pilkington	auto glass	25	*FT, 21 May '96*
GKN	constant velocity joints	40	*FT, 22 July '96*
Tenneco	shock absorbers/car exhaust systems	25	*FT, 28 Oct. '96*
Lucas	brake systems	25	*FT, 8 May '96*
Bosch	brake systems	31	*FT, 8 May '96*
Bridgestone	tires	19	*FT, 19 Jan. '96*
Michelin	tires	18	*FT, 19 Jan. '96*
Goodyear	tires	14	*FT, 19 Jan. '96*
	PETROCHEMICALS		
BP Amoco	PTA	37	
	acetic acid (technology licenses)	70	*BP Amoco, Annual Report*
	acrylonite (technology licenses)	90	
	COMPLEX EQUIPMENT		
Invensys (BTR/Siebe)	control/automation equipment	11	*FT, 24 Nov. '98*

Table 6.8 **continued**

Company name	Sector	Global market share (%)	Source
COMPLEX EQUIPMENT (continued)			
Siemens	control/automation equipment	10	*FT, 24 Nov. '98*
ABB	control/automation equipment	9	*FT, 24 Nov. '98*
Emerson	control/automation equipment	8	*FT, 24 Nov. '98*
Fanuc	machine tool controls	45	*FT, 11 Sept. '96*
Schindler	lifts	25	*FT, 30 Mar. '99*
Otis	lifts	18	*FT, 30 Mar. '99*
Mitsubishi	lifts	13	*FT, 30 Mar. '99*
Kone	lifts	9	*FT, 30 Mar. '99*
FAST MOVING CONSUMER GOODS			
Coca-Cola	carbonated soft drinks	51	*Coca-Cola, Annual Report, '98*
Chupa Chups	lollipops	34	*FT, 31 Mar. '00*
Proctor and Gamble	tampons	48	*MSDW, '98*
Gillette	razors	70	*MSDW, '98*
Fuji Film	camera films	35	*MSDW, '98*
Nike	sneakers	36	*MSDW, '98*
PACKAGING			
Toray	polyester film	60	*FT, 15 May '98*
Sidel	PET plastic packaging machines	55	*Sidel, Annual Report, 1998*
Alcoa/Reynolds*	aluminium	24	*FT, 27 Oct. '99*
POWER EQUIPMENT			
GE	gas turbines (1993–98)	34	*FT, 24 Mar.'99*
Siemens/ Westinghouse	gas turbines (1993–98)	32	*FT, 24 Mar. '99*
ABB/Alstom	gas turbines (1993–98)	21	*FT, 24 Mar. '99*

Source: MSDW, 1998

Notes: * including pacemakers, implantable defibrillators, leads, programmers for treatment of patients with irregular heartbeats.

    ** mergers pending

7. Dominance of Firms based in Advanced Economies

Regions containing a small fraction of the world's population have massively dominated the global big business revolution (Table 6.9). The high-income economies contain just 16 per cent of the world's total population. In 1997 they accounted for 91 per cent of the world's total stock market capitalization, 95 per cent of the *Fortune* 500 list of companies which ranks companies by value of sales, 97 per cent of the *Financial Times* 500 which ranks companies by value of stock market capitalization and 99 per cent of the world's top 300 companies by value of R&D spending. Developing countries are massively disadvantaged in the race to compete on the global level playing field of international big business. The starting points in the race to dominate global markets could not be more uneven. The whole of the developing world, containing 84 per cent of the world's population, contains just 26 *Fortune* 500 companies, sixteen *Financial Times* 500 companies, and fifteen of Morgan Stanley's 250 leading 'competitive edge' companies.

Not only is there a massive imbalance between the 'starting points' in the great globalization race on the global level playing field, but there is also a deeply uneven distribution of business power within the advanced capitalist economies in the big business revolution. The large firms of the USA dominate this process. The leading US-based companies have led the way in the resurgence of big business investment in R&D. The IT sector (hardware plus software) is much the most important category of R&D expenditure (DTI, 1999), with 74 of the top 300 companies by R&D spending in 1998. Of these 53 were US-based companies. No less than 16 out of the top 17 software firms by R&D spending were based in the US. The USA's share of total world FDI outflows rose from 14% in 1986–91 to 27% in 1997 (UNCTAD, 1998: 367). By 1998, North American firms accounted for 37 per cent of the Fortune 500 ranking of the world's leading firms, ranked by sales value. North America was headquarters to 134 of Morgan Stanley's 250 world leading 'competitive edge companies and 254 of the *Financial Times* 500 companies (ranked by market capitalization) (*Financial Times*, 28 January 1999).

8. China and the Extended Global Value Chain: The Choices Facing China

As China's entry to the WTO approached, the country's leaders confronted extremely difficult policy choices. At the extremes, the choice was to either abandon or strengthen industrial policy.

Table 6.9 **Dominance of Firms Based in High Income Countries of the Global Big Business Revolution**

	Population		GNP, 1997 (1)		GNP, 1997 (2)		Fortune 500 companies (1998) (3)		FT 500 companies (1998) (4)		Top 300 companies by R&D spend (1997)		Stock market capitalization (1997)	
	billion	%	$b.	%	$b.	%	No.	%	No.	%	No.	%	$b.	%
HIEs	926	16	23,802	80	21,091	57	474	95	484	97	299	99	18,452	91
L/MIEs	4,903	84	6,123	20	15,861	43	26 (5)	5	16 (6)	3	2	1	1,725	9

Sources: FT, 28 January 1999; World Bank, 1998; 190–1 and 220–1; *Fortune, 2 August 1999* DTI, 1998: 70–80

Notes

(1) at prevailing rate of exchange
(2) at PPP dollars
(3) ranked by sales revenue
(4) ranked by market capitalization
(5) of which: Korea = 9, China = 6, Brazil = 4, Taiwan = 2, Venezuela = 1, Russia = 1, India = 1, Mexico = 1, Malaysia = 1
(6) of which: Hong Kong = 7, Brazil = 2, Taiwan = 2, Singapore = 1, Mexico = 1, India = 1, Korea = 1, Argentina = 1
HIEs = High Income Economies
L/MIEs = Low/Middle Economies

8.1 Strengthening 'Industrial Policy' to Build 'National Champions' that can Challenge the World's Leading Systems Integrators?

Faced with the dramatic widening of the gap between the business capability of China's leading firms compared with the global giant companies, China faced a hugely important turning point in the late 1990s. Reflecting on the failures of industrial policy over the previous decade and a half, China's policymakers could have chosen to learn from the past failures and have attempted to strengthen and improve their industrial policy. This would have been consistent with China's approach towards experimentation in its reform programme, with the incremental transition towards a market economy and with gradual, controlled integration with world economy. Many policymakers and industrialists supported such a path, continuing to argue their case even after the historic US–China Agreement of 1999.

China's strategic options for restructuring its large state enterprises had been narrowed by the late 1990s. Although the room for manoeuvre had been greatly reduced, it was still argued that there were choices that planners could have made to enable a group of large, globally competitive Chinese firms to emerge. China's aspiring global corporations face a far more difficult international business environment than that which confronted Japan and the Four Little Tigers during a comparable stage in their catch-up efforts. However, it is argued that China has the potential advantages of a huge, unified, ancient culture. It contains over one-fifth of the total world population. This is a mighty political force capable of being mobilized in support of such an endeavour. In addition, it has a domestic market that already is one of the world's largest and most dynamic, and that is potentially the largest of any country. It is argued that these factors provide great potential 'leverage', if China's policymakers are willing and able to use them in pursuit of a reinvigorated industrial policy.

The following are some of the measures that have been suggested for a revived and strengthened industrial policy to create large firms that can challenge the world's leading systems integrator companies.

State-orchestrated mergers   One option was to merge the domestic 'giant' companies into just one or two giant firms within each sector. Japan pursued this route in the 1930s by state-led mergers of several leading steel firms to produce Japan Steel, which had a virtual monopoly over the domestic steel market prior to 1939. The state also encouraged the growth of just two giant auto firms in the 1930s, Toyota and Nissan, which accounted for 85 per cent of total production by the late 1930s. The Korean government allowed

Posco to develop in a massively protected domestic market without any significant competition for a long period. In early 2000 the Brazilian state allowed the formation of the giant domestic beverage company, Ambev, produced by a merger of the two leading domestic brewers, Brahma and Antartica: 'The prospect of creating a Brazilian beverages multinational helped win regulatory approval for the merger, despite the fact that the new group will have about 65 per cent of the beer market. In a country with few internationally-known national champions, the national champion argument drowned out potential threats to competition in the domestic market' (*Financial Times*).

Many of Europe's leading private or quasi-private companies of the 1990s emerged from similar structures. In the 1960s Britain merged many different steel, aerospace and automobile firms to form, respectively, British Steel, British Aerospace and British Leyland. In the former two cases these were to form the basis for highly successful private enterprises. It is almost certain that they would not have become successful without the initial merger imposed by the British government. Other Western European countries followed similar industrial policies (for example, France's Usinor Steel Company was formed in this fashion).

As in other countries that pursued this strategy, this path opens up the possibility of domestic monopoly and requires skilful regulation to prevent low levels of efficiency. Due to the relatively small size of the domestic market, such mergers could still result in entities that are relatively small by world standards, given the massive growth in size of the world's leading system integrators. Such mergers do not directly address the problem of poor corporate governance. Nor do they solve the problem of backward technology. However, they provide a more realistic foundation for competition with the global giants than did the previously fragmented industrial structure. The state's implementation of the restructuring of CNPC and Sinopec, the plan to merge China's airlines into three 'giants', its support for a series of trans-regional acquisitions by China Mobile and for large-scale mergers in the power generation sector, were signs that a renewed commitment to industrial policy might be developing.

Increased autonomy for powerful emerging corporations   In Europe in the 1980s and 1990s, a succession of former state-owned 'national champions' were transformed into autonomous, competitive transnational corporations. These included ENI, Repsol, BP and Elf Aquitaine in oil and petrochemicals, Usinor and British Steel in the steel industry, Volkswagen and Renault in the auto industry, and Aerospatiale, Rolls-Royce and BAe in the aerospace industry. The typical pattern was for the appointment of a strong, market-oriented chief executive officer who was subject to strict performance criteria. The CEO was authorized to change business practices radically, gradually privatize ownership rights, and develop an international capability, especially through mergers and acquisitions.

In China in the 1990s, there emerged numerous powerful enterprises. They developed a deep sense of corporate identity and ambition. They were led by ambitious and effective chief executive officers. These included Shougang under Zhou Guanwu, AVIC under Zhu Yuli, Shanghai Petrochemical Corporation under Wu Yixin, Daqing under Ding Guiming, Shenhua under Ye Qing, Yuchai under Wang Jianming, and Sanjiu under Zhao Xinxian. Each of these leaders had a clear understanding of the nature of global competition. Each of them was ambitious to turn their firm into a true global competitive business. However, the enterprises' superior authorities were nervous at the loss of power that might result from these enterprises taking an increasingly independent path. The degree to which these enterprises were allowed to reduce the state's ownership share was tightly controlled. Not all of them were permitted to raise funds from the stock market and none was permitted to reduce the state's share below 50 per cent. Each of them had severe bureaucratic barriers placed in the path of their domestic expansion, and more than one had severe bureaucratic constraints on their international expansion. They each faced serious bureaucratic constraints on large-scale domestic mergers and acquisitions.

If the central government was willing to provide strong support for emerging autonomous enterprises, then the respective corporations would be much better able to raise funds from domestic and international stock markets. China's leading corporations might be able to enjoy strong stock market performance, which facilitates further international expansion. It would also demonstrate the benefits of improved corporate governance to aspiring large corporations.

Government procurement contracts   To this day, state procurement contracts remain an important and highly controversial instrument of industrial policy in advanced capitalist economies. State procurement contracts were an important mechanism of state support for the emerging national champions in aerospace, telecoms equipment and power equipment. China's use of this instrument was relatively limited, and weakened significantly as the influence of market forces grew stronger over the course of the reforms. In the aerospace sector, the central authorities were able to do almost nothing to support the growth of a domestic aircraft industry by ordering domestic airlines to purchase short-haul jet aircraft from the McDonnell Douglas/Boeing or AE-100 ventures. In the power equipment sector, the state's ability or desire to influence the purchases made by power stations declined substantially over the course of the reforms. Increased use of this instrument still remained a logical policy choice for China's leaders at the end of the 1990s.

Using global competition We have seen that China was a major location for multinational investment by large global corporations. These were mainly in joint ventures. However, the very intensity of global competition between giant corporations threw up possibilities for a different strategy that might have been pursued by Chinese industrial planners.

In the 1990s intense global oligopolistic competition in each sector produced firms based in the advanced economies that were technically strong, and which had a strong modern management system, but which fell behind in the global oligopoly race. They lacked the global scale necessary to compete. Such companies included Westinghouse and Mitsubishi Electric in the power equipment sector; Fokker and Fairchild-Dornier in the aerospace sector; Sumitomo, Pirelli and Continental in the tyre sector; Volvo, Nissan, Mitsubishi and even Fiat in the auto sector; Scania, Volvo, MAN and Paccar in the truck sector; Detroit Diesel in the diesel engine sector; Bethlehem Steel, YKK and Cockerill Sambrell in the steel sector; Astra, Rhône-Poulenc and Hoechst in the pharmaceuticals sector; Repsol, Arco and ENI in the oil and petrochemical sector; and Alcatel and Marconi in the IT hardware sector.

In addition, there were a few thrusting new players from other developing countries which lacked the revenue and stock market capitalization to grow into competitive global giants on their own. Such firms included Embraer (Brazil) in the aerospace industry; Daewoo (Korea) and Hyundai (Korea) in the auto sector; Hong Kong Telecom and Singapore Telecoms in the telecoms sector; Samsung (Korea) and Acer (Taiwan) in the IT hardware sector, YPF (Argentina), Formosa Plastics (Taiwan), Reliance (India) and Petrobras (Brazil) in the oil and petrochemical sector, CVRD (Brazil) and Indalco (Indian Aluminium Corporation) in the metals and mining sector.

If the Chinese government had been sufficiently purposive about industrial planning, in the way that Japan or South Korea had been, then it is logically possible for a full-scale merger to have been negotiated between selected large Chinese companies and the respective global partner. Without such a merger, the foreign partner anyway faced the prospect of extinction through bankruptcy or merger with another capitalist giant company. The terms of the merger with the Chinese company could have been constructed in such a way to provide better earning prospects for the foreign shareholders through access to the huge and fast-growing Chinese market. It would have provided the vista of secure long-term rentier income for the foreign shareholders.

The weak multinational would have been offered a minority share in the new entity, but would be ceded full management control. The Chinese partner's equity share would come from a combination of bank loans, stock market flotation, asset contribution and a value placed on privileged access to the Chinese market for a specified period of time. It would have been given privileged access to the Chinese market for a specified period of time, and various supportive policies. For example, in aerospace, a certain proportion of Chinese airliners would be allocated to the new firm established between the Chinese and the multinational, after which point protection would be steadily reduced, and it would have to sink or swim in open competition. The foreign management would be ceded full management authority to run the business in order to make a profit for the Chinese and foreign shareholders.

Thus in the aerospace industry, Xifei (Xian Aerospace) might have partnered Fokker, and Chengfei (Chengdu Aerospace) might have partnered Embraer. In the auto industry, Yiqi might have partnered Daewoo, and Erqi have partnered Mitsubishi. In the auto components industry Yuchai might have partnered Detroit Diesel. In the pharmaceutical industry, Sanjiu might have partnered Astra and Huabei have partnered Rhône-Poulenc. In the steel industry, Shougang might have partnered Cockerill Sambrell, Angang partnered YKK, and Wugang partnered Bethlehem Steel. In the oil and petrochemical sector, Daqing might have partnered ENI, SPC partnered YPF and Yanshan partnered Arco. In the telecoms industry, Guangdong Telecom might have partnered Hong Kong Telecom. In the IT hardware industry, Huawei might have partnered Alcatel or Marconi. Numerous such options still existed at the end of the 1990s.

The key purpose of such international mergers would be 'to liberate the large state enterprises from bureaucratic control, using the management methods of large global corporations' (Wang Xiaoqiang).

Supporting non-SOE national champions   A small group of relatively strong domestic non-SOE firms emerged in the late 1990s. Leading examples of such firms included Haier and Meidi in consumer electronics, Legend in personal computers, Huawei in IT hardware, Baiyunshan in pharmaceuticals, and Jianlibao in soft drinks. These firms were typically led by charismatic CEOs, such as Liu Chuanzhi at Legend and Zhang Ruiming at Haier. They emerged typically in relatively low technology sectors and were able to establish a degree of domestic brand recognition, and in some cases began to penetrate the lower value-added segments of international markets. They employed modern methods of business management. They raised funds from the stock market. They used stock options to stimulate employee enthusiasm. They established genuinely autonomous businesses free from detailed interference from the state. They competed ferociously with the multinational corporations.

These companies often received favourable treatment in the international press. They were sometimes written about by international business schools. For example, the Harvard Business Schools produced a much-read case study on Haier. They were lauded by the populist neoclassical economists within China as examples of the achievements that Chinese firms could make if left to compete on their own on the global level playing field, unaided by state intervention. They were held up as examples of the new shoots that could burst into life once the old world of the state-owned enterprises was destroyed.

However, a closer look at these firms reveals that they typically benefited from a protected domestic market, and from state support through soft loans, state procurement and protected marketing channels. Despite their enormous achievements, these firms were without exception far behind the global leaders in terms of revenue, R&D expenditure, marketing expenditure and global market share. They were all anticipating serious competitive challenges after China's accession to the WTO. Without continued state support, they were most unlikely to be able to build on their considerable entrepreneurial achievements, and mount a serious challenge to the global giants in the respective sectors. Nurturing these firms already demonstrated that 'green shoots' through industrial policy measures was an obvious path to pursue. Such measures included continued protection, continued soft loans, state support for their R&D, and state support for them in their efforts to expand through merger and acquisition.

The mythology surrounding these companies attributes their relative success to their 'success in market-place competition', not to government support. The blunt reality is that, in most cases, relative success required both high entrepreneurial achievements as well as state support. Private discussion with the strategic officers of some of the leading non-state firms reveals great concern about the challenges that await them if China applies fully the WTO Agreement. The leaders of these firms are only too aware of the difficulty they will face in genuinely open competition with such firms as Cisco and Nortel, Coca-Cola and PepsiCo, Whirlpool and Electrolux, IBM and Dell.

State support for technological upgrading   The most successful examples of high-speed technical upgrading in developing countries have taken place through powerful direct and indirect state support. Taiwan provides a vivid example of this form of partnership in a developing country. To this day, almost two-fifths of US technical progress takes place through direct state support for R&D, funded by US taxpayers. In 1994, this totalled no less than $36 billion, around the same size as the entire national product of Malaysia. One can only wonder at the impact on China's technical progress of such a vast infusion of state support for R&D.

In the early days of the reforms, China's central planners enacted a highly successful programme of technical transfer, including a large-scale programme in the power equipment industry. At that point it appeared as if the central planners might mimic the role of MITI in Japan. In fact, as the size of the Chinese market in aerospace, power equipment, autos, pharmaceuticals, high quality steel, oil and petrochemicals, and telecoms equipment grew ever larger, so the degree of state intervention to ensure technical transfer as a condition of access to the Chinese market became weaker. Instead of a centrally coordinated activity, linking procurement, market access and ownership in a rational, explicit and transparent fashion, the technology transfer requirements from multinational companies became increasingly decentralized and uncoordinated. There is no reason in principle why state-coordinated technical transfers should not be revived and greatly strengthened, 'trading market for technology' on a large scale.

Conclusion A key aspect of following such a path was the necessity to create a credible threat of international competition that was sufficient to stimulate change, However, the threat should not have been so severe as to create competition that would prevent any realistic chance of competing with the global giants. Joining the WTO on terms that paid due recognition to the reality of China's developing country and impoverished status was one such possibility. A long transition period to accepting the full impact of WTO rules would have been one part of such a programme. Following such a path would have constituted a coherent path for industrial policy to follow. It would not have involved rejection of the importance of market competition. It would have involved further experimentation and learning from previous policy mistakes. It would have been realistic about the magnitude of the task facing China.

8.2 Abandon 'Industrial Policy' and Become Part of the Extended Global Value Chain?

An alternative view is that China should acknowledge that 'catch-up' at the level of the large 'systems integrator' firm is, with rare exceptions, no longer possible for firms based in developing countries, even huge countries such as China. According to this argument, the only feasible path is to abandon 'old-fashioned' industrial policy aiming at creating 'national champions', and, instead, attempting to develop the country's capabilities within the global value chain. This view argues that these possibilities have been massively increased by the revolution in the nature of the firm during the epoch of the global business revolution.

At the core of the revolution in the global business system lies a revolution within the core 'systems integrator' itself. Within the old 'Fordist', vertically integrated large corporation, the different departments had considerable autonomy and the problem of monitoring performance of subordinate units was a serious and widely discussed issue. Even more difficult were the problems involved in monitoring performance in foreign branches of multi-national companies. National branches of major multinational corporations typically developed a high degree of operational autonomy. Leading multi-national firms often likened their structure to a feudal system, within which the local chiefs had high degrees of independence. New information tech-nology has drastically increased the possibilities for close monitoring of performance within the firm, even across the entire globe. The 'business unit' structure adopted by many firms typically involves constant monitoring of performance in way that was quite impossible even a few years ago. However, surrounding the core 'systems integrator' there has taken place a revolution in the relationship between the core firm and the surrounding business system.

If we define the firm not by the entity which is the legal owner, but rather by the sphere over which conscious coordination of resource allocation takes place, then, far from becoming 'hollowed out' and much smaller in scope, the large firm can be seen to have enormously increased in size during the global business revolution. As the large firm has 'disintegrated', so has the extent of conscious coordination over the surrounding value chain increased dramat-ically. In a wide range of business activities, the organization of the value chain has developed into a comprehensively planned and coordinated activ-ity. At its centre is the core systems integrator. This firm typically possesses some combination of a number of key attributes. These include the capability to raise finance for large new projects, and the resources necessary to fund a high level of R&D spending to sustain technological leadership, to develop a global brand, to invest in state-of-the art information technology and to attract the best human resources. Across a wide range of business types, from fast-moving consumer goods to aircraft manufacture, the core systems inte-grator interacts in the deepest, most intimate fashion with the major segments of the value chain, both upstream and downstream.

Through the hugely increased planning function undertaken by systems integrators, facilitated by recent developments in information technology, the boundaries of the large corporation have become significantly blurred. The core systems integrators across a wide range of sectors have become the co-ordinators of a vast array of business activity outside the boundaries of the legal entity in terms of ownership. The relationship extends far beyond the price relationship. In order to develop and maintain their competitive advantage, the systems integrators deeply penetrate the value chain both upstream and downstream, becoming closely involved in business activities that range from long-term planning to meticulous control of day-by-day production and delivery schedules. Competitive advantage for the systems integrator requires that it must consider the interests of the whole value chain in order to minimize costs across the whole system. It has a powerful incentive to ensure that knowledge is shared in order to reduce systems costs across the whole value chain.

A dramatic expansion of the realm of planning and coordination by the systems integrators has been the establishment of a wide range of online procurement networks by groups of the most powerful firms within given sectors. The first sector to announce such a process was the auto industry. In early 2000, GM, Ford, Renault and Daimler-Chrysler announced that they were going to establish the world's largest electronic marketplace to purchase components (named Covsint) Between them they purchase directly several hundred million dollars' worth of components. This announcement was closely followed by many others, including the aerospace, energy and even the steel industries. The implications of these developments were enormous, not least for the competition authorities. They signalled a massive extension of the realm of planning and conscious coordination over business activity.

The relationship of the core systems integrator with the upstream first tier suppliers extends far beyond the price relationship. Increasingly, leading first tier suppliers across a wide range of industries have established long-term 'partner' or 'aligned supplier' relationships with the core systems integrators. Key systems integrators play an active role in 'industrial planning' through their selection of those suppliers that are to be their trusted partners and with whom they agree to establish a long-term relationship. Trust is an important ingredient in these relationships. In some cases, the most fundamental aspects of the relationship are not even defined through written contracts. In recent years, systems integrators have widely established global procurement offices. This reflects an enormous increase in the central planning function of systems integrators. Leading first tier suppliers use their close relationship with systems integrators as evidence of their long-term business viability in order to support and enhance their business position. Some key aspects of the intimate relationship between systems integrators and upstream firms include the following.

First, leading first tier suppliers plan in minute detail the location of their plants in relation to the location of the core systems integrator. This can apply as much to a leading auto component maker as to a leading packaging supplier to a fast-moving consumer goods firm. It is not uncommon to find the aligned supplier literally supplying key products through a hole in the wall to the systems integrator. Secondly, it is increasingly the case that the aligned supplier produces goods within the systems integrator itself. It is common for leading suppliers of services, such as data systems or even travel agents, to physically work within the premises of the systems integrator. Sometimes there is a large number of employees, perhaps a thousand or more from a given firm, physically within the systems integrator undertaking such specialist functions. Thirdly, leading first tier suppliers plan their R&D in close consultation with the projected needs of the core systems integrator. An increasing part of R&D is contracted out to small and medium-sized firms. This is typically under the close control of the systems integrator. Fourthly, product development is intimately coordinated with the systems integrator. This can apply as much to the development of a new packaging design for a fast-moving consumer goods firm, such as a new design of plastic bottle or can, as to the design of an aircraft engine for a huge airliner. Finally, precise product specifications are instantaneously communicated to the leading suppliers through newly developed information technology. The production and supply schedules of leading first tier suppliers are comprehensively coordinated with the systems integrator to ensure that the required inputs arrive exactly when they are needed and the inventory of the systems integrator is kept to a minimum.

Planning by systems integrators extends downstream also. Manufacturers of complex capital goods, from aircraft and power stations to autos and earthmoving equipment, are increasingly interested in the revenue stream to be derived from maintaining and upgrading their products over the course of their lifetime. New information technology is increasingly being used to monitor the performance of complex products in use, with continuous feedback to the systems integrator in order to construct optimum servicing schedules. Through this pervasive process, systems integrators deeply penetrate a wide range of firms that use their products. However, penetration of the downstream network of firms is not confined to complex capital goods. Systems integrators in the fast-moving consumer goods (FMCG) sector increasingly coordinate the distribution process with specialist logistics firms in order to minimize distribution costs. They work closely with grocery chains and other selling outlets, such as theme parks, movie theatres, oil companies (petrol stations have become major locations for retailing non-petrol products) and quick-service restaurants, to raise the technical efficiency in the organization of the selling process. The FMCG systems integrators often have their own experts working within the retail chain.

In the old vertically integrated large firm, employment frequently totalled many hundreds of thousands of people. For example, in 1990, the world's largest capitalist firm by number of employees, General Motors, employed 750,000 people. Among the world's 100 largest international firms (by overseas assets), 51 had more than 100,000 employees. It is widely thought that the average size of large corporations has sharply declined since the late 1980s due to the impact of downsizing and the relentless pursuit of cost reduction. However, this is far from clear. In 1998, among the *Fortune* 500 companies (ranked by value of sales), the median firm size was 55,000 employees. There were five firms with over 500,000 employees, 27 with 200,000–500,000 employees and 88 with 100,000–200,000 employees. What appears to have happened is that the impact of mergers and acquisitions has frequently stimulated an increase in the total number of employees within the entire merged company, alongside considerable corporate downsizing within each of the merged entities. The functions of the core systems integrator have changed radically away from direct manufacturing towards 'brain' functions of planning the global development of the firm. The proportion of employees working outside the home market has sharply increased. However, the world's leading firms remain very large entities, not only in terms of their revenues, but also in terms of direct employment. Employment remains large, but slow-growing or even declining somewhat alongside rapid acceleration of revenues.

The revolution in the global business system in recent years has meant that a high level of conscious planning of business activity is now undertaken by systems integrators across the whole value chain. A large corporation may have a total procurement bill of many tens of millions of dollars. The total procurement could involve purchases from firms that employ a much larger number of full-time equivalent employees 'working for' the systems integrator than are employed within the core firm itself. In addition, there is typically a large sphere of downstream business activity that is coordinated by the systems integrator. A leading systems integrator with 100,000–200,000 employees could easily have the full-time equivalent of a further 400,000–500,000 employees 'working for' the systems integrator, in the sense that their work is coordinated in important ways by the core firm. In this sense, we may speak of an 'external firm' of coordinated business activity that surrounds the modern global corporation and is coordinated by it.

8.3 China within the Global Value Chain

A major part of the discussion about the impact of the WTO on China has focused on the effect new information technology will have on the economy. A wide range of commentators have argued that the IT revolution will result in the democratization of economic life and hugely enhanced global opportunities for small firms. Klaus Schwab, President of the World Economic Forum, has argued: 'we are witnessing the democratizing [effect] of the information revolution'. Capabilities that 'in the past were possessed only by large and powerful organizations' can now be 'obtained by individuals and small organizations in all walks of life' (Schwab, 2000). He is in no doubt that the net impact on employment in China will be strongly positive: 'These technologies and services can generate many new and rewarding employment opportunities for every nation's citizens'. Experience around the world 'demonstrates beyond any doubt that over time, new information and communications technologies increase the overall level and quality of employment' (Schwab, 2000).

Laurence Lau (Stanford University) has argued that the IT revolution will lead to 'existing demands for goods and services [being] increasingly supplied by new entrants, most of them small and medium-sized start-up firms'. He believes that the IT revolution will cause widespread 'creative destruction' in which 'new firms take away business from the old firms'. Lau believes that in developing countries such as China, there will be 'creation without destruction': 'Developing countries have the ability to leapfrog. There are no vested interests to protect; no existing businesses to be cannibalized; there can be creation without destruction' (Lau, 2000).

In this view, given its massive labour force, with a high level of literacy compared to other developing countries, China can become '*sub-contractor to the world*'. There are argued to be huge opportunities for Chinese SMEs to become outsourced suppliers to the world leading systems integrators in almost every sector. Until now, the fastest-growing activities have been in 'old industries', such as garments, plastic products, luggage, sports goods, assembly of electrical goods, and furniture. However, there are opportunities for Chinese SMEs to provide sub-contracting for global systems integrators in a wide range of 'new technology industries', including components and sub-systems for aircraft, heavy electrical equipment, IT hardware and auto components firms, biotechnology research and drugs testing for global pharmaceutical firms, software services for software firms, and local music, TV programmes, advertising and movies for global media companies.

It can even be argued that as this process evolves, so China's myriad SME firms may form a steadily expanding part of the global corporations' 'external firm'. Over time, Chinese people may form a growing proportion of the managers, scientists, engineers and senior officials of globalizing systems integrator firms. Chinese financial institutions may gradually increase their ownership of 'Western' corporations as Chinese income levels rise and pension funds expand their operation. In the long term, China's weight of population, the high and rising quality of its human resources, and the growing fraction of global output that is produced in China, may cause the gradual '*Sinification*' of the world's business system. As China gradually reassumes its position at the core of the world economy Chinese businesses and employees may transform global capitalism from the 'inside', within the global corporation, and within the 'external firm' that is coordinated by the global corporation. In time China may well return to the position at the heart of the business system that it occupied for one thousand years.

9. Conclusion: The Dilemma for Industrial Policy in China

As China prepares to enter the WTO, its industrial policy stands at a critical watershed. The path it decides to follow will be of great importance not only for China, but also for the future of industrial policy and for character of the global economy in the early 21st century.

The tortoise and the hare   If China had not opened itself to the international economy through trade and foreign investment after the 1970s, the progress in its large enterprises would not have been anything like as great as that which it has achieved. However, the pace of change in global big business has massively outpaced that of China's large enterprises. As the global level playing field is further and further established within China after it enters the WTO, few Chinese enterprises are in a position to compete with the world's leading companies in each sector. Given the differential rate of change in business structures and technological capability, it is hard to imagine that even a much greater length of time under current industrial policies could enable China to produce firms that could challenge the global giants. Would a further ten years of government industrial policy using the same measures as in the past two decades, or using any other industrial policy measures one can imagine, be able to ensure that China's large firms caught up with the global leaders? Is it possible that after a further ten years China's large firms might be even further behind than they are today? Would even a radically strengthened industrial policy, even if it could be applied effectively, be able to achieve 'catch-up' at the level of the large Chinese firm?

Is catch-up at the level of the large corporation possible for any developing country in the new international environment? Chinese industrial policy is caught between the devil and the deep blue sea. On the evidence of the past twenty years, to remain relatively isolated and supported by government industrial policy, even if the policy is more focused, more realistic and more consistently applied, is unlikely to lead to the construction of globally competitive large firms. However, building powerful firms in the face of intense global competition is likely to be extremely difficult. The pace of progress in the business capabilities of the world's leading firms is so great that it is hard to imagine any strategy that could lead to successful catch-up at the level of the large firm on a widespread basis. It is extremely difficult for many people to accept this. However, this is the blunt reality. It may no longer be possible for industrial policy to build powerful competitive large firms based in even the largest and most powerful of the developing countries. If this were indeed the case, then it would require immensely subtle international relations to accommodate this new reality. It would require a radical redrawing of the ambitions of large developing countries, especially, but not only, China. It would require separating the goal of catch-up at the firm level from the goal of advancing national output, structural change, wage employment and the standard of living.

Great subtlety is required in international relations to cope with the new reality   Even for advanced European countries, it is very difficult to accept that 'national champions' may be unable to compete on the global level playing field as individual players. However, whereas individual European countries may have to accept the demise of their national champions, the continent as a whole is breeding a group of regional champions and transatlantic champions. For China, a huge civilization with a proud economic and political history, it is very difficult to accept that it may be unable to emulate Britain, the US, Japan and Korea in building national champions through industrial policy.

Can China cope with US dominance?   US-based firms are by far the most powerful force in the global business revolution. Nowhere is their dominance more pronounced than in the industries of the Third Industrial Revolution, which will be at the centre of global business revolution in the early 21st century. Individual US-based large corporations are desperate to expand their activities in the 'new frontier' for global capitalism in China. The central position of large US-based firms in the global big business revolution will enable its firms to take the lead in the defeat of China's large corporations. This will cause considerable uneasiness among a wide range of Chinese people, including many who are positive about the benefits that capitalism might bring to China. It is impossible to predict in what form this might manifest itself politically, but it is possible that the response could be large-scale and even highly destabilizing to international relations. Forcing China's large firms to compete at high speed on the global level playing field through rapid implementation of the rules of the WTO is a high-risk strategy. Bringing together two forces of such immense differences in strength is highly fissile. The process cries out for care, caution and subtlety.

Is there an alternative?   For there to be an alternative, there has to be a coherent, realistic strategy. It is hard to identify what such a strategy could be in the face of the incredible pace of global change in the nature and business capability of large firms. It is better to 'seek truth from facts' than to live with illusions. There is no point in trying to fight a battle that cannot be won. The heroic age of building national champions through state-supported industrial policy may be over. If this were true, then industrial policy would have been defeated by the full flowering of global oligopolistic capitalism, not by the triumph of small-scale perfectly competitive firms.

The harsh reality of the intensity of the competition that faces China's large firms has been a major factor in the delay in China's admission to the WTO. It now seems unlikely that China will enter until late in 2001, fully two years after the historic agreement with the USA. As China's entry to the WTO approaches, the intensity of debate over the prospects for China's large firms has become ever sharper. It is highly uncertain which path China's industrial policy will take.

- Will China give up industrial policy and accept that, with minor exceptions, in the foreseeable future its large enterprises cannot compete on the global level playing field?
- Will China's leaders accept that for the foreseeable future it must adjust itself to its enterprises becoming part of the global value chain of the world's leading 'systems integrators', headquartered in the advanced economies?
- Will China's leaders, instead, try to revive and strengthen industrial policies that attempt to build powerful indigenous 'systems integrators'?
- Will China try to develop a strategy that uses a renewed and greatly strengthened industrial policy to support the growth of large 'systems integrators', while simultaneously seeking to develop a powerful SME sector that grows within the global value chain of the world's established 'system integrators'?

The outcome will be decided by a complex array of internal and external forces. It is impossible to predict the direction they will follow.

Notes

1   This paper is drawn from Nolan, 2001a and 2001b. Although this paper was written by me, the ideas are the product of research undertaken jointly by myself and Dr. Wang Xioaqiang over the past ten years.

2   US businessman speaking at the China Development Forum held in Beijing in March 2000.

References

Cooper, R., 2000, Speech at China Development Forum, Beijing

Department of Trade and Industry (DTI), various years, *UK R&D Scoreboard*, Edinburgh, DTI

Lau, L., 2000, Speech at China Development Forum, Beijing

Morgan Stanley Dean Witter (MSDW), various years, *The Competitive Edge*, New York, MSDW

Nolan, P., 1997, *Challenging the Established Large Enterprises: The Case of Yuchai Diesel*, China Big Business Programme Case Study, University of Cambridge, Judge Institute of Management Studies

Nolan, P., 1998, *Economic Reform and Institutional Change in the Chinese Petrochemical Industry with special reference to the Shanghai Petrochemical Company Limited*, China Big Business Programme Case Study, University of Cambridge, Judge Institute of Management Studies

Nolan, P., 1998, *The Battle for the Chinese Power Equipment Market: The Case of Harbin Power Plant Equipment Group Corporation*, China Big Business Programme Case Study, University of Cambridge, Judge Institute of Management Studies

Nolan, P., 1998, *The Chinese Army's Firm in Business: The Sanjiu Group*, China Big Business Programme Case Study, University of Cambridge, Judge Institute of Management Studies

Nolan, P., 1998, *AVIC: Internationally Competitive Aircraft Manufacturer, Diversified East Asian Conglomerate or Global Sub-contractor?* China Big Business Programme Case Study, University of Cambridge, Judge Institute of Management Studies

Nolan, P., 1999, *Large Integrated Steel Companies in China's Economic Development: The Case of Shougang*, China Big Business Programme Case Study, University of Cambridge, Judge Institute of Management Studies

Nolan, P., 1999, *Strategic Choices in the Development of the Chinese Coal Industry: The Case of the Shenhua Group*, China Big Business Programme Case Study, University of Cambridge, Judge Institute of Management Studies

Nolan, P., 1999, *Restructuring CNPC and Sinopec: Feudal Fiefdoms or Modern Corporations?* China Big Business Programme Case Study, University of Cambridge, Judge Institute of Management Studies

Nolan., P. and Wang Xiaoqiang, 1999, 'Beyond privatisation: Institutional innovation and growth in China's large state-owned enterprises', *World Development*, vol 17, no 1, 169–200

Nolan, P., 2001a, *China and the Global Business Revolution*, Palgrave

Nolan, P., 2001b, *China and the Global Economy*, Palgrave

Schwab, K., 2001, Speech at Twenty-First Century Forum, Beijing

World Bank, various years, World Development Report, New York, Oxford University Press

7

THE CHALLENGE OF GLOBALIZATION FOR LARGE CHINESE FIRMS[1]
(with Zhang Jin)

I. CHINA AND THE GLOBAL BUSINESS REVOLUTION

China's entry to the World Trade Organization (WTO) is a historic milestone in the process of China's integration with the world economy and business system. Among the many important possible effects is the impact on its large firms. In the course of two decades of struggle, China's large enterprises have undertaken large-scale *evolutionary* change. During the same period, the world's leading firms have undergone a *revolutionary* transformation. This poses a profound challenge for China's large firms at the point of entry to the WTO. During the global business revolution, in order to survive and prosper, the nature of the large firm based in high-income countries altered greatly. The intertwining of China's internal business system change with the revolution in large global firms has been a protracted and complicated process.[2] It is far from over.

A. *CHINA'S REFORMS*

1. Lessons from Other Countries

A succession of 'late comer countries' developed powerful indigenous firms through different measures of industrial policy. These countries included Britain during the Industrial Revolution, the United States and Continental Europe in the nineteenth century, the Republic of Korea, Taiwan Province of China and Singapore in the second half of the twentieth century. From the 1950s to the 1970s, Japan's industrial planners supported the growth of a series of oligopolistic companies that developed into globally powerful firms. After two decades of industrial policy in Japan, the country possessed a whole corps of globally competitive companies. Today, it still has over one hundred *Fortune 500* companies and 83 of the world's top 300 companies by R&D

expenditure (DTI, 2000). In the light of these experiences, it seemed reasonable for China to follow similar policies to support the growth of its own indigenous large firms. The history of other fast-growing, late-industrializing countries suggested that it was realistic to hope that Chinese large enterprises would be able to 'catch up' rapidly with the world's leading firms.

2. China's Ambitions

China began liberalizing the post-Mao economy in the late 1970s. A consistently stated goal of China's industrial policy has been to construct globally powerful companies that can compete on the global level playing field:

> In our world today economic competition between nations is in fact between each nation's large enterprises and enterprise groups. A nation's economic might is concentrated and manifested in the economic power and international competitiveness of its large enterprises and groups ... *Our nation's position in the international economic order will be to a large extent determined by the position of our nation's large enterprises and groups.* (Wu Banguo, Chinese State Council, August 1998.)

China's 'national team' of large industrial firms included: Aviation Industries of China (AVIC) in the aerospace industry; Sinopec and CNPC in oil and petrochemicals; Sanjiu, Dongbei and Shandong Xinhua in pharmaceuticals; Harbin, Shanghai and Dongfang in power equipment; Yiqi, Erqi and Shanghai in automobiles; Shougang, Angang and Baogang in steel; and Datong, Yanzhou and Shenhua in coal mining.

China's chosen global giant corporations were supported through industrial policies, which included: tariffs, which still were significant in many sectors at the end of the 1990s; non-tariff barriers, including limitations on access to domestic marketing channels, requirements for technology transfer and to sub-contract to selected domestic firms as the price for market access; government procurement policy; government selection of the partners for major international joint ventures; preferential loans from state banks; and privileged access to listings on international stock markets.

As the reform process progressed, the Chinese government made it increasingly clear that the country intended also to be able to establish a group of globally competitive large firms in financial services and telecommunications. China Mobile and China Unicom, with massive international flotations, were at the forefront of this process. The Bank of China is scheduled to be the first major international flotation from the Chinese financial services sector. As

China prepares to enter the WTO, the country's commitment to building globally competitive large firms remains undiminished:

> The state will encourage big state-owned businesses to become internationally competitive corporations by listing on domestic and overseas stock market, increasing research and development expenditure, and acquiring other businesses. *The country will develop thirty to fifty large state-owned enterprises in the next five years through public offerings, mergers and acquisitions, restructuring and co-operation.* (Bai Rongchun, Director General, Industrial Planning Department, State Economic and Trade Commission, July 2001.)

3. China's Progress

China's industrial policies to support large firms were successful in the following senses. Large state-owned enterprises avoided the collapse that took place in the former USSR. Industrial output grew at around 13 per cent per annum from the early 1980s to the late 1990s, with sustained rapid growth for large firms. Major changes took place in the operational mechanism of large, state-owned enterprises. They absorbed a great deal of modern technology; learned how to compete in the marketplace; substantially upgraded the technical level of their employees; learned wide-ranging new managerial skills; and gained substantial understanding of international financial markets. China's large firms became sought-after partners for multinational companies. China attracted huge amounts of foreign direct investment. Increasingly, global corporations viewed China as a central element in their long-term strategy. A group of large mainland firms was listed successfully on international stock markets. By 2001, China had eleven firms listed in the *Fortune 500*.

4. China's Difficulties

Achieving gradual reform of China's large state-owned enterprises and nurturing their transformation into globally competitive large firms was a daunting task. It was a very different challenge from that which faced the industrial planners in Japan, the Republic of Korea or Taiwan Province of China. The path taken by China was radically different from that followed in other planned economies, which abandoned industrial policy and attempted to achieve sweeping privatization of the large-scale state sector, and allow the market to decide the outcome.[3] Unsurprisingly, China encountered many difficulties during this long evolutionary process.

a) Policy Inconsistency

As we shall see, within the same industry, radically different reform policies were pursued at different times. For example, in oil and petrochemicals, for many years, the policy was to increase the autonomy of large production units. Then policy shifted totally towards centralized control over large production units. At the same time, completely different policies were pursued in different sectors. For example, while control was being centralized in the oil and petrochemical industry, AVIC was, incomprehensibly, being broken up into two separate entities, each of which was even less able than before to compete with the global giants.

b) Where is the Firm?

The foundation of China's economic reform was to increase 'enterprise' autonomy. The core of most large 'enterprises' was a single large production unit. This had many benefits, including the development of a strong sense of corporate ambition at the enterprise level. However, it caused difficulties in the subsequent attempts to build multi-plant firms with unified central control over individual production units.

c) Impoverished Economy

China is still a poor country, with a relatively tiny middle class. For example, the entire stock of saloon cars is only around five million. A large fraction of domestic demand is for low price, low value-added products for over one billion peasants, internal migrants and poor urban residents. Indigenous firms have to fight a battle on two fronts, on the one hand with global giants in high value-added products, and on the other hand, with domestic SMEs in low value-added products.

d) Local Protectionism

China has a strong tradition of relatively autonomous local government. There has been persistent local resistance to cross-regional mergers, due to fears of downsizing and/or loss of control of a 'local asset'.

e) Inheritance from the Planned Economy

Unlike the other 'late-comer' countries, China's large enterprises inherited huge manning levels, which are extremely hard to reduce without causing social instability. This will remain a profound problem for many years.

f) Incentive to Diversify

The inability of China's emerging large firms to compete in international markets, plus the fact that they each have a huge workforce, produced a high incentive for the individual enterprise to diversify. A single large enterprise could easily have hundreds of 'children' and grandchildren' subsidiaries and related companies. This gives the 'illusion of scale', but beneath an apparently large firm there are typically hundreds of uneconomically small firms and immense problems of corporate governance.

g) Problems for China's Bureaucracy

China's bureaucracy lacked the intense nationalist incentive to build large firms successfully that drove Japanese (and the Republic of Korea) policy-makers. Also, China's leaders are engaged in an intense drive to root out corruption from the country's huge bureaucracy. Corruption undermines the bureaucracy's ability to lead industrial policy effectively.

•h) Ideological Commitment to State Ownership

China remained for most of the reform period committed to state ownership as a goal in its own right, rather than building powerful corporations by whatever means was suitable. It proved hard to achieve the separation of government and enterprise that has been advocated for many years.

5. The Challenge for China

Case studies conducted in the late 1990s in a wide range of sectors (Nolan, 2001) show that after two decades of reform in most sectors the competitive capability of China's large firms is still weak in relation to the global giants. By the simplest of measures of sales revenue, profits and R&D, China's vanguard of leading firms that are intended to 'compete on the global level playing field' are still significantly behind the global leaders. This was found to be extremely marked in the high-technology sectors, such as IT hardware, complex equipment such as power plants, and pharmaceuticals, as well as in 'mid-technology' sectors such as automobile assembly and automobile components. However, even in sectors with apparently less advanced technology, such as steel and coal, there was a significant gap with leading global companies in the high value-added segments of the market. In financial services, it is widely recognized that China's leading commercial banks, insurance companies and accountancy firms lag far behind the global leaders.

At the start of the 21st century, not one of China's leading enterprises has become a globally competitive giant corporation, with a global market, a global brand, and a global procurement system. The Chinese companies included in the *Fortune 500* all faced huge problems of downsizing. China had no less than five of the top ten companies in the *Fortune 500* in terms of numbers of employees (*Fortune Global 500*, 2001). China had just two companies in the *Financial Times 500* which ranks firms by market capitalization (*Financial Times*, 11 May 2001). These were China Mobile and China Unicom, both of which operate in a totally protected domestic environment. The vast bulk of their IT hardware equipment was purchased from the global giants.[4] China did not have one company in the world's top 300 companies by R&D expenditure (DTI, 2000). China did not have any representatives in *Morgan Stanley Dean Witter's* list of the world's top 250 'competitive edge' companies (MSDW, 2000). China did not have a single company in *Business Week's* list of the world's top 100 brands (*Business Week*, 6 August 2001).

B. *THE GLOBAL BUSINESS REVOLUTION*

China's attempt to build large globally competitive firms coincided with the most revolutionary epoch in world business history, possibly even including the Industrial Revolution. The global business system was much more stable during the period during which Japan, the Republic of Korea and Taiwan Province of China were putting into place their industrial policy. China's effort to support the growth of competitive global corporations has taken place at a time of unprecedented change in the international business system, amounting to nothing less than a revolution. Moreover, the high-income countries were willing to tolerate extensive state intervention in these countries, because they were viewed as the front line in the fight against communism. China is regarded by the United States as a 'strategic competitor'.

There were a number of aspects to the global business revolution.

1. Liberalization of World Trade and Capital Markets

The period since the late 1980s has witnessed for the first time the opening up of a truly global market place in goods, services, capital and skilled labour. The only market which still remains bound firmly by nationality is the vast sea of unskilled labour. The world's leading firms have massively increased their production capabilities in fast-growing parts of developing countries. Foreign direct investment (FDI) in developing countries grew from $24 billion in 1990 to $170 billion in 1998. China was by far the main focus of attention, with FDI rising from $3.5 billion in 1990 to $44 billion in 1998 (World Bank, 2001:

315). The struggle among the world's leading firms has now deeply penetrated the most developed parts of the low and middle-income countries.

China is at the centre of this battle. The world's giant firms are struggling intensely with each other for a share of the China market: Boeing and Airbus in aerospace; Pfizer, GlaxoSmithKline, Merck, and Astra Zeneca in pharmaceuticals; Shell, BP and Exxon in oil and petrochemicals; IBM, Siemens, Nokia and Ericsson in IT hardware; Ford, GM, VW and Toyota in automobiles; Alstom, Siemens and GE in power equipment; Coca-Cola and Pepsico in soft drinks; Philip Morris, Japan Tobacco and BAT in tobacco; Nestlé and Unilever in FMCGs; Usinor, Posco and Nippon Steel in steel; Rio Tinto, Billiton and Anglo-American in mining; Morgan Stanley, Goldman Sachs and Merrill Lynch in investment banking; PwC, KPMG and Deloitte in accountancy; Axa, Allianz, AIG, Prudential and CGNU in insurance; Citigroup, Deutsche Bank, JP Morgan Chase, and Credit Suisse in banking; News Corp and AOL-Time Warner in the mass media.

2. Explosive M&A and Concentration

The period since the 1980s saw the world's most explosive period of mergers and acquisitions. Global M&A rose from $156 billion in 1992 to around $3,300 billion in 1999 (Nolan, 2001: 38). The size of the merger boom of the 1990s eclipses that of any previous epoch. It will leave a long-lasting imprint on the global business structure. In almost every sector a small number of focused global producers dominates the world market. Competitive capitalism's inbuilt tendency to concentration and oligopoly has finally flowered on a global scale.

Today, only two firms make large (over 100 seats) commercial aircraft.[5] In pharmaceuticals, the top ten firms account for 46 per cent of world sales. In oil and petrochemicals, a group of just three 'super majors' has emerged, occupying three of the top seven slots in the *Fortune 500* list of the world's largest companies ranked by sales revenue. In power equipment, the top three firms account for almost nine-tenths of the world total of gas turbines installed in the 1990s. In the automobile sector, the top six automobile firms account for over 75 per cent of the global market. In IT hardware, the top three firms account for 71 per cent of the global supply of servers, for two-fifths of the global sales of PCs and three-fifths of global sales of mobile phones. In fast-moving consumer goods, just two firms account for over 80 per cent of global sales of carbonated soft drinks; two firms account for around 70 per cent of global sales of camera film; three firms account for almost one-half of global sales of spirits; and four firms account for 60 per cent of global tobacco sales.

3. 'Cascade Effect'

Not only have the core 'systems integrators' experienced an explosive process of concentration. The deepening interaction between core companies and supplier companies has created an explosive 'cascade' effect that is rapidly leading to concentration and focus among the first-tier suppliers and spilling over even into second and third-tier suppliers. Concentration among leading aircraft assemblers has stimulated concentration among the main aerospace components suppliers: there are now just three makers of large aircraft engines across the world. Concentration among automobile assemblers has stimulated concentration among automobile components makers: the top three tyre makers account for almost two-thirds of global tyre sales; the top two manufacturers of automobile brake systems account for 56 per cent of global sales and the top two firms account for almost one-half of global sales of car air conditioning systems. Concentration among IT equipment makers has stimulated concentration among IT suppliers. One firm ('intel inside') accounts for 85 per cent of global sales of micro-processors, another accounts for 80 per cent of high end routers, another supplies around one half of all optical fibres and another accounts for over nine-tenths of computer operating systems.

In sector after sector, the 'first-tier' suppliers are themselves multi-billion dollar companies with 'global reach'. This makes the competitive landscape even more challenging for firms from developing countries.

4. The 'External Firm'

If we define the firm not by the entity that is the legal owner, but rather by the sphere over which conscious coordination of resource allocation takes place, then, far from becoming 'hollowed out' and much smaller in scope, the large firm can be seen to have enormously increased in size during the global business revolution. In a wide range of business activities, the organization of the value chain has developed into a comprehensively planned and co-ordinated activity. At its centre is the core systems integrator. Through the hugely increased planning function undertaken by systems integrators, facilitated by recent developments in information technology, the boundaries of the large corporation have become blurred. In order to develop and maintain their competitive advantage, the systems integrators deeply penetrate the value chain both upstream and downstream. They are closely involved in business activities that range from long-term planning to meticulous control of day-to-day production and delivery schedules. Competitive advantage for the systems integrator requires that it must consider the interests of the whole value chain in order to minimize costs across the whole system. Far from becoming 'hollowed out' and much smaller in scope, the extent of control exercised by the large firm has enormously increased during the global business revolution (Nolan, 1999).

5. Dominance of Firms Based in Advanced Economies

Firms headquartered in regions containing a small fraction of the world's population have comprehensively dominated the global business revolution (Table 7.1). The high-income economies contain just 16 per cent of the world's total population. They account for 91 per cent of the world's total stock market capitalization, 95 per cent of Fortune 500 companies, 97 per cent of the *Financial Times* 500 companies, 99 per cent of the world's top brands and 100 per cent of the world's top 300 companies by value of R&D spending.

North America is, by far, the world leader in this process. North America has just over 5 per cent of the world's population, but it accounts for 40 per cent of the Fortune 500 firms, 46 per cent of the world's top 300 firms by R&D expenditure (74 per cent of the top 300 IT hardware and software firms, ranked by R&D spending), 50 per cent of the *FT 500* firms, 54 per cent of Morgan Stanley's list of the top 250 'global competitive edge' firms, and 61 per cent of the world's top 100 brands.

Developing countries are massively disadvantaged in the race to compete on the global level playing field of international big business. The starting points in the race to dominate global markets could not be more uneven. The whole of the developing world, containing 84 per cent of the world's population, contains just 26 Fortune 500 companies, 16 FT 500 companies, 15 of Morgan Stanley's list of the 250 leading 'competitive edge' companies, one of the world's top 100 brands and none of the world's top 300 companies by R&D expenditure.

C. *CONCLUSION*

China's rapid move towards 'close' integration with the world economy is occurring at a time of revolutionary change in the global business system. This presents an extreme challenge for China's industrial strategy. As China enters the WTO, there is a series of critical questions that need to be answered both by Chinese and globally powerful firms seeking to penetrate the Chinese market. This raises numerous issues for China's industrial policy-makers. Would privatization of China's large enterprises be sufficient to make them competitive on the 'global level playing field' within the WTO? At what

Table 7.1 **Dominance of Firms Based in High Income Countries of the Global Big Business Revolution**

	Population		GNP, 1997 (1)		GNP, 1997 (2)		Fortune 500 companies (1998) (3)		FT 500 companies (1998) (4)		Top 300 companies by R&D spend (1997)		Stock market capitalization (1997)	
	billion	%	$b.	%	$b.	%	No.	%	No.	%	No.	%	$b.	%
HIEs	926	16	23,802	80	21,091	57	474	95	484	97	299	99	18,452	91
L/MIEs	4,903	84	6,123	20	15,861	43	26 (5)	5	16 (6)	3	2	1	1,725	9

Sources: FT, 28 January 1999; World Bank, 1998; 190–1, and 220–1; *Fortune, 2 August 1999* DTI, 1998: 70–80

Notes

(1) at prevailing rate of exchange
(2) at PPP dollars
(3) ranked by sales revenue
(4) ranked by market capitalization
(5) of which: Korea = 9, China = 6, Brazil = 4, Taiwan = 2, Venezuela = 1, Russia = 1, India = 1, Mexico = 1, Malaysia = 1
(6) of which: Hong Kong = 7, Brazil = 2, Taiwan = 2, Singapore = 1, Mexico = 1, India = 1, Korea = 1, Argentina = 1
HIEs = High Income Economies
L/MIEs = Low/Middle Economies

level in the global value chain can any given large Chinese firm best compete: as a 'core systems integrator', 'first-tier supplier', or lower down the value chain? What role will be permitted for national industrial policy in China within the WTO? Does China's bureaucracy have the capability to administer industrial policy effectively? Does it matter whether China, or other developing countries, have 'national champions' that can compete on the 'global level playing field'? Does the global corporation, with production bases and markets throughout large parts of the world, any longer have a 'national' or a 'regional' identity?

Sections II and III of this paper analyse the challenge of globalization in two very different industries: oil and petrochemicals, and aerospace. The purpose of this detailed examination of these contrasting sectors is to investigate the nature of the challenge facing large Chinese firms in 'strategic' sectors that have formed, and still do form, an important focus of industrial policy in high income countries.

II. OIL AND PETROCHEMICALS

A. *THE GLOBAL SETTING*

1. World Oil and Gas in the 1990s

Crude oil and natural gas remain central to global political economy. The contribution of oil to the world primary energy consumption has remained stable at around 40 per cent. The share of natural gas in the world primary energy consumption rose from 20.3 per cent in 1990 to 24.7 per cent in 2000. The regional distribution of world oil and gas reserves, production and consumption are highly uneven (Table 7.2). This is of special importance for global political economy. The Middle East and the former Soviet Union (FSU) account for 70 per cent of the world total oil reserves and 73 per cent of the world total natural gas reserves. The five countries of Saudi Arabia, Kuwait, the Islamic Republic of Iran, Iraq and United Arab Emirates between them account for over three-fifths of the world total oil reserves. Russia alone accounts for more than one-third of the world total gas reserves. The Middle East is the world's most important oil supplier, accounting for 31 per cent of global production. Seventy-five per cent of its output is exported. The FSU is the world's largest gas producer, accounting for 28 per cent of global production in 2000.

The United States is the world biggest oil and gas consumer (Table 7.2). In 2000, the United States accounted for over one quarter of the world total oil imports and nearly half of the country's total consumption. The United States' share of the world gas production is 23 per cent, but still lags behind

Table 7.2 Geographical Distribution of World Oil and Gas Reserves, Consumption and Production, 2000

Regions & countries	Proved reserves		Consumption		Production		Net imports [exports]	
	Oil (bt)	Gas (tcm)	Oil (mmt)	Gas (bcm)	Oil (mmt)	Gas (bcm)	Oil (mmt)	Gas§ (bcm)
World	142.1 (100%)	150.19 (100%)	3503.6 (100%)	2404.6 (100%)	3589.6 (100%)	2422.3 (100%)	–	–
United States	3.7 (2.8%)	4.74 (3.2%)	897.4 (25.6%)	654.4 (27.2%)	353.5 (9.8%)	555.6 (22.9%)	442.8	101.53
Europe	2.5 (1.9%)	5.22 (3.5%)	752.6 (21.4%)	458.8 (19.1%)	329.0 (9.2%)	287.9 (12%)	389.6	197.33
Mexico	4.0 (2.7%)	0.86 (0.6%)	84.3 (2.4%)	35.5 (1.5%)	172.1 (4.8%)	35.8 (1.5%)	[86.7]	0
S/C America* of which:	13.6 (9.0%)	6.93 (4.6%)	218.7 (6.2%)	92.6 (3.8%)	348.2 (9.7%)	96.4 (3.9%)	[59.7]	[3.51]
Venezuela	11.1 (7.3%)	4.16 (2.8%)	22.6 (0.6%)	27.2 (1.1%)	166.8 (4.6%)	27.2 (1.1%)	–	–
FSU** of which:	9.0 (6.4%)	56.70 (37.8%)	173.1 (5.0%)	548.3 (22.8%)	394.4 (11%)	674.2 (27.8%)	[142.6]	[132.98]
Russia	6.7 (4.6%)	48.14 (32.1%)	123.5 (3.5%)	377.2 (15.7%)	323.3 (9.0%)	545.0 (22.5%)	–	[130.33]
Middle East of which:	92.5 (65.3%)	52.52 (35%)	209.0 (5.9%)	189.0 (7.9%)	1112.4 (31%)	209.7 (8.7%)	[831.7]	[23.44]
Saudi Arabia	35.8 (25%)	23.00 (15.3%)	62.4 (1.8%)	47.0 (2.0%)	441.2 (12.3%)	47.0 (1.9%)	–	–
Iran (Islamic Rep. of)	12.3 (8.6%)	6.05 (4%)	56.9 (1.6%)	62.9 (2.6%)	186.6 (5.2%)	60.2 (2.5%)	–	2.65
Iraq	15.1 (10.8%)	3.11 (2.1%)	–	–	128.1 (3.6%)	–	–	–

Asia Pacific *of which:*	6.0 (4.2%)	10.33 (6.8%)	968.9 (27.8%)	289.3 (12.1%)	380.5 (10.6%)	265.4 (11%)	557.9	22.41
China**	3.3 (2.3%)	1.37 (0.9%)	226.9 (6.5%)	24.8 (1.0%)	162.3 (4.5%)	27.7 (1.2%)	59.9	–
Japan	–	–	253.5 (7.2%)	76.2 (3.2%)	–	–	214.9	72.46
Africa *of which:*	10.0 (7.1%)	11.16 (7.4%)	116.7 (3.3%)	58.9 (2.4%)	373.2 (10.4%)	129.5 (5.3%)	[251.1]	[67.05]
Nigeria	3.1 (2.2%)	3.51 (2.3%)	–	–	103.9 (2.9%)	11.0 (0.5%)	–	[5.61]

Source: BP Statistical Review of World Energy, 2001.

Notes

Figures in brackets () are percentage share of world total; in square brackets [] are net exports.

* South and Central America.

** Former Soviet Union.

*** Data exclude Hong Kong (China).

§ Trade movement of gas transported by pipeline and LNG, excluding intra movement.

bt = billion tones

tcm = trillion cubic metres

bcm = billion cubic metres

mmt = million tones

its share of gas consumption, accounting for 27 per cent of the global total. More than 60 per cent of Europe's oil consumption is met by imports from outside the region. Japan relies totally on imports for its oil and gas supplies (Table 7.2).

China is poorly endowed with oil and gas. Its share of the world oil and gas reserves amount to only 2.3 per cent and 0.9 per cent respectively (Table 7.2). In contrast, China's coal reserves are second only to those of the United States. China was the world's largest producer and consumer of coal in the 1990s. Coal accounted for 67 per cent of China's total primary energy consumption in 1999. It plans to raise the share of gas in total primary energy consumption from the current 3 per cent to 8 per cent in 2010, which will somewhat reduce the share of coal. Coal remains an abundant and cheap source of primary energy for China. During the 1990s, oil and gas consumption increased at a compound annual growth rate of 5.5 per cent and 5.7 per cent respectively. In 2000, China was the third largest oil consuming country after the United States and Japan. After 1993, China became a net crude oil importer. Oil imports reached 71 million tons in 2000 (BP, 2001), equivalent to 31 per cent of China's total oil consumption. It is predicted that by 2005, 40 per cent of China's demand for oil will be met by imports (China Petroleum, June 1999). The issue of oil supply security remains a major concern for China's policymakers.

2. National Oil Companies

At the end of the 1990s, among the world top 25 oil companies ranked by operating performance, fourteen (fifteen if Petrobrás is included)[6] were state-owned national champions, all based in developing countries (Table 3). These national oil companies (NOCs) own the majority of the world oil and gas reserves and are the world's largest oil producers. There have been no cross-border mergers among the NOCs. They are regarded as national assets by their governments. In 1999, the combined oil and gas reserves of these oil companies accounted for 77 per cent and 49 per cent of the total world oil and gas reserves respectively. They produced 48 per cent of total world oil production, compared with 18 per cent accounted for by the global oil majors (GOMs) based in the United States and Europe.[7] Gas production of the NOCs was 449 billion cubic metres in 1999, accounting for 19 per cent of total world gas production, compared with the 424 billion cubic metres produced by GOMs in the same year.

The NOCs are relatively weak in downstream refining and marketing. Their total annual refinery capacity in 1999 was 943 million tonnes per year (mmt/y), compared to the GOMs' capacity of 1064 mmt/y capacity. Refined

Table 7.3 **Top 15 National Oil Companies, 1999**

Company	Reserves Oil (bt)	Reserves Gas (bcm)	Production Oil (mmt)	Production Gas (bcm)	Refinery capacity (mmt/y)	Oil product sales (mmt)	Country
Saudi Aramco	35.50	6040.7	402.2	31.4	99.60	132.50	Saudi Arabia
PDVSA	10.50	4155.1	147.5	41.3	154.80	125.00	Venezuela
National Iranian Oil Company	12.10	23134.1	181.0	53.3	76.70	67.10	Iran (Islamic Republic of)
Pemex	3.89	849.7	167.2	49.5	76.40	82.50	Mexico
Indonesia National Oil Company	1.08	3361.6	48.7	65.1	52.50	59.50	Indonesia
Kuwait Petroleum Corporation	13.20	1492.5	101.3	9.7	53.75	58.25	Kuwait
Algeria National Oil Company	1.21	3860.1	74.0	78.4	24.25	37.50	Algeria
PetroChina	1.51	696.8	106.2	7.0	103.30	48.30	China
Petrobrás*	11.10	302.0	59.6	12.8	97.65	90.90	Brazil
Abu Dhabi National Oil Company	6.95	5553.8	62.0	32.9	11.70	22.75	United Arab Emirates
Iraq National Oil Company	15.40	3109.5	126.4	3.3	17.40	26.00	Iraq
Libya National Oil Company	3.23	1309.6	60.6	6.2	19.00	20.00	Libyan Arab Jamahiriya
Petronas	0.40	1825.8	31.8	52.7	14.50	21.25	Malaysia
Sinopec Group	0.82	307.9	31.5	2.2	118.65	68.80	China
Nigeria National Oil Company	1.85	2105.3	60.8	3.1	22.25	12.55	Nigeria
Total	**118.80**	**58104.5**	**1660.9**	**448.9**	**942.60**	**872.90**	

Sources: Fortune Global 500, 2001, FT500, 2001, company annual reports. *Petroleum Intelligence Weekly*, 18 December 2000. Authors' own research.

Notes: * 49% of Petrobrás is state-owned. bt = billion tonnes; bcm = billion cubic metres; mmt = million tonnes; mmt/y = million tonnes per year.

product sales of the 15 NOCs were 873 mmt in 1999, less than the combined amount of 1063 mmt of refined products sold by Exxon Mobil, Royal Dutch/ Shell and BP Amoco/Arco in the same period.

Among the NOCs, PetroChina and Sinopec Group are at the bottom of the league in terms of oil and gas reserves (Table 7.3). Even their combined oil reserves were only 2.33 billion tons, just 6.6 per cent of those of Saudi Aramco and substantially behind the 3.89 billion tons of oil reserves held by Pemex. Their combined gas reserves of 1005 billion cubic metres were the smallest among the leading NOCs. Both PetroChina and Sinopec rely entirely on domestic reserves for production. In 1999, PetroChina was ranked the eighth largest oil producer in the world (Petroleum Intelligence Weekly, 18 December 2000). The combined oil production of PetroChina and Sinopec Group would rank China as the fifth largest producer in the world. In contrast, the combined gas production of PetroChina and the Sinopec Group was tiny, only 18 per cent of that of Petronas. Downstream, the annual refinery capacity of each of PetroChina and Sinopec Group was above 100 mmt/y, but their combined oil product sales were 117 mmt, at the level of Chevron alone.

3. Merger Frenzy

In contrast to the NOCs, a frenzy of consolidation began to sweep through the global oil majors in the late 1990s. In just two years from 1998 to 2000, the number of major western oil companies was reduced from eleven to six. This fundamentally changed the competitive landscape in the industry.

a) BP/Amoco: August 1998

The consolidation process in the oil and petrochemical industry was initiated by BP's trans-Atlantic merger with Amoco in a $55 billion transaction in August 1998. The combined group placed itself close behind the world leader Royal Dutch/Shell and Exxon in terms of market capitalization, oil and gas reserves and production. The merger greatly strengthened BP's position in downstream marketing in the Mid-West and Eastern United States as well as in the petrochemicals production. The merger is highly significant in that it was one of a series of major transatlantic mergers and acquisitions initiated by European-based companies, including Daimler/Chrysler, Deutsche Bank/ Bankers Trust, Siemens/Westinghouse (non-nuclear power division) and Deutsche Telecom/Voice Stream.

b) Exxon/Mobil: November 1998

Just three months after the BP Amoco merger, Exxon, then the second largest western oil company, announced that it was to merge with Mobil, the third largest, in an $86 billion transaction. The merged company overtook Royal Dutch/Shell as the number one western oil company in terms of revenue, profit, combined oil and gas reserves, oil and gas production, and refining capacity (Tables 7.4 and 7.5). The new company Exxon Mobil has a much wider global spread of assets. It possesses a significant share in some of the world's most important emerging oil areas, including offshore in West Africa and in the Caspian Sea. It owns 60 per cent of the proved gas reserves in Europe and is exploring and developing gas fields in the Asia Pacific Area. Downstream, Exxon Mobil has 33,000 service stations worldwide. Both Exxon and Mobil have powerful global brand recognition. In the fast-growing and profitable lubricant market, Exxon is the world's top producer of lubricant base stocks while Mobil is the market leader in lubricants in both the United States and Europe. Exxon and Mobil also had complementary assets in major petrochemicals such as polyethylene and paraxylene. The merger enabled Exxon/Mobil to overtake Royal Dutch/Shell in financial performance and almost every aspect of operating strength.

c) BP Amoco/Arco: March 1999

Following hard on the heels of the BP/Amoco merger, in March 1999, BP Amoco agreed on a $26.8 billion takeover of Atlantic Richfield Company (Arco). The acquisition of Arco significantly increased BP Amoco's oil and gas reserves. Through Arco, the new company has a much wider global reach with oil fields in Algeria, Venezuela, the Caspian and Russia as well as gas fields in the Gulf of Mexico, the United Kingdom North Sea, the South China Sea, Malaysia, Thailand and Qatar. Moreover, the new company has full operational control of the huge Prudhoe Bay oil and gas field in Alaska. Through Arco, the new company owns 40 per cent of the large Tangguh natural gas site in Indonesia. The acquisition of Arco also gave BP access to the large chain of service stations on the West Coast of the United States, thus effectively establishing a coast-to-coast network across the country. After the acquisition, BP's revenue, oil and gas reserves and production rival those of Shell. It became the world's third largest petrochemical producer after Shell and BASF, with leading technology and market share in acetic acid, polypropylene and PTA. The BP Amoco/Arco deal secured BP's position among the top 'big three' western oil companies.

Table 7.4 **Operating Data Compared: Global Majors *vs* PetroChina and Sinopec, 2000**

| Company | Reserves | | Production | | Refinery throughput (mmb/d) | Oil product sales (mmt/y) | Chemical production (mmt) | Service station number |
	Oil (bb)	Gas (bcf)	Oil (mmboe/d)	Gas (bcf/d)				
Exxon Mobil	11.56	55,866	2.55	10.34	5.64	400.0	25.60	45,000
Royal Dutch/Shell	8.67	50,842	2.27	8.22	2.92	278.5	20.29	46,000
BP	6.51	41,100	1.93	7.61	2.92	188.0	22.07	27,545
TotalFinaElf	6.96	20,705	1.43	3.76	2.41	185.0	15.40†	17,700
Chevron Texaco*	6.83	19,176	2.30	3.70	2.26	233.5	–	39,000‡
ENI	3.42	14,762	0.80	2.50	0.86	53.5	8.50	12,085
Repsol YPF	2.38	14,394	0.64	2.22	1.21	51.4	2.80	7,200
PetroChina	11.0	32,532	2.10	1.38	1.50	56.4	6.70	11,350
Sinopec Corp.	2.95	999	0.68	0.22	2.12	67.0	20.03	20,259

Sources: Compiled from company reports.

Notes

* Figures are combined estimates after announced merger in October 2000.

† Capacity.

‡ Numbers include 8,000 service stations of Caltex.

bb = billion barrels; bcf = billion cubic metres; mmboe/d = million barrels of oil equivalent per day;
bcf/d = billion cubic feet per day; mmb/d = million barrels per day; mmt/y = million barrels per year; mmt = million tonnes.

Table 7.5 **Financial Indicators Compared: Global Majors *vs* PetroChina and Sinopec, 2000**

Company	Revenue ($billion)	Net profit ($billion)	R&D spending ($million)	Market** capitalization ($billion)	Employee numbers (%)	Profit/ revenue ($)	Profit/ Employee
Exxon Mobil	210.4	17.70	936.0	286.4	99,600	8.4	177,711
Royal Dutch/Shell	149.2	12.70	1144.0	206.3	90,000	8.5	141,111
BP	148.1	11.90	599.0	178.0	107,200	8.0	111,007
TotalFinaElf	105.9	6.40	631.0	102.9	123,303	6.0	51,905
Chevron Texaco*	99.2	7.60	922.0	84.5	53,621	7.7	141,736
ENI	45.1	5.30	315.3	48.8	69,969	11.8	75,748
Repsol YPF	42.3	2.20	61.6§	20.6	37,194	5.2	59,149
CNPC	41.7	5.80	–	–	1,292,558	13.9	4,487,000
of which:							
PetroChina	29.2	6.70	212.0	3.5†	441,000	22.9	15,193
Sinopec Group	45.4	0.72	–	–	1,173,901	1.6	613,000
of which:							
Sinopec	39.7	2.30	200.0	1.4‡	508,000	5.8	4,528

Sources: Compiled from company reports.

Notes

* Figures are combined estimates after announced merger in October 2000. ** Market capitalization on 4 January 2001.
§ 1999; † Flotation 10 per cent of company value; ‡ Flotation of 20 per cent of company value.

d) TotalFina/Elf: September 1999

In late 1998, France's second biggest oil group, Total, acquired the Belgian PetroFina in a $7 billion transaction and renamed the new company 'TotalFina'. The acquisition enabled Total to strengthen its downstream businesses in Europe and enhance its international exploration capabilities. The transaction was highly significant in that it demonstrated the fading of national sensitivities associated with the former state-owned oil companies in Europe. Shortly afterwards, TotalFina launched a hostile $43 billion bid for Elf Aquitaine, France's biggest oil group. The takeover was vigorously resisted by Elf Aquitaine but was supported by the French government who owned a 'golden share' in Elf Aquitaine. After months of protracted negotiation, TotalFina and Elf Aquitaine finally agreed to a friendly merger in September 1999. The oil and gas reserves of TotalFinaElf are widely distributed across the world, with 28 per cent in Africa, 27 per cent in Europe, 25 per cent in the Middle East and 20 per cent across the rest of the world. TotalFinaElf's total oil and gas production is close to that of BP Amoco/Arco. The new company has a powerful downstream capability in integrating its petrochemicals with its refining activities around six main hubs. TotalFinaElf greatly strengthened its position as the fourth largest global oil company.

e) BP/Burmah Castro: March 2000

In March 2000 BP Amoco announced that it had agreed to buy Burmah Castrol for $4.7 billion. Castrol is 'one of the great lubricants brands of the world', a name that 'stands for superbly engineered products of the highest quality, and research and development that has consistently kept those products at the forefront of the marketplace' (BP Website). It has become BP Amoco's leading lubricants brand with its products made available through the group's 28,000 retail sites and to BP Amoco's massive worldwide customer base.

f) Chevron/Texaco: October 2000

In October 2000, Chevron and Texaco announced they were to merge in a $42 billion transaction. The new company became the world's fourth largest producer. The combined company has a strong position in most of the world's major and emerging exploration and producing areas. Chevron has low-cost international oil projects offshore Angola and Kazakstan and is a 50:50 equity partner with Petrobrás in the Campos and Cumuruxatiba areas of Brazil. Texaco has made deep-water discoveries offshore Nigeria and is an active explorer and developer in the Unites States Gulf of Mexico, Kazakhstan, deep-water Brazil, Venezuela and the Philippines. The new company became the third largest producer in the United States Gulf of Mexico next to BP and Exxon Mobil. Caltex, the refining joint venture between Chevron and Texaco since 1936, will be integrated into the new company, strengthening the new company's downstream businesses in Asia, Africa and the Middle East. Caltex runs 8,000 service stations. In the profitable lubricant business, the new company accounts for 20–30 per cent of the lubricant additive market and 5–10 per cent of finished lubricant sales in Europe.

g) Conoco/Phillips: November 2001

The consolidation process has been 'cascading' into the mid-sized integrated oil and petrochemical companies. In November 2001, Conoco and Phillips announced a $35 billion merger. Previous to this merger, each company had been making acquisitions fast. Conoco's acquisition of Gulf Canada Resources increased its natural gas reserves and production in North America by 50 per cent. Phillips' acquisition of Tosco increased its refining capacity in the United States by five times and the company becomes the second largest refiner in the United States next to Exxon Mobil. Conoco Phillips will become the world sixth largest energy company in terms of oil and gas reserves and production and the fifth largest global refiner. The merger to grow bigger comes from the pressure to compete with the industry's 'super-major' groups that have an edge in highly capital-intensive projects for the energy world in China, the Middle East and West Africa (*Financial Times*, 20 November, 2001).

h) Repsol-YPF

During the period of large-scale mergers among the western major oil companies, Spain's Repsol launched a hostile, $13 billion all-cash bid for Argentina's YPF in 1999. The deal is highly significant in that it is the first time that a large privatized western oil company has taken over a major, formerly state-owned oil and petrochemical company from a developing country.

Before it was privatized by the government in 1991, YPF had exclusive rights for oil exploration and production in Argentina, though domestic and international private companies had long been allowed to participate in the oil sector. YPF had accounted for around half of domestic oil production. Following its privatization, YPF was restructured for international flotation.

Separated from the non-core businesses, the core businesses from upstream exploration and development to downstream refining, marketing and petro-chemicals as well as electric power were grouped together and formed a joint stock company. In 1993, the new YPF listed in the stock exchanges in Buenos Aires and New York, the largest publicly traded oil company in Latin America.

By 1998, YPF accounted for 51 per cent of Argentina's total oil production. Its three refineries accounted for 51 per cent of Argentina's refining capacity. Its 2,500 service stations across Argentina represented a 37 per cent market share. Under the strong leadership of its CEO, Roberto Monti, YPF had the ambition to build itself from a strong regional player, mainly based within Argentina, into a powerful international company. YPF pursued a series of international projects. In 1995, YPF purchased the United States independent exploration and production company Maxus Energy. It worked together with Petrobrás for a number of exploration blocks in Brazil and to develop gas business in southern Brazil. It also had a joint venture with Petrobrás to develop service station chains in Brazil. In addition, YPF had exploration interests in Bolivia, Ecuador and Venezuela. Through its affiliated companies, YPF also held stake in upstream operations in Russia and in downstream activities in Chile and Peru.

Repsol was the Spanish national champion in oil and petrochemicals. After its privatization in late 1990s, it followed a strategy of international expansion, mainly in Latin America. With 64 per cent of its assets in exploration and development, YPF is a strong upstream player and became an ideal target for Repsol's international expansion strategy, with a focus on Latin America. In January 1999, Repsol acquired a 14.99 per cent stake in YPF from the Argentine government, which still owned 20 per cent of YPF. In April 1999, Repsol launched a $13 billion all-cash bid for all the YPF's shares that it did not already own. Repsol's hostile bid was opposed by the board of YPF. However, the deal was supported by the Argentine government, which had 5.3 per cent of the shares in the company, three other provincial governments with smaller stakes and other private investors. Within only one week, the board of YPF conceded defeat. Chairman Roberto Monti commented, 'We have always maintained a business philosophy based on value creation, and it is the board's view, which I back, that Repsol's bid offers the best alternative for our shareholders in current market conditions' (quoted in the *Financial Times*, 12 May 1999).

The new company Repsol YPF combined YPF's powerful upstream businesses with Repsol's strong downstream capabilities. It became the world's eighth largest publicly traded oil company in terms of oil and gas reserves. Repsol YPF's reserves are close in size to those of ENI. Its assets are spread across the world in Europe, North Africa, Latin America and the United States. It accounts for 59 per cent of refining capacity and 47 per cent of the retail market in Spain, and 56 per cent of the refining capacity and 49 per cent of the retail market in Argentina. It is uncertain if even the new Repsol YPF will remain as an independent player in the new world of super-majors. Rumours have circulated about a possible 'southern European champion', which merged Repsol YPF with ENI, and a possible merger with TotalFinaElf.

4. Conclusion: Competitive Obstacles for Firms Based in Developing Countries

The mergers in the world's oil and petrochemical industry during the global business revolution have created a group of new super-giants that stand in a position of greatly enhanced competitive advantage compared to potential competitors from developing countries. These new super-giants greatly increased their size and their assets base. They have constructed a portfolio of high quality oil and gas reserves distributed around the world. They are able to invest large amounts in R&D to sustain and extend their technical lead over other companies. They have the resources to invest in large-scale information technology systems that can better integrate their extended internal value chain, stretching from exploration to the petrol station. They have developed marketing systems with immensely powerful global brands. They have built massive multi-billion dollar central procurement capabilities with large consequent cost-savings. MSDW estimates that the super-majors, namely Exxon Mobil, Shell and BP, have a capability to sustain their competitive edge in the industry for at least fifteen years (MSDW, 1998).

On the global level playing field, even efficient, ambitious and well-run firms in this sector may be unable to survive as independent entities in the face of the intense competition from the super-majors. Not one integrated oil and petrochemical firm based in a developing country has been able to challenge the global giants in this sector. By far the most successful example was YPF. However, as that case vividly illustrated, privatization, liberalization and high quality management are far from a guarantee of independent survival. Integrated oil and petrochemical firms based in developing countries face formidable obstacles in the ferocious competition with the global leaders. Indeed, in the pursuit of shareholder value, it may be highly rational for the most successful firms in developing countries to be acquired by the world leaders in the industry.

B. *CHINA'S RESPONSE*

In the same period that the merger frenzy swept through the global major oil companies, China's oil and petrochemical industry underwent massive restructuring. After an intense debate on how to reform the oil and petrochemical industry, the Chinese government created two large integrated oil companies through administrative measures.

1. The 1998 Reorganization of China's Oil Industry

In 1998, the State Council undertook a comprehensive restructuring program for China's oil and gas industry with the goal of creating internationally competitive large oil and petrochemical companies. Three objectives were achieved in this asset reorganization. First, through a huge assets swap, the new CNPC and Sinopec became two vertically integrated oil and petrochemical companies with assets across the whole value chain from upstream to downstream. The new CNPC, which had formerly been mainly concerned with the upstream side of the business, now accounted for 66 per cent of both China's oil and gas output, and 42 per cent of its refining capacity. The new Sinopec, which had formerly focused on the downstream part of the business, now accounted for 23 per cent of oil output, 11 per cent of gas output and 54 per cent of refining capacity. With sales revenue of $25–$50 billion each, both of the two groups would have been listed in the world's top 500 companies. Second, the administrative functions of CNPC and Sinopec were separated from their business management functions. As part of the major governmental restructuring programme in the same year, the State Petroleum and Chemical Industry Bureau under the State Economic and Trade Commission was formed to take over the administration functions from CNPC and Sinopec. Third, starting from June 1998, China's crude oil price was pegged to the Singapore FOB prices, which was a significant step in the integration of China with the global oil industry.[8]

2. The Year 2000 Flotation of PetroChina and Sinopec

Closely following the 1998 asset reorganization, CNPC and Sinopec each restructured the company in preparation for international flotation. The businesses and structure of the two companies were fundamentally changed. In each of the companies, core businesses covering oil and gas exploration and development, storage and transportation, refining and marketing, petrochemicals were separated from non-core businesses including enterprises that ran engineering, technical and infrastructure services to core businesses as well as social functions such as schools and hospitals. On 5 November 1999, CNPC grouped together its core businesses and created PetroChina as a joint stock company with limited liability. On 25 February 2000, China Petroleum and Chemical Corporation, known as Sinopec, was established on the core businesses from the old Sinopec, now known as Sinopec Group.

In April 2000, PetroChina listed in New York and Hong Kong (China) Stock Exchange. The initial public offering (IPO) accounted for 10 per cent of the company's total shares, and raised $2.89 billion. Among the shares issued, 32.1 per cent were bought by strategic and corporate investors including BP Amoco, Sing Hung Kai, Hong Kong Cheung Kong Enterprises, and Hutchison Whampoa. After this global listing, CNPC held a 90 per cent of PetroChina's total equity. Six months later, in October 2000, Sinopec listed in the stock exchanges in New York, Hong Kong (China) and London. The IPO accounted for 21.21 per cent of the company's total shares, and raised $3.73 billion. After the global flotation, 56.06 per cent of Sinopec's equity was controlled by its parent company Sinopec Group, 22.73 per cent by the State Development Bank and three asset management companies, Cinda, Orient and Huarong, and 21.21 per cent by overseas investors, including the three largest global oil companies Exxon Mobil, Shell and BP. Exxon Mobil, Shell and BP promised to purchase 20 per cent, 14 per cent and 13.5 per cent respectively of Sinopec's IPO, involving share purchases of up to $1 billion, $430 million and $400 million respectively. ABB Lummus also agreed to purchase $100 million worth of shares. Other overseas corporate investors include Henderson Investment Ltd., Hong Kong (China) and China Gas Company, Cheung Kong Enterprises and Hutchison Whampoa. Both Cheung Kong and Hutchison Whampoa are part of the group of companies owned by Li Ka-shing, whose business empire is based in Hong Kong (China).

3. Business Capabilities

a) Reserves and Output

Within China's total estimated oil reserves in the year 2000 of around 24 billion barrels (Table 7.2), PetroChina owns 11.03 billion barrels, equivalent to those of Exxon Mobil and exceeding those of Shell and BP (Table 7.4). PetroChina's natural gas reserves are 58 per cent those of Exxon Mobil and around 10,000 billion cubic feet more than that owned by TotalFinaElf and Chevron Texaco (Table 7.4). In terms of oil output, PetroChina is already close to the level of the world's leading companies, with an oil output of around 2.1 million barrels per day, compared with 1.93 million at BP, 2.27

million at Shell and 2.55 million at Exxon Mobil. Sinopec is similar to Repsol YPF in terms of oil reserves and oil production but on a much smaller scale in natural gas reserves and production. However, in terms of natural gas output, even the combined production volume of PetroChina and Sinopec lags considerably behind the global giants (Table 7.4).

There are, however, crucial differences between the reserves and output of the two leading Chinese oil companies and those of the global giants. First, the global distribution is strikingly different. PetroChina and Sinopec produce entirely within China. CNPC has international operations in Canada, Venezuela, Kazakhstan, Sudan, Thailand, Indonesia and Malaysia. In 2000, approximately 5.5 million tons of oil were obtained in 2000 from overseas operations, equivalent to just 7.8 per cent of China's total crude oil imports in the same year. CNPC itself retains ownership of these international projects. PetroChina, the floated company, does not have any operations in foreign countries. Sinopec has almost no overseas reserves and production. In the sharpest contrast, BP and Exxon Mobil have production and exploration activities in 27 and 30 countries respectively. Second, the quality of the portfolio of oil and gas assets is very different. China's main onshore oil reserves are declining seriously. Fifty per cent of PetroChina's crude oil reserves are from the Daqing oil field, and one-third of the natural gas reserves are in the Tarim Basin. However, 89 per cent of PetroChina's proved crude oil reserves have already been developed. Daqing is in the secondary recovery stage and polymer flooding has been applied to about 14 per cent of its production. The Tarim Basin is in the remote western part of the country. It will require advanced technology and will involve high transportation costs to ship the gas to the main consuming areas in the eastern part of the country, which raises serious doubts about the commercial viability of the project.[9] Third, the global giants have attempted to construct a global portfolio of oil and gas assets that can make a profit at as low as $10 per barrel of oil. Less than five of PetroChina's oil fields can make a profit when the oil price is at $10–$15 per barrel due to costs induced by difficult nature of the reserves, technological problems and cumbersome management structure.

b) Refining

PetroChina and Sinopec between them have a total of 49 refineries, among which 21 have annual refining capacities greater than five million tonnes. None of PetroChina's refineries and only four of Sinopec's refineries have capacities greater than 10 million tonnes. The utilization rate of refineries owned by PetroChina and Sinopec rose from 61 per cent in 1998, the lowest in the 1990s, to 80 per cent in 2000. This is due to the increasing amount of crude oil available for the two companies' refineries and, to some extent, to the government's campaign to close down small refineries with an annual capacity of less than 1 million tonnes, and refineries out of the state crude oil allocation plan. Since 1999, the State Economic and Trade Commission (SETC) has ordered the closure of 111 refineries over the country (SETC, 1999, 2000). However, the small refineries usually have support from local government for tax revenue and employment. Closing them down has proved a complex task. Despite the government's campaign, an investigation by SETC shows that small refineries in Sha'anxi, Shangdong and Henan that should have been closed are still active (Zhang Zhigang, 2001).

China's total refining capacity was 280 million tonnes at the end of 2000, exceeding the country's total oil consumption by 53 million tonnes in the same year. However, the refining sector needs revamping, upgrading and expanding. First, most of China's refining facilities are equipped to process low-sulphur oil, and are unable to process high-sulphur crude oil from the Middle East except for a few refineries on the east coast such as Maoming and Zhenhai. With more than half of the oil imports from the Middle East, refineries need to add capabilities to use sour crude oil. The effort of PetroChina and Sinopec to increase the capabilities to process sour crude oil requires advanced technology and heavy industry. Second, more stringent environmental regulations for refined products calls for high-conversion refineries. Third, China's accession to the WTO will reduce the tariffs on refined products from the current 6–12 per cent to a uniform rate of 6 per cent. Few of PetroChina's refineries can survive in near-open competition with imported refined products. For Sinopec, the tariff reduction for refined products will reduce its annual revenue by RMB3 billion (approximately US$360 million).

c) Marketing Petroleum Products

After 1999, both PetroChina and Sinopec aggressively expanded their network of service stations all over China. By 2000, PetroChina and Sinopec were reported to own over 11,000 and 20,000 service stations respectively. Each has almost doubled the number that it had in 1999. This expansion has been strongly supported by the government, which granted the two companies exclusive licences to operate new service stations in China. However, the two companies have engaged in a 'blind competitive dash' to acquire service stations, which led to 'less than stringent evaluations of, and inflated price paid for, the service stations' (Zhang Zhigang, Vice Minister of SETC, 2001). Around one quarter of each of the two companies' service stations are franchised retail outlets bearing the companies' brands, 'PetroChina' and 'Sinopec' respectively, and are still run as separate entities. Neither refined products, supplies or the price of refined products are centrally controlled, nor are accounts centrally consolidated, even for the network of service stations owned and operated by the two companies themselves. Between them, PetroChina and Sinopec have over 2,000 wholesale entities. These still have no effective coordination of supply, price or customers. Many of the storage facilities are obsolete. PetroChina and Sinopec still have a long way to go before they develop the logistics expertise of the global giants or possess a comparable brand based on the safe and low-cost operation of a huge logistics system. This is a crucial part of the development of the brand for a globally competitive oil and petrochemical company.

d) Petrochemicals

Ethylene Crackers   By the end of the year 2000, China had a total ethylene capacity of 4.3 million tons, ranking the eighth largest in the world and the third in Asia after Japan and the Republic of Korea (*Oil and Gas Journal*, 23 April 2001). Of the total of 18 ethylene crackers in China, only seven have an annual capacity above 400,000 tonnes (four owned by Sinopec and one by PetroChina) and the other eleven have a capacity of less than 200,000 tonnes. The annual capacity of the largest cracker is 480,000 tonnes, compared to the world's largest at 2.8 million tonnes. Compared with the integrated large sites of the global majors, the average capacity of each petrochemical complex is tiny (Table 7.6). Instead of having a small number of giant, low-cost integrated sites situated in a few concentrated areas, as the global giants do, these 18 ethylene crackers are located at 16 sites in 15 cities.

Product Mix   A high proportion of China's petrochemical and refined products are low value-added products. High value-added petrochemical production only accounts for 30 per cent of total petrochemical production. Only 73 per cent of the diesel produced can be classified as 'first class' and 70 per cent of the lubricants are of middle or high premium quality. By 1997, China could only produce 128 types of synthetic resins, compared to over 10,000 types produced by Japan (Chen Yongkai, 2001). The total petrochemical output and low value-added products has not kept up with the rapid growth of China's economy, which has led to large imports of petrochemicals. By 2000, imports of refined products and major petrochemicals accounted for up to half of the Chinese market (Table 7.7). With further reductions in import tariffs after China's accession to WTO, even these low value-added petrochemical products will face intense competition not only from global majors but also from low-cost producers in the Middle East and South-East Asia.

Table 7.6 **Top 10 Ethylene Producers* *vs* PetroChina and Sinopec Corp.****

| Ranking | Company | No. of sites | Capacity (Million tons per year) | | Company interest (per cent) |
			Entire complexes	Company interests	
1	Dow Chemical Co.	16	12.467	10.076	80.8
2	Exxon Mobil Chemical Co.	14	10.609	7.071	66.7
3	Equistar Chemicals	7	5.265	5.265	100
4	Shell Chemicals Ltd.	6	6.188	4.539	73.4
5	Chevron Phillips Chemical Co.	3	3.674	3.674	100
6	Saudi Basic Industries Corp.	4	5.65	3.95	69.9
7	BP	5	4.151	3.036	73.1
8	Nova Chemicals Corp.	2	3.54	2.968	83.8
9	Atofina	7	3.725	2.378	63.8
10	Enichem SPA	7	3.005	2.196	73.1
–	Sinopec Corp.	5	1.99	1.99	100
–	PetroChina	2†	0.8	0.8	62§

Sources: *Oil and Gas Journal*, 23 April 2001. Authors' own research.

Notes
* As of 1 April 2001. ** End of 2000. ‡ Sites of annual capacity over 350,000 tonnes.
§ Percentage of total capacity of company.

Table 7.7 **Market Share of Imported Oil Products and Petrochemicals in China, 2000**

Imported product	Market share (per cent)
Refined products	20
Lubricants	25
LPG	50
Synthetic resins	48
Synthetic fibres	30
Synthetic rubbers	44

Source: Sinopec.

Technology Both PetroChina and Sinopec have made many important technical advances. However, both companies are still far behind the global giants in their development of world-leading technologies. Whereas the world's leading oil and petrochemical companies each produce more than one thousand patents annually, Sinopec produces only around 300. In the year 2000, PetroChina and Sinopec spent $212 million and $200 million respectively on research and development, about one-fifth to two-fifths of that spent by the 'big three' (Table 7.5). The R&D spending/revenue ratio of Sinopec and PetroChina (0.5 and 0.7 per cent respectively) is no less than that of Shell and somewhat higher than that of Exxon Mobil and BP (0.4–0.5 per cent). However, the global majors are able to spend more on research and technological development in absolute terms due to the sheer size of their sales revenue. Moreover, they are able to purchase greater amounts of the R&D 'embedded' in the products of specialist suppliers to the oil and petro-chemical industry.[10]

The technological capabilities of PetroChina and Sinopec both upstream and downstream are relatively backward. In exploration and production, their oilfield development equipment is at the world level of the late 1980s and their exploration equipment equivalent to the world level of the early 1990s. Oil extracting machinery and oil and gas treatment equipment are either imported complete or assembled in China. Key electronic instruments and software for exploration and production are imported. China's own industrial experts have pointed out that China's capability of technological innovation in upstream oil and gas industry is still at the level of a 'third world' country, which will be a great constraint on the industry's competitiveness and efficiency (*China Petroleum*, January 1999). The technological backward-ness is reflected in the high level of energy consumption in petrochemical production. In ethylene production, PetroChina consumed an average of 872 kilograms of standard oil per ton in 2000 compared to the world average level of 500–690 kilograms. In addition, the percentage loss of ethylene is high. The average ethylene percentage loss in PetroChina's production was 1.3 per cent compared with the world average of 1.0 per cent. The high energy consumption level and high ethylene percentage loss contribute to the high cost of ethylene production. In China energy consumption accounts for 76 per cent of the total cost of production compared to the world average of 63 per cent. Moreover, only 55 per cent of the chemicals from the cracking process in China are further processed and utilized, which is significantly below the level achieved by the world's leading firms in the sector (Chen Huai, 1998: 29).

e) Financial Performance

Revenue   Their sales revenue places PetroChina and Sinopec alongside the leading second tier of global oil and petrochemical companies, but far short of the industry leaders, Exxon Mobil, Shell and BP (Table 7.5).

Profit   In the year 2000 net profits at PetroChina and Sinopec dramatically improved to $6.67 billion and $2.30 billion, compared with $0.33 billion and $0.56 billion respectively in 1999. The gap in net profits with the global giants has narrowed considerably from being only a small fraction in 1999 to almost one-third and one-half that of the 'big three'. However, Ma Fucai, Chairman of PetroChina, cautioned that 80 per cent of the company's increased operating profit in 2000 resulted from the rise in crude and refined oil prices (*Financial Times*, 23 April 2001). Most of Sinopec's revenue increase came from the marketing and distribution of its oil products 'at a time of unusually robust prices' (*Financial Times*, 17 April 2001). The year 2000 may not provide a good guide to the two companies' net profits in the medium term.

Profits per worker at PetroChina and Sinopec are minuscule compared to those at the world's leading companies in the sector. PetroChina and Sinopec each have a workforce four to five times as big as that of the top three global oil and petrochemicals giants (Table 7.5). Downsizing these huge institutions is a complicated and difficult task.

Market Capitalization   PetroChina and Sinopec have market capitalizations that are only a small fraction of that at the leading global companies. If one assumed that the whole company was floated, then at the current share price, the market capitalization of PetroChina and Sinopec would be $35 billion and $14 billion respectively, compared with $286 billion for Exxon Mobil, $206 billion for Royal Dutch/Shell and $178 billion for BP (Table 7.5). Analysts estimate that PetroChina's average annual revenue growth rate in the next five years will be 4.9 per cent, only one-half of that of Exxon Mobil and only one-third of that of the whole oil industry. Industry experts have voiced serious concerns about PetroChina's level of operational efficiency and about the high level of uncertainty in its performance after China's accession to the WTO. PetroChina's P/E/G (price/equity/growth rate) ratio is predicted to be less than 1.0, compared to 1.7 of Exxon Mobil. The shortfall is attributed to the element of 'institutional risk' involved in China (*Finance*, April 2001).

4. Organizational Structure

The organizational structure of PetroChina and Sinopec is superficially similar to that of an international integrated oil company. They have established a board of directors, a senior management team and core businesses segments from upstream to downstream. The superficial similarity conceals important differences.

The global giants have a strong 'one company' corporate identity and culture. Within PetroChina and Sinopec there exist powerful entities that over the years have developed strong independent corporate identities and ambitions. They struggled for autonomy in business management and aspired to become independent competitive companies. Daqing is China's largest oil field. It is now under PetroChina. Over a history of forty years, Daqing developed a strong corporate identity. Its employees took great pride in being 'Daqing people' (*Daqing ren*). Daqing was in many ways like a small country within China. Daqing had the corporate ambition to build itself into a leading oil company able to compete on the world stage, and strongly believed that it should be an independently floated firm. In the 1990s, four companies under Sinopec, including Zhenhai, Shanghai Petrochemicals (SPC), Yizheng and Yanhua were listed separately in international stock markets. Zhenhai and SPC each had a history of more than thirty years and developed strong, distinctive corporate identities. Each devised plans and strategies for development through mergers and acquisitions. Both PetroChina and Sinopec took strong measures during the restructuring to integrate these powerful subordinate companies by centralizing control over planning, personnel, investment and finance. Nevertheless, establishing a unified corporate identity and culture remains a formidable challenge.

The relationship between the two listed companies and their parent companies remains ambiguous. As discussed above, CNPC controls 90 per cent of PetroChina, and Sinopec Group controls 56 per cent of Sinopec. A principle part of the annual income of CNPC and Sinopec Group is from the dividend payment of the two listed companies. In 2000, CNPC received an approximate $3.1 billion dividend payment from PetroChina,[11] accounting for 53 per cent of its net profit. CNPC has retained the non-core businesses as well as social functions employing more than 800,000 people, a large fraction of whose activities are loss-making. The non-core businesses of Sinopec Group employ more than 600,000 people, but none of the businesses in which they are employed made a profit in 1999. To what extent PetroChina and Sinopec have autonomy in decision-making with respect to business strategy, dividend payments and appointment of senior management remains unclear. Of the thirteen directors on the board of PetroChina (including three independent non-executive directors), five concurrently hold top positions with CNPC. Of the ten directors of the board of Sinopec (including three independent non-executive directors and one employee representative director), two also have top positions with Sinopec Group. Ma Fucai, Chairman of PetroChina, and Li Yizhong, Chairman of Sinopec, are each concurrently the president of the respective parent companies. Such a structure has caused concern to be expressed about the respective companies' commitment to creating share-holder value and protecting the rights of minority shareholders.[12]

5. The Competitive Landscape

The global giants are deeply interested in developing their business in China from upstream to downstream. In upstream exploration and development, there were 167 onshore blocks open to foreign companies for exploration and development. By 1999, total foreign investment reached $1.1 billion in onshore upstream and $6.45 billion in offshore upstream (SETC, 2001). There are altogether 70 oil companies from 18 countries participating in upstream activities (SETC, 2001), including the global giants Exxon Mobil, Shell, BP Amoco and other major players such as Texaco and Phillips. In petrochemicals, six global majors will set up six joint ventures in petro-chemical complexes by 2005 (Table 7.8). These projects each involve invest-ment from $2.5 billion to $4.5 billion and all are located in the coastal regions,

Table 7.8 **Proposed Major Sino-foreign Petrochemical Joint Ventures**

Major partners	Ethylene capacity (thousand tons per year)	Investment ($ billion)	Location	Date of completion
Sinopec SPC/BP*	900	2.7	Shanghai	2005
Sinopec Yangzi/BASF*	650	2.7	Nanjing	2005
Sinopec Fujian/Exxon Mobil/ Saudi Aramco	600	2.5	Fujian	2005
Sinopec Tianjin/Dow Chemical	600	–	Tianjin	–
PetroChina Lanzhou/Phillips	600	–	Lanzhou	–
CNOOC/Royal Dutch/Shell*	800	4.5	Guangdong	2005

Sources: *Chemical Week*, 13 October 1999, *Oil and Gas Journal*, 23 April 2001. Authors' research.

Note: * Under construction.

which have the highest average income level in China. Demand for ethylene was around 7.5 million tons in 2000 but total ethylene capacity in China was 4.3 million tons in the same year. It is projected that demand for ethylene will reach 10 million tons in 2005 (*Oil and Gas Journal*, 10 January 2000). If we assume all the joint venture projects start production in 2005, they would account for 42 per cent of total projected ethylene demand in China. In addition, the joint ventures (JVs) will have major associated production capabilities in related petrochemical products, in which the global giants are in most areas technologically far ahead of their Chinese counterparts. From the perspective of the foreign partner in the JV, they each form a part of the respective global business system, typically a single business unit. In this sense, they represent an important growth of the multinational giants within the indigenous Chinese firm.

The global majors have become strategic investors in PetroChina and Sinopec. Equity involvement by the global super-majors was crucial to their successful listing. Before its international listing, Sinopec signed an agreement with each of its strategic investors to develop businesses both upstream and downstream in China. In the upstream sector, Royal Dutch/Shell will partner Sinopec to develop natural gas resources in Inner Mongolia, the Ordos and Tarim Basins. In refining and marketing, Exxon Mobil will establish a joint venture with Sinopec for retail marketing in Guangdong Province, which will involve setting up 500 service stations within three years. Exxon Mobil will study the feasibility of doubling the current refining capacity of 150 thousand barrels per day at Guangzhou Petrochemicals Company. Royal Dutch/Shell will have a joint venture with Sinopec involving 500 service stations in Jiangsu Province. BP will set up a joint venture with Sinopec to acquire, renovate or build 500 service stations in Zhejiang Province. These service stations will have the logos of both BP and Sinopec, and will sell petrol supplied by Sinopec and other refined products supplied by both companies. For the three companies, this was 'but the beginning of their attempts to capture a share of the world's largest retail market' (*Petroleum Economist*, October 2000). In April 2001, PetroChina established a retail marketing joint venture with its strategic investor, BP, in Guangdong Province, with PetroChina holding a 51 per cent equity share and BP holding the remainder. The joint venture will consolidate the 366 service stations owned by PetroChina and the 43 service stations owned by BP in Guangdong. A further 100 service stations will be acquired in 2001. The strategy of the global giants to expand their downstream, high-margin business, each in a different part of the China's high-income coastal markets, is clear.

6. Conclusion

In the evolutionary reform of large state-owned enterprises in China's 'pillar industries', the creation and international listing of PetroChina and Sinopec marked a crucial step in the attempt to create modern, internationally competitive firms. The process of restructuring and flotation was achieved through administrative measures within just one year.[13] This was an immense achievement.

Despite this achievement, substantial question marks remain. Across the whole value chain from upstream to downstream, PetroChina and Sinopec are at disadvantage in terms of the quantity of oil and gas reserves compared with the national oil companies, and in terms of global distribution and quality of reserves compared with the super-majors. They are at a disadvantage in technology and financial strength compared with the global majors. There remains a deep internal battle to establish a cohesive corporate culture to integrate their powerful subordinate companies and establish a truly unified company. The relationship between the floated company and the parent remains unresolved. Across the value chain, PetroChina and Sinopec have been actively forming 'strategic alliances' and establishing joint ventures with global oil and petrochemical companies. How stable will these partnerships be, especially after China's accession to the WTO? Will PetroChina and Sinopec eventually emerge as the 'firm' that is to compete globally? The institutional structure of PetroChina and Sinopec remains in evolution.

The full extent of the challenges facing the Chinese oil and petrochemical industry on the verge of China's entry to the WTO was bluntly spelt out at a meeting convened by the State Planning Commission at the end of September 2001 (Xinhuanet, 2001). The reports to the meeting stressed that this is a 'pillar industry' for China's national economy. They emphasized that acceleration of the trend of globalization and consolidation means that China's petrochemical industry 'faces critical challenges from many aspects'. Experts at the meeting emphasized that China's petrochemical industry was a latecomer to the sector, and that it still had 'low technological and management standards'. The final verdict at the meeting on the state of the industry was blunt:

> The overall technological level of the petrochemical industry of our country lags behind the advanced countries about 10–15 years and has a fairly large gap compared with the world's advanced level. The energy and material consumption level of the majority of the refineries and ethylene crackers is higher than the average level in Asia. The capabilities of technological innovation are weak. Patented self-developed technologies

are few. Development and introduction of high and new technologies and products is weak. Engineering capabilities are weak and lacking in potential for further development.

The institutional experiment in China's oil and petrochemical sector is being closely watched by all concerned to understand the future course of China's industrial strategy regarding large firms and their relationship with the global giants. This sector is held up as a beacon for other sectors to study in restructuring to face the challenge of globalization and consolidation. PetroChina and Sinopec have both successfully restructured and floated on international markets. However, everyone within the Chinese industry is fully aware of the profound challenges posed by globalization and China's deepening integration with the global economy and business system. It remains an open question whether PetroChina and Sinopec will succeed where YPF failed.

III. AEROSPACE

A. *GLOBAL TRENDS*

1. Consolidation

The dramatic change in the demand side of the world's aerospace industry in the 1990s has been a powerful force to drive forward consolidation. After the Cold War, both the United States and Europe drastically reduced their defence spending. In the United States, total defence expenditure fell from a peak of $390 billion in 1986 to $253 billion in 1999, and in Europe (NATO) the total budget fell from a peak of $191 billion in 1990 to $135 billion in 1999 (IISS, 1999, p. 37). Procurement techniques rapidly moved towards those of the civil aerospace world as governments push contractors to lower costs. Alongside the decline in defence procurement, European and United States military aircraft manufacturers have been able to sell to markets that were inaccessible during the Cold War. The fastest growing market for Western arms sales was the Far East, to which arms deliveries increased by one-third in real terms from 1987 to 1998 (IISS, 1999, pp. 281–283). The countries around China substantially increased their arms purchases from $9.1 billion in 1987 to $12.8 billion in 1998, compared with China's purchases of $0.9 billion and $0.5 billion in the same years (Table 7.9).

Until the events of 11 September 2001, the civilian aircraft market had been predicted to grow substantially in the years ahead. Airbus had forecast that over the next two decades from 1997 to 2017, the worldwide airline fleet would increase from the 1998 level of 9,700 to 17,900. Airlines were predicted

Table 7.9 **International Arms Deliveries within East Asia, 1987 and 1998 (millions of constant 1997 US dollars)**

	Total	China	Japan	Taiwan Province of China	Republic of Korea	Thailand	Malaysia	Singapore	Indonesia
1987	9,926	877	1,512	1,408	1,012	581	95	418	351
1998	13,236	469	2,086	6,258	1,366	313	334	887	365

Source: IISS, 1999, p. 283.

to buy 13,000–14,000 new and replacement aircraft over that period with a total value of around $1,200 billion. The predicted market for aero-engines (including original sales and sales of spare parts) was estimated to be around $500 billion in the next two decades (*Financial Times*, 3 September 1998). These forecasts now need to be radically revised. However, even if they are substantially reduced, the market is still very large. Moreover, it is likely that a decline in commercial aircraft purchase will, to some extent, be partially compensated by increased purchase of military aircraft and other military equipment.

The nature of the market for civil aircraft has altered significantly since the 1980s. Privatization, as well as international alliances among the world's airlines, placed great pressure on aircraft suppliers to reduce cost. One major effect of the events of 11 September 2001 may well be to force national governments to end restrictions on foreign ownership of airlines. If so, the current parlous financial state of most of the world's airlines is likely to lead to large-scale global consolidation in the world airline industry, mimicking that among the equipment makers.

a) United States of America

Initiated by the Pentagon, over $62 billion-worth of mergers and acquisitions occurred between 1994 and 1998 in the United States (Table 7.10). The most significant event in this process was the merger between Boeing and McDonnell-Douglas. The resulting extraordinarily high level of industrial concentration received 'strong support from the United States administration (*Financial Times*, 23 September 1997). After the Boeing/McDonnell Douglas merger, Boeing and Lockheed Martin between them accounted for close to one-half of United States defence department contracts, and almost completely dominated military aircraft sales to the United States government (*Financial Times*, 3 September 1998). The merger also resulted in Boeing being the only producer of jet airliners in the United States, the world's largest airline market by far. Moreover, unlike Lockheed Martin, Boeing was now a colossus that spanned both the military and civilian spheres of aerospace production. Boeing accounted for no less than 84 per cent of the world's total commercial aircraft in service (*Financial Times*, 23 September 1997). On 26 October 2001, the Pentagon made a 'winner-take-all' decision and awarded the $200 billion Joint Strike Fighter (JSF) programme, the biggest-ever defence procurement, to Lockheed Martin. The procurement decision 'catapults Lockheed into an unassailable position as the world's top builder of fighter aircraft' (*Financial Times*, 29 October 2001).

Table 7.10 **Principal Mergers and Acquisitions in the United States Defence Industry, 1994–1998 (deals of over $500 million only)**

Acquirer	Acquiree	Value ($ million)	Date
Loral	IBM Federal Systems	1,575	March 1994
Northrop	Grumman	2,100	April 1994
Lockheed*	Martin Marietta*	>9,000	March 1995
Rolls-Royce	Allison Gas Turbine	525	March 1995
Loral	Unisys Defense Operation	862	May 1995
E-Systems*	Raytheon*	2,300	June 1995
Northrop Grumman	Westinghouse Electronic System	3,600	March 1996
Lockheed Martin	Loral	9,500	April 1996
Boeing	Rockwell Aerospace and Defence	3,025	Dec. 1996
Boeing*	McDonnell Douglas**	13,300	1997
Raytheon	Texas Instruments Defence Business	2,950	1997
GM Hughes Defence Business*	Raytheon*	9,500	1997
GEC	Tracor	1,400	1998

Source: *FT*, 3 September 1998.
Note: * For mergers, acquiring and acquired company are shown in alphabetical order.

b) Europe

By the late 1990s, the defence industry had become much more concentrated in the United States than in Europe. The level of government procurement in the United States is far above that in Europe. In 1999, the total defence budget of the United States was more than twice the size of that of the whole of NATO Europe (IISS, 1999, p. 37) and is certain to rise substantially in the wake of the events of 11 September 2001. Moreover, a large fraction of Europe's procurement spending is still conducted by individual countries.

The European military aerospace industry realized that it must unify or perish before the United States challenge. In 1998, the 'national champions' of the United Kingdom, France and Germany, namely BAe, Aerospatiale and Dasa, declared their intention to unify into a single company, the European Aerospace and Defence Company (EADC), with a single management structure and quoted on the stock market. It was intended to incorporate all sectors of the European aerospace industry from military aircraft, guided weapons, space and defence electronics to large civil aircraft (including a restructured Airbus). However, the merger of BAe with GEC-Marconi in January 1999 posed a serious setback to the cause of European aerospace integration. Renamed BAe Systems, the new company became the world's second largest in terms of military revenues (*Financial Times*, 20 January 1999). Despite the serious setback to their plans, in October 1999, Dasa and Aerospatiale-Matra merged into a new giant company called the European Aircraft, Defence and Space Company ('EADS', as opposed to 'EADC'). However, EADS now has serious problems with its management structure leadership (*Financial Times*, 16 November 2001). Moreover, BAe Systems, EADS's partner in Airbus, Eurofighter, now is a full partner with Lockheed Martin in the JSF programme. France is committed to its own Rafale fighter through Dassault and compete for export orders with EADS's Eurofighter. Italy has decided to quit the European programme to build a large military transport aircraft A400M.

In civilian aircraft production, the competition between Airbus and Boeing became more ferocious more than ever during the 1990s. Twice Airbus overtook Boeing in terms of new orders in 1994 and 1999. Moreover, in 2000, Airbus announced that it intended to proceed with plans to build a superlarge aircraft, the A380, to directly challenge Boeing in the most lucrative segment of the market. The A380 is intended to carry more than 500 passengers. From 1996, Airbus began the prolonged attempt to transform itself from a 'Groupement d'intérêt économique' into a limited company floated on the stock market. EADS now holds 80 per cent of Airbus, compared with just 20 per cent for BAe Systems. This made it easier to turn Airbus into a single company. However, the events of 11 September will put severe pressure on Airbus, especially given the large outlays already undertaken on the A380, for which the market now looks much less optimistic than before 11 September. In sum, the final shape of the European aerospace industry is far from certain.

c) Transatlantic Option

The United States has the world's largest arms market by far. Leading European aerospace companies are not only seeking to expand their roles as sub-contractors and risk-sharing partners for the United States giants, they are also considering merging with leading companies across the Atlantic. The possibilities for a 'transatlantic solution' seemed to be growing stronger in 1999. In an effort to prevent the emergence of a 'Fortress Europe' in the arms industry, the United States government is moving towards relaxing its controls on foreign investment in the industry and greater technology-sharing with European-based defence firms. Jacques Gansler (Head of Procurement, Pentagon) announced that the Pentagon was willing to allow European or Asian companies to 'buy major United States defence companies under certain conditions', one of which was that other countries must reciprocate, allowing similar access to their own markets (*IHT*, 8 July 1999). He believed that such mergers would create 'a huge new defense market' and would make it easier for allies who are likely to fight together in future wars to cooperate on developing common weapons (*IHT*, 8 July 1999). If realized, such mergers would radically change the nature of the Euro-US defence industry relationship and have a strong impact on the possible formation of the mooted EADC.

2. Systems Integration

a) Integrating the Supply Chain

Modern aircraft and engines have become so complex that a major aspect of competitive advantage has become the ability to integrate the whole system of supply to produce the final product. The surrounding system of suppliers today constitutes a veritable 'external firm', whose activities are closely co-ordinated and planned by the core systems integrators who design and assemble the civilian aircraft or are the prime contractors for defence industry contracts. For example, Rolls-Royce purchases around 70 per cent of the value of the final product from outside the company. Airbus has more than 1,500 suppliers in 27 countries. Its system of suppliers is truly global, including over 500 United States companies, and suppliers in Singapore, India, Australia, Indonesia, the Republic of Korea, Japan and China. The size of the 'external firm' can greatly exceed that of the core companies. Boeing's 'external firm' employs around three-quarters of a million people across the world, including sub-contractors in China. Rolls-Royce has around 20,000 people in its aerospace division in the United Kingdom, and estimates that around 40,000 people work full-time to supply the company with goods and services.

Organizing global supply networks has become an increasingly important part of the modern aerospace industry. The large scale components purchase that system integrators make from outsourced supply networks has necessitated large investments in IT systems to integrate the supplier networks tightly with the core design and assembly location, and involves increasingly detailed, instantaneous exchange of information. 'Lean production' techniques are essential to cost reduction and control. Rolls-Royce believes that intensified interactions between the core company and the network of over

1,500 first-tier suppliers are the main factors behind the sharp improvements in its system performance.

b) Building Internal Systems Integration Capabilities

Alongside the trend towards concentration among component and sub-system suppliers, the leading systems integrators are themselves tending to become more vertically integrated. This enables them to perform the increasingly complicated tasks involved in integrating complex sub-systems with multiple interfaces (MSDW, 1999, p. 85). For example, Raytheon bought a succession of military businesses in the 1990s, including the military electronics company, E-Systems, the military systems and electronics business of Texas instruments, and the Hughes military electronics business from General Motors. Through the purchase of Hughes, it established a 'near monopoly in United States air combat weapons' (*Financial Times*, 13 January 1997). By the late 1990s, Raytheon had become a huge company with a $20 billion annual turnover, and a wide range of systems integration capabilities in missiles and torpedoes. In Europe, BAe acquired Siemens Plessey in 1997 in order to strengthen its in-house capability in information technology, central to electronics systems integration. BAe's 1999 merger with GEC-Marconi brought a major prime contractor in military equipment together with a major aerospace electronics company. The acquisition dramatically enhanced BAe's ability to develop its systems integration capabilities and compete as a prime contractor for the largest defence programmes, including aircraft carriers and combat aircraft.

3. The 'Cascade' Effect

The intense pressure from global systems integrators compelled the component supply industry to undergo rapid change. In order to meet the demands of the systems integrators, the major components suppliers themselves needed to invest heavily in R&D, and to grow in order to benefit from cost reduction through economies of scale. A powerful merger movement is taking place among first-tier suppliers to the systems integrators: 'More mergers among the smaller sub-scale components and sub-systems manufacturers seem inevitable as the supplier base responds to the pressure being applied by the prime contractors such as BAe, or original equipment manufacturers, such as Boeing' (MSDW, 1999, p. 87). Indeed, leading first-tier systems integrators have themselves become 'systems integrators' of major sub-sections of aircraft.

In the crucial aircraft engine sector, there are now only three engine makers left that have the capability to produce large modern jet aircraft engines, namely Rolls-Royce, Pratt and Whitney of United Technology and GE Engine of GE. In 1997, the market share of civil aero-engine orders in terms of value between them was 34 per cent for Rolls-Royce, 53 per cent for GE and 13 per cent for Pratt and Whitney (*Financial Times*, 6 March 1998).

In 1999, Allied Signal, one of the world's top five aerospace companies, strengthened its already powerful position as a first-tier supplier still further when it announced that it was to merge with Honeywell. The new company's largest single business is aerospace, with about $10.5 billion in annual revenues, 'bringing together Honeywell's focus on sophisticated avionics with Allied Signal's in-flight safety products and systems' (*Financial Times*, 7 June 1999). The new Allied Signal/Honeywell company has 'a strong position in everything from manufacturing cockpit controls to handling aircraft service and maintenance' (*FT*, 8 June 1999). The combined R&D expenditure of the two companies is almost $800 million (DTI, 1998, pp. 60 and 63). Honeywell explicitly pointed to the consolidation of customers as a major reason for the merger (*Financial Times*, 11 June 1999). Only through merger and cost-cutting can companies like Honeywell compete and establish long-run strategic partnerships with the giant customers like Boeing, Lockheed Martin and BAe Systems.

The trend towards concentration is also affecting smaller companies within the industry. In June 1999, Meggitt acquired Whittaker Corporation for $380 million. The company supplies valves, ground fuelling products and fire and smoke detectors to 'virtually every aircraft maker in the West' (*Financial Times*, 10 June 1999). The merger was explicitly driven by the assemblers' push to reduce the number of parts suppliers. Without the necessary scale the two companies felt they would no longer be competitive. Mike Stacey, Meggitt's chief executive commented: 'We are very conscious that bigger suppliers is what it's all about' (quoted in *Financial Times*, 10 June 1999).

4. Embraer

Alone among developing countries, Brazil may be on the verge of building a successful national aerospace industry, though it is still too early to record a final verdict on the endeavour. Embraer (Empresa Brasileira de Aeronautica) was established by the Brazilian government in 1969, as part of its import-substitution-based industrial policy. Early strategies concentrated on aircraft designing, assembling and fuselages production. Although strongly supported by procurement from the government, the company focused on export markets which brought it longer production runs, new ideas for technical change, and exacting performance standards (Goldstein, 2001). In 1994, the company made a loss of $30 million. In the same year, the company was privatized. It was bought by three domestic shareholders, who between them owned 89 per cent of the company's shares. The Brazilian state still retained a 7 per cent holding in the company.

Since then, Embraer has grown rapidly from a small regional manu-facturer into a significant global player in regional jets. Embraer rapidly developed the systems integration skills necessary to assemble a modern air-liner. It purchased all the key components from outside suppliers, including the avionics, flight controls, engines, wings, tail units and fuselage segments. By the end of April 1999, Embraer had achieved 373 firm orders for the ERJ-135 (37 seats) and ERJ-145 (30 seats), and 390 options for the planes. In 1999, the company delivered 97 regional jets, compared to 82 from Bombardier, its main rival, 23 from BAe and 15 from Fairchild Dornier (HBS Case). The company directly employs over 7,000 direct employees and has an estimated further 3,000 employees working in supplier industries in Brazil alone. Furthermore, in July 1999, Embraer announced the launch of a new family of larger jets, the ERJ-170 (70 seats) and the ERJ-190–200 (90 seats). The launch order, the largest ever for regional jets, was placed by Crossair of Switzerland and had a total of 200 aircraft with a total value of $4.9 billion. In October 1999, Embraer announced that a consortium of French aerospace companies including Aerospatiale/Matra, Dassault, Thomson-CSF and SNECMA would acquire 20 per cent of its equity, which would reduce the Brazilian shareholder's total stake to 69 per cent. In July 2000, Embraer was listed in the New York Stock Exchange.

5. Conclusion: Competitive Obstacles for Firms Based in Developing Countries

The aerospace industry is a capital-intensive high-technology industry with high barriers to entry. The profound transformation of the leading aerospace companies based in the United States and Europe in the 1990s created even higher barriers to entry than existed before. Today, major aerospace compan-ies in developing countries face greater obstacles than ever in their attempt to catch up with the world leaders. Aerospace companies based in Europe and the United States benefit from vast military procurement, which together account for around 60 per cent of the world total military procurement. They have massive economies of scale in assembly with long production runs for each aircraft type. They have huge R&D spending and large R&D support from their respective governments (Table 7.11), especially in the United States, which has enabled them to sustain their technological lead: 'The development of the United States aerospace industry was largely government-funded. As late as 1986, close to 80 per cent of all R&D in this industry was

Table 7.11 **Share of R&D Spending Financed by Government for Aerospace, 1970 and 1990 (per cent)**

Country	Share of R&D financed by government		Share of R&D financed by government, excluding defence-related expenditures	
	1970	1990	1970	1990
France	65	49	54	34
United States	58	46	40	26
Germany	45	33	38	30
Japan	28	19	28	18

Source: Fransman, 1995, p. 107.

Federally-supported' (White House, 2000). They have huge financial strength and resources reflected in large market capitalization (Table 7.12), access to export credit guarantees supported by the government and often have the benefit of co-finance of industrial development with the government. They have high capabilities in system integration in both the internal and external firms on a global scale. They have established globally recognized brands both for aircraft and for key sub-systems.

Not one firm from a developing country has succeeded in challenging the aerospace giants of the developed countries either as a systems integrator or a major first-tier supplier. Embraer represents the highest achievements so far for developing countries in the field of commercial aerospace. However, it is far from certain that in the foreseeable future it will be able to compete successfully with the established giants in even the regional jet market, let alone in the market for larger aircraft. Embraer is tiny compared with either Boeing or Airbus, and significantly smaller than Bombardier (Canada), its main direct rival. Moreover, in each of these cases, the aerospace division of each of the companies is part of a much larger group. In November 1999, the WTO ruled against both Brazil and Canada for the subsidies they had given to Embraer and Bombardier. Embraer faces the serious risk of 'head-on competition with Boeing and Airbus in the bottom end of the full-size jet market' (Goldstein, 2001). To these risks are now added the projected general downturn in the civilian aircraft market, with many analysts believing that for short journeys within high income countries, especially in North America, which is Embraer's main market, there will now be a large-scale switch to railways away from regional jets.

Table 7.12 **World Leading Aerospace and Defence Company, 2000**

Company	Assets ($ billion)	Revenue ($ billion)	Profit ($ million)	R&D spending ($ million)	Market capitalization ($ billion)	Employee	Country/Region
Boeing	42.0	51.3	2,128	1,351	53.3	198,000	United States
United Technologies	25.4	26.6	1,808	1,220	34.6	153,800	United States
Lockheed Martin	30.4	25.3	-519	606	14.5	126,000	United States
Honeywell	25.2	25.0	1,659	767	38.7	125,200	United States
Raytheon	26.8	18.3	141	492	10.1	93,696	United States
EADS	38.9	18.0	-835	948	–	88,879	Europe
TRW		16.2		832		102,000	United States
BAE Systems	26.0	14.6	-20	1,382	16.8	85,000	United Kingdom
General Dynamics	8.0	10.4	901	–		43,300	United States
Northrop Grumman	8.3	8.3	608	203		39,300	United States

Sources: *Fortune 500*, 2001. *Fortune Global 500*, 2001. *FT 500*, May 2001. DTI (2000/2001).

Note: Market capitalization by January 2001.

B. *CHINA'S RESPONSE*

1. Ambitions and Successes

The restructuring of China's aerospace industry started at the same time as the world's leading aerospace companies entered a period of profound change. In 1993, Aviation Industries of China (AVIC) was established, assuming responsibility for the management of all the aviation industry assets formerly under the Ministry of Aviation Industry. It was formally turned into an experimental state holding company in 1996. AVIC is directly responsible to the State Council, to whom its senior managers report. It has the entire Chinese aviation industry under its control, with formal responsibility for managing the industry's assets, and formulating the industry's business strategy. The goal of the holding company was to transform the nationwide collection of enterprises into an internationally competitive aviation company:

> AVIC is promoting itself to become a gigantic enterprise group with worldwide fame and influence ... The aviation industry has itself become one of the key high-tech industries with intensive technology and vast infrastructure. AVIC will become an ultra-large industrial group, which combines military and civil aviation, is transnational in operation, high technology and export oriented (AVIC, 1998, pp. 2–4).

In the early 1980s, Deng Xiaoping gave powerful support to the attempt to build a large indigenous jet passenger plane: 'Henceforth, China's domestic airlines should use only domestically-produced airplanes' (Deng Xiaoping, December 1981). By 1985, AVIC had achieved the extraordinary success of building a large civilian airliner, the Y-10, based on reverse engineering of the Boeing 707. It was produced by the Shanghai Aircraft Manufacturing Plant. Two planes were built and underwent extensive flight testing. At this time, Airbus was still in its infancy. China also developed its own turbo-prop regional aircraft, the Y-7, produced by Xian Aircraft Corporation (XAC). The earlier fifty-seat version was developed in the 1960s. An upgraded sixty-seat version entered commercial service in 1986.

Based on assistance from the USSR, China built a large-scale military aircraft industry. By the late 1990s, it had manufactured a total of several thousand military jet aircraft, including large numbers of fighters and bombers. It has continued to build and technically upgrade substantial numbers of military aircraft.

In the late 1980s, China and Pakistan jointly developed a relatively advanced jet trainer, the K-8 Karakorum. In 2000, China for the first time exported an entire aircraft assembly line. It signed a $345 million contract with Egypt to produce 80 K-8E (the export version of the K-8) jet trainers. China will provide Egypt with parts and materials, technical training and service support for the aircraft. In addition, China will help Egypt build five aircraft design and research institutes (*Economic Daily* (*Jingji Ri bao*), 4 January 2000). Myanmar has also ordered thirty of the K-8Es.

These were significant successes for a developing country. However, AVIC faces massive challenges.

2. AVIC's Businesses and Structure

a) Size

In terms of employment AVIC is, indeed, a global giant. It employs over 500,000 people, more than twice as many as Boeing and Lockheed Martin. However, if one looks at AVIC's total sales and profits, the company appears far from being a 'global giant'. The combined total sales of AVIC 1 and AVIC 2 are less than one-tenth of Boeing's and one-fifth of Lockheed Martin's. Moreover, the core aerospace business of AVIC is extremely small, on a par with a medium-sized company such as Vickers (United Kingdom). In 1997, sales of aviation businesses was just $650 million, only accounted for 23 per cent of the total sales revenue and less than one-half the sales value of Vickers (Table 7.13). Even this small total aerospace revenue generated by AVIC was produced by over 100 production enterprises in all branches of aerospace activity (excluding extra-atmospheric rockets). We may assume that the value of the aircraft manufacture, airborne equipment and engine divisions of AVIC in each case are no more than $250 million,[14] with the aircraft division somewhat larger than the other two. Seen in this perspective, AVIC becomes simply a minnow on the world stage. Its engine division produces no more than 2 per cent of the sales value of Rolls-Royce, and its aircraft design and assembly division generates no more than 0.5 per cent of the sales value of Boeing. If AVIC's entire engine division were a separate company, and adopted Rolls-Royce's manning levels, it would employ only around 1,200 people.

b) Non-aviation Production

In line with the policy of 'military to civilian conversion' and the strategy of 'civilian supports military', AVIC had been turned into a vast empire of diversified businesses. In 1979, the share of non-aerospace sales stood at just 7.5 per cent of total sales of the Ministry of Aviation Industry. By 1997, their

Table 7.13 **Relative Size of Selected Aerospace Companies, 1997 and 2000**

Company	1997				2000			
	Assets ($ billion)	Revenue ($ billion)	Profit ($ million)	Employee ('000s)	Assets ($ billion)	Revenue ($ billion)	Profit ($ million)	Employee ('000s)
Boeing	38.0	45.8	-178	239	42.0	51.3	2.1	198
Lockheed Martin	28.4	28.1	1,300	190	30.4	25.3	-519	126
Raytheon	28.1	13.7	523	75	26.8	18.3	141	94
Northrop Grumman	9.7	9.2	407	47	10.1	8.3	608	39
Bae	7.2	10.4	681	44	26.0	14.6	-20	85
Rolls-Royce	3.8	6.9	-45	43	3.9	5.9	83	43
Vickers*	0.5	1.2	83	10	–	–	–	–
AVIC**	7.1	3.1	72	560	–	–	–	–
of which:								
Aerospace	–	0.7	–	–				
AVIC 1	–	–	–	–	4.2	2.52	–	236
AVIC 2	–	–	–	–	3.8	2.35	–	210

Sources: Fortune, 27 April 1998, FT, 22 January 1998, Fortune 500, 2001, Fortune Global 500, 2001. Authors' research.

Notes

* Vickers was acquired by Rolls-Royce in 1999 for $576 million.

** AVIC was split into AVIC 1 and AVIC 2 in 1999.

share had risen to more than 80 per cent. In real terms, the sales of non-aerospace products rose by around 23 per cent per annum from 1979 to 1997. By 1997, AVIC manufactured more than 5,000 types of non-aviation products covering a wide range from automobiles and production machinery to white goods and household appliances. Automobiles, automobile components and motorcycles, together the most important sectors within AVIC's non-aviation sales, accounted for 62 per cent of the total value of AVIC's revenue in 1997 (AVIC, 2000, p. 9).

c) Sub-contract/Sub-system Joint Ventures

Since the late 1970s, international sub-contracts and sub-system joint ventures have grown rapidly in China. By 1995, AVIC had signed contracts for a cumulative total of $1.5 billion worth of sub-contracting work. The principal contracts were with Boeing, for the manufacture of vertical fins, horizontal stabilizers and rear fuselage and with McDonnell Douglas for the manufacture of the nose section and horizontal stabilizers, for the MD-82 and MD-90. In addition there was a wide array of smaller contracts, for aircraft doors, wing sections, turbine disks, blades, bores, rings, atmosphere instruments, meteorological radar, general radar instruments, pumps and valves. AVIC had progressed from purely compensation trade to becoming a competitive global supplier of components, including being the sole suppliers of some items (B-747 wing rear ribs, B-737 maintenance doors, BAe 146 doors, Dash-8 cargo doors and LM2500 turbine disks).

China's aero-engine companies have developed many sub-contracting and some joint venture arrangements with the global industry leaders. Each of the big three engine makers, Rolls-Royce, Pratt and Whitney and GE Engine, has become involved in the Chinese engine industry. However, the arrangements are all still relatively small scale. Chengdu Aero-engine Company (CEC) is China's largest and was a key supplier of engines for China's fighter force. Its largest contracts are with Pratt and Whitney, but the total value of the export earnings from this contract was only $8 million in 1998, amounting to just 2 per cent of the gross value of output at CEC. In 1997 it established sub-contracting arrangements with Rolls-Royce, and is negotiating with GE to sub-contract engine parts. However, neither of these promises to be as large even as the contract with Pratt and Whitney. Xian Aero-engine Company (XAEC) probably has the largest international aero-engine partnerships of any Chinese engine company. In the 1970s it was selected as the location for the manufacture of Spey engines under licence from Rolls-Royce. In 1997 it started a relatively large-scale joint venture to manufacture turbine blades for Rolls-Royce, but total output value will only be around $30 million at full production in the early 21st century (*China Daily Business Weekly*, 11 October 1998).

Despite their substantial growth, China's sub-contracts with the global giants are small-scale. For example, in 1997 sub-contracts were still a less important source of revenue for Xian Aircraft Corporation than either the production of aluminum h-shapes for the construction industry or the manufacture of Volvo buses. AVIC doesn't participate in the decisions over aircraft purchase in China. This limits its ability to place leverage on the global aircraft makers to sub-contract within China. Moreover, the main Chinese aircraft manufacturers are competing with each other to obtain sub-contract work, which weakens the overall industry's bargaining power in obtaining sub-contracts, and in settling the terms for the sub-contracts. In the meantime, China's leading sub-contractors face intense international competition from Israel in military sub-contracting, and from Japan and the Republic of Korea in civil sub-contracting. Another key limitation for China's sub-contractors is their inability to co-finance on a large scale. China's sub-contractors are generally only able to contract for 'Level 3' contracts, compared to the sub-contracts of Japan and the Republic of Korea, which are usually at Levels 4 or 5. The latter usually involves co-financing and co-designing.

d) Structure

Children and Grandchildren The business structure of AVIC is extremely complex, with very limited monitoring and control from the headquarters. Under the commercialization programme, AVIC's subordinate enterprises became substantially responsible for their own development, a dramatic transformation in their method of business operation compared to the 'planned economy' epoch. AVIC has 116 subordinate plants grouped under 56 'children' enterprises. They construct their own business plans, retain profit for reinvestment in state assets, control the way to distribute the wage fund and the size and nature of the bonus, subject only to quite limited supervision from the headquarters of AVIC. The establishment of new 'grandchildren' companies is formally approved by the AVIC headquarters, but the newly established 'grandchildren' report to the 'child' company, not to AVIC headquarters. AVIC has no rights over the income from the companies established by the 'grandchildren' companies. There is a cascade of businesses each with investments in subordinate companies, from 'children', through 'grandchildren', 'great grandchildren', 'great-great-grandchildren' and 'great-great-great-great grandchildren'. The result is a typical East Asian diversified conglomerate, investing in any activity that brings some short-term profit, but without a common focus. This structure raises profound problems for corporate governance and central control as far as the operations of sub-sidiaries and related companies are concerned.

Flotation   The institutional structure of AVIC has changed gradually since the mid-1990s through the flotation of different parts of the Company. By 1998, four subsidiaries of CATIC had floated, including CATIC Shenzhen in Hong Kong (China), and Shenzhen FIYTA Group, Nanguang Group and Shenzhen Tianma in Shenzhen. In addition, Liuyuan Hydraulic Company floated in Shanghai, Nanfang Motor Company in Shenzhen, and XAC International in Shenzhen. The typical flotation is of a minority share in the floated company, with the majority shareholding still held by AVIC through its subsidiary company. For example, in the case of XAC International, XAC held 64.71 per cent of XAC International.

3. Development Setbacks

In military aircraft, it is likely that there was a real fall in the amount of resources allocated to modernization of China's indigenous industry during the economic reform period. The number of military aircraft produced is reported to have fallen significantly (Nolan, 2001). The main thrust of the indigenous military fighter production capability was reported to be the F-8II 'Finback'. However, international experts believe that this aircraft was 'not comparable to contemporary Western or Russian aircraft'. They concluded that 'the failure of the Finback programme forced the PLAAF to seek alter-native aircraft', with Russia as the supplier (Sergounin and Subbotin, 1999, p. 74). At the time of the resumption of military cooperation with Russia in the mid-1990s, China had 'a fleet of 5000 obsolete combat aircraft, most of them based on old Soviet designs such as the MiG-21 and MiG-19 fighter air-craft, and the Tu-16 bomber' (Sergounin and Subbotin, 1999: 74).

In civilian aircraft, the Y-7 turboprop was able to win only a limited num-ber of domestic orders. In the year 2000, just 64 of the Y-7s were in service in thirteen domestic airlines. In addition, the People's Liberation Army used the Y-7 as a transporter. Export orders were negligible. By the late 1990s, a total of only 130 Y-7s had been produced, and new orders had dried up com-pletely. To compound matters, in the year 2000, a Y-7 exploded in mid-air. Following the conclusion of the crash investigation, all Y-7s were taken out of service in June 2001.

China's attempt to build its own indigenous large passenger aircraft, the Y-10, ultimately failed. China's domestic airlines refused to buy the plane. It was extremely heavy compared to the Boeing 707, with high fuel consumption and a very limited range. The test models were, reportedly, only able to fly for around half an hour at a time. Only two of the Y-10s were built. The plane never entered commercial production, and the Y-10 programme was halted in 1985.

After the conclusion of the Y-10 programme, the Ministry of Aviation devised a 'three-step take-off plan', with the goal of building a 180-seater plane by 2010. The plan was to start with the assembly of the McDonnell Douglas 80/90 series of planes, which would provide China with an understanding of the skills needed to assemble a large modern aircraft. The second phase involved the intention to cooperate with a leading manufacturer, in order to jointly design and manufacture a state-of-the-art 100 seater plane, to go into service around 2005. This was the 100-seater Air Express 100 (AE-100) joint venture between AVIC and Airbus. The final phase involved self-design and manufacture of 180-seater aircraft. One by one each of these objectives fell by the wayside.

By September 1998 China's AE-100 programme was scrapped and the planned MD-90 programme was terminated. A year earlier, neither Airbus nor Boeing produced a 100-seater plane, and China had hoped to produce one by 2005. Now Boeing would have a 100-seater aircraft in service by 1999, and Airbus would have one in service by 2002. China would have nothing. The double blows of the termination of the MD-90 programme and the AE-100 programme were perceived outside China to 'deal a severe blow to China's nascent aviation industry' and 'throw into doubt its plans to become a substantial aircraft manufacturer' (*Financial Times*, 5 August 1998 and 6 October 1998). The double blow of the end of both the programmes left China's aircraft industry reeling. Its development strategy of 'three stage take-off' was in tatters. The coincidence of the double blow was remarkable. Many people in the Chinese aircraft industry felt that it had been let down not only by Boeing and Airbus, but also by CAAC, which had refused to order either the MD-90 or the planned AE-100.

4. 1999 Restructuring: Splitting into Two

We have seen that the rapid expansion of AVIC's non-aviation business in the 1990s created a company which consists of a relatively small aircraft firm, by all measures other than size of workforce, within the shell of a vast diversified conglomerate. Moreover, the vast business structure consists of powerful autonomous entities competing with each other for funds, investment and sub-contracting opportunities. The function of the headquarters in monitoring, control, coordination and unifying the whole company to utilize resources and maximize returns is extremely weak. No one within the industry believed this was a viable structure upon which to build either a successful aircraft manufacturing industry or to construct a successful non-aerospace business. The succession of development setbacks intensified the sense of crisis within AVIC. Debate over how to restructure it in the light of its own internal problems and the explosive changes going on in the world industry outside became increasingly intense by early 1999. China's debate over the institutional structure of its aircraft industry took place alongside the similarly intense debate within the European aerospace industry.

By autumn 1998, the strategy for China's aerospace industry was at a critical conjuncture. In early 1999, the Chinese government decided to split AVIC into two fully integrated parts, AVIC 1 and AVIC 2. Each group contains the full range of production and sales of military and civilian aircraft, airborne equipment as well as non-aeronautical products. The stated goal of the reform was the 'break up of monopoly and the fostering of fair market economy mechanism' (*China Daily Business Weekly*, 31 January 1999). Zhu Yuli, AVIC president said: 'The two groups will both compete and co-operate' (quoted in *Financial Times*, 2 February 1999). While the world's leading aerospace corporations were in the midst of an unprecedented epoch of merger and acquisition, the Chinese aerospace industry was being divided into smaller segments. Compared to the global giants, each of China's 'competing aerospace companies' was now even more of a minnow than before the restructuring, each with aerospace revenues of no more than $400 million, and each surrounded by a sea of unrelated businesses in the non-aerospace industry sector.

Instead of one huge diversified conglomerate with no capability to compete with the multinationals, the 'reform' of AVIC in 1999 created two smaller and even less internationally competitive conglomerates. The reform could have separated the vast civilian from the aerospace business, but was unable to do so because this would have provoked such opposition from the subordinate entities who stood to lose many of their most profitable activities. It could have separated engines and avionics from the airframe business, but it didn't. It could have separated military from civilian aerospace, but it didn't. If its main goal was to develop its capability as a sub-contractor, then it might have allowed strong subordinate production units such as Xian, Chengdu and Shenyang to become independent companies that could compete for business with the multinationals, but it didn't. In sum, the prospects for AVIC on the global level playing field were bleak.

Not only did the Chinese government decide to split AVIC into two, it simultaneously decided to split into two the other main branches of the national defence industries, under the State Defence Industries Commission (COSTIND). Thus, the China National Nuclear Industries General Company, the China National Aerospace Industries General Company, the China National Shipbuilding General Company, and the China National

Armaments General Company, were each split into two segments in order to 'foster competition'. Instead of five aerospace and defence industry companies, China's 'restructuring' has established ten much smaller companies.

5. Development Plans

a) Regional Airliner

New Regional Jet Programme   At the end of 2000, it was apparent that China had abandoned the ambition to build a medium-capacity, single-aisle airliner. Zhang Hongbiao, Vice Minister of the Committee of Scientific and Technological Industries for National Defence (COSTIND), announced in November 2000 that China would instead focus on development of a new regional jet. COSTIND will invest $600–$725 million in research and development for the new regional jet programme aiming to build a new 50–70-seater turbofan aircraft to international standards. It is expected to be delivered within six years and will target both domestic and international market. The primary goal of this programme is a successful business venture making full, 'self-reliant' use of all of China's aviation manufacturing technology while looking for international cooperation in investment, design, subcontract production and technical consultancy on the principle of 'risk and benefit sharing'. It is argued that production of regional airliners is the country's 'best bet', frankly acknowledging that China cannot directly compete with the multinational giants: 'We cannot compete with aviation giants such as Boeing and Airbus in financial clout and market share' (Zhang Hongbiao, quoted in *China Daily*, 6 November 2000). CAAC also expressed its support for the programme. 'We specifically encourage the use of domestically made aircraft for short regional flights' (Bao Peide, Vice Minister of CAAC, quoted in *Air Transport World*, January 2001, p. 57).

AVIC 1 has formed a programme management company to oversee resources, production, certification and marketing of the new regional jet named ARJ21. Led by the President of Xian Aircraft Co. and the chief designer of Shanghai Aircraft Design Institute, the company will become a shareholding firm. 'We are willing to form *long-term* and *stable* relationships with *well-established* international companies to work jointly on the new regional jet programme' (Liu Gaozhuo, President of AVIC 1, quoted in *Air Transport World*, January 2001, p. 57, emphasis added).

The market prospect for regional jets in China is promising. Boeing has predicted that around 70 per cent of the total of the 1,800 new medium- and large-sized commercial aircraft purchased by China over the next twenty years would be single-aisle regional jets, such as the Boeing 737 or 717 and the Airbus 319 or 320 (Keck, 2001). Although the prospects for the regional jet market in the high-income countries must now be radically downwardly revised, the prospects for the Chinese market are still bright, as China does not yet possess a high-speed train network that could readily substitute for air travel. The competition for selling regional jets to China is intense, with extensive substitution of regional jets for the fleet of turboprops. In December 1999, Shangdong Airlines placed a firm order with Bombardier Aerospace for five CRJ200s, which are the first CRJs scheduled for service in China. In 2000, the Xian-based Changan Airlines placed firm orders with Bombardier for three 78-seat Q400s that are to replace its turboprop aircraft. In late 1999, Embraer signed a letter of intent to supply ten 50-seat ERJ-145s to Sichuan Airlines (*Air Transport World*, February 2000, p. 23). Hainan Airlines has placed an order with Fairchild Dornier for 39 328-JETs, with 12 aircraft already delivered (*Aviation Week & Space Technology*, 13 November 2000, p. 35). Boeing and Airbus continue to actively market their smallest aircraft to Chinese airlines in an effort to capture the regional jet market. Price competition in all aircraft categories can be expected to intensify following the collapse in the world aircraft market after 11 September 2001. This is good news for Chinese airlines, but bad news for a potential regional jet produced in China. If China is, indeed, successful in designing and building its own regional jet, it will be far behind in the race for its own national market by the time that the first deliveries begin. This will be a huge disadvantage in an already intensely competitive segment of the world aircraft market.

MA-60 (Xinzhou 60) In 2000, Xian Aircraft Company (XAC) launched the MA-60, known as the Xinzhou 60 in China. Developed from the Yun 7–200A, the MA-60 is a 56- to 60-seat turboprop with an extended fuselage, longer range and lighter airframe weight. It is powered by Pratt & Whitney's engines and equipped with Collins avionics. It costs one-third less than comparable Western turboprops. A total of 26 MA-60s have been ordered by Chinese airlines. In 2000, the newly formed Shenzhen Financial Leasing Co. signed an agreement with XAC for 60 MA-60s (*Aviation Week & Space Technology*, 13 November 2000, p. 36).

However, the market prospects for MA-60 are poor. First, there is already intense international competition in the 50–70 seat turboprop market. Strong global market positions are already held by the ATR 42 (produced by Aerospatiale and Alenia), the Dash 8 (produced by Bombardier), and the Saab 2000 as well as the Russian-built An-24 in former Soviet states. A powerful player in this market, Fokker, with the F-50 turboprop, went out of business. China has already imported ATR 42s, five of which were in operation by the late 1990s. Almost 600 ATR aircraft had been sold worldwide by

1998, enabling the company to benefit from economies of scale in a way that the Y-7 was unable to do, and the MA-60 is most unlikely to do. Second, the whole future of turboprop feeder planes is in doubt. In the developed countries, competition for small, local feeder aircraft has come from high-speed trains, a trend that will be accelerated by 11 September 2001. Moreover, there has been a marked shift in airline preference towards jet-engine feeder aircraft. Jet aircraft are preferred for safety, reliability and customer preference. Third, the history of the Y-7, in terms both of its lack of commercial success and question marks about its safety, makes the task of marketing the MA-60 to commercial airlines, which must respond to passenger perceptions and demands, extremely difficult, even within China, let alone internationally.

b) Sub-contracting

Following the collapse of the proposed joint production plans for the AE31X and the MD-90, Airbus and Boeing both responded with offers of considerably enhanced participation by AVIC in the production of sub-systems. Boeing is leading in that strategy with 74 per cent of all parts built in China going to Boeing (*Aviation Week & Space Technology*, 8 May 2000, p. 63). Boeing has offered to make China the second supplier of the wing for the B-717, alongside the current supplier, Hyundai. Airbus agreed that AVIC could participate in the development of its 107-seat A318 programme. In addition, Shenyang Aircraft Manufacturing Co. and XAC will gain work on A320 wing components. Shenyang will make the wing's leading and trailing edge components and build up production levels to four sub-assembly sets per month for all of the wing's leading and trailing edge components. Airbus has agreement with XAC for doors on the A300, A310, A330 and A340 and the fin fairing for the A320 and a variety of components for the A300 and A310 programmes. BAe has discussed with XAC its possible participation in wing manufacture for the A-320. Xian is also expected to become a source for raw material for various components for Airbus aircraft (*Aviation Week & Space Technology*, 5 July 1999, p. 40). These provide the possibility for a significant increase in sales from sub-contracting. However, in the foreseeable future this segment of the industry still seems likely to lag far behind the level of sales and technological sophistication achieved by the sub-contracting industry in Japan and the Republic of Korea.

6. Conclusion

Since the early 1990s, the world's leading aerospace companies have achieved massive competitive advantages through high-speed consolidation and through the development of systems integration capabilities, hugely strengthening their already very powerful competitive position. Moreover, this period witnessed the near-disintegration of the former Soviet Union's civilian aerospace industry and a serious weakening of its military aircraft industry. AVIC has failed to make any inroads on the dominant position of the world's leading corporations.

The institutional structure of AVIC is far removed from that of the global giants. Surrounding the core aircraft business is a vast sea of unrelated non-core business, which raises fundamental difficulties for corporate governance. None of the non-core businesses has achieved sufficient scale to compete with globally successful firms in the respective sectors. In its core aerospace business AVIC is a minnow, without any commercially successful aircraft in either the civilian or military market. AVIC has painfully weak financial resources with which to support R&D and fund new aircraft development programmes. It must support a huge workforce, but many of those with the highest levels of skills in aerospace are leaving the company to work in relatively highly paid jobs outside the sector. It is decisively losing the 'battle for talent'.

To meet its needs for advanced fighter planes, the Chinese military has been forced to rely heavily on imports and domestic production under licence of Russian planes. In 1996, China ordered 200 Russian Su-27 (Sukhoi) fighters. The government has contracted to buy a further 50 Su-30 strike aircraft from Russia (IISS, 1999: 175). China's Central Military Commission is becoming 'more and more reliant on outside sources for new technology and support' (*Aviation Week & Space Technology*, 29 November 1999, p. 33). Exports to China have been a crucial source of revenue for Sukhoi in extremely difficult times for the company.

The Chinese civilian aircraft market is one of the largest and fast-growing in the world. Due to the downturn in the global aircraft market after 11 September 2001, the relative importance of the Chinese market may be even greater. The predicted 1,800 additions to China's commercial aircraft fleet by 2019 will be worth an estimated $137 billion (*Aviation Week & Space Technology*, 13 November 2000, p. 35). China's capability to capture its own large domestic market for civilian aircraft, let alone to penetrate the world market, has proved negligible. China was unsuccessful in its attempt to build a commercially viable turboprop plane. China's large and fast-growing regional jet market is dominated by imports. China was unable to build a commercially successful large passenger jet. China's attempt to partner the multinationals in co-designing and building a large civilian aircraft came to nothing. China's entire civilian aircraft fleet of around 500 passenger aircraft is imported, consisting mainly of Boeings (70 per cent) and an increasing number of Airbuses.

There is no sign that China is in the process of building large, globally competitive first-tier suppliers to the world's aircraft industry in sub-systems such as engines, avionics, airframes, wings, lighting or landing gear.

Since the 1980s, in this, the most 'strategic' of all Chinese industries, the gap between China's 'national champions' and the global giant companies has widened drastically. The Chinese market for commercial aircraft and advanced military aircraft will be dominated by imported aircraft for the foreseeable future.

IV. CONCLUSION

The period since the 1980s has seen dramatic changes in the structure of large capitalist corporations. These changes have established the structure within which competition will take place on the 'global level playing field' in the early part of the 21st century. The period saw an unprecedented concentration of business power. Numerous firms in the high-income countries no longer exist, having merged with or been acquired by the 'winners' in the battle for the global marketplace. Numerous large 'national champions' have now been merged into even larger cross-border firms, either 'European champions',[15] 'transatlantic firms', or, even, European–Japanese or United States–Japanese firms. Almost all of these firms remained headquartered within the high-income countries, were owned mainly by shareholders from, and had senior management drawn mainly from, the high-income countries.

Globalization has dramatically changed the competitive terrain for which developing countries' governments must devise their industrial policies. Of all developing countries, China is the one with the greatest possibility to support the growth of globally powerful corporations that might be able to compete in this new environment. It has a potentially huge domestic market and a powerful and relatively effective state through which to implement industrial policy. However, as this paper has shown, even for China, the task has become far harder and more complex than could have been imagined fifteen or twenty years ago, when the country began its industrial reforms.

In the oil and petrochemical industry, the period saw the creation of a new breed of 'super-major', with annual revenues of $150–$200 billion, and an unprecedented capability to integrate activities across an extended internal value chain. This in turn challenged the existing middle-ranking firms within the industry, provoking a cumulative process of merger and acquisition. These developments drastically altered the benchmark against which China's firms needed to evaluate their progress in system reform. China's planners responded to this revolution through an immense restructuring, which represents a significant triumph for industrial policy in developing countries. In 2000, PetroChina and Sinopec successfully listed in the international stock

market and rose into the ranks of the top ten publicly-traded oil and petrochemical companies. Despite this success there remain deep challenges posed
by the revolutionary change among the world industry leaders in this sector.
For each of these firms growth within the Chinese market is a major strategic
goal. They are already making substantial progress in this objective, and can
be expected to accelerate this progress after China enters the WTO.

In the aerospace industry, the 1990s saw an unprecedented process of high-
speed global consolidation. The process still has a long way to go before some
kind of institutional equilibrium is reached. It not only resulted in a new breed
of immensely powerful 'systems integrators', but also unprecedented business
capability at lower levels of the value chain. Alongside these changes in the
world's aerospace industry, China has had its own 'restructuring' in aerospace
by splitting AVIC into two entities. Chinese policymakers are still groping for
a strategy that will enable the country's aerospace industry to find its place
within this business revolution.

As China is about to enter the WTO, it is crucial that global big businesses
and government policymakers in the high-income countries appreciate the
severity of the challenges that confront China's policymakers and business
leaders, even in key 'strategic industries'. It is not enough to repeat comforting
phrases about the beneficial impact of privatization and the free market.
Privatization and liberalization are far from sufficient to enable China's leading firms to compete on the 'global level playing field'. The 'global level playing field' is not an abstract concept. In the end the marketplace involves a
competitive struggle between firms, which, together with consumers, are the
building blocks of the economic system. For the leading systems integrators
and first-tier suppliers in each industrial sector, this is a competition between
small numbers of identifiable large, often oligopolistic, firms. The struggle is
not between the innumerable nameless small firms of textbook-perfect competition.

The global business revolution has sharply changed the balance of power in
market competition. The 'players' on the playing field occupy far more
unequal positions than they did prior to the business revolution. China's leading firms are in a highly vulnerable position, even in sectors in which China's
policymakers have scored significant successes. Moreover, large Chinese firms
operate in a totally different political-economic environment from that of the
world's leading corporations. China's political leaders have to consider the
huge difficulties that stem from the existence of around one billion poor
people within their boundaries, and the complexities involved in the reform of
China's political system. If China's large firms were to experience widespread
defeat, especially in key 'strategic industries', in the battle on the global level
playing field of the WTO, that would raise profound issues not only for the

Chinese government but also for international relations, and, ultimately, for the large firms headquartered in the high-income countries.

Coping with failure is a massive challenge. Coping with success can also be a challenge.

Notes

1 This paper was originally prepared by Peter Nolan and Jin Zhang for the Third United Kingdom–China Forum in October 2001. Peter Nolan facilitated the discussions for the Industry Committee, Finance and Economy Committee of the Forum. Leaders of major firms from the United Kingdom and China participated in the discussion. Participants include BP, BAe System, Rolls-Royce, BOC, British Airways, Barclays, HSBC, Standard Chartered Bank, Prudential, Royal & Sun Alliance Insurance, Standard Life Assurance, Citigroup Europe, CGNU plc., Pricewaterhouse Coopers, Dresdner Kleinwort Wasserstein, Bank of England, China Petroleum & Chemical Corporation (Sinopec), China Ocean Shipping Corporation (COSCO), China Aviation Industry Corporation Group 1 (AVIC 1), China Aviation Industry Corporation Group 2 (AVIC 2), China International Trust and Investment Corporation (CITIC), China State Development Bank, and Ministry of Finance.

2 Peter Nolan is Director of the China Big Business Programme, based in the Judge Institute of Management Studies in the University of Cambridge. Since 1994, he and Dr. Wang Xiaoqiang have been engaged in research on the transformation of the 'commanding heights' of China's industry, using in-depth case studies to attempt to analyze China's policy of building a powerful 'national team' of big businesses that can challenge the global giant corporations. They have combined their research in China with case study-based research inside the United Kingdom and US-based global corporations. This has attempted to provide a careful benchmarking of the progress and problems encountered in the course of China's industrial policy since the early 1980s. Their research has resulted in numerous books and articles written individually (Wang, 1999, Nolan, 1996, 1999, 2000, 2001a, 2001b, 2002a, 2002b), jointly by them (Nolan and Wang, 1997, 1998a, 1998b, 1999a, and 1999b), and jointly with other members of the research team (Nolan and Yeung, 2001a, 2001b). This paper is a part of that continuing research effort, and the general conclusions reached here draw heavily on these publications.

3 In fact, as is now widely recognized, it did not prove as easy to privatize the large-scale state-owned sector as was originally visualized.

4 In 1999, total IT hardware sales in China reached $20 billion, including mobile infrastructure and handsets; traditional fixed line and broadband switching equipment; optical cable/optical cable fibre; SD and DWDM products. It is estimated that 90 per cent of the IT hardware by value was supplied by the global giants (including Nokia, Motorola, Ericsson, Cisco, Siemens, Alcatel, and Lucent) either through imports or their large production networks of within China.

5 For sources of data used in this and the following paragraph, see Nolan, 2001a: chapter 2, 'The challenge of the global business revolution'.

6 Petrobás (Brazil) is partially privatized.

7 They are Exxon Mobil, Royal Dutch/Shell, BP Amoco/Arco, TotalFinaElf, Chevron, Texaco, Eni, Repsol YPF, and Conoco.

8 Before that, the crude oil price in China was set by the government, which resulted in constant disputes between CNPC and Sinopec, with each lobbying intensely for prices favourable to their own businesses. In line with the restructuring, the State Development and Planning Commission (SDPC) publishes monthly a benchmark crude oil price based on the average Singapore FOB prices. CNPC and Sinopec negotiate a premium relative to the benchmark price.

9 The project would involve the construction of a pipeline 4,200 kilometres long and an estimated total investment of RMB120 billion (approximately $14.5 billion).

10 For example, Schlumberger spends more on R&D than Shell (£324 million compared with £313 million), while Halliburton spends more than ENI (£160 million compared with £146 million) (DTI, 2000: 54).

11 Based on PetroChina's dividend payment of $0.02 per share and the weighted average number of 171,630 million shares issued and outstanding in 2000.

12 The issues of creating shareholder value and protecting minority shareholders are discussed in *China Petroleum*, April 2000, pp. 18–29, and an article 'Oil industry: choices after flotation' in *Finance* (*Caijing*), November 2000. The paper comments: 'For the listed state-owned companies, this kind of structure involves risks that cannot be anticipated. It will affect the profits of a company and distort the behaviour of a company, which in fact jeopardizes the interest of shareholders. As a common problem, it will eventually damage the credibility of the Chinese concept shares (*zhong guo gai nian gu*).

13 For a detailed description and analysis of the institutional evolution of CNPC and Sinopec prior to their international listing in 2000, see Nolan (2001), Chapter 7.

14 A rough guess, assuming approximately one-third of total sales revenue is generated by each of the branches.

15 This term was increasingly used to describe firms such as Alstom, which was formed from the power equipment divisions of Asea (Sweden), Brown Boveri (Switzerland), Alsthom (France) and GEC (United Kingdom).

References

AVIC Economic Research Centre, 2000, Research on Economic Topics of the Aerospace Industry, AVIC Economic Research Centre. Beijing.

Chen Huai, et al 1998, 'Assets restructuring of the Chinese oil and petrochemical industry', *Economic Science Press*. Beijing.

Chen Yongkai, 2001, 'Opportunities and challenges before Sinopec', http://www.worldoilweb.com.

Department of Trade and Industry (DTI), 2000, Research and Development Scoreboard, Department of Trade and Industry. London.

Fransman, M., 1995, 'Is industrial policy obsolete?', Cambridge Journal of Economics, Vol. 19, Oxford University Press. Oxford.

Goldstein, A., 2001, 'From national champion to global player: explaining the success of Embraer', Working Paper CBS-17–2001, OECD Development Centre. Paris.

HBS Case, 701–006, 2000, 'Embraer: the global leader in regional jets', Harvard Business School. Boston, MA 02163.

IISS, 1999, *Military Balance, 1999/2000*, International Institute for Strategic Studies, London.

Keck, E., 2001, 'Commercial Aviation Takes Off', *The China Business Review*, March-April 2001. Washington, DC.

MSDW, 1998, *The Competitive Edge*. Morgan Stanley Dean Witter. New York.

MSDW, 2000, *The Competitive Edge*, April Update, Morgan Stanley Dean Witter. New York.

Nolan, P., 1996, 'Large firms and industrial reform in the former planned economies: the case of China', *Cambridge Journal of Economics*, Vol. 20, No. 1, pp. 1–31.

Nolan, P., 1998, 'Indigenous large firms in China's economic reform: the case of Shougang Iron and Steel Corporation', Contemporary China Institute, SOAS, University of London.

Nolan, P., 1999, 'Coca Cola and the Global Business Revolution: A Study with Special Reference to the EU'. Polity Press, Cambridge.

Nolan, P., 2000, 'Institutional reform of China's oil and gas industry' (in Chinese). *Strategy and Management (Zhanlue yu guanli)*, Vol. 9, No. 38, pp. 1–15.

Nolan, P., 2001a, 'China and the Global Business Revolution'. Palgrave, Basingstoke.

Nolan, P., 2001b, 'China and the global economy'. Palgrave, Basingstoke.

Nolan, P., 2002a, 'Looking at China's enterprises (Zhongguo qiye xing)' (in Chinese). Metallurgical Industries Publishing House. Beijing.

Nolan, P., 2002b, 'China and the global business revolution', *Cambridge Journal of Economics*, Vol. 26, No. 1, pp. 119–137.

Nolan, P., 2002c, 'The challenge of globalisation for China's large enterprises', *World Development*, forthcoming.

Nolan, P. and Wang Xiaoqiang, 1997, 'US defence industry: comprehensive re-organisation within four years – enlightenment for China', (in Chinese), *Strategy and Management (Zhanlue yu guanli)*, Vol. 6, No. 25, pp. 60–67.

Nolan, P. and Wang Xiaoqiang, 1998, 'The Chinese army's firm in business: the case of Sanjiu', *The Developing Economies*, Vol. 36, No. 1, pp. 45–79. Tokyo.

Nolan, P. and Wang Xiaoqiang, 1998, 'Harbin Power Equipment Company and the battle for the Chinese market', *Competition and Change*, Vol. 3, pp. 417–448.

Nolan, P. and Wang Xiaoqiang, 1999a, 'Beyond privatisation: institutional innovation and growth in China's large state-owned enterprises', *World Development*, Vol. 27, No. 1, pp. 169–200.

Nolan, P. and Wang Xiaoqiang, 1999b, *Strategic Reorganisation* (in Chinese), Wenhui Publishing House. Shanghai.

Nolan, P. and Yeung G, 2001a, 'Two paths to the reform of large firms in China', *Cambridge Journal of Economics*, Vol. 25, No. 4, pp. 443–466.

Nolan, P. and Yeung G, 2001b, 'Large Firms and Catch-up in a Transitional Economy: The case of the Shougang Group', *Economics of Planning*, Vol. 34, pp. 159–178.

Sergounin, A.A. and S.V. Subbotin, 1999, *Russian Arms Transfers to East Asia in the 1990s*, Oxford University Press. Oxford.

State Economic and Trade Commission (SETC). 'Notification on distributing the list of the first batch of small refineries that should be closed down', Oil and Petrochemical Section, No. 584, 1999. SETC, People's Republic of China.

SETC. 'Notification on distributing the list of the second batch of small refineries that should be closed down'. Oil and Petrochemical Section, No. 234, 2000.

SETC. *The Tenth Five-Year Plan for Oil Industry, 2001*.

Wang Xiaoqiang, 1998, *Industrial Restructuring*, Wenhui Publishing House. Shanghai.

White House, 2000, 'Supporting R&D to promote economic growth', White House website.

World Bank, 1998, 2001, *Global Economic Prospects for Developing Countries*. Washington, DC.

Xinhuanet. 'Our national petrochemical industry faces a severe situation', 27 September 2001.

Zhang Zhigang, 2001, 'Proceed to regulating the market of refined products', http://www.setc.gov.cn

8

THE CAUSATION AND PREVENTION OF FAMINES: A CRITIQUE OF A. K. SEN

'If this book has the impact it deserves it may save the lives of millions. It is one of the most important contributions to economic thought for many a year' (*Financial Times* review of Drèze and Sen [*1989*]).

1. The Distinctive Nature of Sen's Approach

Sen's explicit aim in his large body of writings on famine is to change policy [Sen, 1981: ix].[1] He argues that former policies were 'deranged' because they were obsessed with the relationship between food output and population [Sen, 1981: 8].[2] The key to his approach is the word 'entitlements'. Physical availability of food at some level is insufficient to prevent famine deaths. People must have some means of ensuring command over food [Drèze and Sen, 1989: 65].[3] In principle Sen's approach is open-ended. He argues that people's failure to obtain food can arise from any combination of trade failure, production failure, 'own labour' failure, or inheritance and transfer failure [Sen, 1981: 2], which means that any influence on the demand or supply side can be included [Drèze and Sen, 1989: 67].[4]

He devotes great attention to the shocking paradox that famine may take place amid plenty [Sen, 1981: 158].[5] The care and power he brings to the examination of this aspect of famine is an important reason for the impact his writing has had.

Sen roots his approach towards famine explicitly in the Marxist tradition of class analysis [Sen, 1981: 4–6].[6] He provides deep insight into the incidence of famine upon different socio-economic groups who possess unequal means with which to obtain food [Sen, 1981: 161],[7] providing vivid examples of the differential way they are affected by economic shocks.[8] Sen emphasizes the contribution that transforming production relations and establishing a new institutional framework might make to preventing famine. His admiration for the apparent achievements of the socialist countries in eliminating famine played an important part in his early writings on the subject. He contrasted the unequal production relations in the cases of famine which he analysed with the apparent success of Chinese institutions, notably the rural people's commune, in eliminating famine [Sen, 1981: 7].[9] Sen has lamented the fact that Chinese reforms in the 1980s led to an apparent decline in the ability of food supply to be guaranteed to all members of the local community [Sen, 1989: 777].[10]

Sen's approach to malnourishment, death rates, life expectancy and famine share a common thread, namely, that policies to stimulate production growth are of secondary importance, indeed may be quite unimportant, compared to institutional changes that redistribute food, income and wealth. This message is appealing because of its simplicity, its apparent moral superiority[11] and because it promises to eliminate hunger and famine immediately [Drèze and Sen, 1989: 251–2].[12]

Sen's analysis has led to the widespread belief that food output does not affect the susceptibility of low income countries to famine. For example, in his 1989 'state-of the art' survey of development economics written for the *Economic Journal*, Nicholas Stern comments on the changes of emphasis in the profession since the 1970s in relation to the choice of Basic Indicators for Table 1 of the World Bank's annual *World Development Report*: 'the index of food availability per capita (as Sen [*1981*], argued, a poor indicator of the probability of famine) was dropped in 1983' [Stern, 1989: 607].[13] Sen's writings have contributed to a marked shift in the economics profession's view of the causes of famine. This has dangerous implications for policy to prevent famine.

2. General Problems with Sen's Approach

'Entitlements' is an approach, not a theory

Sen's approach is normally referred to as 'entitlement theory'. In fact it is an open-ended framework of analysis, not an empirically testable theory. It is rarely noticed that Sen himself recognizes this [Sen, 1981: 162].[14] There is nothing wrong with this, but it does mean that Sen's approach to famines cannot be considered a 'theoretical breakthrough'.

The concept 'entitlement' is analytically useless

Sen does not directly define the word 'entitlement' The nearest he gets to a definition is the statement that an entitlement is the 'specified minimum food requirement' [Sen, 1981: 167]. In other words, people die when they have insufficient food to eat. What he clearly means is an 'entitlement' to life through food intake. In this sense it has no more analytical use than the concept 'entitlement' to life via protection from the elements through access to shelter, via the care of parents when a child, via the absence of war, or access to necessary medical attention.

Sen caricatures previous writers

It is not the case that anti-famine policies have been dominated by a crude obsession with food output per person. For example, the pre-war International Famine Relief Commission in China was indeed concerned about food output but devoted a large amount of effort to improving transport systems and providing income through food-for-work schemes targeted upon the poorest people in famine affected areas, as well as being deeply aware of the vital importance of political factors at all levels [Mallory, 1926].

Sen is cavalier in his treatment of the level at which food availability per person is analysed

He accuses those who take food availability seriously as a contributory factor to famine of focusing on the 'total availability of food – for the nation as a whole, or even the world as a whole [Sen, 1981:42].[15] However, no-one seriously concerned with monitoring even a small country for famine would be content with national level data, let alone world level data.[16] The number of cases in which famine has not been associated at least with local FAD (Food Availability Decline) is minimal.

At one level Sen's argument that FAD is unimportant is irrefutable. Famine need never happen whatever the dimensions of national or regional FAD, provided the average amount of food availability per capita in the world is greater than the minimum necessary for survival, and as long as there is adequate international food redistribution. However, this is useless as a practical guide on how to avoid famine in a given poor country or locality. It is analogous to saying that poverty is simply a problem of distribution because there is enough income available on average at a world level to remove poverty provided income is better distributed. In the absence of politically feasible international redistributions, poor nations have to devise policies to remove poverty and prevent famine mainly through their own efforts.

Famines in the 'socialist' countries are treated strangely

It is hard to understand how someone could write in 1981, as Sen did, of the 'elimination' of famine in the socialist countries. Although there is great argument as to the magnitudes involved, few people then disputed the existence of at least two massive famines under Bolshevik rule in the Soviet Union (in the early 1920s and the early 1930s respectively). The problems being experienced in African socialist countries were already well known by the late 1970s.

Sen [1981] identified China as the clearest case of the successful elimination of famine through institutional change. The Chinese famine of 1959–61 has been a subject of much dispute, and it is true that key facts about it were not known until the early 1980s. Almost simultaneously with the publication of Sen [1981] China was revealed as having unquestionably endured in 1959–61 the worst famine of the twentieth century. That the same institutions which Sen's 'entitlement' approach [1981] identified as the best way to avoid famine through the secure provision of food to all sectors of the population should now be shown to have permitted a catastrophic famine ought to have led to some questioning of the analytical value of that approach.

While it is odd that Sen [1981] devoted no attention to the famines in 'socialist' countries, it is still more odd that almost ten years later Drèze and Sen [1989] devote only a few pages to the Chinese famine and none to the Soviet famine. In the meantime not only had information on the Chinese famine become much more robust but so too had that on the Soviet famines [e.g. Conquest, 1986]. It is simply astonishing that a book published in 1989 by the world's leading experts on famine can contain the following anodyne comment: 'Just as there have been famines in private ownership economies without state guarantees of basic subsistence rights, there have also been famines in socialist countries with their own systems of legality ...' [Drèze and Sen, 1989: 24]. In the twentieth century far and away the largest number of famine deaths have occurred in self-styled 'socialist' systems, and this observation should ring through any analysis of the incidence of famine in the modern world. Closer examination of these famines leads one inexorably towards the great importance of food output decline in causing famine, and the central role of dreadful policy errors by 'socialist' governments in directly causing such declines.

No attempt is made to assess historical trends in the extent of famine

A first priority in a large-scale study of famine should be to establish the dimensions of the problem, and how these might have changed over time and shifted geographically. One searches in vain through Sen's extensive writings for such an account. In one place he speaks of 'the relentless persistence of famines [Drèze and Sen, 1989: 25] and in another of 'some evidence of intensification of famine threats' [Sen, 1981: 42]. The cumulative impression gained from such scattered and elusive statements is that little has changed over a long period in the dimensions of famine. In fact, it is paradoxical that due to the revolution in mass communication, public awareness of famine has increased enormously in a period when its extent has been greatly reduced. The proportion of the world's population living under the threat of famine has never been less than it is today, except possibly in prehistoric times. The threat of famine has been confined principally to parts of Africa. This does not mean the problem is unimportant. One famine in which hundreds of thousands die of starvation is one too many, but emotion should not blind us to the important changes in the dimensions of famine which have occurred. Indeed, understanding why this reduction has happened is important for framing policy to prevent famine in future.

3. Demand for Food

Sen has greatly advanced understanding of why some groups suffer more than others during a famine. Differences within a famine-stricken region in villagers' ownership of assets and the nature of their occupations will determine which households suffer most during a famine. However, this class-based dimension was not absent from the analytical approach adopted by the best 'pre-Sen' investigators of this issue (see, for example, Duby [1968], Mallory [1926], Perkins [1969]).

The main policy conclusion which emerges from Sen's analysis is the importance of ensuring access to food via the provision of effective demand either through employment guarantees, especially public works schemes, or through social security provision.[17] Sen has argued that the system of employment and income guarantee which China operated in her collective farms from the mid-1950s onwards was a major reason for China's success in preventing famine in most years and in ensuring that basic needs in food were met for most of the population [Sen, 1981: 7]. He stresses the achievement of China's food distribution system under Mao, which in normal times was able to ensure food security for most Chinese citizens. This was a major part of the explanation for China's success under Mao in raising average life expectancy to high levels despite a low average income.

It is not necessary to have a system of local food guarantee through employment and income guarantee of a kind similar to that of China and other socialist countries in order to avoid famine in a poor country. Large areas of the developing world which in the 1950s seemed ripe for famine have not experienced such events. Whereas in the nineteenth century famine was a threat which existed for most peasants in most parts of the non-European world (see, for example, Bhatia [1991]) and even in parts of Europe, the threat of famine today has been reduced dramatically in geographical terms. The large parts of the developing world which have so strikingly reduced the incidence of famine have had a wide variety of systems of income and food distribution, some much more unequal than others. Few of the governments in developing countries which have experienced such large reductions in famine have provided extensive systems of employment guarantee or social security provision to the vast mass of rural dwellers or urban lumpen proletariat. It is other factors which have caused famine to decline.

If the 'socialist' system of food distribution is unnecessary to avoid famine, it certainly is not sufficient to do so. Indeed, it can play an important part in causing a decline in food output, thereby itself precipitating a famine. During the Great Leap Forward of 1958–59 China practised a highly egalitarian system of local food distribution which was intended to 'pull out the roots of poverty'.[18] This egalitarian system of food distribution played an important part in damaging peasant work incentives, which in turn was a major factor in the collapse of Chinese food output in 1959–61.[19] In contrast to the prerevolutionary villages, there were only small local inequalities in asset ownership between households, since the major asset in a rural community, land, was 'commonly' owned.[20] However, an equal share of very little is very little, and a huge number of Chinese people starved to death, or died of starvation-induced illnesses, in the immediate aftermath of the Great Leap Forward.

Even in the Soviet Union in the early 1930s, a system of fairly equal local food distribution existed. Though not as egalitarian as the Chinese system,[21] income distribution within the Soviet collective farms was based on the 'work-day', the value of which was kept within narrow bounds, which meant that income inequalities within the collective farms were smaller than within the pre-revolutionary villages. Employment was guaranteed to all Soviet farmers, and indeed, work was an obligation ('he who does not work shall not eat'). Despite this system, around seven million peasants perished from starvation in the early 1930s, with probably a greater degree of local equality of suffering ('kulaks' excepted) than would have been the case in a pre-revolutionary famine: in 1932–33 in rural Ukraine (the worst hit of all the Soviet Union's republics), 'the poor begged from the poor ... and the starving begged from the starving' [Conquest, 1986: 246].

Maoist China and the Soviet Union under Stalin are the two most striking examples of countries which put into practice systems which guaranteed a fairly even local distribution of food, either directly or through employment guarantees and the methods of income distribution. These examples demonstrate that such systems which appear to conform so closely to the institutions which Sen identifies as the best guarantee against famine are far from a sufficient condition for preventing mass starvation. Indeed, much the largest famines of the twentieth century have occurred in countries which operate such systems, namely the Soviet Union and China. Were it not for the enormity of these two famines alone, the 'famine history' of the twentieth century would look strikingly different.

4. Food Supply

Sen intersperses his writings with the sentence (in one form or another): 'It is not my purpose to deny the importance of food production' [Sen, 1981: 159]. However, his doggedness in searching out examples which appear to have allowed famine to happen without FAD, his determination to show the small connection between FAD and famine in the Chinese case (1959–61), his lack of emphasis on the importance of food output having kept up with population, and his overall apparent lack of interest in the factors that have affected or might in the future affect per capita food output, all draw the reader towards the conclusion that food supply plays a minor role in shaping policy towards famine prevention. For example, Robert Solow's review of Drèze and Sen [1989] interprets them as follows: 'The key to understanding famine, according to Dreze and Sen, is to realise that that it has little to do with shortages of food' [Solow, 1991: 22].

Devising policies to raise food output in poor countries in the face of large population growth is a central task in avoiding famine

Throughout Sen's writings on famine there is rarely a mention of population growth. There is an occasional statement about world food supply pointing out that world food output per capita has grown quite satisfactorily over the past few decades as though it were the most natural thing to have happened.[22] The level of food output per person is taken as a 'given' requiring no further thought for future policy to avoid famine. This complacent view is extremely dangerous in its implications for policy formulation to prevent famine.

The total population of the developing countries grew from 2.1 billion in 1960 to over 4.1 billion in 1990 [UNDP, 1992: 166–7]. It was widely felt that such huge increases in population in developing countries would produce a Malthusian crisis.[23] In fact, despite the persistence of massive malnourishment, widespread famine in developing countries did not occur, despite drastic shrinkage of the amount of arable area per person in these countries.

Instead, the Malthusian spectre was yet again postponed by technical progress, this time in the shape of the Green Revolution.[24] Over large parts of the developing world huge investments in new industrial inputs occurred, with improved seeds, better irrigation, and greatly increased application of agro-chemicals.[25] This required finance for investment, knowledge to be able to use the new inputs, availability of inputs at a price farmers could afford, and incentives for those with capital to invest in the new technology. It is true that the regional impact of the Green Revolution within countries was strikingly uneven, and within the more advanced areas the benefits from the new technology were unequally distributed. However, its achievement was enormous. Instead of the widely anticipated decline in per capita food output, over most of the developing world food output more than kept pace with the vast growth in population.[26]

Africa is the only region of the developing world where in most countries food output per capita fell in recent decades. Without the tremendous progress in agricultural output which occurred in the most populous developing countries, notably India and China, limiting their need to purchase food on international markets and to request food aid from the advanced capitalist countries,[27] the susceptibility of Africa to famine would have been even greater than it has been.

Without this striking example of technical progress and its application, poor countries would have been forced to turn to international markets for their food supply much more than they have done[28] and to hope for adequate supply from the advanced countries. This in turn would have had large ripple effects upon international prices as more marginal lands were brought into production in the advanced economies. There would have been large consequential effects upon the balance of payments and growth prospects of poor countries. Domestic food prices would have been powerfully affected, reducing the possibility for more disadvantaged groups to feed themselves and with large effects upon the overall growth process. In other words the scenario of many African countries in the last two decades would have been played out on a much grander scale. The net effect of this is that the likelihood of widespread famine would have been increased greatly. The capacity of governments to purchase food with which to supply potential famine areas would have been reduced due to likely price increases in both domestic and international markets. The ability of vulnerable peoples to purchase food would have declined.

The world's population is projected to rise to around eight billion in the year 2025 (that is, around double the present figure), with most of the increase occurring in the developing world [*World Bank*, 1990: 228–9]. A fundamental part of any strategy to avoid famine in the period ahead, until total population begins to stabilize at some point in the 21st century, must be to learn from the lessons of the past few decades and seek to continue and improve upon the successes of this period in achieving output growth in agriculture in the developing world. This will almost certainly involve even more government action than in the past to promote the spread of the Green Revolution to areas with smaller amounts of capital per person, fewer human skills, higher transport costs, lower irrigation ratios and more variable rainfall than advanced areas such as Punjab in India or the Pearl River Delta in China. One hopes that the natural environment of poor countries will be able to withstand the onslaught of such huge increases in biochemical inputs, and that the water table is of sufficient size and/or renewability in most areas to provide the necessary quantities of water. However, it is far from clear that this will be the case. If the answer is negative, then the widespread famine threatened in the 1960s will indeed finally come to fruition. One has to hope that Sen's confidence is well founded: 'it seems unlikely that the real dangers in the near future can lie in the prospect of food output falling short of the growth of population' [Drèze and Sen, 1989: 32]. However, even if the environment indeed is able to take the strain, a huge amount of policy action is required to ensure that the complacent conclusion which Sen makes does come to fruition.

As countries move to higher levels of income and economic sophistication it is possible to experience FAD without famine since food imports can be paid for by non-food exports. Drèze and Sen [1989: 32–4] observe that some countries have experienced FAD but not famine.[29] On this basis they argue that famine in Africa may 'only, superficially appear to be a problem of food production and supply.' What they fail to note [Drèze and Sen, 1989: Table 2.4] is that the average per capita income in 1988 in Sub-Saharan Africa was just US $330 compared to US $5,550 in the list of seven 'other' countries which they select in which FAD has occurred without famine [World Bank, 1990: 178–9]. Moreover, the average population of these latter countries is just six million. It is not legitimate to conclude from this analysis that FAD might not play a large part in causing famine in a low income country.

The correct policy conclusion from this analysis is not, as Drèze and Sen imply, that food output does not matter in poor countries. It is rather that poor countries can only begin to worry less about food output once they are successful in raising their incomes and increasing their foreign exchange earnings: growth is the best long-term policy to eliminate famine. However, for a long time to come most African countries will have low incomes and in those circumstances policies which neglect food output are likely to lead to greatly increased likelihood of famine.

Policy errors, mainly in the 'socialist' countries, which have precipitated large declines in food output have been the main cause of famine deaths in modern times

The importance of FAD in contributing to famine is nowhere more in evidence than in the Chinese famine of 1959–61. In Sen [1981] China appeared as the paragon of how to avoid famine. In the early 1980s it became clear that a massive demographic disaster had occurred in the aftermath of the Great Leap Forward of 1958–59. Careful estimates by a number of Western demographers suggest that the 'excess' deaths attributable to the famine may have been as high as 30 million [Ashton et al., 1984]. Sen [Drèze and Sen, 1989: section 11.3] subsequently acknowledged that there was a large fall in food output in China in this period, but argued that if China had been a country with democratic institutions like India, then this colossal FAD would not have led to famine.[30] The central government may have been ignorant of the true state of Chinese agriculture until late in the day.[31] Indeed, it continued to take actions which worsened the situation, such as exporting grain [Walker, 1984]. The Great Leap Forward occurred in the wake of the tough campaign within the Chinese Communist Party to purge those who had spoken out during the Hundred Flowers campaign of 1957. Many local officials hid the true extent of the agricultural disaster following the Great Leap Forward and this exacerbated the problem. There was, indeed, no free press to report the true state of affairs.[32]

Without such a collapse of food output as in fact occurred (Table 8.1), large-scale government action would not have been necessary to try to avert a famine. Sen's discussion of this most disastrous of modern famines relates entirely to the government's response once the FAD had happened, not to analysis of the factors that produced the collapse in food output which precipitated the famine.

The extent of the FAD in China was extremely wide (Table 8.1). Out of 29 provinces and municipalities only one escaped a decline in total grain output from the pre-Great Leap Forward peak to the post-Great Leap Forward trough. In 14 provinces, the decline was between 20 and 40 per cent; in eight provinces the decline was between 40 and 50 per cent, while in one province the decline was greater than 50 per cent. The situation might have been less serious for the government if the major surplus-providing provinces had been hit less badly. In fact, the opposite was the case. The two most important provinces by far in inter-provincial grain trade pre-1958 were Sichuan and Helongjiang. Between them they accounted for almost two-fifths of the total net provincial grain exports during the period 1953–57 (Table 8.1). The fall in grain output in these two provinces was 49 per cent and 46 per cent respectively, and in the case of Heilongjiang this followed stagnation in total grain output after the mid-1950s. The largest surplus-providing province during China's First Five Year Plan, namely Sichuan, was also that which suffered the worst loss of life during the famine. The six provinces of Sichuan, Heilongjiang, Inner Mongolia, Hunan, Jilin and Jiangxi, between them accounted for 70 per cent of the total inter-provincial net grain surplus during the First Five Year Plan. Their total decline in grain output during the famine (from peak to trough) was 38 per cent. The largest net grain importing provinces in 1953–57, Hebei and Liaoning, also suffered large falls in grain output, making 'belt-tightening' for them extremely difficult.

Even during the First Five Year Plan, when China's grain output merely stagnated, as opposed to collapsing (Table 8.1), the central government, despite the absence of democratic institutions, and with the full weight of the Communist Party at its disposal, still found it difficult to maintain grain 'exports' from 'surplus' provinces at a level necessary to feed the cities and earn adequate foreign exchange for the industrialization programme (Walker [1984: 92–5]: 'Grain struggles and political power'). To transfer grain from less badly affected provinces against a background of an FAD of the dimensions of 1958–59 would have required an extraordinary degree of administrative power, even if the government had possessed perfect information about the distribution of output. It seems most unlikely that a 'democratic' government would have been able to do a better job of extracting food from areas which were themselves suffering the worst decline in food output that the country had experienced in modern times.

The more deep and widespread FAD is in a poor country, the more difficult it is likely to be for the government to obtain surpluses of grain from less badly affected areas and transfer them to worse affected areas. If the FAD is sufficiently serious, areas with larger output per person are likely to resist selling to the government, let alone allowing increased taxation of grain, in order to feed themselves at an acceptable level. In India today the state of Punjab supplies about two-fifths of the government's grain purchases. How much freedom of manoeuvre would India's democratic government have if, in the space of two to three years, alongside a national fall in food output of one-third, spread widely across all states, Punjab suffered a 50 per cent fall in output?

Sen argues repeatedly that monitoring food output per person is of little use in understanding the susceptibility of countries to famine, and indeed ridicules the value of such an exercise. The above analysis suggests that this is a problematic view: the Chinese government would not have been 'deranged' to have monitored food output per person on a national, regional, provincial, or even better, a county basis.

It is hard to gauge the degree to which early government acknowledgement to the international community of the impending crisis could have prevented

Table 8.1 Grain Output in Chinese Provinces (m. tonnes), 1955–65

Province/city	1955	1956	1957	1958	1959	1960	1961	1962	1963	1964	1965	Net provincial grain exports (+)/ imports (-) (m.tons) av., p.a. 1953–57	Change in output pre-'58 post-'58 peak to trough (%)
Hebei	7.71	6.82	8.19	8.38	7.40	6.23	5.92	6.63	5.52	7.47	9.65	-1.11	-29
Shanxi	3.73	4.34	3.57	4.62	4.07	3.37	3.54	3.75	4.17	4.89	4.63	+0.04	-27
Inner Mongolia	3.33	4.66	3.03	4.83	4.34	3.59	3.44	3.26	3.38	4.30	3.82	+0.78	-33
Liaoning	6.17	7.43	5.87	7.00	5.90	3.60	4.04	4.60	5.67	5.63	6.71	-1.66	-52
Jilin	5.57	4.94	4.29	5.29	5.27	3.95	3.99	4.37	5.02	4.92	5.25	+0.64	-28
Heilongjiang	8.21	7.93	6.65	8.78	8.51	5.34	4.75	5.83	6.98	7.05	8.83	+1.43	-46
Jiangsu	11.79	10.82	10.64	11.28	9.93	9.60	9.04	9.65	11.15	13.50	14.43	+0.35	-23
Zhejiang	7.61	7.51	7.62	7.89	7.79	6.65	6.54	7.13	8.37	8.71	9.21	+0.42	-17
Anhui	11.53	9.09	10.27	8.85	7.01	6.75	6.29	6.71	6.98	8.12	9.67	+0.32	-45
Fujian	3.90	4.43	4.44	4.46	4.00	3.30	3.24	3.59	3.94	4.34	4.56	+0.03	-27
Jiangxi	6.27	6.49	6.55	6.62	6.27	6.06	6.10	6.04	6.38	7.00	8.02	+0.73	-9
Shandong	12.76	13.72	11.26	12.26	10.49	8.30	8.41	9.10	9.93	11.33	13.32	negl.	-35
Henan	12.50	12.11	11.80	12.65	9.75	8.87	6.85	9.03	7.88	9.51	11.66	+0.25	-46
Hubei	8.96	9.83	9.86	9.87	7.65	7.98	7.34	9.60	10.63	10.43	12.41	+0.05	-26

Table 8.1 continued

Hunan	11.27	10.36	11.32	12.28	11.09	8.02	8.03	10.25	9.09	10.87	11.02	+0.55	-35
Guangdong	9.24	9.88	10.07	9.76	8.31	8.14	8.29	9.30	10.19	10.60	12.28	+0.29	-19
Guangxi	5.97	5.90	5.85	5.86	5.45	4.97	5.00	5.23	4.74	6.10	6.67	+0.14	-21
Sichuan	19.61	21.56	21.31	22.46	15.82	13.40	11.55	14.35	17.01	18.00	20.56	+1.84	-49
Guizhou	4.26	4.87	5.36	5.25	4.23	3.16	3.25	3.66	3.72	4.56	4.90	+0.29	-41
Yunnan	5.42	6.01	5.83	5.44	5.07	4.89	5.00	5.35	5.37	6.07	5.87	+0.16	-19
Tibet	—	0.17	—	0.18	0.18	0.21	0.23	0.24	0.27	0.27	0.29	—	—
Shenxi	4.52	5.44	4.44	5.14	4.74	4.10	3.76	4.00	4.41	4.48	6.08	+0.14	-31
Gansu	3.31	3.80	3.15	3.40	2.90	2.01	1.95	2.10	2.90	3.03	3.71	+0.11	-49
Qinghai	0.59	0.61	0.59	0.59	0.52	0.41	0.39	0.41	0.61	0.63	0.67	negl.	-36
Ningxia	0.63	0.76	0.56	0.70	0.63	0.47	0.49	0.48	0.71	0.75	0.83	—	-46
Xinjiang	1.47	1.58	1.46	1.96	1.98	1.98	1.74	1.65	2.18	2.56	2.62	negl.	-17
Beijing	0.73	0.57	0.78	0.84	0.58	0.55	0.61	0.79	0.85	0.97	1.19	-0.89	-38
Tianjin	0.63	0.57	0.72	0.47	0.52	0.47	0.47	0.44	0.65	0.67	1.17	-0.63	-36
Shanghai	1.13	1.22	1.02	1.17	1.10	1.16	1.15	1.27	1.40	1.71	1.74	-1.97	-6

Sources: State Statistical Bureau, [1990; cols. 1–11 and 13], and Walker [1984: Table 29, col. 12].

loss of life through starvation. The largest relief effort of the twentieth century probably was US government assistance to the Soviet Union during the famine of 1921–22. At the peak of its operations the American Relief Association was reported to be feeding more than ten million people each day [Volin, 1970: 174], and as a result a large number of lives was saved. However, even in this case it has been claimed that as many as five million people in the Volga Valley and Southern Ukraine starved to death [Patenaude, 1991].[33]

Assuming the Chinese government in the late 1950s had been willing to acknowledge the dimensions of the problem, and that the international community had been willing to provide assistance,[34] there still would have been substantial obstacles confronting any relief effort. None of the provinces worst hit by the famine was coastal. Indeed, as usual in Chinese famines, the worst affected provinces were those in central and northern China,[35] so that the logistics of famine relief would have been especially difficult. The improvements in transport between the late nineteenth and early twentieth centuries did much to reduce loss of life from famine in the disaster affecting north China in the 1920s. However, the regional spread of the FAD and the numbers of people involved in the disaster of 1959–61 greatly exceeded even the extent of that of 1920–21. In view of the magnitude of the FAD in China, the size of the population affected and the difficulty of identifying the famine-stricken localities,[36] it is unlikely that even a democratic regime of the Indian type could have avoided extremely large loss of life once the FAD had occurred. Moreover, however well organized or well intentioned the government might be, its capacity to relieve famine was critically dependent upon advances in transport (see below).

Drastic FAD was at the heart of the second largest famine of the twentieth century, namely that in the USSR in 1931–33 (Table 8.2). There was also a large decline in food availability during this famine (Table 8.3). As in the Chinese case of 1959–61, there is no doubt that the number of famine deaths could have been reduced substantially by an early government acknowledgement of the dimensions of the decline in food output and an international appeal for food aid. However, as the example of the Soviet famine of 1921–22 demonstrated, even huge international food aid could not prevent massive loss of life in a relatively poor country with still poorly developed communication systems.

The lesson for poor countries to learn from the Chinese and Soviet famines is the necessity of avoiding inappropriate institutional experiments which might lead to a decline in food output of such dimensions that even well-intentioned government action to attempt to alleviate the famine threat from FAD might not be able to prevent large loss of life.

Table 8.2 **A Comparison of the Severity of the Chinese Famine of 1958–61 and the Soviet Famine of 1933–34**

						Decline in population, peak to trough	
						(a) million	(b) %
		1932	1933	1934			
USSR	Total population (m.)	161.9	162.9	156.4		4.7	3.7
	Death rate (no./1000))	29.5	71.6	21.7			
		1958	1959	1960	1961		
China	Total population(m.)	660	672	662	659	13	1.9
	Death rate (no/1000)	12.0	14.6	25.4	14.2		
1. Sichuan province	Total population (m.)	70.8	69.0	66.2	64.6	6.2	8.8
	Death rate (no/1000)	25.2	47.0	54.0	29.4		
2. Anhui province	Total population (m.)	33.9	34.2	30.4	29.9	4.3	12.6
	Death rate (no/1000)	12.3	16.7	68.6	8.1		
1+2	Total population (m.)	104.7	103.2	96.6	94.3	10.2	9.7
3. Henan province	Total population (m.)	49.4	49.8	48.2	48.0	1.8	3.6
	Death rate (no/1000)	12.7	14.1	39.6	10.2	1.8	3.6
4. Guizhou province	Total population (m.)	17.1	17.4	16.4	16.2	1.2	7.0
	Death rate (no/1000)	13.7	16.2	45.4	17.7		
5. Gansu province	Total population (m.)	12.8	12.9	12.4	12.1	0.8	6.2
	Death rate (no/1000)	12.1	17.4	41.3	41.3	0.8	6.2
1–5 province	Total population (m.)	184	183	174	171	13	7.9

Source: State Statistical Bureau (ZGLST JHB) [1990] and Ellman [1991].

Table 8.3 **Soviet Gross Value of Agricultural Production, 1913–36 (Preliminary Estimates) (Indices, 1928=100) (at constant prices)**

	Grain and chaff		Potatoes/ Industrial vegetables crops		All arable		Livestock	All agriculture	
	High	Low			High	Low		High	Low
1909–13	109	105			93	91	83	90	88
1913	126	125	70	143	102	99	87	96	94
1925	99	100	95	88	92	92	91	92	92
1926	104	105	95	72	96	95	98	97	96
1927	98	98	90	91	95	95	100	97	97
1928	100	100	100	100	100	100	100	100	100
1929	98	98	100	94	97	97	86	93	93
1930	104	104	103	118	100	100	65	87	87
1931	84	90	104	131	95	98	56	81	82
1932	83	88	94	128	88	91	47	73	74
1933	97	103	114	138	98	101	51	81	82
1934	102	108	115	131	100	102	61	86	87
1935	109	119	139	156	113	118	73	99	101
1936	90	95	103	181	104	107	76	93	95

Source: Wheatcroft et al. [1986: 281].

Democratic institutions are not necessary to prevent famine

Sen has argued that the main reason for India's lack of a major famine since Independence has not been the fact that food output growth has kept pace with population, but rather the fact that India's democratic institutions have given 'voice' to India's masses via newspapers and the broadcasting system. Although the masses may be malnourished the government does not dare to let them starve to death for fear of the political consequences this would cause in a system with universal suffrage and contested elections.[37]

Is it indeed the case, as Sen comes close to arguing (see, especially, Sen [1982]), that the existence of democratic institutions constitutes a sufficient condition for India to have avoided mass starvation since the 1950s? Is it even a necessary condition? A large part of the developing world coped with huge increases in population after the 1940s yet managed to avoid famine, and reduced drastically the proportion of its population dying through famine compared with previous epochs. Amongst these were countries of widely different political complexions. Indeed, most of them for most of this period can be considered as one type or another of undemocratic regime. For example, it can hardly be argued that the reason Indonesia was able to experience a growth rate of population of well above two per cent annum from the 1960s through to the late 1980s, without experiencing a major food crisis and famine, was that it had a democratic political system. For most of this period it did not. After the 1950s Indonesia moved away from 'a highly unstable less-than-perfect democracy' to a system that was 'basically stable but democratic largely in name only' [Sundhaussen, 1989: 454]. Rather, it seems plausible to argue that the main reason was the successful growth of food output. Indonesia raised its inputs of chemical fertilizer per hectare from 13 kilograms in 1970–71 to 107 kilograms in 1987–88. High yielding seed strains were adopted on a wide basis and Indonesia's farmers were given adequate incentives to invest in the new technology.

A common element across countries with a wide diversity of political systems is agricultural progress which has enabled food output to keep pace with, or slightly exceed, the high growth rate of population, and has meant that farm output has declined less than formerly in the face of bad weather. Alongside this has gone a widespread rise in income, foreign trade ratio and improvement in transport.

Growth of farm output makes it easier for the government to build up food stocks to help avoid famine

The capacity of the government to obtain food stocks with which to supply people threatened with famine is related in part to administrative capacity. One of the reasons for the Chinese government's ability in most years since 1949 to avoid a famine was its success in establishing tight control over grain marketing, which enabled it to have larger per capita grain stocks at its disposal than the pre-revolutionary government to meet the needs of peasants in grain-deficit areas. The government established this control in the early 1950s prior to collectivization (see especially Walker [1984]). However, output growth also plays an important role in enabling the state to build up buffer stocks. Stagnation in grain output after the mid-1950s made it difficult for the Chinese government to obtain the food surpluses it needed from grain surplus areas [Walker, 1984] and in the post-Mao period the rapid growth of agricultural output enabled there to be a large rise in government grain procurements [Walker, 1984]. Alongside the Green Revolution in India the public sector's grain stocks rose from around two million tons in the mid-1960s to around 17 million tons in the early 1980s, greatly assisted by rapid growth in output from surplus areas, notably Punjab [Mellor, 1988: 73].

5. Markets, Information and the Movement of Food

Information about impending famine can be provided through the market mechanism as well as through the press

The mass media are not the only mechanism through which information can be conveyed about an impending famine. The market is also an important mechanism for conveying information. The Chinese system of political economy under Mao did not just have a highly centralized political system. It also had a Stalinist economic system with no role for markets: capitalism (buying and selling for profit) was likened to a 'dog in the water' which should be 'beaten with a stick and drowned'. This was the Stalinist conception of planning in which the whole economy was treated as a single factory. The consequence of such a system was that information flows which a market system (imperfect as it might be in a poor country) is able to provide were missing. The better integrated such economies become, especially through the growth of transport, the more easily will such information spread.

In his contrast of India and China, Sen stresses the capacity of information to flow through a free press in India. This undoubtedly matters a lot. Restriction on reporting freedom in China in the Maoist period was an important factor explaining the poor information the planners received. However, information can also flow through the market mechanism, in the shape of price changes and the movement of information with people whose job is connected with commerce. Both such important sources of information were eliminated in the Maoist variant of the Stalinist planning system. As was pointed out above, most developing countries are governed by one variant or another of authoritarianism, with more or less restriction on the freedom of the press, yet they have experienced a drastic decline in famines. What they have in common, in addition to policies to sustain or raise food output per person, is a functioning market mechanism, however imperfect, through which information of an impending or actual FAD may be transmitted.

The level of development of the transport system is an important determinant of a country's susceptibility to famine

A major part of the Sen interpretation of famine is the small importance attached to transport.[38]

One of the most striking changes in the developing world over the last century, and especially since the 1940s has been the huge expansion of transport systems, frequently through government action. This has had the effect of making national and international markets more integrated. Instead of a local FAD driving up food prices beyond the reach of all but the relatively well off, the chances are increased for poorer people to obtain food through the market process: whatever purchasing power they have, small as it might be, will be able to obtain more food in this way due to more integrated markets and smaller regional price differentials. The growth of transport systems was an important factor in the drastic reduction in famine in early modern Europe, and there is no reason to think that the mechanism should work fundamentally differently in developing countries. A further element in the impact of transport expansion is that, in the event of a local FAD, national and international authorities are able more quickly to move food to assist potentially famine-stricken people. However, the impact of transport growth does not end here. An important survival response to famine is migration. The more developed transport systems are, the more easily are people able to migrate away from the famine-affected area.[39]

Perkins' [1969] careful analysis of Chinese famines demonstrated the great impact which, even in pre-revolutionary China, advances in modern transportation, limited as they were, had upon the susceptibility of the country to famine. China's worst famines have tended to occur in the Northwestern, wheat-growing part of the country, which has always suffered from its inaccessibility and from the great variability and low average level of its rainfall. In the great northern drought of 1876–79, Perkins estimates that 13 million people may have starved to death in the provinces of Shenxi, Shanxi, Hebei, Henan and Shandong. However, communications with these areas were so poor that it was months after people were in severe difficulties before the capital and coast even heard of the distress. In the drought of 1920–21 similar conditions prevailed in North China, but less than half a million people died: 'The major difference was the arrival of the railroad providing a cheap and rapid means of transport' [Perkins, 1969:166]. However, in the drought of 1928 in the same area at least three million people seem likely to have perished from famine in one province alone, Shenxi [Ho, 1959: 23], so that advances in transport had reduced – but far from eliminated – the possibility of famine deaths. Other factors too form part of the explanation.

Those parts of Africa which have suffered worst from the famines of the 1970s and 1980s have tended to have poor transport. However, Sen does not regard transport as part of the explanation for the Ethiopian famine of the early 1970s, to which he devotes considerable attention. The worst hit region was Wollo province. He argues that the province had two main highways running through it and that most of the relief camps were set up along the highways. 'Underdeveloped roads would not explain the starvation in these famine affected regions' [Sen, 1981: 94]. However, what Sen fails to tell his readers is that the 'two main roads running through the main famine-affected areas' are extremely poorly connected with the surrounding countryside, much of which is extraordinarily difficult terrain to cross even under normal circumstances: 'The central plateau [in which much of Wollo is situated] ... is frequently rent asunder by river beds and narrow valleys, by cracks, fissures, and deep gorges' [Ulendorff, 1973: 23]. In Ethiopia at the time of the terrible famine of 1971–74, this huge country (more then one-third the size of India) had just 14,000 miles of road, of which just 1,250 miles were asphalted, all-weather roads. Three-quarters of all farms were more than half a day's walk from the nearest road. There was estimated to be a total of just 50,000 trucks and cars in the whole country [Halliday and Molyneaux; 1981]. To get food from the roads to the starving and widely dispersed peasants was extremely difficult. It was at least as difficult for starving peasants to move from the areas in which they were starving to the 'two main roads'. It seems inconceivable that if successive Ethiopean governments had been able to divert a greater fraction of their expenditure from military struggle towards infrastructure building, the country would not have been in a better position to avoid famine.

In the Sudan, the collapse of food output in 1990–91 in inaccessible areas with large populations meant that even with good intentions from the Sudanese government and generous responses from Western governments, the chances of avoiding large-scale famine were small:

> It is a distance of 2,000 kilometres or more from the ports to the further parts of of the interior [where a large proportion of the famine victims lived]. In a country which is so starved of fuel that entire fleets of lorries stand idle for days on end and where spare parts and new tyres are virtually unobtainable, the obstacles are overwhelming ... Within the next few weeks the rains should start to fall ... The better the rain, the more impossible the tracks into the interior; huge areas of the most affected regions will be beyond reach. In the remote possibility that the required quantity of relief reaches Sudan, much of it will be impossible to move. It will remain stacked up this side of the floods; on the other side, untold thousands of people will perish [Dimbleby, 1991].

Of course, the provision of good transport is insufficient to avoid famine, but it is a necessary part of a strategy to do so. The Chinese case analysed by Perkins (above) shows clearly the necessity of improved transport. Equally, the disaster of 1959–61, with greatly improved transport provision than pre-1949,[40] shows that this is far from a sufficient condition to prevent famine.

Warfare is of great importance in causing famine

Wars get more attention than transport in Sen's analysis, but not much more (mentioned on five pages in Dreze and Sen [1989]). In his discussion of the Ethiopian disaster of the early 1970s the subject gets no mention, yet civil war was a central feature of life in the country under both Haile Selassie and the Dergue. The areas worst affected by famine in both the 1970s and the early 1980s were those also worst affected by warfare. War has direct effects upon food output, availability of information to the government, transport systems and the functioning of markets, as well as indirect effects via its impact upon government expenditure, limiting the government's ability to improve the national, and especially the agricultural, infrastructure, and often contributing directly to its deterioration. Civil War in the Soviet Union, following hard on the heels of the First World War, played an important role in the Soviet FAD and famine of the early 1920s. Large parts of China were affected by warfare at different points in the nineteenth and twentieth centuries, with undoubted negative effects upon food output, transport systems and the functioning of markets. It is hard to disentangle the impact of direct slaughter during the war from other demographic effects, both direct (including migration, changes in the sex ratio, and postponed marriages), from the indirect affects upon food supply. By far the greatest demographic event in modern China's history, exceeding in importance even the Great Leap Forward disaster, was the Taiping Rebellion, which devastated large areas of central and southern China between 1850 and 1864.[41] Most recently, civil war was at the heart of the Somali famine of 1992.[42]

Conclusion

The 'entitlement' approach does not constitute a methodological advance upon the best previous analyses of famine. The word has a scientific ring, but it is analytically useless. The main reasons that Sen's analysis has had such an impact are the power of the paradox that people can die amid plenty and the wish quickly to solve problems of famine and malnutrition through institutional change and associated redistributive measures.

Sen's analysis of the causes of famines and his contribution to famine-prevention policy is one-sided in its selection and interpretation of the evidence. He urges a plurality of strategies to be considered in preventing famines, but in practice neglects some of the most important aspects of policy. This matters because his influence has been enormous in setting the agenda for economic research on this subject in the 1980s and doubtless will continue to be so in the 1990s.

Distributional arrangements, especially those at the local level, are crucial in determining who suffers most during a famine, and it is here that Sen's contribution is most valuable. He is most helpful in thinking about ways of avoiding famine once FAD has occurred. However, this advance in the analysis of famine is achieved at the cost of leading policymakers away from devising methods of avoiding such a situation (FAD) in the first place.

One should be extremely careful in advocating institutional change as a means to prevent famine. Poorly designed institutional changes may handicap the long-run growth of income and food output. Even more seriously, changes in distributional arrangements which are intended to provide members of a community with an equal capacity to be 'positively free' to live a long life, might have so drastic an impact upon incentives as to precipitate a famine on their own through their effect on output. The Chinese case alone provides strong evidence that these are not unlikely occurrences.

Availability of information is necessary if governments are to be able to relieve potential famine once FAD has happened. Sen's analysis has made people more aware of the importance of information flows in affecting the degree of impact a given decline in output has upon mortality. However, Sen underestimates the importance of the market compared to a free press in providing information about impending famine.

Investment in transport infrastructure is also a necessary condition of famine reduction, both because transport is part of the process of market widening which enables people to raise their per capita income, but also because markets are the conduit through which information about impending famine is conveyed so that food supplies might reach regions suffering from FAD. Without adequate transport, food supplies will not reach famine-stricken areas in sufficient quantities, however open and well-intentioned the government. Sen's persistent underemphasis of its importance is incomprehensible, especially as it is an area that government policy can so readily affect. None of the processes which might prevent famine is likely to operate so well in an environment of political turbulence, especially warfare: a necessary, but not sufficient, condition of famine avoidance is stable and effective government.

Contrary to the strong impression given by Sen's writings, food output is of prime importance in preventing famine in low income countries with rapidly growing populations. Food availability in most poor countries, especially large ones, needs to be ensured through policies that enable food output to keep up with population growth and avoid large fluctuations in output. The wide array of measures which might affect the growth of food output, including institutional arrangements, price policy and the supply of farm inputs, are essential elements of famine prevention in poor countries. However, policies which reduce human fertility are also part of the reason why some societies are better able than others to maintain food supply per capita.

FAD at some level is part of the explanation for most famines. Monitoring average per capita food availability at a properly disaggregated level is an essential part of famine relief strategy, in case policies to ensure the provision of food through self-production or via the market are unsuccessful. The main lesson of famines in the twentieth century is that wild government-led (or government-imposed) institutional changes which might produce collapses in food output should be avoided. This has happened more than once in 'social-ist' countries. Indeed, the worst famine of the twentieth century was caused by a collapse of food output, precipitated largely by institutional change which was, paradoxically, intended to eliminate starvation by sharing more equally the available food supply. Even the most honest, resolute government can only hope to mitigate the worst effects of, but not to avoid, famine under such circumstances.

Of course, the surest way to avoid famine is to industrialize successfully, and raise income from $500 per capita to $5,000 per capita, but that is not of much use in shaping policy for countries that are still at low levels of per capita income.

Notes

1 'I am immodest enough to believe that the analysis presented in this monograph has a certain amount of relevance to matters of practical concern' [Sen, 1981: ix].

2 'The mesmerising simplicity of focusing on the ratio of food output to population has persistently played an obscuring role over the centuries, and continues to plague policy today much as it has deranged anti-famine policies in the past' [Sen, 1981: 8].

3 'Famines develop from entitlement failures suffered by a large section of the popula-tion. Those who cannot establish command over an adequate amount of food have to perish from starvation' [Drèze and Sen, 1989: 65].

4 'Seeing famine prevention as an entitlement protection problem draws our attention to the plurality of strategies available for dealing with it. Just as entitlements can be threatened in a number of different ways there is also typically a number of feasible routes for restoring them' [Drèze and Sen, 1989: 67].

5 'It is possible that severe famine conditions can develop for reasons that are not direct-ly connected with food production at all; ... [s]hifts in ... entitlement relations can pre-cipitate gigantic famines without any impulse from food production' [Sen, 1981: 158].

6 'In understanding ... outbursts of famines, it is necessary to look at both ownership pat-terns and exchange entitlements and the forces that lie behind them. This requires careful consideration of the nature of modes of production and the structure of economic classes as well as their interrelations' [Sen, 1981: 6].

7 'Market demands are not reflections of biological needs or psychological desires, but choices based on exchange relations. If one doesn't have much to exchange, one can't demand very much, and may thus lose out in competition with others whose needs

may be a good deal less acute, but whose entitlements are stronger' [Sen, 1981: 161].

8 For example, 'the class basis of destitution' in the Great Bengal Famine; 'the economic background of the destitute' in the Wollo region during the Ethiopean famine of the early 1970s; 'occupational distribution, intensity of destitution', and 'exchange entitlement of labour power' in the 1974 Bangladesh famine [Sen, 1981: 70–75, 96–104, 140–50].

9 'The elimination of starvation in the socialist countries – for example China – seems to have taken place even without a dramatic rise in food availability per head, and indeed, typically the former has preceded the latter. The end of starvation reflects a shift in the entitlement system, both in the form of social security and – more importantly – through systems of guaranteed employment at wages that provide exchange entitlement adequate to avoid starvation' [Sen, 1981: 7].

10 'Since the reforms, food availability per head has gone up radically, but the delivery system [of health care and food to different sections of the population] has undergone some changes, including contraction in some respects, and there seems to have been some decline from the previously achieved peak of high life expectancy and low death rate. While the Chinese economic reforms must be praised for what they have achieved – the increase in production has been altogether remarkable – there is need to reassess the lessons of the Chinese reforms, especially when attention is shifted from production, GNP and output per head to the basis indicators of the freedom to live long and related positive freedoms' [Sen, 1989: 777].

11 His approach is politically 'correct' in relation to the mainstream of intellectual discourse in the USA, and Sen's writings in the *New York Review of Books* have had a large impact on a wide audience of US intellectuals.

12 'Public support programmes ... make it possible to do something immediately about conquering deprivation and raising the quality of life without having to wait ... before ploughing back the fruits of economic growth into improved health and longevity' [Drèze and Sen, 1989: 251–2].

13 I am grateful to Paul Aiello for drawing my attention to this quote.

14 'The entitlement approach provides a general framework for analysing famines rather than one particular hypothesis about their causation' [Sen, 1981: 162].

15 Interestingly, Sen himself does just this in Dreze and Sen [1989: 31–2]. See also the discussion of this point in section IV below.

16 As Mallory argued in relation to China in the 1920s: 'Most famines, particularly those due to drought, can be anticipated if there is a proper crop-reporting system. Crop estimates can be made throughout the growing season, and a sufficiently accurate appraisal of the situation arrived at to forecast the probable yield over the whole country. If such information were collected by county officials in China and forwarded promptly to the central government, plans to meet any impending disaster in the regions where crop failure was threatened could be drawn up well in advance' [Mallory, 1926: 167].

17 In respect to the latter, Sen argues: 'social security arrangements are particularly important in the context of avoiding starvation. The reason why there are no famines in rich developed countries, is not because people are generally rich on average ... but [because of] the guaranteed minimum values of exchange entitlements owing to the social security system' [1981: 6–7]. This is an odd view of the historical process of famine elimination in the advanced economies, since in most countries the establishment of social security systems occurred long after famine had ceased to be a problem.

18 Drèze and Sen [1989: 211] make the odd statement that during the Great Leap For-

ward in China public distribution at the local level was 'comprehensively disrupted'. What certainly was disrupted was the pre-Great Leap Forward system of distribution, which paid more attention to distribution according to work accomplished, as opposed to distribution 'according to the number of eaters'. However, in its place over much of rural China was put a thoroughly egalitarian form of food distribution, alongside continued employment and income guarantee. Dreze and Sen's vagueness on this point, which is so important, is puzzling. At no point in their account [Drèze and Sen, 1989: 210–15] do they draw attention to one of the most striking facts about the Great Leap Forward; indeed, from their perspective, arguably *the* most important fact, namely that the worst famine in modern times, perhaps in the whole of human history, occurred in a system that at the local level provided the most thoroughly egalitarian access to local food supply to all members of the local community, that is, distribution principally according to the number of eaters.

19 Other factors included incentive and management problems stemming from the huge size of collective farms; excessive diversion of labour to non-farm tasks such as backyard iron and steel furnaces; administrative orders to reduce the area sown to grain in the belief that the grain problem had been 'solved'; and enormous construction of technically infeasible irrigation works which often collapsed during heavy rain, inundating farmland. All these errors were, to a greater or lesser degree, the result of failures in policy by the central government, under the influence of Mao Tsetung's optimism about the capacity of institutional change to produce economic progress (see for example, Nolan [1988]).

20 Of course, even in this period, despite the formal rules for relatively equal sharing of food supplies, the horror of starvation most probably was not in fact shared equally at a local level. At the very least, the 'usual' inequalities of intra-family food distribution applied, and probably too there were other local inequalities in outcomes.

21 Indeed, distribution mainly according to the number of 'eaters' was, after a debate within the leadership, decisively rejected (see especially Davies [1980: Ch. 7]).

22 '[T]here has not been any declining trend in food availability per head in the world as a whole in recent decades, [and] it seems unlikely that the real dangers in the near future can lie in the prospect of food output falling short of the growth of population' [Drèze and Sen, 1989: 31–2].

23 'The battle to feed all of humanity is over ... The famines of the 1970s are upon us – and hundreds of millions of people are going to starve to death before the decade is out' (Paul Erlich, quoted in Arnold [1988: 39]).

24 The term 'Green Revolution' does not even appear in the subject index of Drèze and Sen [1989].

25 In the low income countries (excluding India and China) as a whole inputs of chemical fertilizer per hectare of cropland rose from 7 kilograms in 1970–71 to 32 kilograms in 1977–78, and in middle income countries, from 33 kilograms in 1970–71 to 65 kilograms in 1987–88 [World Bank, 1985: 184–5, and 1990: 184–5]. In the two most populous developing countries, India and China, chemical fertilizer input per hectare rose from 14 and 41 kilograms, respectively in 1970–71 to 52 and 236 kilograms respectively in 1977–78 [World Bank, 1985: 184–5, and 1990: 184–5]. In India the net irrigated area expanded by 37 per cent from the early 1960s through the early 1980s [Mellor, 1988: 68], while in China, an already high area under effective irrigation rose by no less than 63 per cent from 1957 to the late 1970s [Ministry of Agriculture, 1989: 318].

26 The reported growth in average per capita food output in low income countries

(excluding India and China) from 1969–71 to 1986–88 was four per cent; in India the growth was eight per cent; in China the reported rise was no less than 53 per cent; in middle income countries the growth over the same period was nine per cent [*World Bank*, 1983: 158–9; *World Bank*, 1990: 184–5].

27 In the case of India, for example, net food grain imports fell from a peak of over 10.6 million tons in 1966, prior to the Green Revolution, to under one million tons in the early 1980s [Mellor, 1988: 73], and for the first time in modern history India in the 1980s briefly became a net food grain exporter.

28 Food grain imports by low income countries rose from 23 million tons in 1970–71 to 32 million tons in 1987–88, and for the middle income countries the comparable figures were 33 million tons and 65 million tons [*World Bank*, 1985; 1990].

29 'Some of the Sub-Saharan economies have indeed experienced famine in the middle eighties, and they did also have considerable declines in food output per head in the middle eighties ... On the other hand, several economies elsewhere have experienced comparable or even greater declines in food output per head ... without any problems of the kind which have afflicted these African countries' [Drèze and Sen, 1989: 34].

30 'Given its system of public distribution, China did not lack a delivery and redistribution mechanism to deal with food shortages as the famine threatened in 1958 and later. Despite the size of the decline in food output and the loss of entitlement of large sections of the population, China could have done a much better job of protecting the vulnerable by sharing the shortages in a bearable way ... What was lacking when the famine threatened China was a political system of adversarial journalism and opposition' [Drèze and Sen, 1989: 212].

31 There is still no unambiguous evidence on the degree of central government knowledge about the true state of agriculture in different parts of the country in the immediate post-Great Leap period.

32 Dreze and Sen argue: 'A relatively free newspaper system may be the most effective "early warning system" a famine prone country can rely on' [Drèze and Sen, 1989: 264].

33 I am indebted to Michael Ellman for supplying me with this reference.

34 Which is far from certain in the atmosphere of great hostility towards China at that time.

35 For a discussion of the regional pattern of Chinese famines in history, see especially Buck [1937: 125–8].

36 Although 'excess deaths' may have been in the order of 30 million, the number of people close to starvation would have vastly exceeded this figure. It is difficult in a famine to predict precisely who among those close to death are the ones who will indeed end up dying. Thus, once a large FAD has occurred the amount of food required to prevent famine is much greater than that required to feed the number who do indeed die of starvation.

37 'India's success in eliminating famines since Independence is not primarily the result of raising food output per head ... Indeed the increase in availability of food per head has been fairly moderate ... The main difference [with pre-1947] has been brought about by an administrative system which compensates the loss of entitlements as a result of such calamities as droughts and floods by providing employment giving the affected population renewed ability to command food in the market. The process is further helped by using substantial stocks held in the public distribution system which can be brought in to supplement what the creation of income does in regenerating lost entitle-

ments ... No government at the centre – or at the state level – can get away without extreme political damage if it fails to take action against famines. The presence of active opposition parties and a relatively free news distribution system provides the political triggering mechanism that the Famine Codes in their original form lacked' [Sen, 1989: 774–5].

38 See, for example, the discussion of the alleged unimportance of transport in his analysis of the Wollo famine in the early 1970s [Sen, 1981: 93–6]. So little does transport figure in Sen's analysis that in their large volume on hunger and famine [Drèze and Sen, 1989] not only is not one of the 13 chapters or 67 sub-sections devoted to the issue but it does not even appear in the subject index.

39 Not only does the transport system affect the capacity to shift food to suffering areas, but it is also an important avenue through which information about impending or existing FAD can flow.

40 From 1952 to 1962 the length of railways expanded from 23,000 to 35,000 kilometres, and the length of highway from 127,000 to 464,000 kilometres [SSB, 1989: 489].

41 While the direct carnage was awful, the indirect effects through famine-induced deaths may have been at least as great. The impact was, through one channel or another, to reduce the estimated total population from around 410 million in 1850 to just 350 million in 1873 [Perkins, 1969: 216].

42 A report from the combined major aid agencies working in Somalia suggests that at least 300,000 people (that is, around four per cent of the population) died in the drought of August 1992 (BBC Radio 4, 19 August 1992). As might be expected deaths were heavily concentrated in the vulnerable age groups, particularly the very young. The same report believes that as much as one quarter of the under-five population may have perished in this famine. A large proportion of the worst affected people are thought to be located in remote areas poorly connected to transport facilities, so that even if the international relief effort did eventually get off the ground, it would be very hard to avoid large loss of life.

References

Ashton, B., Hill, K., Piazza A. and R. Zeitz, 1984, 'Famine in China, 1958–61', *Population and Development Review*, Vol.10, No. 4.

Arnold, D., 1988, *Famine*, Oxford: Basil Blackwell.

Bhatia, B.M., 1991, *Famines in India* (revised edition), Delhi: Konark Publishers (first published 1963).

Buck, J.L., 1937, *Land Utilisation in China*, Nanking: University of Nanking, reprinted in 1964 by Paragon Book Company, New York.

Conquest, R., 1986, *The Harvest of Sorrow*, London: Hutchinson.

Davies, R.W., 1980, *The Soviet Collective Farm, 1929–30*, London: Macmillan.

Dimbleby, J., 1991, 'Squabbling to the Death', *The Observer*, 21 April.

Drèze, J. and A. Sen, 1989, *Hunger and Public Action*, Oxford: Clarendon Press.

Duby, G., 1968, *Rural Economy and Country Life in the Medieval West*, London: Edward Arnold.

Ellman, M., 1991, 'A Note on the Number of 1933 Famine Victims', *Soviet Studies*, Vol. 43, No. 2, pp. 375–9.

Halliday, F. and M. Molyneux, 1981, *The Ethiopean Revolution*, London: Verso Books.

Ho, P.T., 1959, *Studies on the population of China, 1368–1953*, Cambridge, MA: Harvard University Press.

Mallory, J.W., 1926, *China – Land of Famine*, New York: American Geographical Society Special Publication No. 6.

Mellor, J.W., 1988, 'Food Production, Consumption and Development Strategy', in R.E.B. Lucas, and G.F. Papanek (eds.), *The Indian Economy*, Oxford: Oxford University Press.

Ministry of Agriculture of the People's Republic of China, 1989, *Complete Statistics on China's Agricultural Economy (Zhonguo nongcun jingji tongji daquan) (1949–1986)*, Beijing: Nongye chubanshe.

Nolan, P., 1988, *The Political Economy of Collective Farms*, Cambridge: Polity Press.

Nolan, P. and J. Sender, 1992, 'Death Rates, Life Expectancy and China's Economic Reforms. A Critique of A.K. Sen', *World Development*, Vol. 20, No. 9, Sept.

Patnaik, U., 1991, 'Food Availability and Famine: A Longer View', *Journal of Peasant Studies*, Vol. 19, No. 1, Oct.

Patenaude, B., 1991, 'American Famine Relief Recalled', Meeting Report, Kennan Institute for Advanced Studies, Washington, DC, Vol. 8, No. 11.

Perkins, D.H., 1969, *Agricultural Development in China, 1368–1968*, Edinburgh: Edinburgh University Press.

State Statistical Bureau, 1990, *Collected Historical Statistical Materials on each Province, Autonomous Region and Directly Administered City (Lishi tongji ziliao huibian)*, (1949–1989) (LSTJHB), Beijing: Zhongguo tongji chubanshe.

Sen, A., 1981, *Poverty and Famines*, Oxford: Oxford University Press.

Sen, A., 1982, 'How is India Doing?', *New York Review of Books*, 16 Dec.

Sen, A.K., 1989, 'Food and Freedom', *World Development*, Vol. 17, No. 6.

State Statistical Bureau (SSB), various dates, *Chinese Statistical Yearbook (Zhongguo tongji nianjian)*, Beijing: Zhongguo tongji chubanshe.

Stern, N., 1989, 'The Economics of Development: A Survey', *Economic Journal*, Vol. 99, Sept., pp. 597–685.

Solow, R., 1991, 'How to Stop Hunger', *New York Review of Books*, 5 Dec.

Sundhaussen, U., 1989, 'Indonesia: Past and Present Encounters with Democracy', in L. Diamond, J.J. Linz and S.M. Lipset (eds.), *Democracy in Developing countries: Asia*, London: Adamantine Press.

Ullendorff, E., 1973, *The Ethiopians*, London: Oxford University Press (first edn., 1960).

United Nations Development Programme (UNDP), 1990 and 1992, *Human Development Report*, New York: Oxford University Press.

Volin, L., 1970, *A Century of Russian Agriculture*, Cambridge MA: Harvard University Press.

Walker, K.R., 1984, *Food Grain Procurement and Consumption in China*, Cambridge: Cambridge University Press.

Wheatcroft, S.G., Davies, R.W. and J.M. Cooper, 1986, 'Soviet Industrialisation Reconsidered: Some Preliminary Conclusions about Economic Development between 1926 and 1941', *Economic History Review*, 2nd Ser, Vol. xxxix, No. 2, pp. 264–94.

Will, P.-E., 1990, *Bureaucracy and Famine in Eighteenth Century China*, Cambridge: Cambridge University Press.

World Bank, various dates, *World Development Report*, Washington, DC: Oxford University Press.

EPILOGUE
ADAM SMITH AND THE
CONTRADICTIONS OF THE FREE
MARKET ECONOMY: A NOTE

Adam Smith provides a principal source of inspiration for free market economists across the world. In fact, Smith himself had grave doubts about the
ability of the free market to meet human needs. He believed that the market
was a two-edged sword, with unique dynamic qualities but also with deep,
inbuilt contradictions. Free market economists rarely, if ever, acknowledge his
penetrating and realistic analysis of the inherent contradictions of the market
economy. Yet Smith has left a rich legacy of ideas in this sphere, which are
even more relevant to the pressing issues that face the world today than they
were when he wrote his key works.

First published in 1776, the *Wealth of Nations* is the most influential book in
the history of economics, arguably more so even than Marx's *Das Kapital*. It is
a huge work of more than one thousand pages and, apart from specialist
scholars of Smith, few people negotiate the whole text. Few economics under-
graduates read the book and indeed many professional economists, while
freely making use of the idea of the 'invisible hand', have never read any part
of it. It is widely assumed that the *Wealth of Nations* 'proves' that the free
market, guided by the 'invisible hand', is the best arrangement for organizing
economic life. Smith's other great work was the *Theory of Moral Sentiments*, published in 1759 and revised by Smith in 1761. Many economists have never
heard of this work and fewer still have read it. Far from being an 'early work',
which was superseded by the *Wealth of Nations*, the *Theory of Moral Sentiments* is
intellectually inseparable from the former work. While their main topics are
different, the books share the same fundamental passion about the moral
foundations of social life. At the heart of both is an explicit recognition of
fundamental contradictions within the market economy. In them, Smith
demonstrated that the free market is an immensely powerful force for

impelling economic progress, but one that has profound contradictions. He gave little clue as to how these inconsistencies might be resolved, but felt it was his duty to point them out.

In the *Wealth of Nations*, Smith identified two powerful drivers of economic progress, the division of labour and the accumulation of capital. The foundation of Smith's 'growth model' was the division of labour, discussion of which occupies the first few chapters of the *Wealth of Nations*. Smith's famous enunciation of this principle declared: 'The greatest improvements in the productive powers of labour, and the greatest part of the skill, dexterity and judgement with which it is any where directed, or applied, seems to have been the effects of the division of labour'.[1] Smith considered that the fundamental driver of the accumulation process was the pursuit of profit: 'It is only for the sake of profit that any man employs a capital in the support of industry'.[2] The possessors of capital direct their stock of capital towards those industries that yield the greatest profit and are therefore 'likely to be of the greatest value': '[B]y directing that industry in such a manner as its produce may be of the greatest value, he intends only his own gain, and he is in this, as in many other cases, led by the invisible hand to promote an end which was no part of his intention'.[3]

Smith believed that these principles were the key to 'economic development', or the 'wealth of nations': 'Little else is required to carry a state to the highest level of opulence from the lowest level of barbarism, but peace, easy taxes, and a tolerable administration of justice[4]... The natural effort of every individual to better his own condition, when suffered to exert itself with freedom and security, is so powerful a principle that it is alone, and without any assistance, not only capable of carrying on the society to wealth and prosperity, but of surmounting a hundred impertinent obstructions with which the folly of human laws encumbers its operation...'[5]

The system appears to be an elegant, harmonious integration of individual self-interest and social interests. However, this is far from the case. Alongside Smith's rigorous analysis of the growth process was a deep awareness of the internal contradictions of that same process. Both the division of labour and the pursuit of profit each contained deep internal contradictions from an ethical standpoint, the one from the perspective of man as a producer, and the other from the perspective of man as a consumer.

Man as Producer

While the division of labour promoted productivity growth, the basis for long-term improvements in the 'wealth of nations', it also has deeply negative consequences for the mass of the population. Smith believed that people are born with relatively equal capacities for self-expression and self-realization. He considered people's capability for self-realization to be largely dependent on their social environment, especially their work environment, not on inherited differences: 'The differences of natural talents in different men is, in reality, much less than we are aware of; and the very different genius which appears to distinguish men of different professions, when grown up to maturity, is not upon many occasions so much the cause as the effect of the division of labour. The differences between the most dissimilar characters, between a philosopher and a common street porter, for example, seems to arise not so much from nature, as from habit, custom and education'.[6]

In the course of industrial advance, opportunities arise for greatly enhanced divisions of labour that were not present in agriculture: 'The nature of agriculture, indeed, does not permit of so many subdivisions of labour, nor of so complete a separation of one business from another, as manufactures'.[7] Smith believed that the advantages of the enhanced division of labour included increased worker dexterity and reduced time lost in passing from one task to another, on account of greater occupational specialization; the greater possibility for applying mechanization to specialist tasks; and the associated opportunities for technical progress in the production of new types of machines by specialist machine-makers.[8] However, a major advantage of the enhanced division of labour was the possibility it presented for 'saving time' by increasing the labourer's work intensity: 'The habit of sauntering and of indolent and careless application, which is naturally or, rather, necessarily acquired by every country workman who is obliged to change his work and tools every half hour, and to apply his hand in twenty different ways almost every day of his life; render him almost always slothful and lazy and incapable of any vigorous application even on the most pressing occasions'.[9]

For Smith, the division of labour was a two-edged sword. It promoted the advance of productivity, but at a high price. He was brutally realistic about its consequences for the mass of workers: 'In the progress of the division of labour, the employment of the far greater part of those who live by labour, that is the great body of the people, comes to be confined to a few very simple operations, frequently to one or two. But the understanding of the greater part of men are necessarily formed by their ordinary employments. The man whose life is spent in performing a few simple operations, of which the effects too are, perhaps, always the same, or very nearly the same, has no occasion to exert his understanding, or to exercise his invention in finding out expedients for removing difficulties which never occur. He naturally loses, therefore, the habit of such exertion, and generally becomes as stupid and ignorant as it is possible for a human creature to become.'[10] Smith warned that 'in every improved and civilised society, this is the state into which the labouring poor, that is, the great body of the people, must necessarily fall, unless government takes some pains to prevent it'.[11] The only 'solution' that Smith was able to offer to this deep contradiction was the establishment of 'little schools' in each parish or district, 'where children may be taught for a reward so moderate even a common labourer may afford it'.[12]

Smith considered that great inequality and class conflicts were unavoidable in a society based on private property: 'Wherever there is great property, there is great inequality. For one very rich man, there must be at least five hundred poor, and the affluence of the few supposes the indigence of the many'.[13] Smith warned that without substantial 'trickle down' of the fruits of economic progress to the mass of the population, a society would be morally unsatisfactory and at risk due to the threat of social instability: 'Servants, labourers, and workmen of different kinds, make up by far the greater part of every great political society. But what improves the circumstances of the greater part can never be regarded as an inconvenience to the whole. No society can surely be great and flourishing of which the far greater part of the members are poor and miserable. It is but equity besides, that they who feed, clothe, and lodge the whole body of the people, should have such a share of the produce of their own labour as to be themselves tolerably well fed, cloathed and lodged'.[14]

However, Smith believed that it would be difficult to obtain cooperative solutions to the great differences in socioeconomic interests in an economy like that of late eighteenth-century Britain: 'The affluence of the rich excites the indignation of the many, who are often driven by want, and prompted by envy, to invade his possessions'.[15] He concluded that it was a critical duty of the state to protect property-owners, upon whom rested the key instruments for economic progress: 'The acquisition of valuable and extensive property, therefore, necessarily requires the establishment of civil government ... Civil government presupposes a certain subordination ... [which] gives some men some superiority over the greater part of their brethren'.[16]

Smith considered that the realities of the labour market were basically antagonistic: 'The workers desire to get as much as possible, the masters to give as little as possible. The former are disposed to combine in order to raise and the latter in order to lower the wages of labour'.[17] In late eighteenth-century England, the balance of power in the labour market was tipped decisively towards the masters: 'The masters, being few in number, can combine much more easily; and law, besides, authorises or at least does not prohibit their combinations, while it prohibits those of the workmen. We have no acts of parliament against combining to lower the price of labour; but many against combining to raise it. In all such disputes, masters can hold out much longer ... Many workmen could not subsist a week, few could subsist a month, and scarce any a year without employment'.[18]

Smith believed that class stratification was a necessary condition of economic progress, facilitating the accumulation of capital and the division of labour. However, he acknowledged that this contained the high possibility not only of class conflict, but also of 'corruption of moral sentiments', through the construction of social values that justified 'neglect of the poor and mean': '[T]he disposition to admire, and almost to worship, the rich and powerful, and to despise, or at least, to neglect persons of poor and mean condition, though necessary to maintain the distinction of ranks and the order of society, is at the same time, the great and most universal cause of the corruption of our moral sentiments'.[19]

Man as Consumer

We have seen that one of the central forces in Smith's growth model was the accumulation of capital, and that the central motive for the application of capital was to obtain profit derived from the use of capital. He believed that behind this lay an even deeper psychological drive, namely the desire to acquire 'wealth and greatness'. However, Smith considered that this fundamental driving force of economic progress contained its own 'deception', or inbuilt contradiction: 'The pleasures of wealth and greatness... strike the imagination as something grand and beautiful and noble, of which the attainment is well worth all the toil and anxiety which we are apt to bestow upon it. And it is well that nature imposes upon us in this manner. It is this deception which rouses and keeps in continual motion the industry of mankind'.[20] Smith enumerates the dramatic effects of the application of this 'industry', impelled by the 'deception' of the pursuit of 'wealth and greatness': 'It is this which first prompted them to cultivate the ground, to build houses, to found cities and commonwealths, and to invent and improve all the sciences and arts, which ennoble human life; which have entirely changed the whole face of the globe, have turned the rude forests of nature into agreeable and fertile plains, and made the trackless and barren ocean a new fund of subsistence, and the great high road of communication to the different nations of the earth. The earth by these labours of mankind has been obliged to redouble her natural fertility, and to maintain a greater number of inhabitants'.[21] It is deeply paradoxical that the driving force for economic progress should be considered to be a 'deception'.

Smith believed that the pursuit of 'wealth and greatness' was a 'deception', because, beyond a certain modest level of consumption, additional consumption brought no increase in happiness, and often brought unhappiness: 'In the langour of disease and the weariness of old age, the pleasures of the vain and empty distinctions of greatness disappear ... Power and riches then appear to be, what they are, enormous and operose [sic] machines contrived to produce a few trifling conveniences to the body, consisting of springs the most nice and delicate, which must be kept in order with the most anxious attention, and which, in spite of all our care are ready every moment to burst into pieces, and to crush in their ruins their unfortunate possessor'.[22] Smith compared 'power and riches' to 'immense fabrics' that 'require the labour of life to raise': '[They] threaten every moment to overwhelm the person that dwells in them, and which while they stand, though they may save him from some smaller inconveniences, can protect him from none of the inclemencies of the season. They keep off the summer shower, not the wintry storm, but leave him always as much, sometimes more exposed than before, to anxiety, to fear, and to sorrow; and to diseases, to danger and to death'.[23]

Smith was deeply critical of the pursuit of 'frivolous consumption', believing that it brought no increase in happiness: 'How many people ruin themselves by laying out money on trinkets of frivolous utility ... All their pockets are stuffed with little conveniences ... They walk about loaded with a multitude of baubles ... If we consider the real satisfaction which all these things are capable of affording, by itself and separated from the beauty of the arrangement which is fitted to promote it, it will appear in the highest degree contemptible and trifling ... [W]ealth and greatness are mere trinkets of frivolous utility, no more adapted for procuring ease of body or tranquility of mind than the tweezer-cases of the lovers of toys'.[24]

Smith believed that the only worthwhile social goal was the pursuit of happiness. In his view, this was to be attained through 'tranquillity', not the pursuit of 'power and riches': 'Happiness is tranquillity and enjoyment. Without tranquillity there can be no enjoyment; and where there is perfect tranquillity there is scarce anything which is not capable of amusing'.[25] In Smith's view, the attainment of happiness did not require high levels of consumption: '[I]n the ordinary situations of human life, a well-disposed mind may be equally calm, equally cheerful, and equally contented ... [I]n the most glittering and exalted situation that our ideal fancy can hold out to us, the pleasures from which we propose to derive our real happiness, are almost always the same with those which in our actual though humble situation, we have at all times at hand and in our power ... [T]he pleasures of vanity and superiority are seldom consistent with perfect tranquillity, the principle and foundation of all real and satisfactory enjoyment'.[26]

Smith believed that a good society was one in which people attained happiness through fulfilling basic human needs, not in the vain pursuit of unlimited wants. He considered that there was a clear choice: 'Two different roads are presented to us ... the one by the study of wisdom and the practice of virtue, the other, by the acquisition of wealth and greatness ... the one of proud ambition and ostentatious avidity, the other, of humble modesty and equitable justice ... the one more gaudy and glittering in the colouring, the other more correct and exquisitely beautiful in its outline'.[27]

Smith considered that human psychology required social cohesion as the foundation of a good society in which all citizens could achieve happiness: 'All the members of human society stand in need of each others assistance ... Where the necessary assistance is reciprocally afforded from love, from gratitude, from friendship, and esteem, the society flourishes and is happy. All the different members of it are bound together by the agreeable bonds of love and affection, and are, as it were, drawn to one common centre of mutual good offices'.[28] The foundation of such cohesion was 'benevolence': '[T]o feel much for others and little for ourselves, to restrain our selfish, and to indulge our benevolent affections, constitutes the perfection of human nature; and can alone among mankind produce that harmony of sentiments and passions in which consists their whole grace and propriety'.[29]

Benevolence, not the pursuit of 'wealth and greatness', allows the construction of a sense of duty which, in its turn, enables the realization of social cohesion: 'The regard to those general rules of conduct, is what is properly called a sense of duty, a principle of the greatest consequence in human life, and the only possible principle by which the bulk of mankind are capable of directing their actions ... Without this sacred regard to general rules, there is no man whose conduct can be much depended upon ... By acting according to the dictates of our moral faculties, we necessarily pursue the most effectual means for promoting the happiness of mankind'.[30] Smith believed that unless a society was 'just', there was a grave danger that it would disintegrate into chaos: 'Justice, on the contrary, is the main pillar that upholds the whole edifice. If it is removed, the great, the immense fabric of human society, that fabric which to raise and support seems in this world, if I may say so, to have been the peculiar and darling love of Nature, must in a moment crumble into atoms'.[31]

Conclusion

Smith's analysis of the market mechanism was an attempt to lay bare the fundamental laws governing economic development. At the same time that he sought to identify these principles, he devoted scrupulous attention to the underlying contradictions of the market economy. While he did believe that the free market was the fundamental driver of economic progress, he demonstrated that this driving force contained profound internal contradictions from the point of view of people as both producers and as consumers. In respect of both issues, Smith insisted that the dynamism of the free market economy should be considered alongside its deep ethical shortcomings. He was unable to answer satisfactorily how the latter shortcomings could be resolved, but his intellectual honesty and driving sense of moral purpose led him to lay bare these contradictions clearly and passionately.

His analysis of the contradictions of the market economy are highly relevant to fundamental issues facing the world today. These include:

- the nature of work for almost one billion people in developing countries employed as 'lumpen labour' in the non-farm sector for US$1–2 per day;
- class conflict between capital and labour in developing countries that are still in the early phase of capitalist industrialization;
- the 'degradation of work' in rich countries for a large fraction of the service sector workers, who work under intense pressure from 'remorseless monitoring' made possible by modern information technology, in order to increase 'labour intensity';
- the erosion of a sense of social cohesion as 'state desertion', in order to provide a 'good investment environment' for global capital, becomes widespread across countries at all levels of development;
- widespread consumer fetishism promoted by the immense marketing expenditure of global giant firms, and commercialized global mass media;
- and even the very sustainability of life on the planet as fast-growing parts of developing countries move towards the immense per capita consumption levels of the advanced capitalist countries.

Notes

1 Smith, 1776, vol 1: 7.
2 Smith, 1776, vol 1: 477.
3 Smith, 1776, vol 1: 477.
4 This famous sentence in fact is not contained in the *Wealth of Nations*. It is from Adam Smith's Essays, quoted in Edwin Cannan's Introduction to the 1904 'Cannan' edition of the *Wealth of Nations* (Smith, 1776: xl).
5 Smith, 1776, vol 2: 49–50.
6 Smith, 1776, vol 1: 19–20.
7 Smith, 1776, vol 1: 9.
8 Smith, vol 1, 1776: 9–14.
9 Smith, 1776, vol 1: 12.
10 Smith, 1776, vol 2: 302–3.
11 Smith, 1776, vol 2: 303.
12 Smith, 1776, vol 2: 306.
13 Smith, 1776, vol 2: 232.
14 Smith, 1776, vol 1: 88.
15 Smith, 1776, vol 2: 232.
16 Smith, 1776, vol 2: 232.
17 Smith, 1776, vol 1: 74.

18 Smith, 1776, vol 1: 74–75.
19 Smith 1761: 61.
20 Smith, 1761, 183.
21 Smith, 1761, 183–4.
22 Smith, 1761: 183–4.
23 Smith, 1761: 184.
24 Smith, 1761: 180–181.
25 Smith 1761: 150.
26 Smith, 1761: 149–150.
27 Smith, 1761: 62.
28 Smith, 1761: 85.
29 Smith, 1761: 25.
30 Smith, 1761: 161–3, 166.
31 Smith, 1761: 86.

References

Adam Smith, 1761 [1982], *The Theory of Moral Sentiments*, (revised edition), Indianapolis, Liberty Classics edition.

Adam Smith, 1776 [1976], *The Wealth of Nations*, Chicago, University of Chicago Press, Cannan edition.